The Changing Church

DUQUESNE STUDIES

Theological Series

6

THE

CHANGING

CHURCH

by

Bertrand van Bilsen, O.F.M., S.T.D.

Adapted by

Henry J. Koren, C.S.Sp., S.T.D.

DUQUESNE UNIVERSITY PRESS
Pittsburgh, Pa.
Editions E. Nauwelaerts, Louvain

DUQUESNE STUDIES
Theological Series

Henry J. Koren, C.S.Sp., S.T.D., Leonard A. Bushinski, C.S.Sp., M.A., S.T.L., Leonard J. Swidler, Ph.D., S.T.L., editors.

Volume One—*Albert Dondeyne*, FAITH AND THE WORLD. XI and 324 pages. Second impression. $5.00.

Volume Two—*Peter Schoonenberg, S.J.*, GOD'S WORLD IN THE MAKING. IX and 207 pages. $4.95.

Volume Three—*Leonard J. Swidler, editor,* SCRIPTURE AND ECUMENISM. VII and 197 pages. $4.95.

Volume Four—*William H. van de Pol*, S.T.D., ANGLICAN-ISM IN ECUMENICAL PERPECTIVE. V and 293 pages. $6.75.

Volume Five—*John H. Walgrave*, O.P., S.T.D., PERSON AND SOCIETY. 182 pages. $4.25.

Volume Six—*Bertrand van Bilsen*, O.F.M., S.T.D., THE CHANGING CHURCH. 433 pages. $7.95.

Nihil Obstat
 Very Reverend Donald W. Kraus, S.T.D., Ph.D.
 Censor Deputatus

Imprimatur
 ✠Most Reverend Vincent M. Leonard, D.D.
 Vicar General—Chancellor
January 10, 1966

Contents

Gratis

95471

5

7

Preface

It is not easy to present a synthesis of the manifold changes that are taking place in the Church, to place them in their historical context and to analyze their bearing on the future. Too many things are still in a state of flux, for, in the words of Pope Paul VI, even the drawing to a close of Vatican Council II is "not the end but the beginning of many projects" in the Church. Nevertheless, the author has attempted to offer such a picture in this book because it seemed imperative to him that an over-all view be made available. Too many of our fellow-believers—including many priests— are bewildered by the rapid "updating" of the Church; they see familiar old practices disappear and notice that the younger generation despises much of what they themselves held most sacred. Silently they wonder whether the Church has lost its bearings.

Both young and old, however, realize that a new era has dawned for the Church. It is an era of enormous possibilities for a renewed vigorous Christian life, but an era beset also by great dangers. Negativism, the mere rejection of moldering forms of Christianity, is a strong temptation. It could easily lead to a spiritual form of nihilism, unless there be a forceful accent on the positive values of the renewal. This book attempts to present such a positive account. Conceived in terms of the existential involvement of all believers in their Church, it addresses itself to the whole ecclesial community, to both priests and laity. For the entire people of God shares in this pastoral concern.

The book's original edition appeared on the eve of Vatican Council II, but its author seems to have enjoyed a kind of prophetic insight into the forthcoming decisions of the Council. For this reason only relatively minor changes needed to be made in the English edition scheduled to be released after the conclusion of the Council. They were mainly concerned with inserting the decisions of the Council and bringing the bibliography up to date. In addition, I have left out some passages that were of interest only to Holland and added others referring to situations in the English-speaking world. Finally, on a few occasions, I have abbreviated an extended passage because a decision of the Council had eliminated the need for a long plea in favor of a particular reform. The full responsibility and blame, if any, for such changes remains, of course, mine.

HENRY J. KOREN, C.S.Sp.

Duquesne University
January 2, 1966

The first draft of the translation was made by the Reverend Walter van de Putte, C.S.Sp.

Introduction

1. The Changeable and Unchangeable Character
of the Church

That the Church is changing is a fact that has become evident to many during the past decades. The Catholic Church is no longer to the same extent and in the same way a monolith of certainties in every field, as it was, for instance, in the first quarter of this century. Many things which were once seemingly inseparable from being-a-Catholic are now considered of lesser importance or are discarded; sometimes they are even abolished by higher authority.

Undoubtedly there are people who become anxious and uncertain under the impact of the changes and who wonder —though not always voicing their fears—whether the Church is not being knocked loose from the rock of Peter. "Where are we heading?" is a question many Catholics ask themselves. Others, on the contrary, are of the opinion that there is still too little movement, that there are not enough changes, that too many things are not yet sufficiently adapted to the times. But it is precisely the latter who are not shaken in their conviction that the Church is indeed the rock amid the breakers, the candle in the darkness, God's sign that brings salvation to the world.

This problem raises many questions. We can no longer avoid asking ourselves what is the reason and the origin of the change. Nor may we neglect to ask how far this change can go or rather how far this process of change ought to go. Every society has a certain constitution, a definite structure that most of the time is developed even in detail. The members of the society become accustomed to that structure and quite often do not realize that formerly it was different and that it could again be changed. But if we consult history we may find that quite a number of variations have existed in the same society. Certain times are characterized by a desire for rest and a fixed order, but there are also times that manifest a dynamic spirit in which very important changes are realized.

This applies also to the Church; the Church has always manifested either fixity or movement. We had become accustomed to a structure of Christ's Church in which everything, even in its smallest particulars, had its definite place. But the spirit of our time is no longer satisfied with that. However, the Church is a special kind of society and, unlike ordinary societies, we are not permitted to change its *essential* structure.

The Church is Christ's Church, it is the mystical body of our Lord Jesus Christ. But it is just as much and completely human at the same time. Our Lord became like unto us in all things except sin. His Church similarly is fully human and, insofar as it is composed of sinful men, it is not able to avoid sin itself. The Church has entered mankind, and by this fact she is completely human. Because of her human character the Church will also constantly change in shape and structure, and these changes will not confine themselves to outward appearances. In that human character of the Church lie the possibilities of change. This is even the basis for her obligation to change over and over again, if she does not want to renounce her duty to become embodied in all times, peoples and cultures. Change and adaptation always remain a vital necessity for the Church.

It is often difficult for us who live in this dynamic age to distinguish the essential from the accidental, the immutable from that which can and sometimes should be changed. We

12

live in a time of transition, and such a time is characterized by unrest and tensions which frequently prevent us from obtaining a correct view of the problem confronting us. These belong to the nature of such a time. On the other hand, we must look upon that unrest and those tensions as manifestations of life which, in the end, lead to good results. May Heaven protect us against a situation in which the whole of human society is on the march and progresses in the economic, social and cultural fields while the Church is satisfied with "remaining herself."

There are people who are quick in claiming that "religion is changing." They are ill at ease and feel cut loose from their anchorage. They lose their security when they see that this or that change has been introduced in the ordinary course of things in the Church. Most of the time the changes affect only more or less accidental structures, in the strict sense of this term. The average Catholic feels the pulse of what is taking place in the Church precisely in the changes made in these structures, but he is often unaware of what lies behind those changes.

The ordinary Catholic is often forgetful of the fact that the Holy Spirit continues to be active in the Church, in the ecclesial community including the laypeople, in an invisible and unfathomable way; he forgets that there continues to be a development in man's believing understanding of the treasure of faith. He likewise does not know that a correct view of particular truths of faith can be temporarily missing, even for a long time, and that these truths may have been presented in a one-sided fashion. This, for instance, has been the case regarding the very nature of the Church, the general priesthood of all the faithful and hence the place of the layman in the Church. Similarly, many causes have led to a narrow-minded practice of the sacraments, especially of the Eucharist, and given rise to spiritual aridity.

A sudden and unprepared acquaintance with new ideas and trends that consider certain practices an enrichment of the faith and regard others as its deterioration and impoverishment, can be disturbing to many good people. On the contrary, a well-planned introduction to those problems can forestall difficulties and, what is even more important, may open new perspectives. We must and can meet the present situation with a healthy optimism. Pessimism and a constant harping on dangers are never a good norm of conduct in pastoral care.[1]

2. Structural Changes

Structural changes in the Church are not concerned only with changes in organization and administration or changes in the external appearance of the Church and her worship; they go deeper. These more profound structural changes are, naturally, the most important, although the changes in organization that occur in actual Church life are the first to be noticed. That is why we shall begin by discussing the latter and then proceed to examine the structural changes that are directly concerned with the spiritual realm.

In the life of faith there is a growing and fuller realization of what it means to be a Christian. In a very general way the view can be formulated in the following manner. To be a Christian means a living union of love between God and man; this union was initiated and is maintained by the incarnate Son of God, our Lord Jesus Christ. All of us who died, were buried and rose by our baptism in and by and with our Savior, have thereby become brothers and sisters of the Incarnate God, of Jesus Christ, and also of one an-

---

[1]See also F. X. von Hornstein, "Optimismus und Pessimismus in der Seelsorge," *Anima,* vol. 5 (1950), pp. 239-245.

other. and have become children of the Father. We form one Body, the mystical body of Christ, which we call the "Church" because it is the community of the Lord (*Kyrios*). We, the Church, realize that we live in this world to glorify the Father, and that in this lies our greatest happiness, a happiness guaranteeed for time and eternity. The life in God through Christ demands, of course, a corresponding attitude of life, an attitude which must find concrete expression in deeds. In all this we must always keep in mind that we as persons live in a community and that therefore this community, namely, the Church, plays a great role in the forms assumed by our Christian life.

Let us develop this general description somewhat more in detail.

Man's true relationship with God manifests itself more fully. The true and complete structure of man's relations with God has at times been too much forgotten. By this we mean, in the first place, that Christians speak mostly in a very general way about "God"; moreover, we also use the words "Christ" and "God" indiscriminately. For example, when we speak of "the dear Lord" it is usually not clear that we mean Jesus Christ. By God's salvific will we are children of the *Father* by and in God's *Son*, who became man, in the power and the love of the *Holy Spirit*. We are connected and united with the Triune God and in that union it is the Word of God who takes the central place: we are Christians, that is, we have been baptized—have died and risen—in Christ. We live and labor through our Lord Jesus Christ. This living connection and union of life is what we call "grace."

Secondly, a danger constantly threatening man is his inclination to approach almost everything solely from the *human* standpoint. In a certain sense—which is not our present meaning—this is unavoidable because we happen to be men. But what we mean is this: Christ, by His life, passion, death and resurrection, has glorified the Father and thereby worked out our salvation. Now this must also be our attitude of life: salvation comes to us by the glorification of the Father. Our life is *worship* in which thanksgiving full of love predominates. When we keep this in mind, it implies another attitude toward the Eucharist (which means "thanksgiving") and the other sacraments; these we then see no longer exclusively as *means of salvation,* but fully as worship, as the high points of our Christian life which *is* worship. Moreover, this will of necessity make us realize that the sacraments at the same time have a social aspect.

The Church acquires another dimension in our life of faith. In the actual life of faith the Church becomes, much more than has been the case until now, the *community* of all the baptized for the honor of God and the salvation of men. Christ is the vivifying Head and all of us are hierarchically ordered in faith and unity in that community, each one in his proper place. In this community love for God and for one another is the universally predominant factor. We realize that an almost exclusive emphasis on the *individual* union of every man with God is an unacceptable limitation of the total reality of Christian life. Hence it would be better to express this reality in this way: we are all, everyone personally, children of the Father in and by and with our Lord Jesus Christ, in the community of His mystical body, the Church. Until recently the emphasis was almost exclusively on the vertical direction without a simultaneous accent on the horizontal dimension.

One-sided emphasis on morally good conduct that fails to do justice to man's true relationship with God is making way for a more total vision of Christian life. We live in a typically Christian relationship with God, a bond of being. This

16

bond of its very nature demands a corresponding attitude of life: our morals must correspond to our being-Christian. Hence the duty of good moral conduct flows with logical necessity from our being-Christian. However, Christian life is first a mode of being and then also a mode of doing. We must not narrow down our Christian life to morally good behavior aimed at an eternal reward. We shall make an even greater mistake if we narrow down the duty of moral goodness that flows necessarily from our being-Christian to a few concrete points or duties. We do not mean, of course, that concrete duties are unimportant. All we want to say is that they must be viewed and realized within the context of the whole of good moral conduct, and this in turn must fit into the totality of our being-Christian.

3. Division and Method of this Book

As a result of the new "climate" there arise many concrete problems. We will deal with them in their interconnection as follows:

In Chapter One, under the title "Catholic Reformation," we will examine the growth and development of the new "climate."

Chapter Two, called "Changes in the Organizational Structure of the Church," will be a study of the hierarchy and the layman, intra-hierarchical changes (decentralization), changes in the pastoral structures of diocese, parish, and other units, the supra-national character of the Church and its regional diversity.

Chapter Three, "Structural Changes in the Life of Faith," concerns a number of questions that are intimately connected with the question of organization, but with which, for methodical reasons, we prefer to deal separately and after the questions discussed in Chapter Two. These are, for instance, questions dealing with the community and the person, the service of the Word and the liturgy of the Eucharist, the sanctification of work and daily life, ecumenical tendencies.

Chapter Four will examine the "Pastoral Consequences" that flow from the changed situation. Here, in the first place, is the question: What is pastoral care? Pastoral care seems to be a thing whose importance needs no explanation and is self-evident; yet it, too, is affected by the changes that are taking place in the Church. In this connection we will consider the true ideal of the priesthood, particularly in relation to the new accent that is placed upon Sacrament and Word and also in relation to the changing position of the layman in the Church.

It is impossible to predict all the changes that will ultimately result from Vatican Council II. We should not yield to pessimism, even if some cherished idea has not been accepted by it. A Council is not a panacea for all ills, and should even refrain from trying to create an "order of affairs" designed to remain for several centuries. A General Council is the voice of the Church of a particular moment.

It has been evident in the sessions of the Council that the contemporary voice of the Church is clearly expressed by the Fathers gathered in it. There is diversity among them as there is diversity in the Church herself. But in the midst of diversity the one Church of Christ is clearly heard. There is no uniformity concerning all concrete questions on the practical and disciplinary level, and theological controversies are a normal phenomenon in a Council. But the one Church of Christ can, in her unity of faith, give the beginning of an answer to the questions that are put to her by men of the present time. In spite of differences of opinion and regional diversity, differences springing from nationality and character, the Council has already enacted many salutary decrees and introduced measures that will improve the organization and management of the Church on the various levels.[2]

Our study of the problems concerning the changes and renewal in the Church will be made from a pastoral standpoint. Pastoral theology is one of the most recent branches of theology. It makes use of the achievements of the other theological branches, dogmatic theology and moral theology, as well as biblical exegesis, canon law and liturgics. Starting from such data, pastoral theology, with a certain amount of autonomy, studies the nature and properties of pastoral care (the theology of pastoral care); at the same time, it observes phenomenologically the actual situation of the Church, especially in relation to pastoral care; finally, it tries, on the basis of theological and factual data, to provide orientation for the present time. This orientation aims primarily at the priest but pertains in principle to all other Christians, whether they be religious or lay people, for all of them have a role to play in this pastoral task.

This book, then, contains no dogmatic, moral, exegetical, juridical or liturgical studies. It wishes to examine how those various fields are being affected by our present spirit of renewal, and it may serve to show in what direction our efforts should be applied for a more profound spiritual renovation. It stands to reason that we shall have to get ac-

[2]There exists an abundant literature about Vatican Council II. To name only a few titles, Hans Küng, *The Council: Reform and Reunion,* Sheed and Ward, 1962; Hans Küng, ed., *Council Speeches of Vatican II,* Paulist Press, 1962; Bernard Häring, *The Johannine Council,* Herder and Herder, 1963; Anthony D. Lee, ed., *Vatican II, the Theological Dimension,* Thomist Press, 1963; Michael Novak, *The Open Church,* Macmillan, 1964; Robert McAfee Brown, *The Challenge to Reunion,* McGraw-Hill, 1963; Wolfgang Seibel, *The Pastoral Goal of the Council,* St. Mary's, Kansas, 1965.

quainted with the actual situation of the Church and its pastoral task, as they are seen in the total context of human society. A complete pastoral study evidently requires data borrowed from sociology and psychology so that we may know the factual situation and factual relationships. Pastoral theology itself cannot supply these data. When, therefore, we say that we will approach the problems of the changing Church from the standpoint of pastoral concern, we mean that we do not want to write as sociologists or psychologists but want to take into account the contributions of these specialists in our pastoral approach to the problems.[3] Neither do we wish to write a complete treatise of pastoral theology. We simply want to look at things through pastoral eyes and throw some light upon certain features of the changes that are takig place in modern Catholic life. This method is in harmony with the spirit of Vatican Council II which Pope John XXIII called a "pastoral council."

---

[3]It is striking how much the "pastoral" Second Vatican Council insists on the relevance of psychological and sociological studies. See, e.g., the *Decree on the Pastoral Office of the Bishops in the Church*, Ch. II, art. 14 and 17; the *Declaration on Christian Education*, art. 1; the *Decree on Priestly Education*, II, art. 2 and 3; IV, art. 11; VI, art. 20; the *Decree on the Adaptation and Renewal of Religious Life*, art. 3 and 12; the *Decree on the Apostolate of the Laity*, Ch. VI, art. 32; the *Constitution on the Church in the Modern World*, art. 29.

CHAPTER ONE

Catholic Reformation

1. The Historical Origin of Today's Renewal and Adaption

Sixteenth Century Roots

The life of the Church is a real life with all the dynamics proper to life. There is movement in the Church, a life of constant change and growth, although she remains always herself in the most proper sense of the word. The Church is constantly in the process of *reformation*. This reformation is a continuous phenomenon, though it comes more to the fore in one period than in another, and it also has different external characteristics. This permanent phenomenon is very strong in our own day and is activated by forces both from above and from below.

Reform movements usually start from below. The fact that Church leaders show interest in the movement of reform indicates that these tendencies have reached a rather advanced stage of development. The Church will always require a twofold activity: on the one hand, private initiative, and on the other, decisions of the authorities. These two need one another. There will always be a certain tension between them, for the authorities have, almost necessarily, an inclination to conservation, a desire to preserve what is in existence. Conversely, private initiative must be on its guard not to discard too many things.

We can say without exaggeration that the movement of renewal that is taking place in the Church has its roots in the time of the Reformation and its antecedents. The Church's reform, which made a strong, though hampered, start in the late Middle Ages, is now pushing forward through God's help and our cooperation. The present situation certainly has historical connections with the sixteenth century and, hence, it will be worthwhile to take a closer look at that period. But before doing that let us reflect on the following statements of Dr. Polman: "The interior restoration of the Church that took place in the sixteenth century is directly connected with the fifteenth century's striving for reform in head and members: for the reformation of the clergy, the salt of the earth, that had lost its power, and for the reformation of the people by way of that reform." "The international Catholic reformation already had its tradition long before the proclamation of the Protestant reformation; and side by side with this new phenomenon that Catholic reform continued to follow its own way."[1]

The sixteenth century, then was characterized by a two-fold tendency toward reformation: a Catholic reformation and the movement of the Reformers which finally came to stand in opposition to the Church. Both movements had their roots in the fifteenth century. The whole movement had an explicitly religious character: it was in no way a movement toward irreligiousness. On the contrary, "the reconstruction began from the bottom; in some areas lower authorities—preachers, writers and pious people—had for a long time proclaimed and accepted the necessity of a renewal of life before the higher ones—the popes, cardinals and bishops—understood their task in this respect. It was precisely the

---

[1]"Vruchten van de katholieke hervorming," *Cultuurgeschiedenis van het Christendom,* Amsterdam, 1950, vol. 3, ch. 8.

endless procrastination of the Eternal City, which was certainly the principal object of the required reformation, that constituted the most severe trial for anyone in Europe who strove for improvement. Renaissance-minded Rome was too attached to its sins to give preference to the ascetics, who preached mortification of the senses, over the humanists who advocated a refined and luxurious life."[2]

Many were able to wait in long-suffering patience for the time when Rome would come to its senses. Others did not believe in the practice of such patience. And precisely on this account a split occurred in the movement of reform. The Reformers and their movement became divorced from the Church, and the Catholic reformation quite naturally acquired a greatly defensive character and a certain one-sidedness. This split has affected and has left its stamp on the Church during the last centuries.

THE ONE-SIDEDNESS OF THE COUNTER REFORMATION

The Catholic reformation of the sixteenth century is known in history under the name of "Counter Reformation." This term is correct in great measure although it does not do it full justice. The Catholic reformation of those days became to a great extent a *reactionary* reform because of the appearance of the Protestant Reformation. This, for instance, was the case with the Council of Trent. This Council was very important and most beneficial to the Church; but it is impossible to deny that it was to a great extent characterized by a defensive attitude on account of the situation in which it was held.[3]

For this reason some points were particularly emphasized because they were denied by the Reformers. Other points

---

[2]*Ibid.*

[3]For the Council of Trent see Hubert Jedin, *History of the Council of Trent.* 3 vols., Herder, 1957 ff.

were *de facto* left very much in the background, particularly those which were strongly or too strongly stressed by the Reformers. It was necessary to make every effort and use all means to safeguard and keep unstained all the doctrines that had been assailed. But this tendency also acted as a brake on the movement for a complete reform. There were important initiatives at Trent with respect to both the formulation of the doctrine and Church discipline, particularly regarding the clergy; but the life of faith as such acquired a strongly one-sided, Counter Reformation character.

To demonstrate this we can offer the following striking examples:

The place of the laity in the Church. Because the hierarchical priesthood was rejected by many reformers who recognized only the general priesthood of all the faithful, Trent saw itself obliged to sharply define the hierarchical priesthood. The Council achieved most meritorious work in this respect; but in reality the general priesthood of the laity, and therefore also the layman's place in the Church, was put in the background, at least in popular theology and in preaching. For a long time it was considered dangerous and open to suspicion to speak about that general priesthood and the layman's own place in the Church.

The view regarding the Church thus became improverished. There was a one-sided emphasis on the institutional, hierarchical character of the Church, thus theology and preaching paid little attention to the Church as the community of Christ.[4]

The doctrine and practice of the Eucharist provides another example. Because of the Reformers' intrepretation of Christ's

---

[4]Cf. Hans Küng, "The Charismatic Structure of the Church," *Concilium,* vol. 4 (1965), pp. 41 ff., concerning the importance of the Christian people's charisms.

presence under the appearances of bread and wine, Trent
felt obliged to clarify this dogma once and for all, as well
as the sacrificial character of the Eucharistic celebration
which was also combated by the Reformers. Trent's definition of these aspects of Holy Eucharist was of enormous
importance. However, in Eucharistic practice, in preaching
and devotion, the real presence was so strongly emphasized
that the Mass was practically no longer, or scarcely, experienced as the communal memorial supper of our Lord
Jesus Christ. The accent was put on the presence of Christ.
People attended Mass as a rite that was instituted for this
purpose. And when people went to communion on rare occasions, mostly outside of Mass, they considered it almost
exclusively as "Christ coming in our heart." The rules for
the Eucharistic fast were worked out in minute details and
were interpreted with particular severity. The length of the
desirable or even required thanksgiving was calculated according to the probable duration of Christ's physical presence
in the communicant. The adoration of Christ received enormous prominence as Benediction with the Blessed Sacrament.

It is also necessary to recall that the Protestant Reformation itself was to a great extent a reaction against the conditions of that period. For instance, in the late Middle Ages,
excessive value was attached to gazing at the Sacred Host,
which we certainly cannot approve. People scarcely thought
of going to Communion, so that the Church in the thirteenth
century felt it necessary to impose the obligation of communicating once a year. Many people entered a church just
before the Elevation and left immediately after it. Hence,
the ruling that the faithful had to be present on Sundays at
least at the three "principal parts" of the Mass: the Offertory,
the Consecration and Communion. Sometimes cries of "higher,
higher" were heard in the church during the Elevation. Some
people believed that to have seen the Sacred Host was a

guarantee against all accidents during that day; some thought that time stood still for those who had seen It, so that a day was added to their lives. There were even people who believe that such a sight would give them a better appetite during that day.

It stands to reason that we must take into account these and similar phenomena when we try to judge the Reformers' aversion toward the real presence of our Lord in the Eucharist. It is to be regretted that the Catholic corrective reaction against faulty practices and beliefs was not more vigorous. As a consequence of the defensive character of the Council of Trent, the one-sided emphasis of the Middle Ages, though many abuses were done away with, has been prolonged and preserved even to our own day. This defensive attitude shaped the character of Catholic piety at the time of the Counter Reformation. Books dealing with the "spiritual life" developed this even further. Popular extracts of those books diffused this same spirit among every strata of society. Thus the one-sidedness of the Counter Reformation became, not a new phenomenon, but a confirmation of an existing situation, at least to a great extent. And this trend was strengthened by the Counter Reformation, and given a better chance of success.

However, we must not look only at the negative side of that movement. The Counter Reformation also gave a powerful impetus and vigor to the Church. The bloom of that period, viz., the second half of the sixteenth century and the seventeenth century, produced many great saints and new spiritual movements; also a new flourishing of the faith among ordinary priests and the faithful came about.

Nevertheless, it is not unjust to point to particular important examples of one-sidedness. This situation was bound to eventually create difficulties, because this spiritual constellation unavoidably produced tensions and spiritual mustiness, especially among the less devout. The good which we had a right to expect, and which was actually achieved, is the fact that there arose a cry for reform which was to prompt further correction without causing an actual break with the past. But, at the same time, it could not be expected that all one-sidedness would be avoided and that the living Church would succeed in creating perfect order among the human beings of which it is composed.

Unsuccessful Renewal Efforts

There have always been efforts to combat such manifestations of one-sidedness. But they obtained little permanent success. One reason was that those who combated that one-sidedness were quickly suspected of being in league with the Protestants. And surely the periods of the Jansenistic struggle and the Enlightenment were not the most favorable climate for a healthy movement of reform. In fact, during the Jansenistic struggle and the time of the Enlightenment, there were attempted adaptations that bore the clear mark of those movements, although we must be on our guard against seeing things as either white or black. In view of the purpose of this book we need not delve more deeply into the attempts at renewal that were made during the seventeenth and eighteenth centuries.[5]

Modernism, when viewed in the perspective of the oncoming efforts of reform, has a tragic history. Progress in the historical field led to disconcerting discoveries. A mania for studying ancient Christianity was generated. Many came to the wrong

---

[5]For the liturgical movements of renewal see E. B. Koerker, *The Liturgical Renaissance in the Roman Catholic Church,* Chicago, 1954; M. J. Taylor, *The Protestant Liturgical Renewal,* Newman, 1963; L. Sheppard, *The Liturgical Movement,* Hawthorn, 1964; W. Trapp, *Vorgeschichte und Ursprung der liturgischen Bewegung vorwiegend in Hinsicht auf das deutsche Sprachgebiet,* Regensburg, 1940, pp. 5-190; O. Rousseau, *Histoire du mouvement liturgique,* Paris, 1945.

conclusion that everything is historically determined; they thought that dogmas were crystallizations of a particular time, that they thus required, not only a new formulation for the present time, but also a different content. Some persons were too strongly affected by the idea that the truth of religion had become estranged from life and were not sufficiently adapted to it. The adherents of modernism considered religious *experience* to be the most important thing. In those days, the sudden, unprepared and immature contact of faith with science caused a short-circuit. The Church reacted strongly, especially at the beginning of this century. But a less gratifying result was the appearance of integralism, which gave rise to the regular heresy hunts, still remembered by the older members of the present generation. Needless to say, this did not bring about a solution of the questions that were pending.

After the era of Modernism came a period dominated by a kind of fear. Now, however, those themes are once more taken into consideration and we seem to have entered upon a time that is more favorable to a healthy progress. Historical studies have become more mature. There is no longer the same danger of short-circuits. We face the unsolved problems as men who have been warned. Pope Pius XII in his 1950 encyclical *Humani Generis* sounded a few warnings but, at the same time, clearly and strongly spurred on further study. At the present time there are greater possibilities. We are able to study the Protestant Reformation with greater freedom and wih less need for a defensive attitude. At the same time, historical studies have given Protestant circles a better understanding of Catholic ideas.

THE CORE OF TODAY'S MOVEMENT FOR REFORM

At present we see that in theology, pastoral care and the practice of faith the emphasis falls on aspects that previous centuries had left in the background. In particular, there is an emphasis on the Church as a community, as the body of Christ, on the place of the layman in the Church, and on the Eucharist as the memorial banquet of the community. There is also a growing consciousness of the Church as a world-church; there is more interest in the tragedy of the separation of the Eastern Churches. We feel more responsibility toward the plight of the Church in South America and realize better that the young churches in Asia and Africa will not fail to affect the too Western character of the Church.

Thus, the present movement of renewal and adaptation that desires to be a movement of Catholic reformation, is not something that has suddenly dropped from the skies. It possesses an evident historical continuity. It is absolutely necessary to have a feeling for history if we wish to realize where we stand in the course of human history. We are justified in looking upon that historical perspective as the hallmark, the condition of culture and civilization. It is impossible to have a genuine religious renewal, one that is more than mere demolition, without an appreciation of the value of history. Arthur Koestler once remarked that many young people seem "to be born without a navel," which means that they lack all historical perspective and all interest in history. This is an alarming phenomenon; nevertheless, this lack of understanding of historical continuity confirms the idea that we are in a period of transition toward a new period in the history of the world and the Church. For the fact that so many, especially the young, no longer feel a connection with the past, clearly shows that a new era has begun that differs clearly from the one that went before.

A new era does not begin suddenly on a particular day. A clear-cut division is always arbitrary. One who lives in a time of transition can have a strong feeling of its presence that not infrequently comes close to certainty. And that strong presumption is undoubtedly characteristic of the present generation's attitude toward life, although many people have not yet crossed the threshold, psychologically speaking. There are even extreme cases of men who are still living peacefully in the spirit of the old time as if nothing had happened around them. But those who feel almost certain that they have crossed the threshold into the new era, are unable to say when exactly that took place because such a clearly-marked threshold simply does not exist.

No one can tell us precisely when the present movement for renewal began in the Church. And the march did not start at the same time on all fronts. There were starts in the nineteenth century, but these again had their connections with earlier movements; in particular, there were social ideas that came to the fore rather late under the pressure of circumstances and there were beginnings in the liturgical realm during the early part of that century. World War I definitively marked the end of the nineteenth century era.

That war, like every great war, undoubtedly has acted as a shock; it produced principally a feeling of uncertainty. Old values and established situations lost much of their significance but there was still little interest in new or renewed values. This mentality could also be observed in the Church. During the twenties a number of revolutionary ideas were launched, but they were principally directed against the existing order; they offered poor perspectives for the future. Then, during the thirties, certainly a period of crisis in every respect, there resulted a feeling of dissatisfaction and powerlessness.

World War II caused a much greater upheaval than the First. To a great extent it spelled the bankruptcy of old values. With one blow this also became clear within the Church; and, over many hesitations, more than a few readily took the step forward. They lost their attachment to old values. This, naturally, produced at first a rather disorderly situation in the Church. In contrast with what happened after World War I, however, the movement did not waste its strength in mere criticism but developed into a positive renewal. This renewal was, of course, accompanied by growing pains, which even today are far from finished.

CRITICISM AND RECONSTRUCTION

We are justfied, then, in calling the present situation sound and full of hope. Roughly speaking we can divide the years after World War II into two periods with respect to the movement of renewal in the Church: the period of *criticism* and the period of *reconstruction*. Of course, there was an intermingling of criticism and construction, but it is true, nevertheless, that that first the one, then the other, mentality was predominant. This we hope to be able to show in what follows.

Shortly after the war it was customary and rather necessary to sound a loud and vigorous alarm. In a small circle there had grown the realization that many things needed to be changed. Change and renewal were necessary, for instance, in theology, liturgy, preaching, catechesis and pastoral care, in family life, education, and in the cultural and social spheres. Although many lived in a mood of uncertainty, few felt the urgent need of changes; hence they had to be aroused by strong words. It was necessary to awaken the community at large. There is no doubt that the means used to arouse the sleepers were sometimes rather rough. The *criticism* of existing conditions had the upperhand. Added to this was the fact that the critics had no clear idea of what was to be done once the sleepers were well awake and how the task was to be tackled. The critics were against many things, but it was not very clear what they were actually *for*. Much of the criticism of those days appears unreasonable to us now; but other things with which we are now impatient were then left peacefully alone.

The first cries of alarm came from France. The small book of Abbé H. Godin (in collaboration with Yves Daniel) made a great impression during the first years after the war. Godin, the first leader of the priests-workers, set minds aflutter by asking the uncomfortable question, "Is France pagan?"[6] All who were keenly aware of the situation of the Church at the time desired to read the book, and translations appeared in German, English and other languages. What was the reason? Was it only because in Europe, and later in America, there existed a particular interest in the situation of France? Evidently, there was something in that book, especially in its tone of alarm, that was valid for the Church as a whole and also for anyone's particular situation. In Holland there appeared publications such as *Unrest in Pastoral Care,* and the alarm was sounded by the very title of the new review *The Eleventh Hour.*

In the liturgy the cries for adaptation and change grew increasingly louder. The existing social and political organizations were critically examined and provisional modifications were introduced because the circumstances demanded them. A wave of unrest passed through a great section of the Church in Europe, and even in countries with a supposedly flourishing Church it was realized that there was no basis for the smug feeling that at least in our land "all was well." And thus many were prompted to make a salutary self-examination.

We find an echo of that situation also on a higher level in the Church. The numerous allocutions and encyclicals that characterized the pontificate of Pius XII, particularly those

---

[6]*France, pays de mission?* English title: *France Pagan,* New York, 1950.

that appeared around the year 1950, were not without emotional coloring, a rather uncommon thing in pronouncements of the Holy See. This slight emotional element we find especially surrounding the encyclical *Humani Generis* of 1950.[7] This encyclical was meant to serve as a guide amidst the "dangerous novelties" (the term "poisonous novelties" was also used). One instinctively places that encyclical alongside Pius X's encyclical *Pascendi* of 1907,[8] which came at the peak of the modernistic struggle. On September 23, 1950, about one month after *Humani Generis,* Pius XII sent the clergy the letter *Menti Nostrae* in which he renewed his attack on the "spirit of novelty" that "is being diffused in an ever greater and more disturbing manner" and "especially among priests . . . less equipped with doctrine and of less strict lives."[9]

However, there was no intention of blocking true progress, as appears from an allocuation of the Pope, on September 23 of the same year,[10] to the professors belonging to the Order of Discalced Carmelites. In this discourse the Pope complained that *Humani Generis* had been wrongly interpreted as a wish to stem all wholesome development. It is indeed evident that a great difference exists between *Humani*

---

[7]*Acta apostolicae sedis* (hereafter abbreviated as *A.A.S.*), vol. 42 (1950), pp. 561-578. Concerning this encyclical, see *Nouvelle revue théologique:* Jean Levie, L'encyclique 'Humanis generis'," vol. 42 (1950), pp. 785-793; F. Taymans, "L'encyclique 'Humani generis' et la théologie," vol. 43 (1951), pp. 3-20; A. Hayen, "L'encyclique 'Humani generis' et la philosophie," *ibid.*, pp. 113-137; G. Lambert, "L'encyclique 'Humani generis' et l'Ecriture sainte," *ibid.*, pp. 224-243; G. Vandenbroek, "L'encyclique 'Humani generis' et les sciences naturelles," *ibid.*, pp. 337-351. See also Gustave Thils, "The Encyclical 'Humani generis'," *American Ecclesiastical Review,* vol. 124 (1951), pp. 183-189; Gustave Weigel, "The Historical Background of the Encyclical 'Humani generis'," *Theological Studies,* vol. 12 (1951), pp. 208-230.

[8]*Acta sanctae sedis,* vol. 40 (1907), pp. 642 ff.

[9]*A.A.S.,* vol. 42 (1950); English text in N.C.W.C. ed., p. 39.

[10]*A.A.S.,* vol. 43 (1951), pp. 734-738.

Generis and Pius X's *Pascendi* and also Pius IX's *Quanta Cura* with the "Syllabus" of condemned errors attached to it (1864). About these, Professor L. J. Rogier remarks that: "Particularly around the time of the publication of the famous encyclical *Quanta Cura* with the annexed *Syllabus of Errors* (1864) it seemed indeed that the power of the Church had come to lie quite one-sidedly in defense, condemnation and negation."[11] He also speaks of a "chain of condemnations" pronounced over all experiments to reach a better system of Christian thinking.[12] But a more positive spirit of the Holy See was evident even in *Humani Generis.*

Nevertheless, the year 1950 can in a certain sense justly be called a year of crisis. The crisis was reflected not only in the attitude of the Holy See, it was also evident in the lower strata of the Church. In those years there existed a rather widespread pessimism with respect to the Church, religion and the possibility of a sane human community. This pessimism was fostered by alarming sounds about the condition of the Church and mankind; but, in reality, it had its foundation in the awareness that we had failed in many respects in spite of our feverish activities.

A very striking example of that is seen in Virgil Gheorghiu's book *The Twenty-Fifth Hour* which appeared in 1950.[13] This book received great praise because it gave a masterly description of the situation of the world. The poor guiltless Romanian farm hand who is dragged from one camp to another, while no one, whether Germans or Americans, can put an end to this because man has lost control over his own systems, is the personification of modern civilization. The description is powerful but also utterly pessimistic. The title of the book,

---

[11]*In vrijheid herboren,* The Hague, 1952, p. 144.
[12]*Ibid.,* p. 153.
[13]Knopf ed., 1950; Heinemann ed., 1950.

The Twenty-Fifth Hour, tells us enough; we have lost our last chance. As Christians we can and must recognize the reality that is presented in that book, but with a more profound sense of reality, it is impossible for us to accept its pessimism. However, at the time when that pessimistic book appeared, the movement of renewal had more or less bogged down. People did not feel able to cope with the situation. They saw but little light amid the darkness. The past they had renounced, more or less, but the future seemed very uncertain. And on top of that came a strong warning on the part of the highest Church authority. It would have been possible for the whole movement of reform to run aground or at least to come to a standstill for a number of years. But this is precisely what did not take place.

TENDENCIES IN THE REFORM MOVEMENT

The number of men who had been won to the idea of "renewal" appears to have become larger than it was in the first years after the war, although those men, quite naturally, belonged to the upper strata of the Catholic community. Soon, however, the ideas of "renewal" and "adaptation" became familiar to all Catholics, although they reacted very differently to them. Some were or still are impatient, others suspicious, or hopeful, sceptical or anxious, or again they may be entirely opposed to any change. The principal gain, however, is that some light has dawned in the darkness. People have begun to see a little more clearly in what direction the Church will have to develop. Substantial gains have already been made in the fields of theology, Bible exegesis, and liturgy; and the religious practices of Catholics are gradually becoming affected by those changes.

A typical example of the change in attitude was shown in an article by Viktor Schurr that bore the title "The Church on the Offensive."[14] The questions raised became more and more orientated to the future rather than remaining merely critical of the past. This development in a positive direction was one of the reasons why the sharp criticisms of faulty ideas and conditions gradually met with a growing opposition. It was only one of the reasons, for excessive conservatism also played a role in that opposition. Anyhow, many people, while sincerely desiring a renovation, got tired of so much negative criticism. And when more positive perspectives came in sight, they became less and less inclined to waste their time in criticism.

Not only was there evidence of a development in a more positive sense, but people also acquired a greater appreciation of the hierarchy of values. They attained a better perception of the interconnection of things, and the core of the questions became more clearly defined. They passed beyond the stage where it was thought that although a multitude of things had to be done, it was not clear how all those things were related to one another. The discussion left the periphery to concentrate on the core of the problem. It became evident that the power of the renewal movement lay in the new approach to the realms of theology and biblical exegesis. It was a question of a new approach, not of an "old" and a "new" theology.

The reaction of the Holy See to the movement of renewal also changed. The theme of "preserving tradition" has, of course, never been absent, and especially after *Humani Generis* it sounded its warnings ever more distinctly; but there was also evident an element encouraging progress. The most striking evidence of this encouragement is found in the fields of biblical science, the liturgy and morals. Although we should perhaps make an exception regarding the declarations

---

[14]"Kirche im Angriff," *Paulus,* vol. 25 (1953), pp. 14-29.

in the field of biblical science,[15] we can say that all the really stimulating statements and far-reaching decisions came after 1950. Regarding liturgy, we have of course the encyclical *Mediator Dei* of 1947,[16] but all the concrete renovations came after 1950. The number of papal allocutions that concern professional morality are innumerable.

In this respect we must note, first of all, an evident tendency to approach the life of the Christian in its concrete reality; this is manifest in the numerous allocutions addressed to professional groups. Secondly, there is an endeavor to determine a standpoint with respect to modern warfare and all sorts of new discoveries, which is expressed especially in medical ethics.[17] This endeavor to establish a standpoint in relation to the problems of our time is strongly present in almost all the allocutions of Pius XII. The question of the splitting of the atom, international problems, such as the unification of Europe, movies, sports, legal questions regarding the relation of guilt and punishment, general problems such as that of man's dignity— all these received suitable attention in the positive sense.[18] And, precisely, the important statements of a positive nature are mostly dated after 1950. Nearly all the great discourses concerning justice and law date from the

---

[15]The encyclical "Divino afflante spiritu," *A.A.S.*, vol. 35 (1943), pp. 297-325; the letter of Jan. 16, 1948, to Cardinal Suhard, *ibid.*, vol. 40 (1948), pp. 45-48.

[16]*Ibid.*, vol. 39 (1947), pp. 521-595.

[17]Cf., e.g., Sept. 23, 1949, *A.A.S.*, vol. 41 (1949), pp. 557-561; Sept. 13 (1952), *ibid.*, vol. 44 (1952), pp. 779-783; Sept. 7, 1953, *ibid.*, vol. 45 (1953), pp. 536-607; Oct. 13, 1953, *ibid.*, vol. 45 (1953), pp. 744-754; Oct. 8, 1953, *ibid.*, vol. 45 (1953), pp. 673-679; Sept. 11, 1954, *ibid.*, vol. 46 (1954), pp. 587-598; April 7, 1955, *ibid.*, vol. 47 (1955), pp. 275-281; Feb. 24, 1957, *ibid.*, vol. 49 (1957), pp. 123-147; Sept. 12, 1958, *ibid.*, vol. 50 (1958), p. 738.

[18]Cf. Dec. 6, 1953, *A.A.S.*, vol. 45 (1953), pp. 794-802; Dec. 5, 1954, *ibid.*, vol. 47 (1955), pp. 60-85; Oct. 3, 1953, *ibid.*, vol. 45 (1953), pp. 730-744; Dec. 24, 1956, ibid., vol. 48 (1956), pp. 5-22.

last six or seven years of the pontificate of Pius XII. The same can be said about those that deal with social problems; as also those that belong to the large field of what can be called "pastoral concerns."

But when we study the discourses concerning the discoveries in the medical field and other modern problems, we see clearly that the center of gravity lies in the years that followed 1950. And what strikes us is that the problems are treated in so much detail and so concretely. The Pope is not satisfied with general recommendations or warnings; and we note that he deals with actual problems in a very positive way. The tendency to defend and issue clear warnings occupies a secondary position.

It should not astonish us that so many concrete modern problems were discussed in the fifties, for it was precisely during those years that these problems begged for a solution. However, the attitude of the Holy See could have been different. The pope could have remained more or less negative regarding those problems or could have contented himself with warnings against present and possible dangers; but he did the opposite. This is a very important fact; it shows that the entire problem was alive throughout the Church, for the Holy See is not an island in the Church. Although those problems arise "from below" in a different, and especially in a more spontaneous way, it is a healthy sign and a proof of the power of the renewal efforts that the highest organ of authority in the Church occupied itself actively and positively with those problems.

TENSIONS AND DEFECTS

It is perfectly obvious, then, that presently a powerful tendency toward renewal is at work and that it is taking an ever more positive direction. However, this process does not operate in a rectilinear and harmonious way, nor without jolts.

Many people remain aloof from the trend to renewal or imagine they have found their way by simply abandoning a number of values. Even within the movement of renewal itself there is no unanimity and there are numerous problems and tensions.

Many people simply try to make themselves "free." They strip established ideas of their true meaning and give them an entirely new one that harmonizes with a purely secularist, if not outright materialistic, ideology. In some spheres of public life it is no longer possible to distinguish between Christians and non-Christians. Some seem to think that they "can serve two masters," and many adopt an attitude toward life that is far removed from God's commandments and the teaching of the Gospel.

More than ever before, mankind is in a spiritual crisis, and unfortunately many are scarcely aware of the fact that they are slowly falling into a spiritual nihilism. There is a growing mental division among men and it is necessary for us not to be blind to this situation but to be fully conscious of it.

Within the Catholic world, which is generally well disposed toward spiritual renewal, there also are many tensions. Not infrequently there are tensions between "conservatives" and "progressives," though these words are sometimes used as invectives and have a variety of meanings. We may not underrate the danger of conservatism. Although it is true that, historically speaking, the conservative spirit has frequently prevented aberrations, it is also true that that spirit has often obstructed genuine progress.

Let us recall, for example, how slowly the Catholic reformation started in Luther's and Calvin's time. Much evil could have been prevented then by a quicker renewal. Similarly, the idea of social justice was held back much too long. The conservative spirit contributed greatly to the "scandal of the nineteenth century," the massive loss of the working classes to the Church in several countries. Yet even now there are still people who speak with nostalgia of the "good old days" that existed before 1914. What characterizes the conservative spirit is certainly an excessive clinging to the spirit of a particular era. This is due mostly to the fact that these "conservatives" lack a solid interior anchorage and are short-sighted. That is why it is also necessary to be on one's guard against becoming too involved in the spirit of *our* time. Experience shows that people who were most impetuous "progressives" fifty years ago now are not infrequently the worst conservatives because they are immovably fixed in the methods which they protagonized in their youth.

Besides the Christians whose mind and heart still cling to the past, there are those who wish to free themselves from it and desire to be Christians of the present time. This is the only possible point of view that a Christian should adopt. The people who are now living, in present circumstances, must come to Christ; they must be brought to Christ. The Church is unchangeable in her nature; she is static and the core of her being must be protected and "conserved." But precisely for that reason she must also be changeable, dynamic in her structure, her appearance in the world; she must go along with and be involved in her time, she must be progressive.[19] It is on this level that the struggle for a Christian existence in our own time takes place.

Here we notice a great number of fortunate phenomena. Over and over again we have heard the call "back to the sources!" It is indeed necessary to learn and relearn the pure and true core of Christianity. Precisely through knowledge and experience of its *supratemporal* character, it will be possible for Christianity to be of our time. But it is equally

---

[19]Cf. Karl Rahner, *The Dynamic Element in the Church,* Herder and Herder, 1964; François Houtart, *The Challenge to Change: The Church Confronts the Future,* Sheed and Ward, 1963.

fortunate that we are seeking forms that *suit our own time* with respect to the liturgy, the proclamation of the Gospel and Christian life. It is necessary, however, that going "back to the sources" and "adaptation of Christianity to our own times" go hand in hand. Naturally it is not so easy to obtain quickly the proper balance between the two. On the one hand, "back to the sources" might mean a going "back" to the situations and forms of the Church in the first centuries, with their Greco-Roman pattern of culture. This would be a fruitless endeavor; and those who try to do it will cause serious trouble. Although such a movement might call itself modern, it is in reality that conservatism of people who are too enamored with ancient history; they speak a language that differs from ordinary conservatism but are in reality identical with them.

On the other hand "contemporary" Christianity is sometimes too oblivious of the supratemporal dimension and of the continuity of history. We must avoid chaining ourselves to the circumstances of our time. One who does this commits the same fault as the immovable conservative. Hence the terms "conservative" and "progressive" are unsuitable to indicate differences of opinion, for they can represent a variety of meanings.

It is true that one can discern at least *two directions* among the Christians who are fully in favor of a Christianity adapted to our time. These people have not bound themselves to a time that is gone; they want to live as members of a supratemporal Church, but as it should be lived in our own time. However, by that very fact, they feel at the same time the tension between the supratemporal and the present. It is easy to discover a difference in emphasis among the "progressive" Christians. There are many who feel so happy to be free from old worn-out forms that they hesitate to bind themselves to the equally limited forms of our own day; they

41

are somewhat fearful and hesitant when faced by recommended new forms. Ultra-conservative elements make use of this situation to discredit these people in the minds of other "progressives," who are less afraid and sometimes too quick in accepting new forms. However, it does not do to pelt one another with historical terms of abuse such as "integralist" and "modernist." The term "integralist" was not infrequently used, especially at the beginning of the movement for renewal. Anyone who did not belong to a movement that announced itself as "progressive" was quickly suspected of belonging to the ghostly army of spies and informers that flourished at the time of modernism, even though one abhorred integralism as much as his opponents.

We may not underestimate the *danger of parties and fronts* in the movement of renewal. In our time there exists the same danger as in earlier times of tension and clamor for reform: there arise oppositions within the Church which are a mixture of a doctrinal and personal (or even political) antithesis. When communications between opposite groups are not energetically kept open, there arise parties that take delight in accusing one another of heresy and then tend more and more to extremes. This is a thing that has always taken place in the Church. The Reformation is a clear case of it. The parties became increasingly antagonistic and accused one another of heresy in most coarse terms. At the end neither party could turn back. A dialogue was out of the question. Condemnation alone remained.

The tragic story of modernism, with its antithesis of integralism, presents a similar picture, even when we leave the bitter question of Jansenism out of consideration. At the beginning of the present century there were indeed people who swerved from the right course in their efforts to adapt the Church to the times. But matters were pushed to extremes by the pernicious influence of integralism. Not only did the

integralists cause great grief to many excellent priests and
laypeople by accusing them unjustly of insincerity in their
teaching; but integralism also caused those who had trans-
gressed the lines to become hardened and embittered. Moreover, that formation of parties, integralism in particular, considerably slowed down the development of the biblical sciences and theology.

The danger of forming fronts and parties is not wholly
imaginary even in our present movement of renewal, although
it is perhaps not as great as in years gone by. The danger of
"closing the ranks" exists in many countries. It has existed
for a long time in France. The French bishops felt obliged to
act energetically, especially against conservative elements.
But there were also mishaps "on the other side." We are
thinking of the difficulties with the worker-priests, also of
what happened with respect to the group *Jeunesse de l'Eglise*
and in general of the relation of the Church with the workers
and with Communism. There are serious tensions also in
Italy—more than one would expect from superficial observation.

Not only on the part of "conservatives" are there tendencies
to push matters to extremes and to lead, at least practically,
to the formation of fronts and parties. We cannot help
noticing that it is precisely on the side of the "progressives,"
at least among some groups, that there is too much readiness
to speak about oppositions, even about insurmountable oppositions, and about people "with whom it is no longer possible to speak." There is also too great a use of slogans which
express more a superficial posture, a fashion, than an internal
conviction. If we wish to arrive at a true renewal of Christian
life, we must be open to one another. It is certainly an unhealthy situation when Catholics show true openness toward
humanists and Protestants but not toward their fellow Catholics, even though these may be old-fashioned. It is not a

healthy phenomenon to speak all the time of the good qualities of our separated brethren and the bad qualities of many Catholics. This attitude, which probably has some connection with an inferiority complex and a degree of immaturity, creates resistance to a sound renewal and adaptation; it also fosters the spirit of partisanship.

This tendency to form fronts and parties is furthered by a number of "side effects" that accompany the movement of renewal in the Church. We do not mean the decline of the life of faith, the noiseless falling away from the faith and, in general, the dechristianization of society. These are really the counterpart of the renewal; in times of unrest there is always both a new flowering and decadence. By "side effects" we mean certain facts and tendencies that present themselves as a renewal but in reality are not that at all. These phenomena show a false flag. Many people are more or less afraid of identifying those phenomena because they are likely to be shut up with the retort: "You are a conservative!" And this is feared so much more when influential newspapers and periodicals use such words as invectives. Thus there exists an element of unfreedom in the most necessary dialogue about renewal and adaptation. This is an unhealthy phenomenon in our Catholic community. It should remain possible for both sides to speak out and state clearly what they think of the situation. Hence it should also remain possible to point to the true nature of some elements which falsely present themselves as "progressive," without being stigmatized as an ultraconservative.

One of the "side effects" of the renewal, which we now have in mind and which causes great confusion, is the very *imprudent way of speaking adopted by some priests*. Not a few of the faithful become confused by such behavior. Many are incapable of digesting such things and become bewildered. Others find in them a stimulus for their own deviating ideas.

But there are also protests. And not only on the part of the so-called simple Christians. Many a Catholic intellectual is often scandalized by the unqualified "modern" statements made by priests in the pulpit, in the press and in more or less private conversations.

"Getting involved in the reality of modern life," as it is called by some priests, must also be called imprudent. Some priests lose themselves in activity; they want to go wherever people go and do what they do, casting off every restraint. This attitude causes surprise not only among those who are out of touch with the spirit of their time. The priest has his particular function to fulfill; he is not the whole Church. There are also laypeople who can represent the Church much better in certain fields.

Another phenomenon of puberty that accompanies the renewal, manifests itself in *laypeople*. In the past few years there have been a number of articles in newspapers and reviews that were very critical of ecclesiastical authorities and defended daring theological views without helping their solution in the least. If some priest protested against irresponsible writings, the answer came quickly: "Is a layman not permitted to say what he thinks about the hierarchy?" and "Has a layman not the right to study theology?" The ready reply to both questions is that, of course, he has those rights, but that is not the point. The fact that these questions are asked as a reply to criticism of "daring" utterances, shows a definite lack of maturity and an adolescent mentality. While one can and must be mild in judging such symptoms, they are a source of difficulties.

The greatest danger, however, of the movement toward renewal is that it remains *too much limited to an upper layer*. In the past, this situation has often made movements of renewal end in failure. They often remained restricted to an elite and did not affect the ecclesial community as a whole.

45

The whole People of God must be involved in that renewal. It is not because diocesan papers and Catholic periodicals have much to say about the renewal or because wonderfully worded Constitutions and Decrees are sent out from the Council or the Pope that renewal is actually taking place.

For example, in many parishes the renewal manifests itself only in the disappearance of certain traditions and devotions. Their clergy feel uncertain and this uncertainty inevitably affects the parishioners themselves. Such a situation is not exactly a desirable effect of a spiritual renewal. There are, of course, also parishes in which there has been a great reawakening. In most of them there exist excellent relations between pastors, assistants and laymen; there is contact, dialogue and sincere discussion.

The attitude of the faithful toward the Bible, formerly considered by some as a "Protestant book," is gradually changing, although a few are still scandalized when they hear about Bible Vigils. But it is well know how much ignorance remains, not only about the Old Testament which for many is unexplored territory, but even with respect to the New Testament which many Catholics have never read from beginning to end. Yet knowledge of the Bible is necessary for a fully Christian life today. Fortunately our sermons are becoming more and more scriptural. So is our school catechesis.[19a]

Ignorance of the content and form of expression of Holy Scripture, we now realize so well, is one of the great obstacles in the way of liturgical renewal. Reading scriptural texts in the vernacular will not help the faithful if the words are not explained to them in a homily. And without that explanation, such reading might lead to misunderstandings or boredom. The liturgy is wholly scriptural; and only if Holy Scripture

---

[19a]Cf. *Fundamentals and Programs for a Renewed Catechesis*, Duquesne University Press, 1966.

is appreciated will the liturgy be appreciated and participated in intelligently. It is also necessary to foster a proper
concept of the Church and of the Sacraments, for the liturgy
is the social worship of the Church, and the sacraments are
the liturgical channels by which the graces of Christ are
distributed.

PREREQUISITES FOR A GENUINE RENEWAL

Standing as we are in the midst of the urge for renewal,
it is impossible to give a definitive evaluation of this movement. While accepting it in a positive way, we must dare
to look at the tensions, the side effects and the shortcomings
present in that movement. No one will blame us if we abruptly end here this survey of the growth of the Catholic reformation, for this renewal is still going on and has not reached
any stage that could even provisionally be called a kind of
terminus.

In conclusion, we may be permitted to mention four virtues
that should mark the urge for genuine renewal:

1. A Sense of Responsibility. Although a sense of responsibility for one's own person can sometimes be wanting, a con-
scientious Christian is usually well aware of this responsibility.
But is it not true that we are much less aware of being responsible for the community, the Church, and all mankind,
in all our attitudes and activities? Everyone of us must consider himself personally responsible for cooperating in the
renewal, for helping mankind in its efforts to get out of the
present spiritual crisis. Wailing over the "evils of the present
time" and then peacefully withdrawing into one's shell are
unworthy of a Christian. Of course, not all are able to engage in external activities. But even aside from direct apostolic work, there are many possibilities; for instance, we can
avoid the extreme individualism that all too often has dominated our prayers and sacramental life. Whoever has a true

47

sense of responsibility will find ways to do what he can for the present renewal.

2. *Courage to Look at the Crisis.* We must dare to look at and accept the fact that we are passing through a crisis even in the realm of religion. Perhaps it may seem unnecessary to be reminded of that, for only the totally blind are unaware that many things are going on in the world and in the Church. But that is not what we mean. We must dare to see and recognize the crisis that tends to renewal as such. In the first place, we must dare to accept that we face not merely some disconnected great or small events, things "that will blow over," but are in the presence of a coherent phenomenon that certainly will result in profound changes. In many fields it will be necessary to free ourselves from our own familiar little world and from many religious practices and customs. We must dare to take a leap into the future.

3. *Courage to Make Experiments.* It is necessary to have the spiritual courage to make experiments. The courage to discern the crisis in religious life is necessary, but not enough. We must examine how we shall translate our ideas of renewal into practice; this means that things must be tried out and also that we must accept the risk of making mistakes at the beginning. The courage to make experiments means more than abolishing a number of customs under the pressure of circumstances, for instance, in the life of the parish, in the family, in convents, seminaries and monasteries. In order to avoid the creation of a vacuum, parents, priests, sisters, youth leaders, etc. themselves must look for new ways. The right ways, however, will not be found at once. A new experiment is not yet a new form of Christian living. The road to the future will be strewn with unsuccessful experiments.

4. *Translating New Ideas Into Action.* There are already a number of achievements in the religious sphere that are the

result of the modern changes and the renewal of the religious mentality. There are things about which, at least for the time being, there is almost perfect agreement; here the stage of experimentation is almost over. But unfortunately, we are still far from having translated those accepted ideas into *practice*. Let us take as an example the new community approach toward the Eucharist. In some parishes the social character of the Eucharist is indeed manifest, but in many others the community character of the Mass was hardly noticeable until the new liturgy almost forced both clergy and people to change their practice. Even now, aren't there still parishes where, in spite of all the literature on the liturgy, the clergy and laypeople stick to ancient customs and practices that make the Mass appear as a spectacle and receiving Communion during it a private devotion?

In spite of so much that has been said and done, especially under the powerful initiative of Pope John XXIII, we are still at the beginning of the movement of renewal with its return to the sources and its *aggiornamento*. What the Church will be like at the end of this century is difficult, if not impossible, to foresee. We already know the importance of the mutually connected factors of the media of communications and the spirit of ecumenism. The whole world has become one world by those media and it is now possible to influence the minds of all mankind for better or for worse. Then there is the ecumenical movement which, when properly defined, does not aim at the immediate return of separate Christians to the fold of Mother Church but prepares the way through dialogue and prayers for a better understanding of the sources of division and the nature of mutual differences; a movement which prompts Catholics to renew and reform first of all themselves and thus to present to separated Christians a proper image of the Church. When eventually a one and undivided Church is achieved through the grace of God, it will most certainly differ greatly from what we can now imagine.

2. The Central Position of the Church as Community

THE ROOTS OF THE SOCIAL CRISIS IN THE FEUDAL AND INDIVIDUALISTIC ERAS

There exists a general crisis in man's social consciousness which has deep roots in history. On the one hand, there is still at present a very serious deficiency of social consciousness; on the other, there is also, though only half perceived by many, an ardent desire for a more developed community life. This phenomenon is not peculiar to the Church but is universal. It presents an apparently contradictory appearance; it cries out for community, for human relations, also for human relations with a fixed structure; but, on the other hand, it also cries for room to allow one to be oneself.

It is only at first sight, however, that that appearance is self-contradictory. History reveals that the German feudalism which arose in the early Middle Ages had an enormous influence until the end of the eighteenth century, and even after that. The whole of society was built on it. Individualism, which became so strongly opposed to feudalism precisely in the eighteenth century, had its roots in the later Middle Ages when great emphasis was put on the value and the freedom of the person. This emphasis became constantly greater and reached a very strong though one-sided apex in individualism.

For a long time, and in a certain sense even today, the feudal structure and way of thinking and, on the other hand, the individualistic structures and mentality have continued to exist side by side and mingled with one another.[20] Feudalism

---

[20]See, e.g., for feudalism, Martin G. Plattel, *Social Philosophy*, Duquesne University Press, 1965; for individualism, see Remy C. Kwant, *Phenomenology of Social Existence*, Duquesne University Press, 1965.

as a mode of thought is now completely dead, whereas the individualistic mentality still exercises great influence that finds expression also in social structures. But for a long time there has also existed a strong reaction against individualism. Strict individualism was itself a reaction and, on that account, fell into exaggerations: exaggerations that had unfortunate social results, especially for the weaker social groups. Among the more successful social groups, i.e., those which could lead a wealthy life thanks to economic liberalism, it led to self-satisfaction. It is easy to understand that their smug and self-satisfied attitude has been called a "bourgeois" mentality. For it is precisely in the bourgeois circle, who unleashed the French Revolution and established the individualist-liberal society, that the feeling of success and self-satisfaction was predominant.

In our days there is a repugnance for everything that is feudal or proceeds from it: a dislike for a rigid hierarchical social structure with a small group at the helm and a large group that must obey and follow. There is an equal repugnance for the bourgeois individualistic system in which there is no question at all of community and "equal" opportunities exist only for those who are economically strong. As a result there is presently a real crisis and it is often impossible to understand one another when we speak of society and community. The terms have ambiguous and controversial meanings. They evoke in some minds reminiscences of the old feudal system, although they may not even know the latter word. For others they evoke the spectre of a collectivistic mass in which man's personality is lost. On the other hand, some people equate the stress on personality with individualism.

And yet it is certain that there exists a general desire for relations worthy of men, for human relations in which we know we are really together as men; in other words, there is a desire for community. We can reject the particular social structure that is called feudalism and yet have a longing for community. It is possible to reject individualism and yet strive for the unfolding of personality, namely, in community. The so-called deficiency of social consciousness and the desire for a more human community, when seen against the historical background, are only a seeming contradiction.

Those tensions are also present in the Church. In her, too, the desire for community is also alive. In fact, all sorts of social structures have influenced the mentality and the shape of the Church. In particular the German feudal social structure has exercised considerable influence on the life of the Church. A general social influence is really something one should expect, since the Church like Christ has become totally incarnate in human life. We simply must accept that the social life of the Church in one era differs greatly from that of another era. And so it is evident that the present call for a community structure is in great part the product of our modern democratic ideas.

However, the Church should never become completely equated with the state and society. We are not permitted to call the Church a democracy in the strict politico-social sense, and she cannot become a democracy in that sense. But neither is she a monarchy or anything else in the political sense. The Church has her own structure, a structure that is based on Christ's work of salvation. However, in this structure certain features become prominent, features that are *de facto* closely connected with the structure of the society in which the Church is established. In this sense it is clear that we are presently opposed to all sorts of remnants of the feudal structure. We say thus that our repugnance springs from the idea of democracy, but in a broader and deeper sense, viz., the democratic idea as an expression and incarnation of the desire for an authentic humanity in which the person is fully appreciated within the community.

In the Church there is an equally great aversion to the bourgeois individualism which, in its turn, has left profound traces in the Church. But in this case it is more a question of a mentality than of structures. From the structural standpoint the Church reminds us much more of the feudal structure than of individualism. Whatever one may think, historically speaking, about the feudal structure,and no matter how many healthy elements were present at the beginning of the feudal period, that structure no longer fits our present society. The feudal structure with its "lords" and "serfs," in the strict sense of feudalism, continued to exist until the French Revolution; and even after that it retained its influence in large sections of the world. That social structure has undoubtedly exercised great influence on the Church; it has been very influential in preventing the emancipation of the laity. It is also largely because of the influence of the feudal structure that the hierarchical functions in the Church were not seen from the standpoint of the community, that is, as functions in service of the community. Rather, they were looked on as a tenure belonging to the functionary, as a kind of possession obtained from a "feudal lord" much as the great feudal lords put their vassals in possession of a holding or feudal estate.

During feudal times the bishops, from the political standpoint, were the vassals of the sovereign; and from the spiritual standpoint they were more or less vassals of the pope, although the political element had no doubt a considerable influence. The bishops in turn had their own "serfs," the priests, who were put in possession of a parish, often as a reward for services. The latter, in turn, looked upon the parishioners more or less as upon serfs; and from the social standpoint this is what they were most of the time. Hence those parishioners had nothing to do but obey.

This set-up, of course, has disappeared. But there remain all sorts of regulations, practices, situations and especially ideas that are still alive and that strongly remind us of that feudal structure. The appointment of functionaries must still be followed by a "taking possession of" or "being installed" in a see, a parish, a function. Typical also is the granting of a function for life. Making a functionary thus irremovable is certainly not advantageous to the interests of the community he is supposed to "serve," but seems exclusively for the benefit of the "possessor."[21] This whole idea of a "possession" that is entrusted to a vassal by a lord, is clearly a remnant of the feudal system, and even today there are places where it causes serious difficulties.

Add to this the fact that this feudal structure was a Western, a European, and even a German feature. Now that the Church is face to face with other social structures of every kind, not only in the West but in the whole world, the demand becomes more and more urgent that the Church should eliminate those traces of feudalism.

We must even ask ourselves if the blotting out of all vestiges of feudalism will not be necessary for the future spiritual encounter with communism when this system has lost some of its virulent anti-religious spirit. This has happened with liberalism, especially with respect to religious freedom which at first was conceived and applied quite differently from its present-day sense. It will be necessary for the Church to reflect deeply on her own nature and task, and when she takes account of existing social structures she must endeavor

---

[21]The *Decree on the Pastoral Office of Bishops in the Church* of Vatican Council II stresses that "bishops should stand in the midst of their people as those who *serve*" (Ch. II, art. 16). "requests" them to resign when old age or other serious reasons makes them less capable of exercising their pastoral office (Ch. II, art. 21). The same invitation is extended to pastors (Ch. II, art. 31).

to foster the general tendency to give greater influence to the people, to the whole community. Adaptation to existing conditions does not mean that the Church should abolish leading ecclesiastical functions, or that appointment to them should be made by popular vote, for even in democracies there is often only indirect representation. She should rather keep in mind that "community" means a whole composed of smaller interconnected and adapted groups, having centers of direction and government; in any case, "community" does not mean a formless mass, but a properly ordered whole.

The structure of the Church, in respect to its fundamental pattern that came from Christ, is very well suited to that purpose. And now there will be great possibilities to develop the Church more as a community. For the episcopal function and the episcopal college, the truly apostolic office, will be brought into greater relief in the Church, as a function that has its own competence and significance, though always in union with and under the direction of the Bishop of Rome.

In fact, however, the Church does not yet function well as a community. The active interest of church-goers is generally small in contrast with the lively interest of Mormons, Seventh Day Adventists and Jehovah's Witnesses. There are still many Catholics who consider it normal not to think and work together with the Church, but to simply follow orders and directions. Others, on the contrary, think it right to contribute to a dialogue within the Church, but are more or less convinced that they will not be permitted to do so, and, therefore, keep quiet and become peripheral Church-members.

In this respect it is also quite understandable that a certain anticlericalism exists within the Church itself. The structure of the Church, influenced by feudalism, almost necessarily brought with it an overemphasis on the clergy. In several European countries there was a violent reaction against that form of "clericalism." Many looked upon the clergy, identified them with the Church itself as a "ruling class," and turned away from the Church. Others, including many priests, basing themselves on a better view of the Church, resisted that clericalization while trying not to oppose the proper and necessary function of Church authority.[22]

There are many possibilities for changing that situation, but it stands to reason that first the mentality existing in the Church must be patiently and perseveringly modified and a profound study made of the nature of the Church in relation to the society in which she exists. The Church, particularly as community, is strongly connected with the sociological structures of society. The Church, in today's world, standing amidst so many nations and peoples, must do everything possible to adapt herself to the structures of those nations and peoples. She must not try to introduce elements that come from a former and, in fact, very limited structure of society, into peoples of different mentality and different times. On the contrary, she must try to give shape in various sociological structures to what constitutes the heart of her community life, namely, the union of all in Christ as children of the Father. Those structures can vary greatly in the present world, and on that account the Church will have to limit the number of concrete regulations precisely in order to foster the community life of those peoples. But when we look at the present situation of the Church, we cannot help noticing that precisely in this matter there still exist great obstacles. As the Church is now, it remains difficult to experience her as a true community, despite the fact that everyone would like to do so.

---

[22]Cf., e.g., "Der Kampf gegen den Klerikalismus," *Herder Korrespondenz,* vol. 8 (1953-54), pp. 530-537; and "Katholisches Denken und Klerikalismus," *ibid.,* 575-582.

THE CHURCH AS COMMUNITY

When we survey the greatly varying tendencies in the Church, we see that in one way or another they are centered around the mystery of the Church and, in particular, around the Church as community.

Already during the two decades between the world wars, there was an increasing interest in the mystery of the Church, especially in theological circles. This interest became much greater in the thirties, as is evidenced by the large number of popular theological writings about this question. The term "mystical body of Christ" became fashionable in those years. The encyclical bearing the same name (1943) can justly be called the fruit of that growing interest in the Church, although no modern theologian believes that this document— or even the *Constitution on the Church* of Vatican Council II—has said the last word about the Church. Nevertheless, this encyclical has certainly acted as a powerful stimulus in a movement that was already under way.[23]

The most evident characteristic of these studies, ideas and conversations about the Church is the fact that we are gradually rediscovering a balance between the Church as an institution and the Church as community. There is no longer so great an emphasis on the Church as a hierarchical institution. That emphasis was understandable from the historical standpoint. Because the Reformers denied the hierarchical office in the sense in which it was understood by the Catholic Church, the Council of Trent reacted by giving an unambiguous expression of that office. This emphasis on the institutional character of the Church was propagated in theological writings, in the popular preaching of the Counter Reformation, and has continued to live until our own times.

---

[23]A.A.S., vol. 35 (1943); Joseph Bluett, *The Mystical Body of Christ. Text and Analysis*, America Press, 1943.

It led to a very narrow viewpoint among Catholics and even among those who lived outside the Catholic Church. The Church for most people is the pope, the bishops and the pastors. This view is now on the decline; there is a growing awareness that the Church is a true community: she is the People of God which is the sign of salvation for the world, the People of God that is not only a symbol of God's goodness and a sign that awakens and exhorts, but a sign that indeed can and undoubtedly will bring salvation to all who desire to accept it.[24]

The relations within the Church herself also are affected by this new and different attention to the Church. For a number of years there have been discussions regarding the relationship between the hierarchical office and the ecclesial community; the relationship between the ordained priesthood and the general priesthood; the relationship between priest and layman. And we can truly speak here of a discussion. What has been brought to the fore, especially in popular writings, conferences, and dialogues, has not always been properly balanced. We may probably call this an advantage, for that question, which had not been discussed for centuries —at least not in this way—may thereby be helped to reach maturity. It is to be hoped that the dialogue regarding the proper relation between the office and the faithful, between the office and the community, will still remain a more or less open question for many years.

Insofar as everyone must accept the fundamental role of the hierarchical function in the Church, the question is not an open one. And about this there exists no real difficulty. Every Catholic accepts the true function of the office in the Church. No Catholic entertains the desire to abolish that

---

[24]Cf. Vatican Council II's *Constitution on the Church,* Ch. I, art. 8.

58

office; no one wishes to diminish and limit it or to place it under supervision. However, there are all sorts of attempts to envision that office in its pure state; they would like to purify and free it from a variety of accessory tasks that are not essential to it. The task of the priest in the early Church was fully circumscribed, but by custom and tradition all sorts of things were added to it. About these we now doubt whether they are truly priestly functions. A number of functions that are now fulfilled by priests are now looked upon as functions that really belong to laypeople, or that at least need not be performed by priests.

The great difficulty, however, concerns the definition and establishment of the position and place of the layman in the Church. At the present moment there is an almost universal acceptance of the view that the Church is a large community of the baptized, who all, therefore, have a share in Christ's priesthood in virtue of baptism and confirmation. But within this one community there is a small, serving group which, precisely because of its serving function, has a special share in Christ's priesthood and obtains this priesthood through ordination, in virtue of the official conferring of an office by the Church. In this way we avoid breaking up the Church, as it were, into two groups: the ruling clergy and docile laypeople. Although this principle is now generally accepted, this whole question of the relation between the office and the faithful has not yet been fully clarified.

This question we shall examine in more detail later. But what we are interested in presently is this question of the relation of the priest and the layman in the Church as it arises from another view of the nature of the Church than the one we have been familiar with until now: it rests on a growing interest, an increasing appreciation of the Church as a community, of the Church as the People of God.

The problem of the Church and the world[25] is connected with this question of priest and layman. This problem is now no longer looked upon as exclusively a matter of the relationship of Church authority with civil authority, and it is certainly not seen in a defensive or negative sense. But that question is now presented rather from the standpoint of the ecclesial community as such: How do we as Christians stand in this world? How must we value this world? How must we Christianize it? How must we accept it and what things of this world must we reject?

When we put the question regarding the relation of the Church and the world in this way, the position of the layman in that problem comes much more strongly to the fore. For it is rightly said that it is precisely the layman who is always and in every respect in touch with what we are accustomed to call the "affairs of this world." It is the layman who is active in politics, who is engaged in industry, in medical science, who is occupied with scientific research, and so on. Hence precisely in virtue of this different idea of the nature of the Church we have now another view of the relation of the Church and the world, and it is a broader view.

The realm of worship and piety also is greatly influenced by the idea of community. Great tensions developed in the liturgy in the course of the centuries. On the one hand, the official liturgy showed a social, though formalized, structure; on the other, there existed a strongly individualistic piety. There was no genuine consciousness of an ecclesial community which as a community celebrates the liturgy, but merely a coexistence of two juxtaposed realities: an official,

---

[25]Cf. Albert Dondeyne, *Faith and the World,* 2nd impr., Duquesne University Press, 1964, and Gill and Son, Dublin, 1964; Gerard Philips, "The Church in the Modern World," *Concilium,* vol. 6 (1965), pp. 5-22.

but lifeless liturgy and a narrow, one-sided, devotional, individualistic piety.

The realization that we worship and celebrate the liturgy as an ecclesial community, that all our piety, even our personal piety, must be founded on the celebration of the liturgy of the Word and the Sacrament, has now begun to spread among the clergy and laity of the Church. But this is a laborious process. A deviation developed and grown strong in the course of centuries cannot be corrected overnight. It is evident, however, that the new concept of the Church greatly stimulates the liturgical movement of renewal.

The parish also became the object of growing attention in the decade before World War II when there developed a new interest in the Church. The parish, in those days, was thought of principally as being the core of the mystical body of Christ. On that account a particularly strong emphasis was placed on the parish as community. We observe, in those years, an almost complete identification of the mystical body of Christ and the parish, in the sense that in the thought of those days there was no room for any other form of community or of pastoral care than the parish.

Pastoral care itself is also seen at present from the standpoint of the community. While this view is not new, at least insofar as the parish is concerned, things are quite different from what they were before the war. First of all, the study of pastoral care as it exists throughout the Church is now coupled with a critical study of actual structures, a critical study from the sociological standpoint. We start no longer simply from an *a priori* theoretical consideration that the parish is a community *because* it is part of the mystical body of Christ and even its principal incarnation. We now study very thoroughly to what extent the parish as it is corresponds

61

to that community structure. And we are thus immediately confronted with a great number of doubts.

Recently, a shift is taking place on a more theological level: the bishop and the diocese are receiving greater attention than formerly. Although this shift is, no doubt, influenced by sociological discoveries, it is due especially to the fact that we have acquired a better insight into the nature of the Church. Because there is a better understanding of the Church there is also a better understanding of the apostolic function of the bishop and, hence, also of the significance of the greater unit called a "diocese," which is under the direction of the bishop. From this naturally arise a great number of very practical questions. But also in regard to pastoral care, it is quite evident that, when we speak from the standpoint of the community, we proceed on the basis of a richer and broader concept of the Church.

Finally, there is a growing realization that pastoral care is no longer the exclusive task of the priest. And this is not the same idea that existed in the first years of "Catholic Action," namely, that the layman should help the priest because there were too few priests. Today the necessary contribution of the layman is based directly on the idea that the layman as a member of the Church has a share in the Church's work of salvation. Hence it can be said that the broadening of the concept of the Church brings with it also a broadening of the concept of pastoral care.

COMMUNITY AND PERSON[26]

One can say that the last decades were marked, as far as the Church is concerned, by a reaction against individualism. And it was truly a *reaction*: the whole emphasis was placed

---

[26]For a general study of this topic see H. P. Walgrave, *Person and Society. A Christian View,* Duquesne University Press, 1965.

on the community. But it must be said that the emphasis was somewhat undifferentiated. The impression was given, not infrequently, that the Church had little interest in the person and in the development of personality. Many spoke rather vaguely about the "parish community." Massive gatherings, mass demonstrations, gigantic congresses were the order of the day. Great and powerful organizations meant very much to the Church but there is no doubt that they also contributed most to the neglect of the person.

This more or less "reactionary" emphasis on the community is evident in the field of liturgy and piety. There had been a great degeneration in liturgy and piety in the direction of extreme individualism, and it is understandable that at the beginning liturgical reformers sometimes went too far in stressing the communal character of piety and worship. It is also quite natural that many of the faithful developed a certain fear or dislike for liturgical innovations precisely because there seemed to be no more room for personal piety. A great many reactions against the new liturgical ways undoubtedly sprang from an individualistic mentality. But it must be recognized that there was also an element of "reaction" in the liturgical movement itself; for it spoke sometimes too unqualifiedly about the community and paid too little attention to the personal piety of the faithful.

At the present stage of development we find, beside an emphasis on the community, a strong emphasis on the *person*. Man wishes to be himself, not a number in a faceless crowd. We can see a certain tension between the underscoring of the person and the stressing of the idea of community. This tension might sometimes appear to be an opposition between the person and the community. But in reality, when the person is emphasized, this does not mean a reaction against the idea of community but against being a faceless number in the mass. And it is only insofar as he identifies the community with the mass, that one could get the impression today that less attention is paid to the value of the community because there is a greater respect for the person.

Whether the emphasis lies on the community or on the person is merely a matter of a different facet of one and the same tendency. Conflict can arise only insofar as one of the facets makes us forget the other. A proper concept of community very emphatically calls for a respect of the person and the opportunities for unfolding and developing the personality. And the reverse is equally true: it is not possible to form a true community when the components of the community are not really persons. This fact is perfectly evident in the Church at the present time. Very many endeavors to foster the community end in failure because, as we commonly express it, "people are not ready for it." This not-being-ready means in great measure that they are not accustomed to contributing their share by thinking, speaking and acting for themselves, by bearing personal responsibility and being personally concerned about the Church. This situation is noticeable in all strata of the Church: in priests, religious and laypeople.

The present emphasis on the human person is of priceless value for the formation of a true community spirit. But "community" must then be understood as a complex whole: an orderly totality of persons, of smaller and larger groups who, together, each having its own responsibility, form a true and properly functioning community.

It cannot be denied that one of the most important spiritual phenomena of our time is the great importance that is attached to the human person. Man was created by God to be the ruler of creation; the living and lifeless creatures in his world are at his service. Man is raised by God to the dignity of a child of the Father and a brother of Jesus Christ,

the Incarnate Word of God. In and by Christ man has risen
high in dignity.

This is the Christian view of the value of human personality. It is a theocentric view that has a higher esteem for
man than any anthropocentric view. Modern science, following another road, also comes to a high esteem of the human
person. It is with gratitude that we must accept the attain-
ments of modern science. It would not be reasonable to allow
some exaggerations and partialities to lessen the significance
and the Christian freedom of man. The foundations of that
human worth are and remain God's work of creation and
salvation. Pope Leo the Great's admonition in the liturgy of
Christmas eve remains fully actual: "O Christian, realize your
dignity!"

CONCLUSION

Ecclesial consciousness, the realization of what the Church
is, is the central point in the new and developing pattern of
spiritual life and pastoral care. It is easy to show that this
Church-consciousness, as the foundation of pastoral care and
the spiritual life, is in clear contrast with the mentality of
the period that is now coming to a close. However, in spite
of that sharp contrast, we must not see the whole matter in
terms of black and white. Though there is an evident difference in mentality, we must also recognize that there is continuity in the life of the Church. Moreover, there is always a
flowing, transitional line between various periods.

When we look backwards we see clearly that, for instance,
the mentality of the third century differs greatly from that
of the ninth century. But we have to stand at a certain dis-
tance from the facts in order to appreciate such differences,
and this is especially true when the evidence is not very
patent. The closer we are to a certain time the more difficult

it is to make judgments about it. And it is certainly a dangerous undertaking for us who are still living in the twentieth century to draw a clear distinction between the nineteenth and the twentieth centuries. Hence it is astonishing that contemporary man so strongly feels that he is living in a different period. This goes to show that the change must already have struck deep roots. Vatican Council II bears an eloquent witness to this general feeling when, speaking about man's growing sense of personal dignity and responsibility, it says: "We are witnesses of the birth of a new humanism, one in which man is first of all defined by this responsibility to his brothers and to history."[27]

---

[27]*Constitution on the Church in the Modern World,* Part II, Ch. II, art. 55.

CHAPTER TWO

Changes in the Organizational Structure of the Church

THE tensions present in the Church are more easily noticeable in her organized life. These tensions and the changes that flow from them have a more profound underground, but one naturally first notices them in the visible and organized expressions of Church life. Here we meet first of all the present vitality of the Church. It is precisely those external features of renewal and change that call forth a number of questions whose solution will lead us to the foundations of that movement. That is why we consider it preferable to speak first about the changes in the organizational structure of the Church and after that to deal with the changes in the spiritual structure of the Church.

1. Hierarchy and Laity

THE LAYMAN IN CHURCH AND SOCIETY IN FEUDAL AND POST-FEUDAL TIMES

The changing relationship between hierarchy and laity is one of the most important features that strikes our attention in the organizational picture of the Church's history. With respect to the ancient Church, it is not possible to speak of the existence of tension between the hierarchy and the laity, in the strict sense of the word. The Christian community accepted guidance as a matter of course; it accepted the ecclesiastical office. It was also considered natural for laypeople to take an active part in Church life and to do their share in theological thinking.

A problem could arise only when there was a further development of the hierarchical function and particularly when the clergy became a social class. Now this has been the case increasingly and in a very special manner since the rise of feudalism. The specific characteristic of the feudal structure resulted in a society in which there was a small group of rulers, of men who had authority. Hence, when tensions arose between the clergy and the laity, it was not a matter of tension between the clergy and the large body of the faithful, but between the clergy—mostly the pope and bishops—and that small ruling social group.

With respect to the Middle Ages and their problem of hierarchy and laity, we must avoid transplanting our modern concepts to that time. The "layman" of those days was in fact a totally different person than the "layman" about whom *we* speak in the relationship between priest and layman. In those days it was clearly a question of relations between the leaders of the hierarchy, the leaders of the clerical class, and the feudal rulers. These feudal lords exercised a great influence on the Church. With varying degrees of success, the Church was constantly trying to diminish the influence of those laymen on her councils, ecclesiastical appointments and on the ownership of Church property. It is certainly unjust to invoke the attitude of the Church in those matters as an example of the Church's attitude toward the layman. If it is done nevertheless, the dialogue about hierarchy and laity is doomed to failure.

The struggle between the hierarchy and the "laity," in the sense we have explained, was coupled already in the Middle Ages with doctrinal discussions that aimed at diminishing one another's influence. In the twelfth and thirteenth centuries we note the increasing influence of the hierarchy and particularly of the papacy. Nevertheless, the bishops were often appointed by the rulers, and on that account those lords had great influence on the bishops and thus also on the priests. But the popes maintained their independence for a long time, although we know the tragic history of the so-called Babylonian captivity in Avignon.

It is certain that one reason for the increase of papal power, even over bishops, was that the pope alone was able to restrain and reduce somewhat the influence rulers and other lords had on the life of the Church at that time, an influence that already several times had proved disastrous. This struggle between the papacy and the rulers, we notice, was not merely a struggle for power; it was also accompanied on the part of rulers by an effort to spread ideas that tended to give greater power to the faithful in the Church; and this influence was, on account of the conditions of that time, strongly colored by the power of the rulers themselves.

There was, however, also another factor that favored new ideas regarding the place of the hierarchy in the Church. These ideas aimed at restricting its function and role, at giving more freedom to the faithful and securing for the latter an opportunity to exercise greater influence in the Church. In the fifteenth and sixteenth centuries a loud cry for reform was heard and it is a fact that both the papacy and the rest of the hierarchy acted as an obstacle to that reform. That eagerness for reform strongly favored the new and older ideas concerning the need of restricting the powers of the hierarchy. It is well-known that the Reformers attacked the hierarchy at its very core and took away from the ecclesiastical office even that which, in the eyes of the Church, constituted its deepest meaning. We also know how the Church reacted to all that. In opposition to the errors and the continued attempts of rulers to obtain or maintain influence in the Church, she put the office of the hierarchy in a clear light and repressed the influence of the laity as much as possible.

REFLECTION ON THE LAYMAN'S POSITION IN THE CHURCH IN A DEMOCRATIC SOCIETY

At present there is a new reflection about the relationship of hierarchy and laity. This reflection takes place in an entirely different social situation. The layman of today is totally different from the laymen against whom the Church of the Middle Ages saw herself obliged to struggle. We can and must look at things as they are before us and, in this respect, we must forget the ideas we have inherited from the past.[1]

In Holy Scripture we do not find the word "layman" (*laikos*) nor the equivalent of the word "cleric" (*clericus*). But there is an abundant use of the word *laos* with the explicit meaning of "People of God," as contrasted to the pagans, the "unholy" peoples. This meaning was maintained in the tradition of the Church; but beside that there is also a clear distinction of the "clergy," on the basis of a divine regulation. Soon there was added the concept of "religious" (*religiosus*).

With respect to the content of these ideas, the situation was as follows: little was said about the content of the

---

[1]Concerning the relationship between hierarchy and laypeople and especially the position of the laymen in the Church, see Vatican Council II's *Constitution on the Church;* Yves Congar, *Lay People in the Church,* Newman, 2nd ed., 1965; *Laity, Church and World,* Helicon, 1961; John D. Gerken, *Toward a Theology of the Layman,* Herder and Herder, 1963; Hendrik Schillebeeckx, *The Layman in the Church and Other Essays,* Alba House, 1964; Max Thurian, *Consecration of the Layman,* Helicon, 1963; Gustave Thils, *Mission du clergé et du laicat,* Brugge, 1945; Karl Rahner, *Theology for Renewal: Bishops, Priests, Laity,* Sheed and Ward, 1964; George H. Tavard, *The Church, the Layman and the Modern World,* Macmillan, 1959; Jacques Leclercq, *Christians in the World,* Sheed and Ward, 1961.

"layman"; he was evidently a Christian who sanctifies himself in the world; to be a "cleric" was not looked upon as a *state* of life but as a *function;* to be a "religious" was a *form* of life.

In spite of this threefold division, which is not at all adequate, we must be particularly on our guard against forgetting what they had in common. All the baptized, be they clerics or religious, religious clerics or neither one nor the other, are "laypeople" in the deepest sense of the word, namely, children of the People of God. From the midst of this people a group is chosen which must fulfill a definite and important *function* in the ensemble of that People of God. That is, the members of this group can say: "The Lord is the part of my inheritance," and they are "enslaved for divine ministries" (*divinis ministeriis mancipati*). But these functionaries remain full, and we may say pre-eminently, members of the People of God. Hence they have a special place in that people only in virtue of their function. And both the clergy and laymen, taking this term now in the narrow sense, can, for the sake of their own perfection, adopt a certain form of life on account of which they are called "religious," a form of life which, however, is also important to the Church as such. Hence the question regarding the place of the layman in the Church is one that directly concern *all* Christians. To be a cleric and to be a religious are merely specifications affecting certain groups.

We see then that the "theology of the layman" is an important chapter in the doctrine concerning the Church. If we wish to get a somewhat clear picture, it is necessary to distinguish two aspects in the *one* Church; this is a point that has been particularly stressed by Yves Congar. The Church is the community of all in Christ, and this community is expressed in the word *ecclesia* (assembly). The Church, therefore, is a "community of salvation," but the

71

Church is also the ensemble of the means of salvation, which we express by the words "institute of salvation." This is one of the essential points in the theology of the laity. This is only a distinction though a very important one. The concept of the Church as a community was powerful in the Church, from the time of the Fathers to the Counter Reformation. But that idea did not in the least detract from the idea of the Church as an institute of salvation. The idea of the Church as the "body of Christ" was related not only to the spiritual community of the saved but equally to the visible organism. The Church is the body of Christ according to two aspects: as a community and as an institute of salvation. Seen from the theological standpoint, the Church is first an institute of salvation before she is a community of salvation. But we must not see this so much as a matter of historical succession, but rather in the sense that the Church is continuously under construction until the return of the Lord when the final completion will take place.

Hence, when we look at it from the theological standpoint, the ensemble of the means of salvation by which men can be sanctified precedes the community of men who are sanctified through their union with God in Christ. This situation will last until the end of time. The Church is *both* a community with God in Christ *and* the means to realize that community. That which is a means will disappear at the end of time. Then the Church will be no longer in a process of construction, but she will be the completed Church. It is clear that the task of the hierarchical priesthood as such lies in the Church as an institute of salvation. But we must still discuss to what extent the layman has a task in the latter, and we must not forget that the priest also remains always a "layman," a member of God's people.

First, however, we must give our attention to the question that plays a role in that matter, namely, to the relation between the *Church* and *the world*. This is the question: the Kingdom of God will some day be finally achieved; but what role do the Church and the world play in bringing about its fulfillment? This is a question of great interest at the present time. Is this world merely a piece of scenery before which the divine drama is enacted, or does the surrounding world contribute something toward the fulfillment of the Kingdom? And how? Gustave Thils has written a good summary of this question.[2] It is impossible to deny that there exists a certain duality, a certain internal and external tension between the Church and the world. But is this duality an insuperable dualism? Does everything we call "the world," everything we do in the natural, "profane" field, have absolutely no significance for the development of the Kingdom of God? Is it perhaps only an obstacle?

In broad lines we can distinguish two views: 1) the dualistic-eschatological view, which no doubt can invoke many texts of the New Testament especially from St. Paul; 2) the incarnational view. Although this twofold division leaves out many nuances and is somewhat artificial, there certainly are two directions and both can become guilty of exaggerations. The more eschatological view can, so to say, "leave the world alone." The incarnational view, which desires to christianize the world and earthly relations, can be guilty of exaggeration by pursuing, for instance, a "social Christianity" that ends in a "heresy of activity" and a strange mingling of spiritual and profane affairs. It will be necessary to find the correct synthesis.

This question is particularly important for the topic of "the hierarchy and the laity." For, it is especially the layman

---

[2]*Transcendance ou incarnation?*, Nauwelaerts, 1950.

who lives in the world and who, therefore, has or has not the task of christianizing the world and its conditions; it will or will not belong to him to make use of worldly relationships for his own sanctification and for the construction of the Kingdom. This does not mean that the priest has no task in that matter. The world that is still partly unredeemed and sinful is destined to be permeated by the Incarnation; the Incarnation aims at salvation, everything is directed to salvation. The end of time will fulfill all things, but it is a *fulfillment,* not a suddenly finished structure, and the construction is already under way. Salvation is partly a fact and partly an expectation.

THE ONE CHURCH OF PRIESTS AND LAYMEN

On the basis of the preceding ideas we can try to determine the position of both hierarchy and laity. As to the hierarchy, the Church is at the same time community with God in Christ *and* a means to realize this community. The hierarchy, the hierarchical priesthood, is connected with the fact that the Church is an institution of salvation, by which the community is constantly being formed. She "makes" the faithful. The priests, as such, are primarily servants and representatives of Christ. Priests must bring man to the fullness of the Incarnation. They are the ones who are the principal builders of the temple. As to the layman, those who thus receive the fullness of the life of grace must as community—and community implies person—permeate the world and its relationships. Until the return of the Lord, the Kingdom is not completed; the Church remains the seed and beginning of the Kingdom. The faithful must realize the Kingdom in their hearts and do their best to make Christ's influence permeate the world. This task belongs to all the "laity," hence also to the priests.

74

Special attention must be given to the community of priest and layman in the *one* Church, for this has special consequences for the so-called division of labor between priest and layman. There is indeed a proper field of work for the hierarchy; but, in the strict sense of the word, there is no proper field of work for the layman because we are all "laymen," i.e., we belong to the *one* people of God. It is for this we were anointed and consecrated by baptism and confirmation. The priest must try to fulfill properly his own task. Consequently, there are many tasks—for instance, the christianization of professional life—which the priest has as "layman," i.e., as member of the Church, that he must leave to laymen, in the narrow sense, as far as their direct execution is concerned.[3] There is, thus, in reality a true division of labor on the basis of the proper task of the hierarchical priesthood. While we must not allow this division of labor to be overlooked, there is, nevertheless, no split in the Church between the hierarchy and the laity. In reacting against the former lack of attention to the place of the layman in the Church, we should not try to maintain the old distinction and, at the same time, throw full light on the layman, for in this way we would merely drive the hierarchy and the laity farther apart.

We have said that the temple of the Church is constantly under construction as the institute of salvation and that this constitutes precisely the typical task of the hierarchical priesthood. But the question then presents itself whether the members of the Church who are not in the ranks of the hierarchical priesthood, who are not called to that function of service, and whom we therefore simply call "laypeople," contribute anything to the construction of the temple. Let us try to answer this question.

---

[3]Cf. *Constitution on the Church*, Ch. III, art. 31 and 36.

In the first and in the last place, it is Christ who builds the temple of the Church; He is the only and true high priest, He who is enthroned at the right hand of God's majesty in heaven. We are all in Him, in whom we were immersed by baptism, in whom we were incorporated, in whom we participate in divine life; hence all "laypeople" are *priests*. How must this be understood? We read in St. Paul: "I exhort you therefore, brethren, by the mercy of God, to present your bodies as a sacrifice, living, holy, pleasing to God—your spiritual service" (Rom. 12:1). And St. Peter tells us: "Be you yourselves as living stones, built thereon into a spiritual house, a holy priesthood, to offer spiritual sacrifices acceptable to God through Jesus Christ" (1 Pet. 2:5). St. Paul also said: "that I should be a minister of Christ Jesus to the Gentiles, sanctifying the gospel of God, that the offering up of the Gentiles may become acceptable, being sanctified by the Holy Spirit" (Rom. 15:16). That worship, and the priesthood which corresponds to it, is really the worship of a *holy life*. Hence it does not lie on the liturgical, the sacramental plane. The New Testament and the whole of tradition give evidence to that.

But is that all? We distinguish in the priesthood of Christ: the priesthood in the narrow sense (*ministerium*), the kingship and pastoral function (*imperium*), the office of prophecy or teaching (*magisterium*). In virtue of the sacrament of ordination, the functional hierarchical priest has a share in all three aspects of that threefold priesthood of which the priesthood in the so-called strict sense, the priesthood that expresses itself principally in the sacrifice of the Cross and the sacrifice of the Mass, is the most essential. Has the layman also some share in this? Or is the priesthood of the laity confined to the spiritual priesthood which, nonetheless, is a real priesthood, and of which Scripture speaks?

According to Paul Dabin,[4] tradition clearly shows that there is more to it than that. There is a clear tradition of a sacramental priesthood that springs from baptism, and of which the highest act is participation in the Eucharistic Sacrifice. But regarding the connection with baptism, especially regarding the manner, there is no perfect agreement in tradition. Some, following Origen, have taught that the lay priesthood is connected with confirmation. St. Thomas Aquinas teaches, on the contrary, that it is connected with baptism. Dabin is of the same opinion but thinks that it is necessary to take the celebration of baptism as a whole, that the priesthood is expressed outwardly by the anointing *after* baptism and is manifested by the anointing with chrism in confirmation. Congar says that it is, in any case, connected with baptism although it is not clear precisely how. Vatican Council II, however, has put its seal of approval on the statement that "the baptized, by regeneration and the anointing of the Holy Spirit are consecrated as a spiritual house and a holy priesthood."[5]

It follows that, although we must call the priesthood of the laity sacramental, it is nevertheless clearly distinguished from the other sacramental priesthood, from the functional, hierarchical priesthood which has its source in the sacrament of ordination. In virtue of this sacrament of ordination, the priests have a *function* in the Church which is not had by the laity. The priests administer the sacrifice and most of the sacraments in the person of Christ. But this does not do away with the fact that laypeople have a sacramental priesthood that exists alongside the ordained priesthood. It would be of particular importance to find out how this

---

[4]*Le sacerdoce royal des fidèles dans la tradition ancienne et moderne,* Editions universelles, 1950

[5]*Constitution on the Church,* art. 10.

77

priesthood is expressed in the central act of worship, the Eucharistic Sacrifice. One thing is certain; it is in a way that differs essentially from the hierarchical priesthood; but we may certainly say that the layman "joins in the offering of the Eucharist."[6]

Hence we can make a distinction between the special, sacramental priesthood of the ordained priest, the priest who has an office, and the general spiritual, real and sacramental priesthood of the laity. We are permitted to say then that the layman, though he has no office in the Church, has nevertheless an *active* place in the Church in virtue of his priesthood. This active role finds expression, not only in the most essential aspect of the priesthood, the ministry or priesthood in the narrow sense, the administration of the sacrifice and the sacraments, but also in the other aspects: the kingship and pastoral office (*imperium*) and the office of prophecy and teaching (*magisterium*). How is the priesthood of the laity expressed in the pastoral office? It is the hierarchy which determines the structure of the Church, insofar as it has not been determined by Christ. However, regardless of the structures adopted, it must imply the people's participation, a cooperation from above and from below. In the office of teaching also we must expect an *active* witnessing from the laity.[7]

With respect to the layman's increasing participation in Church matters, his way of life, his business, position, or intellectual work, the term "laicization" is sometimes used. This term can be misunderstood. If it is taken to mean that part of the Church and the life of its members is being divorced from a spiritual foundation, it points to something

---

[6]*Ibid.*, art. 10.

[7]For the universal priesthood see E. J. de Smedt, *The Priesthood of the Faithful*, Paulist Press, 1962.

wrong, to a condition that should be branded as "secularization." But it can also be taken to mean that a situation, a work or a position is one in which the layman now plays a role that remains in full harmony with his task in the Church, even though formerly that work or function used to be done by a priest. It then remains fully ecclesial in spite of having been "laicized."

2. Changes Within the Hierarchy

A natural consequence of the older views and historical events affecting both the Church and political society was the concentration of the administrative power at particular junctions, especially at the top. In the Church, in that respect, we note how the papacy and the Roman Curia as its organ of administration developed into an almost all-embracing instrument of government. It is similarly natural that our present tending toward the democratization of society should bring with it a desire for decentralization, for a less top-heavy Church government. But this desire is not merely a result of the present democratic mentality; it also fits in perfectly with the greater emphasis on the Church as community. Theological and sociological considerations here go hand in hand.

A desire for decentralization was frequently expressed even before Vatican Council II. There have been demands to give greater powers to individual bishops, to regional councils of bishops, and especially to the apostolic college of bishops. These will no doubt continue to be among the most important subjects of consideration in the present movement of *aggiornamento.*

The Roman Curia has been praised for its devoted work but it has also been criticized for extreme conservatism. In any case it could no doubt be relieved of much of its heavy load of affairs especially now that the Church is spread far and wide and that rules must be adapted to the various conditions of regions and peoples. Dissatisfaction has also been expressed in the lower strata of the Church, on the part of priests, religious and laypeople, on account of the many hardships that are caused in our present world by an over-centralized system.

In all this there is no desire to impair the fundamental structure of the Church which was dictated by a divine ordinance. It is rather a matter of finding out what structures actually exist in the Church government that owe their origin and foundation to a different sociological pattern dating from a different period of time, or to a different concept regarding the value of the human person, a concept which can perhaps be attributed to the more limited possibilities open to man in a former stage of his development. Further, it is precisely the "democratic" idea that demands regional diversity, because situations differ greatly according to country and democracy is not a sort of dogma that must be applied everywhere. Moreover, it is felt that the Church in this way will function better as community, as desired by Christ.

THE HISTORY OF GRADUAL CENTRALIZATION

If we wish to judge this question properly, it will be necessary to study the present situation of centralization as it actually presents itself, how it has grown, and what its controvertible aspects are. We admit that there is significance in the fact that a general feeling exists concerning a particular situation in the Church; but it is necessary, nevertheless, to subject such a situation to a critical examination. "Centralization" is the accused in this process and it has the right to receive a fair trial.

The Holy See, in the course of its long history, has drawn many matters of administration to itself, and in this it certainly made use of an undeniable right. There is no doubt that the pope as supreme shepherd of the Church has the right to occupy himself actively and with full authority with all Church affairs. And this he actually has done. The "Holy See" is a concept that has acquired a very vast content. The "Holy See" refers to the pope and the Roman Curia which assists him as an organ of government. The Roman Curia is itself composed of a number of "ministries" that deal with certain important Church matters; such as the Secretariat of State, the Holy Office (whose name has now been changed), the Congregation of Rites, the Propagation of the Faith and the Rota.

According to present law, the pope exercises his power personally or by means of his organs of government, even in many details. The appointment of bishops has been reserved to the Holy See. This reservation was preceded by a long development in which the choice was made by the clergy and the people, by the clergy alone, by the chapter of canons or by the king; and it is especially on account of the latter that we can see the reasonableness of reserving this appointment to the pope. Many other appointments are also reserved to the pope. Canon Law is still principally a papal code of law in which, therefore, the pope himself regulates most Church affairs. Thus a departure from that law, by dispensation, except in specified cases, is reserved to the Holy See. On that account, for example, in virtue of Canon Law and apart from a system of delegations, all dispensations for marriage have to be requested from Rome, regardless of where the parties concerned might live in this wide world.

The same problem exists also, for instance, in regard to religious who must have recourse to the Holy See for innumerable questions. Moreover, in accord with the practice of the Sacred Congregation of Religious, most religious constitutions require recourse to the Holy See in cases of dispensation. And we know also to what extent—even after the new *Constitution on the Liturgy*—the ordering of the liturgy has been reserved to the highest authority of the Church. This, then, is the situation that existed until Vatican Council II in almost every field of Church life. It still continues to exist in many areas, although there are good reasons now to expect a change.

But there are also complaints about too little "centralization." Sometimes astonishment is expressed at the fact that dioceses often have their own rules and practices in important Church matters, e.g., dispensation for mixed marriages. Some people are afraid that too much decentralization will lead to excessive diversity in the Church and hence will not help the preservation of unity. In any case, the problem of administrative decentralization has two sides.

It stands to reason that the Church at the beginning, though recognizing the supreme authority of Peter, did not have governmental centralization in the strict sense of that word.[8] It is equally normal that the Church showed a more strongly organized pattern when she reached a certain stage of development. The communities received a more firm internal organization; among other things, gradually a clearer distinction was made between bishops, priest and deacons. And the mutual relations between various communities were more specifically defined. But this cannot yet be called centralization in the strict sense. By centralization we mean here a particularly strong development of the highest organ of government, together with a gradual shrinking of the radius of activity of the lower organs of government.

---

[8]For the situation in the early Church, see Hilaire Marot, "The Primacy and the Decentralization of the Early Church," *Concilium*, vol. 7 (1965), pp. 15-28.

We are permitted to say that that centralization reached its apex with the Council of Trent, which put its seal upon a centuries-old tendency at a time when there was a particular need for a strong government. This tendency received powerful confirmation at Vatican Council I, in connection with the proclamation of the dogma of papal infallibility.

However, centralization began already to develop in the second flowering of the Roman Empire. In fact, we see that the development of centralization ran parallel with the estrangement of the Eastern and the Western churches. This estrangement, no doubt, was due also to polical causes. The patriarchates played an important role in that whole process of estrangement. Seen from the standpoint of centralization, the patriarchates are a sort of intermediary form: they were under the pope but above a great many archbishops and bishops.

Of the four great patriarchates that existed in the Church, three belonged to the Eastern Empire and hence were known officially as "Eastern" patriarches. Only the Patriarch of Rome, who was also the head of the whole Church, belonged to the West. "Rome," the Western Latin patriarchate, was therefore *the* Western Church. Because of the frictions between East and West there also arose difficulties between the Eastern patriarchs, especially the Patriarch of Constantinople, and the Pope, who was at the same time patriarch of the West. The Patriarch of Constantinople, who was bishop of the territory comprising the imperial court, found it difficult to accept a position that was subordinate to the bishop of decadent Rome. In addition, theological controversies played a great role. The breach between East and West grew wider. The West came to stand alone precisely while the Bishop of Rome, Patriarch of the West, claimed—rightly so—that he was the head of the whole Church. When the break became definitive after centuries

83

of struggle, the Eastern patriarchates stood thereby outside the unity of the Church, and the one, Catholic Church was reduced to the patriarchate of Rome.

In this way relations that could be considered normal within a patriarchate, namely, a strong centralization under the government of the patriarch, became the situation of government in the *whole* Church. This condition was accentuated even more by the actual development of the West, that is, of Western Europe, namely, by a "Christendom" ruled by pope and emperor. This idea had already caused endless difficulties in the Middle Ages, but one of its final results was that in the sixteenth century the central authority of the pope had become very strong and led to the growth of the Roman Curia.

DECENTRALIZATION VIEWED FROM THE PRACTICAL, THEOLOGICAL AND ECUMENICAL STANDPOINTS

For various reasons this situation can hardly be maintained or rather it has already become untenable.

From the practical standpoint of technical administration, we meet with all sorts of difficulties. The Church has spread widely and grown numerically. It has become clearly impossible for the strongly centralized government of the Holy See to occupy itself with all kinds of details. At the time when the Church was confined to Western Europe, and when the population of that part of the world was considerably smaller, it was possible to maintain this more or less patriarchal structure. But since the spread of the Catholic, but in fact Western, Church throughout the world, that has become an impossibility. To ask Rome to solve all kind of questions arising anywhere from Iceland to Patagonia, from Finland to New Zealand now seems supremely impractical.

The matter of dispensations for marriages can serve as an example. A whole system of delegation had to be developed giving bishops powers that they do not have by virtue of Canon Law. Such a system is evidently only an emergency measure and shows that in practice the official system cannot be fully maintained. Even so, many problems remain reserved to the Holy See; for example, matrimonial cases, which sometimes drag on for years when they are submitted to Rome. Here, too, much more could be left to be determined on the local level, at least with respect to the preparation of the final decision.[9]

From a more theological standpoint, we can also bring forward a good number of objections to the present system of administration. In our own day more attention is given to the Church as community and a more harmonious relation is sought between the Church as institution and the Church as community. This means as a natural consequence that the local church, the Church centered around the bishop, will demand more and more attention. A real community life in the sense of orderly interhuman relations is not possible on a world-wide scale. The whole Church can live a community life only if the local churches live as communities. This tendency to emphasize the local church does not exclude loving and continuous contact with Rome. But it does demand a greater emphasis on the authority of the local bishop, so that the bishop does not appear only as a vicar of the pope who has to refer to Rome for innumerable things and even relatively trivial matters. Hence, the Church as community demands a strengthening of the episcopal authority.

---

[9]For the revision of Canon Law see P. Huizing, "The Reform of Canon Law," *Concilium,* vol. 8 (1965), pp. 95 ff. (also bibliography).

From the ecumenical point of view also, the present system appears defective. On the part of the Eastern Catholics united with Rome, there were already difficulties on the occasion of the introduction of the new Code of Canon Law for Oriental Churches. They complained that there were too many traces in it of the Western centralizing system, by which the historical position of the patriarchs was weakened. It is a well-known fact that many bishops of the Eastern Orthodox Churches are repelled precisely by the present system of papal power; in any case, they are more averse to the actual centralized government than to the doctrine concerning papal authority and infallibility.

"In their eyes submission to the Pope and to the Vatican system of government means slavery to a tyrannical and arbitrary power that in principle goes counter to all ancient and venerable traditions. It was thus that the Ecumenical Patriarch Athenagoras, speaking to the representatives of the Greek newspaper *Elephteria,* said in November, 1960: 'The Catholic Church has made an absolute ruler of the pope.' The conservative Russians who had emigrated from Russia based their rejection of the Council on the wrong supposition that bishops participating in a Catholic Council had only a consultative voice, and this, they said, is contrary to tradition.

"Some Orthodox, in order to explain their rejection of the primacy, sometimes point to the actual consequences of submission to Rome. The Greek lay canonist Hamilcar Alivistatos, for instance, criticized the new Canon Law for Oriental Churches in the following terms: 'The tendency to uniformity and levelling is becoming all too evident. The integration of the Uniate Churches leads to a complete assimilation and a total disappearance of what is proper to Orthodoxy, at least insofar as one may still speak here of Orthodoxy.' The Greek Metropolitan and theologian Chrysostomos Konstantinidis wrote: 'The Uniates who are now in the Catholic

Church lead a life of total subjection. They have preserved only a few external elements of their own Eastern character.' Such statements are not free from exaggeration. But it is a fact that the Orthodox see it that way and their fears are not entirely without foundation."[10]

On the Protestant side, there was a group of people in the German Evangelical Church who were at least very sympathetic toward a real supreme authority of the pope in the one Church of Christ; but they begged "Rome" to do away with the present "curial" system. Although this small group cannot unqualifiedly be considered representative of the German Lutherans,[11] their questions are surely important for us. In contrast with the *Sonderkirchliche* (those who favor separate churches), they seek "Catholic truths." Hence they want to ask "Rome" whether particular phenomena found in her can be understood as "Catholic" in the sense of "universal-Christian." With respect to the primacy of the pope, they say: "It is a Catholic truth that the Church of Christ on earth stands and must stand under one leadership. Jesus said in the plural to the Apostles: 'He who hears you, hears me' (Luke, 10:16), but then he entrusted his all-embracing pastoral office to one particular apostle and called him the 'rock' (Peter), which was to be a foundation and a protection of the Church against the gates of Hell (John, 21:15ff.; John, 1:42; Matt., 16:18). It is unthinkable that the mission of the many would continue whereas the pastoral office of the one would cease. This testimony of Revelation puts

---

[10]Cf. Wilhelm de Vries, "De orthodoxe christenen en het Concilie," *Streven,* Jan. 1962, pp. 313-320. See also Ivan Zuzek, "Oriental Canon Law: Survey of Recent Development," *Concilium,* vol. 8 (1965), pp. 129 ff.

[11]This group composed of Hans Asmussen, Richard Baumann, Ernst Fincke, Gustav Huhn, Max Lackmann and Wulfgang Lehmann, has circulated a number of letters concerning this question under the title *Die Sammlung.* Our quotation is taken from the seventh and last letter.

before the evangelical *ecumene* the question, where that office is present in her. 'When, according to ancient Church tradition, the Bishop of Rome claims that he possesses that office as successor of Peter, evangelical Christianity can no longer evade the question whether that claim is in harmony with the testimony of biblical Revelation concerning the office of Peter. The divine necessity of giving an affirmative answer to that question does not yet mean that we must approve the development which brought with it the fact that that authority sometimes degenerated into a worldly authority and one that exercised an unchristian control over consciences. But this affirmative answer likewise does not excuse us from seeking an answer to a question that is still open today, viz., how that authority must be placed in the right relation to the authority of all bishops and their churches. Nevertheless, it is certainly wrong to reject the unity of the leadership in the Church.' The bishop is not an administrator with the title of 'bishop' but the teacher of his diocese and the one who has the task of preserving unity with the other dioceses."

What is striking in this testimony is, not only the exceptional positive attitude toward the office of Peter, but also the fact that there still remains so much dread concerning certain aspects *de facto* connected with the highest office in the Church.

Similar voices can be heard in England. In other Protestant circles the fear of papal power is much more profound. Their arguments, however, usually refer to certain aspects of the actually existing structure of the supreme office which, for us, are not essential but which, for them, are subjects of great aversion.

The view, then, that the present system can hardly be maintained certainly has solid arguments in its favor, and it is in no way contrary to a profound respect and complete acceptance of the supreme authority of the pope in the Church.

It would be foolish, and a sign of a lack of historical sense, if we were to expect that the present system of government of the Church will be profoundly changed overnight, even as a consequence of Vatican Council II. While we must admit that the change is more rapid in our own day, the formation and development of a new structure takes time, and in all probability the structure will not be totally new. In addition to certain elements that cannot change, other things will remain, although perhaps in a different form and for a different function. History cannot be disowned. We have every reason, however, to expect that the Council and its aftermath will at least lay the foundations for thoroughly adapting the Church's apparatus of government to the modern situation.

Western Patriarchates

When we approach the governmental relations within the Church by placing ourselves as it were on top and, from there, looking at the various levels, the first question we encounter is that of the patriarchates.

The great Oriental patriarchates are separated from the Church. As a consequence, there are a number of sees that have two occupants, for example, the sees of the patriarch of Antioch and the patriarch of the Armenians: one patriarch separated from and the other united with the Holy See. Nevertheless, the Catholic Church possesses patriarchy, although in fact only with respect to the Eastern Churches, because in the West the pope alone can be designated as a patriarch. The "patriarchates" of Venice, Lisbon, Jerusalem, etc., are purely honorary titles without any real meaning. But we might ask ourselves if the institution of the patriarchate does not contain greater possibilities.

Together with a desire for decentralization there is the wish for closer cooperation between the bishops of one country, or of several countries that have much in common, and even between the bishops of one continent. Such a cooperation should be institutional, in order to make it lasting and fruitful. In fact, apart from the relatively small Oriental churches that are in union with the Holy See, there exists in reality no intermediary between the Holy See and the several thousand local bishops. The position of the archbishop is not strong from the standpoint of Canon Law, but Vatican Council II has now decreed that the archbishop's rights are to be redefined—and presumably strengthened— by new norms.[12] Even then, however, in large countries there may be ten or more archbishops. If one of these is called the "primate," this title is purely honorary. It would certainly be desirable to have a more solid organizational unity between a number of ecclesiastical provinces, so that similar pastoral problems of a particular country or countries could obtain a co-ordinated solution.

A measure of greater organizational unity is given in the so-called "episcopal conferences." According to the *Decree Concerning the Pastoral Office of Bishops in the Church* of Vatican Council II, such a conference "is, as it were, a council in which the bishops of a given nation or territory jointly exercise their pastoral office."[13] But, provisionally at least, even decisions approved by a two-thirds majority of a conference's bishops do not have any juridically binding force save "in cases prescribed by the common law or determined by a special mandate of the Holy See."[14] On the other hand,

---

[12]*Decree on the Pastoral Office of Bishops in the Church,* Ch. III, art. 40, 1.

[13]*Ibid.,* Ch. III, art. 38, 1.

[14]*Ibid.,* Ch. III, art. 38, 4.

it is to be expected that very few bishops would simply disregard decisions approved in this way by their conference. The various episcopal conferences are encouraged to communicate with one another in order to promote and safeguard the common good.[15] Moreover, with the approval of the Holy See, "bishops of many nations can establish a single conference,"[16] as is already done in South America.

In connection with these pastoral conferences of bishops pertaining to the same general territory we would now like to make a plea for western patriarchates. Their introduction would seem to offer many advantages. Regarding relations with the Oriental Churches, it would be a distinct asset if the governmental structure in the Western Church lay on the same level: the Oriental Churches would feel themselves in a more "normal" and less privileged situation, and they would, besides, be assured a proper understanding of the position of their patriarchs. These patriarchates could also be a blessing for the rest of the Church. Powers of government that are now concentrated in Rome could thus be spread to lower levels. A great many cases that are now reserved for the jurisdiction of Rome could very well be handled by the patriarch. This would guarantee a more prompt transaction of many affairs; it would also more easily safeguard regional differences and give more opportunity for regional diversification.

According to this way of thinking, we see the possibility of patriarchates in Europe, Africa, North, Central and South America, sections of Asia, Australia, etc. This would certainly be advantageous for the harmonious structure of the Church; for it would insure both a strong and a diversified

[15]*Ibid.*, Ch. III, art 38, 5.
[16]*Ibid.*, Ch. III, art. 38, 5.

government. The pope, as Bishop of Rome, should not be patriarch of Europe at the same time. On account of his unique position he should stand above the entire Church and should not be bound in a particular way to any part of the Church. In this way the Diocese of Rome would also acquire a unique place.

By introducing the intermediary structure of patriarchates, the work of the Roman Curia could be greatly limited; and this would certainly facilitate their efficient and prompt handling of affairs. The cardinalate would also acquire a different character in such a structure. The cardinalate is too deeply rooted in Church history to readily disappear in favor of the patriarchate. In fact, the College of Cardinals has already developed into an advisory college for the pope, as supreme head of the Church; and many cardinals have, besides, been taken up directly into the Roman Curia which is the pope's organ of government. The cardinalate, in a certain sense, limps on two ideas. There are still traces of its historical origin as the college of the principal priests of the Roman *diocese*: the Curia cardinals, the great number of Italian cardinals, the titular churches of which the cardinals are nominal "pastors." Even their right to choose the pope developed from the right of the Roman clergy (and people) to choose the Bishop of Rome, but for many centuries the College of Cardinals has had also a function in the universal government of the Church. Already in the Middle Ages bishops, first of Italy and later also of Europe in general, became members of the College of Cardinals, besides the bishops of the seven "suburban" dioceses around Rome. We also note that in some way or other there were always a number of non-Italians among the Curia cardinals. The right to elect a new pope was also regarded more and more as the choice of the head of the universal Church who would at the same time be Bishop of Rome.

That the College of Cardinals should be entirely divorced from its Roman origin and become an advisory body for the pope is in line with historical development. The structure of the diocese of Rome could be organized like other dioceses. In this way more or less folklorish customs like that of the "pastorate" of the cardinals could disappear. One could envisage a College of Cardinals in which the patriarchs would be cardinals by right and other cardinals would be chosen by the pope from among the bishops and priests whom he considers particularly fit for that function, and some could be directly at his service in Rome for the government of the universal Church. Such a development of the cardinalate is in line with history and it would be more easily achieved that way than by other solutions that would do away entirely with the cardinalate.

In the supposition that patriarchates would be formed, it would not be necessary to change anything essential regarding the position of archbishops. They could have more frequent contacts with the patriarch; and the latter would maintain more frequent relations with them and consult them more often than the other bishops.

In such a structure the local bishop stands, in a certain sense, at the bottom of the ladder. And yet he is, in the whole structure of the Church, the most important functionary, the foundation, the basis of the whole structure of the Church. We must, however, keep in mind that a non-local handling of many affairs has also great advantages: stubborn customs do not play so great a role, the local bishop is not "personally" involved in certain difficult situations, a narrow viewpoint can be avoided and political influences can be eliminated. These are, in fact, some of the reasons that have actually led to the gradual formation of the present centralized system. But we must not forget the other side of this centralization: delay of decision, the inevitabe bureaucracy, which actually means very often that problems of a profoundly human nature are torn loose from the sphere of human relations.

As we have already pointed out, the system that has existed until now has proved untenable, since it was found necessary to create a whole system of delegations. Thus a beginning has already been made with the restoring of faculties to the bishops, and this movement will probably continue. So-called "quinquennial faculties" could become normal faculties of the bishops deriving from their office. It was realized that such delegations were necessary. If so, it is a juridical anomaly to maintain a fiction of "faculties granted for five years" when in reality they are always prolonged beyond that limit. We can expect that other faculties will also normally belong to the bishops in the near future.

The bishops generally have frequent contact with their archbishop, who has principally a coordinating function. If we add to that the function of patriarchs, who by right would have a number of powers that are now reserved to the pope and that would not be granted to local bishops, we would then have a hierarchical structure in the Church, a harmonious construction of governmental organs, a balanced organism.

The complete unity of the Church continues to rest on unity with Peter and his successors in the see of Rome. The pope can intervene wherever he thinks it necessary, especially for the preservation of unity, and we are not permitted to limit his powers in this respect. It is not the business of local churches, no more than that of patriarchs, to determine the limits of papal power. But a strongly centralized system is certainly not demanded by any dogma. The dogmatic doctrine concerning bishops points rather in an opposite direction. It would also mean an increase of dignity if the Holy See directly occupied itself only with truly important affairs.

POPE AND BISHOPS

The formal appointment of bishops is completely reserved to the pope; in fact it is the pope who appoints the bishops. That the right of appointing bishops was ultimately reserved to the Holy See is understandable when we recall that there often were many local difficulties in connection with the choice of a bishop, that local rulers and other authorities frequently interfered, and that there sometimes were tendencies to break away from Rome. In practice, it is quite impossible that all bishops everywhere in the world owe their appointment to the personal choice of the pope. The Roman Curia naturally plays a great role in this, but an even greater role is played by those who live in the diocese concerned. There exist all sorts of customs and privileges which modify somewhat the sole right of the pope to appoint bishops. Sometimes cathedral chapters have the right to propose the candidates. In some countries the choice is made by the canons and the pope merely confirms that choice; this exists, for instance, in some dioceses of Switzerland. In mission lands all missionaries are asked, beforehand, to express their opinion; in other words, there exists an evident need to consult also the lower strata in the nomination of bishops. This custom could lead to the development of a greater "influence of the people," so that both the laity and the clergy would have a more direct share in the choice of their bishop. No one will object to the pope having the last word in that appointment, but it is a much expressed desire that the faithful have more influence in that matter.

The College of Bishops and the Bishops' Synod. The relationship of the bishop to the head of the universal Church has not yet been fully clarified, at least not in practice.

Bishops certainly are not mere "vicars of the Roman Pontiffs, for they exercise an authority that is proper" to themselves.[17] Together with the pope, moreover, they constitute the "college of bishops." This episcopal college "is also the subject of supreme and full power over the universal Church, provided we understand this body together with its head the Roman Pontiff and never without this head." (The pope himself, of course, has full, supreme and universal power over the Church.) In this college the bishops "exercise their own authority for the good of their own faithful and indeed the whole Church" either by way of an ecumenical council or through "collegiate action." As a member of the episcopal college, the individual bishop is "obliged by Christ's institution to be solicitous for the whole Church" and to "promote every activity that is of interest to the whole Church." With respect to the preaching of the Gospel the bishops "are obliged to enter into a community of work among themselves and with the successor of Peter, upon whom was imposed in a special way the great duty of spreading the Christian name."[18]

How these and other points contained in the *Constitution on the Church* will be worked out in detail remains to be seen. The lines of development, however, clearly show that the episcopal college will assume increasing importance in the government of the universal Church. On September 5, 1965, Pope Paul VI instituted the Bishops' Synod as a central and perpetual institution "representing the complete Catholic episcopate" through members elected by the episcopal con-

---

[17]*Constitution on the Church,* Ch. III, art. 27, p. 30. For a study of the episcopacy see Karl Rahner and Joseph Ratzinger, *The Episcopacy and the Primacy,* Herder and Herder, 1963; Paul Anciaux, *The Episcopacy in the Church,* Alba House, 1965; Karl Rahner, *Bishops: Their Status and Function,* Helicon, 1965.

[18]*Constitution on the Church,* art. 22-24.

ferences in various parts of the world. The Bishops' Synod has as its aim "close union and valued assistance" between the pope and the bishops, to secure the necessary and pertinent information on affairs touching the internal life of the Church as well as its activity in the world of today, and to facilitate "agreement on essential points of doctrine and on methods of procedure." This Synod is not subject to the Roman Curia but "directly and immediately to the authority of the Roman Pontiff."[19]

The Roman Curia. Among the many wishes for reform voiced at the Council, the desire for a reorganization of the Roman Curia occupies an important place. The central offices of the universal Church need to be adapted to the needs of our time, especially with respect to their methods of procedure. In particular, the Council said, the composition of the various departments of the Curia must become more representative of the universal Church; less Italian, therefore. On the other hand, a mere replacement of Latin officialdom by an international bureaucracy would not lead to more dialogue with the Church at large. The Council, therefore, desired that especially diocesan bishops be chosen as members of the Curia. Laymen also should be heard to give them "an appropriate share in Church affairs."[20] In accordance with the Council's wishes Pope Paul VI has announced a reorganization of the Roman Curia.

FUNCTIONAL RESTORATION OF THE DIACONATE AND THE LOWER ORDERS

Another point worth noting is the exclusive place that the priesthood has acquired among the clergy. All other lower

---

[19]A.A.S., vol. 57 (1965), pp. 775 ff.
[20]*Decree on the Pastoral Office of Bishops in the Church,* Ch. I, art. 9.

functions have practically disappeared, namely those of deacon, subdeacon and minor orders. When those functions are exercised it is done by priests or laypeople, but ordination for these functions is merely a preparation for the priesthood.

For a number of years the desire has been expressed for the re-establishment of the functional significance of the ordinations that are below that of the priesthood.. There has been a great interest in that question especially in German-speaking territories.[21] This interest was principally concerned with the diaconate, although there was also a slowly increasing general interest in the lower orders, by which we mean all those below the priesthood. Thus, during an international congress of sacristans, a plea was made for the conferring of minor orders (the four lowest ordinations) on sacristans and other minor functionaries of the Church.

This question is approached from different standpoints, but primarily from the practical side; namely, from the problem of the shortage of priests, particularly in places where Catholics are dispersed among non-Catholics and in mission countries. This approach is good but insufficient, although it is easy to understand why the question is considered from that standpoint. The same thing is happening here as with the lay apostolate: at the beginning the lay apostleship in general and "Catholic Action" in particular, were based on the need of such help because of the scarcity of priests. But when

---

[21]One of the first protagonists for the reintroduction of the functional diaconate was the layman Josef Hornef of Fulda, who wrote numerous articles about the question and, in 1959, the book, *Kommt der Diaken der frühen Kirche wieder?* Among the most representative studies of this question we may name W. Schamoni, *Married Men as Ordained Deacons,* Templegate, 1955; Karl Rahner, *Diaconia in Christo,* Herder, 1962; W. Croce, "Die niederen Weihen und ihre hierarchische Wertung," *Zeitschrift für katholische Theologie,* 1948, pp. 258-314; P. Winninger, *Vers un renouveau du diaconat,* Paris, 1958.

the lay apostolate began to develop, the question was examined more thoroughly and it was understood very soon that the basis for lay apostolate lies in the position which the layman has in the Church, and hence that it rests ultimately on the very nature of the Church. The question about the diaconate is now undergoing a similar development. Though many are still moved by predominantly practical reasons, there are already signs of a more profound examination of that question. By way of an inventory we could say that this question comprises the following elements:

Theologically speaking, there are no objections against the functional re-establishment of the diaconate and the other lower orders. On the contrary, there are important scriptural and theological reasons that favor such a restoration. A restoration would be a help toward a better and more profound ecclesial consciousness. In particular the organic structure of the Church would appear to better advantage and the excessive clericalization that has developed in many fields could thus be restrained. This, then, implies the restoration not only of the diaconate as a true function but also of the other lower orders. The latter could be more or less numerous, for their number is wholly at the discretion of the Church. In particular, the re-establishment of the diaconate will call special attention to the loving service of the Church, to the religious foundation of Christian charity, and also to the unity of sacrifice, preaching and charity.

From the practical-pastoral standpoint we must, of course, pay attention to the possibilities which the restoration of orders below the priesthood makes available to the Church. One may even ask whether the shortage of priests would not thereby acquire a totally different aspect.

A historical sketch of the lower orders is necessary if we want to understand the whole question properly. History

99

shows how well all the orders constituted together a connected whole; it also shows that all the orders did not arise
as "means of obtaining grace" nor exclusively as a preparation for the priesthood, but they arose as functions that
fulfilled an actual need.

The beginnings of the diaconate are sufficiently known (cf.
Acts 6:1-6). The deacons are frequently mentioned both in
the letters of St. Paul and by the oldest ecclesiastical writers.[22]
The number of deacons varied in the early Church. The
large churches clung to the number seven, in conformity
with the number of the first deacons in Jerusalem; but the
smaller churches were satisfied with a lesser number that
met the smaller needs of their community. There was generally opposition to having more than seven in a community,
but eventually, especially in the East, that rule was finally
discarded. Thus, already at the beginning of the fourth
century there were nine deacons at Alexandria, in Edessa
in 451 there were thirty-nine, and Constantinople had one
hundred deacons in the sixth century. In Rome the city
was divided into seven sectors under Pope Fabian (236-
251), and there, for a long time, they adhered to the classical number of seven deacons. Each of the deacons was at
the head of a "neighborhood house" for the care of the
poor and the sick; but slowly there developed the custom
for each church to have its own deacons, so that in Rome
also there were no less than one hundred deacons in the
year 520.

Although the care of the poor and the widows gave rise
to the diaconate, liturgical functions and the office of preaching were attached to it from the beginning. We see that

---

[22]Phil. 1:1; 1 Tim. 3:8 ff.; St. Clement, *ad Corinthios,* ch. 42; St.
Ignatius, *ad Magnesios,* 6; *ad Trallianos,* 2, 3; *ad Philadelphenses,* 4, 7;
ad Smyrnenses, 8; *ad Philippenses,* 5; St. Justin, I *Apologia,* chs. 65, 67;
Tertullian, *de baptismo,* ch. 17; *de praescriptis,* ch. 41.

the first deacons, Stephen and Philip, already baptized and preached (Act 6:10; 8:5, 38). Toward the end of the first century we have the testimony of Ignatius of Antioch who tells us that they are not deacons of food and drink, but servants of God's Church.[23] And so it has remained in the Church.[24]

The deacons gradually acquired a share in the administration of the Church. Already in the second and third centuries there were deacons who were special assistants and ministers of the bishops.[25] In the fourth century we have the first traces of a function that resembles the later office of an archdeacon; it was held by St. Athanasius who was deacon of Bishop Alexander of Alexandria, from 319 to 328, and who appeared as such at the Council of Alexandria (321) and later at the Council of Nicaea.[26] But as early as the second century, one of the deacons was the special procurator of the bishop for the government of the churches and the care of the poor; as we would say, he was the treasurer of the diocese. He was in fact called "the episcopal deacon."

Nevertheless, these important activities did not yet constitute an official function. It was only toward the end of the third and the beginning of the fourth centuries that the change occurred. We meet then with the name "archdeacon." Slowly this office developed into what we now call the office of a vicar-general, and in reality it was even higher than that. From the fifth century on, this was fully the case. To the archdeacon was entrusted the training and supervision of the young clerics. When the see was vacant,

---

[23] *ad Trallianos*, 2, 3.
[24] St. Justin, I *Apologia*, ch. 65; St. Hippolytus, ch. 3; *Didascalia*, II, 57; *Constitutio apostolica*, III, 16; Tertullian, *de baptismo*, ch. 17.
[25] Eusebius, *Historia Eccl.*, 4, 30; 5, 1.
[26] Theodoretus, *Historia Eccl.*, I, 25.

it was usually the archdeacon who governed the diocese. Those deacons gradually grew so powerful that they came to look upon a promotion to the priesthood as a degradation; yet this promotion was used by many a bishop to get rid of an over-ambitious archdeacon, at least when the bishop still had the power to do so.

Meanwhile, the ordinary deacons remained faithful to their function of service, and, although many priests and also bishops sprang from their midst, the diaconate remained an independent function for many centuries. They had plenty of work: to asist at liturgical worship and in the work of preaching; to maintain order during liturgical services; to receive the gifts of the faithful; to announce to the catechumens and penitents at what time they had to leave the church; to take care of the poor and the sick; to attend to the instruction of the catechumens and to assist at baptism. They were permitted to baptize in urgent cases when no priest was present and the bishop gave his consent.

They also administered church property. In small churches (dioceses and "parishes") they performed that considerable task alone for a long time, which sometimes made them more influential than even the priests. But when the faithful became more numerous, especially in densely populated cities, other functionaries became necessary, especially because, as we have said, tradition for a long time forbade the appointment of more than seven deacons. That is why they had to get assistants. These assistants were at first laymen who aided in worship, the administration of church property and the care of the poor. But gradually a certain system developed for the ranking of those helpers and they were reckoned among the clergy insofar as a permanent function was conferred upon them in a church ceremony. Quite naturally the first helpers were *sub*deacons. It is possible that there were some already in the second century; it is certain that they existed in the third century.

St. Hippolytus' *Apostolic Tradition,* at the beginning of the third century, mentions subdeacons and lectors. The four minor orders existed already in the third century. According to a letter of Pope Cornelius to Bishop Fabius of Antioch in the year 251, the Church of Rome at that time had seven deacons, seven subdeacons (one for each deacon), forty-two acolytes, fifty-two exorcists, lectors and doorkeepers (*ostiarii*).[27]

The subdeacons assisted at the altar in lower functions, helped in administration and care of the poor, whereas the deacons were entrusted with the general administration and supervision of those functions. The acolytes in turn were assistants of the subdeacons. Thus in Rome there were seven subdeacons (who were themselves assistants of the deacons), each one with six acolytes at his service.

The function of exorcist arose at about the same time, because abuses made it necessary to entrust the exorcism of the devil to official ministers for, at the beginning, exorcism was sometimes practised by "ordinary" Christians with charismatic gifts. It was not without resistance that this office was incorporated into the ordinations and it was not introduced everywhere, especially in the East. Moreover, before long, exorcisms became reserved to higher ministers.

The lectors acquired an important place in the early Church. The reading of Sacred Scripture, especially of the letters of the Apostles, was often entrusted to competent laymen in the earliest times of the Church, as was also done in the synagogues. This became an established office in the second century and acquired an ecclesiastical rank

---

[27]Eusebius, *op. cit.,* 6, 43, 11.

in the third century. The ancient ecclesiastical writers who give testimony to that function are legion; e.g., Justin, Tertullian, Hippolytus and Cyprian. In the fourth century we find the growing custom of appointing (ordaining) to the office of lector boys who were still too young for other functions (ordinations). For example, the boy who was later to become Pope Damasus functioned as lector at the age of thirteen. This explains why "schools of lectors" (*scholae lectorum*) arose in several churches of Rome, Lyons and Rheims. In the seventh century these became "schools of chanters" (*scholae cantorum*) when the readings were entrusted to the deacon and subdeacon.

The office of doorkeeper also sprang from the diaconal and, respectively, the subdiaconal function. In the fourth century almost every church had its doorkeeper, and as early as the third century he belonged to the clergy. Other functions have also existed, such as the sacristan (*sacrarius*) and gravedigger (*fossarius*), which were sometimes counted among the orders. But these disappeared rather early. However, it is important for us to note this possibility of changes in these minor orders. The tonsure, which was of monastic origin, was in use from the fifth century when it was administered together with the first ordination; from the seventh century on, it was conferred in a separate ceremony.

The clergy rose gradually to higher orders. Many remained at a certain level while some rose to the episcopacy, always ascending step by step. This was strictly adhered to and indicates clearly that the diverse ordinations were considered as true offices and functions.

In the fourth century, under Pope Siricius (385), it became the rule that those who had been ordained lectors in their early youth were subsequently promoted to acolyte and subdeacon; then, when they had reached their thirtieth year, they were ordained deacon and finally bishop. We leave out here the question of the relation between priest-hood and the office of bishop, but it is a fact that for centuries deacons were directly ordained bishops.

In the fifth century Pope Innocent mentioned that clerics should remain for a suitable time in minor orders and must show by their lives that they are suited and worthy to be admitted to higher orders, especially to the priesthood.[28] There were exceptions, of course, but it was the rule to ascend by gradual process. It is probable, however, that the clergy did not receive all the lower orders before they were advanced to a higher rank and that they received only the more important ones—such as the order of lector, acolyte and subdiaconate. The subdiaconate now belongs to the higher orders, but not in the East, and for a long time the matter remained uncertain in the West. St. Ambrose point-ed out that some were more suited to be lectors, others to be chanters of the psalms, others more suitable for the function of exorcists or for the care of the church. Each one should be given the function that is suitable for him.[29] The required age of lectors was very young. There were even eight-year-olds who received that function. The age of twenty was held to be very suitable for acolytes and subdeacons, thirty years for the diaconate and thirty-five for the priesthood. As the beginning, the age of forty-five was required for bishops; but in practice this became thirty years.

Celibacy, which became fairly general toward the end of the third century, at least in the West, was required only of the higher clergy. At first it was demanded beginning with the diaconate. At the beginning of the fourth century it was expressly prescribed for the first time by a Council.[30]

---

[28]Letter to the Bishop of Nucera, P.L., 20, 604.
[29]*Liber I de officiis,* ch. 44.
[30]The Concilium Eliberatanum of 305.

This has been strictly maintained ever since, although previously married men were tacitly permitted to continue their married state. Pope Leo the Great, in the middle of the fifth century, required celibacy also of the subdeacon. This became more or less the practice in the sixth century but it was not universal. In any case, married subdeacons were permitted to continue to live as husbands but were excluded from higher orders. On the other hand, celibacy was not required of the lower clergy.

DEACONESSES

In connection with the matter in question and the contemporary examination of woman's position in the Church, it is important to examine what significance must be attached to the deaconesses mentioned in the earliest times of the Church. In the first centuries, and even in apostolic times, there were women—widows, virgins and deaconesses —that had a particular task and position in the Church.[31] The deaconesses especially demand our attention here, for they fulfilled an *office*, while widows and virgins lived in a particular *state of life*. The deaconesses were chosen from among the widows and virgins. They took care of the poor and sick women and, in general, had those tasks which could not well be fulfilled by men (deacons), at least not according to the ideas of those days. They had to visit sick women; they had to be present at the conversations between a bishop or priest and a woman; they had to guard the special door for women in the churches. On that account they also had liturgical functions: the deaconesses did the anointing in the baptism of women. Perhaps they even brought the Eucharist to pregnant women during Easter night.

---

[31] 1 Tim. 3:11; 5:9-16; Rom. 16:1.

The rite by which they were appointed was very similar to the ordination of deacons: the bishop, in the presence of the priests, deacons and deaconesses, laid his hands upon her and, in a prayer, the Holy Spirit was invoked upon her. Wonderful texts of those prayers have been preserved. For example:

> Eternal God, Father of our Lord Jesus Christ, Creator of man and woman, You who have filled Maria, Debora and Holda with Your Spirit, You, who have not thought it below your dignity to make Your only Son to be born of a woman; You who in the tabernacle-tent and the Temple of the Old Covenant have appointed women as guardians of Your holy portals, look down upon this Your servant, who is destined for the diaconate: grant her the Holy Spirit, purify her of all corporal and spiritual stain, so that she may be able to fulfill the office that will be entrusted to her, for the honor and praise of Your Christ, with whom may honor and adoration be given to You and to the Holy Spirit forever. Amen.[32]

Some texts say that a stole was laid around her neck and that she received the Chalice at Communion.

The nature of that rite has been the subject of great controversy for a long time. Some authors do not hesitate to call that rite a true ordination and, hence, count the deaconesses among the clergy; but most authors are against that interpretation. However, there are still open questions in this matter. It is perfectly clear that the ancient Church considered ordination as a *function,* an *office.* As there arose a need for definite functions, these were filled; and the ministers of those functions were appointed by an official church ceremony. There was also an evident need for functions by women. That function, namely, of the deaconess, arose and those women were officially appointed by

---

[32]*Constitutiones apostolicae* (4th to 5th century).

the Church in a solemn church ceremony. We must ask ourselves if the distinction we make between a function that is an ordination and a function that is not an ordination really existed at that time.

The subordination of woman, that is so clearly expressed in St. Paul, did not necessarily have to prevent the complete recognition of the deaconess' ordination and function, for it was only a subordinate function. The subordination of woman was made sufficiently clear by the practice of not granting her the episcopal or the priestly office. There is, in fact, no trace in history of a woman becoming a bishop or a priest. The constant tradition of the Church has always rejected this.

Even the office of deaconess met with great opposition in the Church, and this is understandable in view of the mentality of those days. One of the great objections was that deaconesses meddled with too many things, an objection that was also made in respect to the deacons. Deaconesses began to disappear in the West in the sixth century, but remained longer in the Oriental Churches. At the time of the Reformation, the office of deacon, in the Protestant sense of the term, was revived and this office was also entrusted to women. Thus there were deaconesses in Amsterdam in the sixteenth century. But they disappeared again at the end of the same century. In the nineteenth century the office of deaconess was reintroduced in Germany, the Netherlands, England and the United States; they took care of the sick (Holland), acted as evangelists and performed liturgical functions (England).

It is worth noting that the function of the deaconess was in reality a consequence of the subordinate and isolated position of the woman in those ancient days. Bishops and priests in many cases were unable to come in direct contact with women. That is why the office of the deaconess was created. Even among Christians the respect for women was often not

108

very great. New Christian reasons were invoked to keep the woman in a lower position. The sin of Eve was a strong argument for that attitude. Tertullian, in the second and third centuries, desired that all women should always conduct themselves as a kind of penitent Eve and should dress accordingly. St. Augustine had similar opinions. "Don't you know, that you are an Eve . . . it is on account of your deadly crime that the Son of God had to die." On the other hand there were Church Fathers, for example St. Ambrose, who were led to milder ideas by the thought of the Mother of God.

THE COUNCIL OF TRENT

History reveals that there was much more organic differentiation in the structure of the Church during the centuries to which we have referred. Thus the division of labor among the ministers of the Church was also more rational; everything was not put on the shoulders of the priest as long as the lower orders, beginning with the diaconate, remained true functions. The concept "clergy" was also quite different. Because many more Church members were occupied in Church affairs, there was not so sharp a distinction between the clergy and laity. On the other hand, after a few centuries the clergy was thought of as an "estate." The above-described system also had bad points. Deacons, especially the "episcopal deacon" who later became the archdeacon, acquired great power; and not infrequently, until the eleventh and twelfth centuries, he was *the* man in the diocese. It is necessary for us to keep this development well in mind now that we look forward to the functional re-establishment of the diaconate.

After some centuries little remained of that organic system of functions. Particularly the minor orders ceased increasingly to be true functions; they were mere steps to the priesthood. In many cases the priesthood was granted too lightly, while diocesan bishops were often not even priests and, of course, not true bishops.

The Council of Trent took up that question.[33] The Council considered that the separation between order and function was an evil and it desired particularly to restore the four minor orders as autonomous Church functions. It wished those functions to be exercised by those who were ordained for them and by no one else; and on the other hand, one who had received the lower orders had to exercise them. This was particularly true for future priests. The Council attached great importance to this as an element of education and did not consider mere school education sufficient. However, the number of seminarians was, of course, too small to enable them to perform those functions in all churches; besides, according to the explicit will of the same Council, seminarians remained in the seminary during the greater part of the year. Hence, the Council laid down the rule that married men could also receive minor orders. They would then also be true *clerics* and would have to wear the tonsure and the spiritual garb. Trent thus distinguished two kinds of clerics: first, those who were on the way to higher orders, particularly the priesthood; secondly, those who remained in minor orders throughout life. It is evident, then, that the Council looked upon the orders as being functions.

It was soon realized, however, that the various minor orders no longer signified any real task. They had remained outside the process of development for many centuries and had been preserved in a purely artificial way. They had, in fact, no pastoral significance. The Council tried to put new life into those functions but also adhered strongly to the original content of those orders. And that rigid pattern offered too

---

[33]Cr. Croce, *art. cit.* (footnote 21).

few possibilities. It is precisely necessary for those lower functions to have great flexibility, for they must be adapted to ever changing needs in the Church. Here was a case of "putting new wine in old goatskins." For this reason the endeavors of the Council of Trent ended in failure. The minor orders remained merely steps toward the priesthood. And the question of the functional restoration of the subdiaconate and the diaconate was entirely left out. Nevertheless, it is significant that Trent took steps in the direction of restoring the minor orders. It is very important that we study the reasons for that failure.

The same thing happened in this matter as in many others: so many problems clamored for a solution that the Fathers of the Council of Trent were buried under them; there was especially the necessity of restoring Church discipline and clearly defining sound doctrine. On account of all that, very many questions received no solution or remained "frozen" in a few fundamental rules, as happened also with the whole of the liturgy. This was also the fate of the functional restoration of the minor orders: the Council fixed and kept the four minor orders, and also the subdiaconate and diaconate; it reasserted the Church's right to revive lower orders and tried to save the four minor orders in particular from this formalistic decadence.

THE NEED OF SERVICE FUNCTIONS

It can be expected that the restoration of the diaconate by Vatican Council II will be instrumental in solving the problem of functional orders to the advantage of the entire Church.

When we discuss the question of the restoration of the diaconate and other orders as autonomous functions, we must first ask ourselves if there is a real need for such a restoration and to what extent it is necessary. And it is important to start from the fundamental fact that orders are really functions. The question is focused, of course, on the diaconate, and it is with the diaconate that that restoration ought to begin. To begin with the minor orders would be a wrong start. The diaconate is pre-eminently the "serving function" in the Church. History tells us that it was from the diaconate that the lower functions arose, with the exception of that of the exorcist which is of a peculiar nature; and all, just like the diaconate, are strongly marked with the character of serviceability. Hence, it is this spirit that should be present in all lower functions. It is only on the basis of the diaconate as a function of service that it will be possible to determine what other lower functions will be necessary.

There is in our own time an evident need of service functions that are lower than the priesthood. There exists a large field of charities, and here the Church has a permanent task, although the needs and the forms of charity differ greatly according to time and place. Charity had a definite place in the Church from the very beginning, and in early Christianity the deacon and his helpers had a particular place in the administration of that charity. In our own day we need works of charity on the parochial and diocesan levels and that of other relatively independent Catholic organizations. Many are engaged in that work either professionally or on a voluntary basis, and it is an ideal vocation for Christians.

Church life, as all human life lived in our present world, brings with it an increase of administrative work. Yet this does not need to degenerate into bureaucracy. Organization is natural and necessary, but its administration is a burden, particularly for parish priests. A number of parishes already employ lay men and lay women to help in the work of administration.

But there are also functions that are more directly concerned with pastoral care and that are being entrusted to

112

laypeople, both men and women. This has been the practice for a long time in the field of the liturgy; there are sacristans, organists, singers, Mass servers. There is an evident development in this field. In some places a properly so-called *schola cantorum* has been formed; the singers exercise a true liturgical function. In some dioceses the function of Mass server has developed into the more extensive function of "acolyte" for older boys. When boys are properly instructed and realize their close association with the divine mysteries, many appreciate that privilege and a number may be prompted to follow a vocation to the priesthood.

The participated Mass requires the service of a reader and commentator; there is need of a "deacon" who gives directions to the faithful, assists the priest at the altar and acts as an intermediary between the people and the celebrant. There is also a need of assistants for distributing communion to the faithful and for the administration of baptism. These functions were, until recently, performed by the priest alone or, as in baptism, the housekeeper was occasionally asked to act as a sort of deaconess.

The need for assistants in liturgical functions is much greater in mission countries. It is impossible for the priests to visit all the mission-posts every Sunday. The catechist then leads the Christians in prayer and song and gives instruction or even a homily. But more is necessary to maintain and develop religious life. And this the catechist is unable to do. The same situation exists in regions where Catholics are widely scattered, in dechristianized countries that have few priests, and on a continent like South America that is very poor in priestly vocations.

Catechesis is a most important pastoral work. Many priests apply themselves to it with zeal because people like to see catechesis given by the official ministers of the Church. This work demands an enormous amount of time and energy, and some priests make it their almost exclusive task. In Catholic schools, Sisters and laypeople also perform that work excellently; sometimes lay teachers can exercise even a greater influence on the pupils than the priests because they are closer to the pupils. In more recent times secular institutes have been organized that consecrate themselves entirely to that important work. On the other hand, great hope is placed on an ever greater influence of societies like the Confraternity of Christian Doctrine in the United States, which is so very necessary to meet the demands of the rapidly increasing number of children who are unable to attend Catholic schools.

Many laypeople consecrate themselves either completely or in their syare time to other tasks that are directly pastoral. Well known is the Legion of Mary founded by Frank Duff. Catholic men and women visit homes, especially those that the priest would be unable to visit. Others are active in works that are for the benefit of youth. There is also a growing need of men who—as is done by the Jocists—bear Christian witness in their own milieu and are able to influence workers in various trades, because of their direct contact with the workers.

Many more examples could be given to show the great need for such functions and to record the fact that organizations have already been formed to meet that demand. Let us merely mention here the German men and women who help the priest in pastoral work (*Seelsorgehelfer* and *Seelsorgehelferinnen*). Those functions have no official and certainly no ritual character; yet in many cases they are exercised in a ritual way, that is, they are virtually liturgical functions. On the other hand, there are official functionaries for the liturgy, but they have no opportunity to exercise their proper functions because they are quickly raised to higher orders. It even happens that, by a "kind dispensation of the Holy See," the higher orders are conferred within a few days or even hours. Thus the functions of the lower orders are fulfilled by priests and laypeople. Other functions have arisen that did not exist formerly because there was no need for them; in fact, these functions have grown far beyond and above the traditional orders.

Is this need of lower functionaries in the Church a consequence of the shortage of priests? We believe that this is only partly true and only in certain regions; it is not true for the Church generally. There is a real shortage of priests in South America, in most mission countries and in some territories where Catholics are widely scattered. Thus it is understandable that it was from the German "diaspora" territories that the first cries went up for a functional restoration of the diaconate. But when we look at the question from a more general standpoint, and include also that of the lower functions, it does not seem that the shortage of priests is the true reason.

We can rather turn the argument around. Because the lower functions were not filled, the priests became overburdened with all kinds of tasks that do not really belong to their office. As a consequence, even in countries where the Church is well-established and which are in every respect well-developed—and precisely even in such countries—there exists a frightening lack of priests. In reality, however, it is largely a lack of men who put themselves, wholly or in part, at the special service of the Church and, in her, of their fellow-men. Every priest who is engaged in the ministry knows that he has to do all sorts of things. That is why many have invoked the help of laypeople. But if we really wish to have a harmonious development of the Church, it will be necessary to introduce new functionaries *within* its hierarchical structure.

The Church has the authority to do this, and she has actually done it in the past. The ritual appointment by the bishop for the exercise of a function gives to that function and to the work a deeper dimension, because it is the Church which gives that official appointment as connected with—we may certainly say—the exercise of Christ's priesthood. An official status would give more security and greater standing in the Church to those functionaries. But above all, such a greatly developed hierarchical organization of the Church corresponds more to her community structure. The dividing line between the "laity" and the "clergy" would thus become less pronounced. There would remain, of course, a clear distinction between clergy and laypeople, but it would be principally a spiritual and functional distinction, much less a difference of social status or class. All sorts of people would then also belong to the clergy; people who live, nevertheless, among the laity and share their life. These lower clerics would, in turn and by virtue of their function, have much contact with the priests who through them could also have an easier connection with the world of the layman. Such a structure corresponds much more to the inner nature of the Church. And this is really the principal and most profound argument in favor of the restoration of the diaconate and the other lower orders.

With respect to the lay apostolate, however, difficulties are bound to arise in connection with the restoration of the diaconate. Proponents of the independent diaconate claim that many laymen desire to have their work for the Church crowned by an ordination to the diaconate or the reception of one of the lower orders.[34] But it is also true that many

---

[34]Cf., e.g., Hornef, *op. cit.* (footnote 21), pp. 21 ff. Pope Pius XII, in his allocution of October, 1957, to the World Congress of the Lay Apostolate, emphasized that the diaconate is not a lay function and that its exercise therefore cannot be called a function of the lay apostolate. See also Herbert Vorgrimler, "Restoring the Diaconate," *Herder Correspondence,* January, 1964, p. 13, and Chapter Three of the *Constitution on the Church* of Vatican Council II, no. 29, p. 33.

laymen, especially those who are engaged in Catholic Action on a more or less full time basis, do not at all desire the diaconate, because they think that such a diaconate will lower the proper value of the lay state.

It would seem that there is here a certain confusion. For it would indeed be wrong to think that full value is denied to the lay apostolate unless it is crowned with an ordination; for this shows a mistaken tendency toward clericalization. But the re-established diaconate is not a matter of finally giving the right place in the Church to the lay apostolate. It is not at all a question of lay apostolate but of the right place and proper functioning of the ordained priesthood, which now has too many functions to be able to fulfill them properly. Spreading the priesthood over several offices, which would be exercised without the intention of some day advancing to the priesthood in the strict sense, would be advantageous to the exercise of the hierarchical function. This diffusion is something taking place *within* the office and it does not in the least jeopardize the lay apostolate. It would certainly be wrong for those who are engaged in the lay apostolate to be opposed to a better functioning of the office of priesthood because they imagine that it would do harm to their own apostolate. In such a case two questions are mixed up that should be kept apart.

A Renewal of Lower Orders
But Not a Simple Restoration

The restoration of the diaconate and other orders is certainly feasible. But we must insist that the ideal is *not* the restoration of the situation that existed in the first centuries. When we speak of a "functional restoration," we mean expressly the restoration of functions. It would really be impossible to maintain the four minor orders and "let them function once more." Much that had meaning formerly is now meaningless. The minor orders will need to receive new content. It will be necessary to ask if one or more should not be abolished and replaced by others. The Church has the power to do so and no one has doubts about that. The question that has long been a subject of debate, viz., the relationship of the subdiaconate and minor orders to the sacrament of the priesthood would remain untouched even if lower offices are adapted in such a way that they can function properly in our time.

In connection with the ideas of the Council of Trent, we could now arrive at two kinds of clergy. Let us repeat once more that we should discard our conventional ideas about the clergy: both kinds are human beings who are in a particular way at the service of the Church and, in her, of their fellow-men. The "lines" of the orders for the two groups of clergy need not run completely parallel, in the sense that the only difference between them would be that the priest had advanced farther than the others who remain fixed at a certain stage. On the contrary, we should distinguish two clerical lines that are somewhat divergent: 1) those who are unwilling or unable to become priests; 2) those who desire to become priests and are called to the priesthood. The sequence of the two here is dictated by purely practical reasons; otherwise we would have to repeat certain things we want to say.

Before going more deeply into the examination of those two lines, we should like to plead for the abolition of the exorcist function *as an order,* with respect to both lines. The function was added to the orders somehow, but already at an early date the exorcists were obliged to relinquish their function to higher officials. It is the established rule in our own day that, in case of a necessary exorcism, it is a priest who must exercise that function, and even he then needs the special permission of the bishop. It does not seem that this rule will ever be changed. Why then should we preserve a rather questionable relic like the order of exorcism in an artificial way?

When we now reflect upon the orders, that is, functions, that could be available to the first kind of clergy, we must first take an inventory of the functions that are actually performed by laypeople today or that could be exercised by them: Mass servers, acolytes, singers, sacristans, readers, commentators, catechists, administrators, those who devote themselves to Catholic charities and perhaps still others. This must be our starting-point. We must confront those functions with the existing series of orders and with the diaconate. Where can we maintain the historical line and where must we abandon it?

The order of acolyte could simply be maintained, with the understanding that it is destined for those who fulfill the more important lower functions in liturgical celebrations. This order could be received at the age of seventeen or eighteen, and the acolytes could continue to exercise that function when they become adults.

But what would prevent the Church from raising the function of Mass server that is now exercised by younger boys and, as a function, actually precedes the order of acolytes? It could be made the first order. It is truly a valuable function, and in olden times there were no objections against conferring upon boys even the order of reader. Of course, this ordination would have to be preceded by a period during which the boy would be an "aspirant" for this order, and one could require the minimum age of ten years for this ordination.

The lectorate is now receiving a new meaning on account of the function of reading Holy Scripture in the vernacular; there is every reason for making it an official function by ordination.

119

The singers, members of the *schola cantorum,* fulfill an important church function. This function of "cantor" should become an order. This would, moreover, be useful in creating a proper attitude among choir members; they would thus better understand the meaning of their function as ministers in liturgical worship.

The "doorkeeper" (*ostiarius*) easily reminds us of the sacristan. The latter does indeed fulfill the ancient function of the ostiariate but he does much more than that. Thus it might be a good thing to drop the ostiariate and replace it by the broader *order* of sacristan. A proper training could be given to aspirants to that order and the ordination would give them inspiration and dignity. The idea proposed in the international congress of sacristans in Vienna, to give sacristans the four traditional minor orders appeals much less to us, although it is not necessary to react to such a proposal as an old sacristan did, who remarked: "I guess they want to give those orders to us to make us wash the purificators!"

The subdiaconate and the diaconate should be considered together. And the question is then concerned with the diaconate, for the subdeacon is his assistant and helper. There are certaintly good reasons for advocating the re-establishment of the diaconate as an autonomous function for the exercise of important liturgical functions and for catechetical, charitable and administrative work. Here we can fully return to the original meaning of the diaconate, and we can speak of a real restoration in a twofold sense. These functionaries will need a thorough education that is truly adapted to their function; hence it should not be a simplified seminary education. They could be made to advance to the diaconate by way of the minor orders and the subdiaconate.

However, it would not be necessary that the deacons should pass through all those lower orders. This is generally not necessary. The main thing is that they be fit for the function, as was already declared by St. Ambrose. One who is suited for the function of acolyte or lector is not *per se* fit to be a cantor; and it is often impossible for one man to exercise a variety of functions. It is not necessary for a sacristan to be also a singer, an organist, a reader or acolyte.

It stands to reason that celibacy would not be *per se* obligatory for those servants of the Church who are not destined for the priesthood, as was already sanctioned by the Council of Trent for those in minor orders. The *Constitution on the Church* of Vatican Council II permits married men to receive the diaconate. Today, of course, there is no longer any difficulty regarding clerical dress, especially for those in minor orders.

Finally, particular attention should be given to the proposal that a distinction be made between two kinds of deacons: those who are totally consecrated to that work, and those who have an ordinary job besides their function of deacons. As there are advantages and disadvantages attached to both situations, it is certainly advantageous to propose that distinction.

The administration of tonsure could be the sign that the candidate is destined for the priesthood. It would then be reserved to the second group of clerics. And in case a candidate of the first group desired to go over to the second group—which evidently is not to be prohibited—tonsure could then be received as a sign of that change.

There is a special difficulty in respect to the many girls and women who totally or partially devote themselves to the service of the Church. While we will not enter here into the question of the woman as minister of the Church, it seems desirable that more relief and distinction should be given to the functions of those women. That this could

121

be done in a ritual ceremony is evident from what we learn in the history of the deaconesses.

Regarding the second group of clerics, namely, those that are destined for the priesthood, tonsure, as we have already remarked, could be the external sign of that intention, and the right to wear clerical garb could also be given to the candidate at a specified time. There would also be no valid objection against giving the minor orders at an earlier time than is now the custom, for if any candidate renounced his destination to the priesthood, he could still continue to exercise the ministerial function of his order. Such a situation would have great advantages, for there are a number who eventually feel called, not to the celibate priesthood, but to the state of marriage, or who are incapable of completing the necessary studies. These could then still continue to exercise their orders in the Church.

Is it necessary that the cycle of orders—which are obligatory as an ascent to the priesthood—should be the same as for the first group that does not have that destination? Some, of course, might already have received the order of Mass server and/or acolyte before entering the seminary. But would it not be sufficient for future priests to pass through the following orders before they receive the priesthood: reader, acolyte, subdeacon and deacon? Surely it is not necessary for them to receive once more the office of Mass server and certainly not that of sacristan. For practical reasons, however, perhaps some seminarians should be ordained as sacristans and a whole group as cantors, that is, as members of the *schola cantorum*.

Where there are fewer orders to be received, there is a greater possibility to exercise their specific functions. But that possibility becomes even greater when the lower orders, those of acolyte and reader, are already conferred during the first years of senior seminary. The objection that these

122

seminarians may discontinue their studies would no longer be valid, for they could go over to the other group of clergy. There is a greater difficulty in regard to the subdiaconate because a definitive acceptance of celibacy is still attached to it. But would it be improper to transfer that commitment to celibacy to the diaconate, especially since, in the supposition of two kinds of clergy, the subdeacon could continue to exercise his function?

The spreading of the various functions leading to the priesthood over a longer time also makes it possible for seminarians to exercise their functions for some time in a sort of apprenticeship, for instance, in parishes, so that they would be gradually introduced into pastoral work. That they will be ordained to the priesthood one or two years later is certainly not an objection; in the meantime, they have worked for the Church and will be more mature when they become priests.

The present tendency to decentralization is not based on a desire to diminish the power of the pope or the position of the hierarchy in general. The supreme power of the pope and the place of the hierarchy, as they have been clearly established in the teaching of the Church after a development of centuries, is fully accepted. But what is aimed at is a greater equilibrium in the organization of the Church. There are many possibilities for improvement in that respect within the frame set by religious doctrine. In fact it is the doctrine concerning the Church that underlies the efforts to arrive at a greater harmony in its relations.

3. Changes in the Structures of Pastoral Care

One very important aspect of the changes in the organization of the Church is concerned with modifications in pastoral structures. By "pastoral structures" we mean the framework within which the life of the Church runs its course and in which its office bearers exercise their functions. We shall speak in turn about the diocese, the parish, and other pastoral structures.

The Diocese: the Local Church and Its Bishop

Emphasis on the Local Church. The fundamental and most important structure is the diocese or rather the "local Church."[35] The custom of calling a diocese a "Church" has practically disappeared. It was only in official ecclesiastical terminology, for example, on the occasion of the appointment of bishops, that that name continued to be used. The disappearance of that ancient name was very significant. A diocese was seen much more as a subdivision, an administrative part, than as an independent unit within the greater whole of the universal Church; thus the stress was placed on the universal Church.

It is likewise very significant that in our own time the term "local Church" is coming into use again. It is a matter for rejoicing that Pope John led the way in that direction. In those local Churches the bishop forms the Church by means of celebrating the sacraments and proclaiming God's word. Without the bishop there is no local Church. In this respect it is also advantageous that in mission countries so-called apostolic vicariates are disappearing more and more. No doubt, political factors are also playing a role in this, for it is desired that the Church should, as soon as possible,

---

[35]Cf. Fernard Boulard, "Vers la communauté diocésaine," *Les cahiers du clergé rural,*" Paris, no. 120 (1950), pp. 317-323 and no. 143 (1952)), pp. 454-458; J. Colson, "Qu'est-ce-qu'un diocèse?", *Nouvelle revue théologique,* vol. 75 (1953), pp. 471-479; J. Frisque, "La place de l'évêque dans la vie chrétienne," *Eglise vivante,* vol. 6 (1954), pp. 275-292; Cipriano Vagaggini, "The Bishop and the Liturgy," *Concilium,* vol. 2 (1965), pp. 7-24; Joseph Pascher, "Relation Between Bishop and Priests According to the Liturgy Constitution," *ibid.,* pp. 25-31.

become independent in those countries. It is typical, nevertheless, that it is considered necessary precisely for that independence that there should be residential bishops as soon as possible everywhere instead of papal vicars endowed with episcopal dignity.

The position and status of the bishop has passed through many developments in the course of history. A favorable development has taken place during the last centuries; nevertheless the question "What does the bishop mean for his people?" remains very real. Do we not think too much of the bishop as being the great administrator, the one who appoints pastors and is needed for ordinations, for the administration of confirmation, and for the consecration of churches? And yet it is precisely the bishop who is our shepherd, our "pastor." With due respect for the parish, we must say that the diocese forms a more solid bond between the faithful than the parish.

When Christianity began to gain a firm footing in ancient times and the ecclesiastical office became more developed, a bishop was appointed in every place that had some importance and he celebrated the Eucharist, administered the other sacraments and proclaimed the faith. In this he was assisted by the *presbyterium,* the "college of priests." These priests had also become sharers in Christ's priesthood by ordination; in particular, they shared in the central power of the priesthood, the power to celebrate the Eucharist. But only the bishop had the fullness of the priesthood. The presbyters were his assistants. This was beautifully expressed in the arrangement of the seats around the altar. Behind the altar was the seat of the bishop—not a "throne"—from which he announced the word of God: his *cathedra.* On both sides of the bishop were seated his first assistants, the "ministers of the second order," the presbyters. By mandate of the bishop, the priests also offered the sacrifice of the

125

Mass and administered the sacraments. They celebrated the Eucharist, as is still done, "in union with our bishop" (*una cum Antistite nostro*), and proclaimed the word of God.

As the Church expanded, the priests were sent out to the surrounding countryside to celebrate the Eucharist and do whatever the bishop considered necessary and did not reserve to himself. It was perfectly evident that the bishop was the center and the starting point of pastoral care and that he was in no way a sort of administrative overlord. In reality, however, the numerical growth of the Church, the increased size of dioceses, and also the influence of feudalism, made the bishop become a remote figure, distant from the people. Thus the proper concept of the bishop as the pastor was somewhat lost from sight. This was evidently a wrong development. The bishop is and remains the heart of all pastoral concerns. That is why the cathedral is the center of the diocese, especially when the bishop celebrates the Eucharist and announces the word of God there. It is the diocese that is pre-eminently the small community within the larger community of the universal Church.

Changes are possible and have taken place in the episcopal office, but not every form of development is good. An example of a change in the wrong direction is that at one time it became a mere honor and source of income, as was the case with many court bishops who practically never resided in their dioceses. The episcopal office has a core, a foundation, that is of divine origin. Christ's ordinance demands that the bishop be always a true shepherd whose chief concern it is to celebrate the sacraments, to proclaim the word and take care of pastoral work. That core must always be preserved, however much the circumstances may change; that is also the norm for judging whether a particular development is right or wrong. While today's bishop differs from a fourth-century St. Augustine and his fellow

126

bishops, we easily recognize them as bishops. But the same cannot be said of the younger sons of rulers to whom dioceses were assigned.   ,

Lingering Traces of Feudal Times. In our own day there are still traces of the development of the episcopal office that took place in the feudal period. The bishop at that time was simultaneously the temporal ruler, and not infrequently he was more temporal ruler than bishop. We continue to speak of the bishop's "throne" but forget that that throne was rather the throne of the sovereign. It is more correct to speak of the "seat" or "chair," the *cathedra* on which the bishop is seated as shepherd and teacher of the community.

The whole outward appearance of the bishop continues to remind us of a monarch or prince bishop. The bishops, in the course of time were clad with the royal purple, a privilege that was absolutely reserved to the sovereign, and they were also covered with the royal ermine. The bishop has in fact a twofold attire: the liturgical garments and the purple mantle with the train and ermine cap of the sovereign. When the bishop visited a church, he was received at the door as the sovereign, but sitting down on his "throne," he took off his princely garments, and left the throne robed in episcopal vestments to begin the celebration of the Eucharist. We still perform this ceremony of the "vesting" of the bishop at the throne, which is a time-consuming affair now devoid of meaning.

The episcopal coat of arms clearly has a princely origin. And in Europe the bishop's residence is often still called the "episcopal palace." Fortunately, the reality that used to hide behind those symbols has greatly disappeared, although some people still like to speak of the "princes" of the Church. It is interesting to note the difference in the definitions of the word "bishop." The old *Catholic Encyclopedia* has the following: The bishop is "an ecclesiastical dignitary who possesses the fullness of the priesthood to rule a diocese as its chief pastor, in due submission to the primacy of the pope." The *Grosse Herder* encyclopedia has the much more exact: "Successor of the apostles in their office of teacher, priest, shepherd, and head of a part of the Universal Church."

The Essential Position of the Bishop. It is pleasant to note that the essential position of the bishop in God's Church is being emphasized in our day. We need not regret that we have left behind the time when many bishops were at the same time temporal rulers or at least were reckoned among the great lords of the country. Not without difficulty, there is now a growing appreciation of the bishop that is much more profound, for it values him precisely as a bishop. The figure of the bishop as a shepherd and pastor thus becomes more significant, and this will serve to create a greater spiritual bond between bishop, priests and laity. The bishop is behind everything the priest does, and it is from the bishop that the priest receives his mission. Sometimes the bishop comes directly in contact with the people. When, for example, he strengthens the Christians, mostly in their youth, by confirmation, he commissions them to bear witness to Christ and His Church. By confirmation and in connection with baptism the Christian is given special power to manifest the Gospel to the world. It is the bishop who personally strengthens the Christian and gives him this commission, and, through the bishop, it is Christ who gives us that mission and share in the task of God's Church upon earth.

This better understanding of the bishop's truly pastoral office and of the personal mission of every Christian can lead to greater mutual cooperation, to a better understanding of the Church as true unity in Christ and to a better realization of what it means to be a Christian. Commissioned by Christ and in union with Him, the bishop is our shepherd. In the bishops we are directly connected with Christ who sent his apostles into the world, clothed with power to celebrate the Eucharist, to administer the other sacraments and with the mission to "go and teach all nations."

We may call all bishops "vicars of Christ,"[36] although the Bishop of Rome particularly deserves that name as successor of Peter who was the leader of the apostles. All priests, diocesan and religious, whether they are active in or outside a parish, participate in the power and the task of the bishop.[37] They, too, by their participation in the priesthood, are Christ in the Church, vicars of Christ, in close union, however, with the bishop as his assistants. Obviously, the diocesan and religious clergy attached to parishes occupy a special place in the diocese, precisely because they represent the bishop in a particular, influential and extensive way. Precisely, however, because the parishes have an important place *in* the diocese, it is wrong to "absolutize" them. The parishes derive their importance from the great community of bishop and diocese that is based on a divine origin.

The theology of the episcopal office is still in the process of development and, undoubtedly, this development will be greatly stimulated by the decisions and discussions of Vatican Council II. This development may also clarify the relation between the bishop and his priests and the members of his community, in which there remain all sorts of practical difficulties. There can be no question, however, of returning to the situation of the first Christian centuries. Such a return is always impossible. Hence it would be fruitless to try to establish the same pattern of contact between bishops, priests and people as existed in the first centuries. The ecclesiastical patterns of that age were, like those of all other periods, strongly determined by the form of society in those days. Similarly, we must reject the feudal episcopal pattern. Today

---

[36]*Constitution on the Church*, Ch. III, art. 27.
[37]*Ibid.*, Ch. III, art. 28.

we must try to realize the leading idea of the bishop as shepherd and first "minister" (*leitourgos*) of the "local Church" in a way that is appropriate to our time. In a modern society, the leaders are no longer "lords" but top-ranking "servants" of the community. Whence the *Constitution on the Church* specifies that the bishops "have taken up the service of the community" constituted by the faithful;[38] they stand "in the midst of their people as those who serve."[39] This idea of service appears to underlie also the modern desire for a compulsory retirement age from active duty of ecclesiastical servants of the community.

Diocesan and Parochial Collegiality. The collegiality of the bishops in reference to the universal Church must find its counterpart at the level of the diocese between the bishop and his local church composed of priests and laity. It should be extended also to the ordinary parish level. Otherwise an imbalance would result. For this reason the *Decree on the Pastoral Office of Bishops in the Church* says: "Let the bishop call the priests in dialogue, especially about pastoral matters. This should be done not only on a given occasion but at regularly fixed intervals."[40] "To put this into effect," the *Decree on the Ministry and Life of Priests* adds, "there should be—in the manner suited to today's conditions and necessities, and with a structure and norms to be determined by law—a body or senate of priests representing all the priests. This representative body by its advice will be able to give the bishop effective assistance in the administration of the diocese."[41] The first of these two decrees provides also for a special "pastoral commission" to examine all matters of pastoral concern and draw up norms regarding them. The

---

[38]*Ibid.*, Ch. III, art. 20.
[39]*Decree on the Pastoral Office of Bishops in the Church*, Ch. II, art. 16.
[40]*Ibid.*, Ch. II, art. 28.
[41]*Ibid.*, Ch. II, art. 7.

laity's participation is foreseen both in this pastoral commission and in the diocesan curia.[41a]

The laity are "permitted and sometimes even obligated to express their opinion on those things which concern the good of the Church."[42] Priests "must sincerely acknowledge and promote the dignity of the laity and the part proper to them in the Church. . . . They must willingly listen to the laity, consider their wants in a fraternal spirit, recognize their experience and competence in the different areas of human activity, so that together with them they will be able to recognize the signs of the times."[42a] In the United States, where there exists an extensive system of Catholic schools of every kind, it is to be expected that laypeople, and especially parents and educators, will also assume an increasingly greater role in all matters dealing with Catholic education.

Tendency to Smaller Dioceses. It is certain that the theological considerations of the episcopal office will have to seek support in sociological studies. How can we in our time give concrete form to the idea that the bishop is not a distant administrator and ruler, but a shepherd who is close to his flock and the genuine pastor of his community? All we can say is that patience is needed here, for time alone can provide us with the answer. Perhaps the only point about which there is a kind of universal agreement on a practical level is that it is necessary to reduce the size of dioceses. This agreement is supported by sociology: communities should not be too large; but on the other hand, modern man is no longer connected to his locality by strong bonds. In order to make a diocese a viable community and give life to the parishes in it, it may be necessary to create dioceses that are territorially rather small, for instance, a

---

[41a]*Ibid.*, Ch. II, art. 27.
[42]*Constitution on the Church*, Ch. III, art. 37.
[42a]*Decree on the Ministry and Life of Priests*, Ch. II, art. 9.

city and its suburbs, a connected whole of small towns and villages or a large rural territory with a town as its center, so that they can function as an "organic unit."[43]

The bishop himself should be able to make pastoral visitations, direct and coordinate all apostolic works and know well the priests, religious and laypeople who are engaged in diocesan projects. On the other hand, a proper functioning of the episcopal office requires also that the diocese be not *too* small, for otherwise it could hardly possess all the organs required for an efficient pastoral care.[44] The experience of countries where there were, or still are, many small dioceses has shown this to be true. Vatican Council II leaves it to the episcopal conferences to examine the opportunity of revising diocesan boundaries and to propose their recommendations to the Apostolic See.[45] It stands to reason that natural population units with their organic structure, as well as psychological, economic, geographic and historical factors, are to be taken into consideration.[46]

In any case, in the study of the Church's pastoral structures, it is of the utmost importance to put the position of the bishop in the center. To begin with the parish is to begin without a proper foundation. The bishop's office is fundamental in a discussion of the parish and other pastoral structures.

THE PARISH: ITS HISTORY, STRUCTURE AND CONTEMPORARY SITUATION

It is in the parish that the faithful most directly meet the Church. There are many degrees of actual encounter with the Church, but even the most negligent believers meet the

---

[43]*Decree on the Pastoral Office of Bishops in the Church*, Ch. II, art. 23.
[44]*Ibid.*, Ch. II, art. 23.
[45]*Ibid.*, Ch. II, art. 24, 2.
[46]*Ibid.*, Ch. II, art. 24, 1.

parish on the occasion of baptism, first communion, marriage and at the hour of death, or they meet at least the parish priests. It is understandable, therefore, that the parish receives the principal attention in discussions about pastoral concerns.

History of the Parish. Very instructive and even necessary for a proper understanding of present parochial problems, is a survey of the history of the parish. This part of pastoral history is of supreme importance. The parish is not at all the creation of modern times, for instance, of the Counter Reformation; nor is it, in its proper nature, a product of the feudal period. The parish has its roots in the most ancient history of the Church.[47]

The Church at the beginning was found principally in cities. Almost every large or small town in which there was a group of Christians gradually received, with the development of the episcopal office, its own bishop. We are still struck by the great number of dioceses (or titular dioceses) in the countries where Christianity had its first development, namely in Asia Minor, Greece, North Africa, Italy, and the south of France.

The bishop was assisted by a college of "presbyters," elders, priests. They were the ordinary helpers and counsellors of the bishop. They assisted him in the celebration of the Eucharist and sat at his side, to the right and the left of the bishop's chair. Together with the bishop they laid their hands upon those to be ordained: "Do not neglect the grace that is in thee, granted to thee by reason of prophecy with the laying on of hands of the presbyterate" (1 Tim. 4:14).

However, the priests did not receive any territory of their own, but they stayed with the bishop in the town or

---

[47]For the history of the parish, see B. Kurtscheid, *Historia juris canonici,* vol. I, Rome, 1941; W. Croce, "The History of the Parish," *The Parish from Theology to Practice,* ed. by Hugo Rahner, Newman, 1958, pp. 9-22; A. Schrott, *Seelsorge im Wandel der Zeiten,* Graz, 1949.

city. The bishop entrusted to them whatever he was unable to do himself, especially when the communities became too large. They were allowed to baptize and preach with the permission of the bishop. St. Ignatius of Antioch (died 107) already mentions that the priests celebrated the Eucharist instead of the bishop, together with the other priests.

But when the Christians increased in number, this situation became a source of difficulties both in the city and in the country. Before the time of Constantine, there were only small house churches in the cities. In order to make all at one with the bishop, a rite was introduced, in virtue of which the pope in Rome and the bishop elsewhere sent a part of the consecrated Bread to the other gatherings to signify the unity of all in the one Bread. For the Christians were firmly convinced that it was principally in this that their mutual unity consisted. In a letter to Decentius of Gubbio in 416, Innocent I speaks about that practice as "a very old Roman custom." At that time, moreover, everyone went to the church of his choice. It is true that very soon, particularly in Rome, there developed fixed centers, the "title churches," which were cared for, in the name of the bishop, by priests designated by him.

In the countryside where no bishops and priests resided, the difficulties were evidently greater, for there too the Christians grew in numbers, though more slowly than in the cities. It is not improbable that already in the second century chapels sprang up outside the towns which had a bishop's church; but there is no evidence at all that a priest resided near those chapels to celebrate the Eucharist, proclaim the word and administer the sacraments. A priest now and then came from the city to the chapels. Around 300, however, the custom was introduced of establishing priests at least in the most remote villages. This was the beginning of the parishes.

In the territories which we now call "the East" with respect to the Church, another solution was at first attempted. The nature of this unsuccessful attempt to solve the problem serves to illustrate the great value attached to the office of the bishop. From the middle of the third century we find, particularly in the East, no ordinary country priests but so-called "rural bishops." Bishops were appointed in all villages of some importance that lay around the episcopal city; they were called "rural bishops" (*chorepiscopi*) or "bishops of the fields" (*episkopoi tōn agrōn*) in contrast with the city bishop. Such a rural bishop was, for instance, St. Gregory Thaumaturgus (died 270) who, when he was made Bishop of Neocaesarea, had only seventeen faithful under his care. Since the fifth and sixth centuries there were also a few "rural bishops" in the West. They were assistants of the bishop "in pontifical matters," co-adjutors, who lived in territories where no diocese could be formed. Hence they were not resident bishops. This particular form of "rural bishops" owes its origin to the Anglo-Saxon missionaries. For example, Eobanus was the "rural bishop" of St. Boniface in the fourth century.

In the East there was a most unfortunate multiplication of rural bishops; this great number was not advantageous to a good administration of the Church that was in need of greater unity. Moreover, very many of those bishops were insufficiently trained and they were no credit to the episcopal office. Measures were taken already in the fourth century to limit their number. And in a rather short time they were replaced by priests.

In the fifth century there were already a good many parishes—as we understand the term today—in rural areas.[48] Theodoretus of Cyrus in a letter to Leo the Great (440-461)

---

[48]Cf. Croce, *art. cit.*, pp. 12ff.

reported that eight hundred parishes had been erected in his province. Pope Zosimus (417) protested against the undue enlargement of parochial territories, which goes to show that the boundaries of the parish were slowly becoming fixed. In this decentralization, care was taken not to endanger the rights of the episcopal office. This is also attested by the fact that the bishop had the right to make a yearly visitation to the country parishes and to hold provincial synods. The rights of the pastor were thereby limited. Thus he did not have the faculty to impose public penances and to administer the boundaries of the parish were slowly becoming fixed. the public reconciliation of penitents. He was also allowed to preach and baptize. The administration of church property of the parish remained in the hands of the bishop. The bishop gave the pastor a definite part of its income. By retaining the administration of the church property, the bishop assumed, of course, responsibility for the care and maintenance of the parochial churches in the rural districts. Thus the parishes were closely connected with the diocese in that ancient parochial system. And this connection proved very beneficial.

The migrations of nations that took place in the same fifth century when the parishes began to take root, soon and permanently prevented the sound development of the parishes. When the Germanic tribes overran the Roman empire they destroyed most of the parochial churches existing at that time. After the baptism of Clovis (436), the German tribes, starting with the Franks, began to accept Christianity. Very many new churches were built, but—and here was the beginning of trouble—not only bishops, but especially the king, the nobles, and wealthy landowners began to build churches. In the beginning the bishops gratefully accepted any help in the process of reconstruction after the upheaval of the migration. However, the builders considered those churches as their personal property. In this way there arose the system of "private churches." This system was radically opposed to the situation that existed before the migration of nations, and it did not merely affect material affairs.

The feudal lords built churches on their own lands. They sold and exchanged those churches at will and retained the income derived from them. Quite a number built churches merely for the sake of additional revenue. They took it upon themselves to provide a priest for their church. Often they simply retained some roving cleric who happened to come around, or even took one of their servants to the bishop for ordination. Most of the time the latter complied, because there was no alternative. The feudal lord then continued to treat the priest as a servant and dismissed him according to his pleasure. Such priest-servants had very little to do in the ecclesiastical line and were obliged to work as servants in the house and on the land. There was no question of systematic pastoral care; there was no preaching and no religious instruction. The "pastors" themselves were scarcely able to read or write. They celebrated Mass, gave many blessings and were also sacristans.

The bishops were not satisfied with this situation. They tried for a long time to take measures to straighten out things. It is precisely these measures that explain the origin of many rights pastors have even in our own day. The bishops organized cathedral schools, which were in reality a kind of seminary for priests, and there a better instructed clergy received their formation. The bishops themselves owned large tracts of land; on these they built as many churches as possible but their number remained only a small fraction as compared to that of other churches. They gave greater rights to those churches: in them alone could baptism be administered and they alone were true parochial churches. The bishop was able to attach better priests to them. Also introduced was the obligation for the faithful to go to Mass in those churches on the principal holydays, and it was then forbidden to offer Mass in the smaller chapels. Marriages and funerals could be held only in those churches. There existed a close spiritual bond between the pastor and his parishioners: he had to take care of them "from the cradle to the grave" (Council of Aachen, 836). And very precise boundaries were given to the parishes.

Those "baptismal churches," as the episcopal churches were called, were not numerous; and because they were the only true parochial churches, the parishes were very large. A parish often included several villages with their churches and chapels, sometimes as many as eight or ten villages. This was an unbearable situation. Obviously it was necessary to establish new parishes. New villages were founded and they received a parochial church. But some of the already existing "private churches" attached to castles also received parochial rights, though with a certain dependence on the mother-parish; i.e., they had no right to baptize or to hold funerals and part of their income had to be handed over to the mother-parish church. The necessity to give parish rights to "private churches," however, enhanced the power of this system, for the appointment of the pastor of those "private parish churches" belonged to the owners of the church. This situation became even worse when the sovereigns began expropriation on a large scale. Charles Martel was the first to secularize church property on a large scale. He was in need of land to be given to his vassals. He therefore forced the bishops to give up their landed property. The laypeople who received such property, considered it privately owned by them and this applied also to the churches that stood on that land. In this way many former "episcopal" churches became "private" churches that were no longer dependent on the bishops with respect to administration and finances.

Thus the struggle against the system of "private churches" was unsuccessful; and the bishops gradually gave up the fight. Pope Zacharias in the year 746 still requested of Pepin that the "mass priest" of "private churches" be appointed by the bishop, but a few years later he was satisfied with the rule that the bishop should examine the candidate who was presented by the landowner. The *Concilium Germanicum,* which St. Boniface called in 743, specified only that every priest must give an account of his ministry to the bishop during Lent, that he must go to the episcopal city for the Holy Chrism and that he must be willing to let the bishop make a visitation of his church.

But all those regulations, if they were observed, did not touch the heart of the matter. The system of "private churches" was not affected as such. It was finally officially recognized in the Synod of Frankfurt (794). Louis the Pious demanded even that the bishop be obliged to ordain the candidates presented to him, provided they were irreproachable in faith and morals. This system of "private churches" was also recognized in 826 by Pope Eugene II in a Roman Synod. And so it remained far into the late Middle Ages. Even Gregory VII, who fought so violently against the lay investiture of the higher clergy, did not dare to attack the system and the appointment of the lower clergy by laymen.

Alexander III (1159-1181) tried to find a new solution for the problem. He changed the right of "private churches" into that of "patronage." This meant that the landowner would no longer be the owner of the church, but would merely exercise a "right of disposal." The right of free appointment was likewise changed into a right to present candidates. But in practice all this meant only a change of names. There was as much arbitrariness regarding the disposal of church goods as before. In one way it was even worse than before. It was possible to obtain as many rights of patronage as one might desire. Many monasteries were economically almost bankrupt and they saw a chance to remedy their situation by means of patronage. One or more parishes were attached to the monastery and their revenues now went to the monastery. The monastery then presented to the bishop as pastor of the parish a lowly paid secular priest, or what was even more economical, one of their own monks.

In spite of the fact that many private churches became parish churches, the parishes remained excessively large, both in villages and in the cities. In the episcopal cities, until the eighth century, there was usually only one parish church, although in the large cities of the East and the West, such as Alexandria, Antioch and Rome, there were already several churches in the fifth century, and in Rome even at an earlier date. These were auxiliary churches of the episcopal church and they could not be considered, in the full sense of the term, parish churches. Gradually more churches were established also in other cities. A priest was appointed for every one of those churches but did not have all the rights of a parish priest. After some time, however, some churches, first in the suburbs, later in the cities themselves, received full parochial rights. In many cities the latter development began already in the Merovingian period. From the tenth to the twelfth century this became universal practice. The faithful retained the right to go to the Cathedral as the "general parish church of the diocese." Sometimes there was an obligation to be present at the cathedral on particular days. The parishes, however, remained much too large, usually for economic reasons. Thus, in 1227, Bremen, which was already a very important city, had only one parish.

140

In villages the situation was often even worse on account of the privately owned churches and, later, the system of patronage. Every division of a parish meant a lower income. That is why the owners, or the holders of patronage fought with might and main against the foundation of new parishes.

The number of parishes remained small in the Middle Ages. And, proportionately, the number of priests directly engaged in the pastoral work was small, although the absolute number of priests was very large. There was also no question of systematic pastoral work. Pastoral duties were largely determined by the very great number of obligatory holydays and celebrations of fraternities and gilds. The obligation of the faithful to go to Mass in their parish church was misused as a means to obtain revenue.

In the thirteenth century there came a reaction against that "system" of pastoral care, led by the new Mendicant Orders, especially the Dominicans and Friars Minor. With them began a new period in the history of the parish. The priests of those orders, among other things, also went around to preach. They spread everywhere, preaching and holding popular religious exercises, especially in the cities where they established themselves in public churches and monasteries. Canonically speaking, no objection could be made against them, for they had received their mission to take care of religiously neglected people directly from the pope. However, such a pastoral activity was contrary to the accepted view that pastoral care belonged exclusively to the parish clergy, and this gave rise to a violent struggle. The secular clergy appealed to the rights of the parish. Pastors forbade their parishioners to go to hear the sermons, for instance, of the Friars Minor, and to give them alms for their support. The faithful were permitted to go to Mass in the churches of the Mendicants only after they had first gone

141

to Mass in their own parish church. Whoever failed to observe
this order was threatened with excommunication and refusal of the last sacraments. But the Mendicants did not
give up, for they knew that they were supported by the
popes. They felt they were sent, as St. Francis of Assisi had
expressed it, "to help the secular clergy and do the things
the seculars were not able to do." This struggle lasted three
centuries and is looked upon as one of the reasons why the
Reformation could get such a hold on large portions of
the population.

The principal merit of the Council of Trent (1534-1564)
in regard to parish life was that it put strong emphasis on
the pastoral character of the parish priest in contrast with
the material-juridical character that it had in the later Middle Ages. The Council ordered the pastors to reside in
their parish, a thing many had not done until then; they
merely collected the revenue and let another priest do the
work in the parish, paying him a very moderate salary.
(Among these auxiliary priests there were often good shepherds.) The Council determined also that the parishes had
to have well-defined boundaries "in order that the pastor
might be able to know his parishioners."[49] The parish should
not be too large nor cover too much territory. The evil
conditions of that time were caused in no small measure
by the indefiniteness of the parish boundaries and the existence of numerous personal, non-territorial parishes. The latter
were an infringement of the normal rule that demanded territorial parishes, and this infringement had largely been caused
by reason of self-interest rather than pastoral efficiency. Trent
made it difficult to erect those non-territorial parishes. The
Council also determined precisely what the rights of pastors

---

[49]Session XIV, *de reformatione*, Ch. IX.

were, and the right of religious to be engaged in pastoral work was also maintained and confirmed by the Council.

Trent introduced great improvements. In many cases its decisions were translated into practice. But the parishes remained much too large, and the resulting inadequacy of pastoral care which, however, had its source also in other causes, remained a great problem. This problem assumed calamitous proportions when, in the period of the Enlightenment, intensive pastoral care became a vital necessity.

In the nineteenth century it was especially the large city that presented the major problem for pastoral care. Man was in imminent danger of getting lost in the impersonal crowd and he became a prey of a process of dechristianization. Much becomes understandable to us when we note the enormous growth of city parishes. In Paris, for instance, shortly before the French Revolution, the parish of St. Sulpice hand ninety thousand parishioners and its pastor had forty-three assistants. In the whole of Paris there were then about three thousand priests but only nine hundred were engaged in pastoral work. In modern Paris, still 97% Catholic in 1906, there were then 184 parishes for 3,640,000 Catholics. Every parish had an average of from twenty to thirty thousand parishioners. We say, on an average, for besides the already named parish of St. Sulpice there was one, Notre Dame de Clignacourt, that has 120,000 parishioners. It was simply impossible for all those people to go to Mass on Sundays, even with the help of monastery churches. Yet that parish was then subject to intensive socialistic propaganda. The situation was almost the same in many other European cities, especially in Catholic countries.[50] In coun-

---

[50]Cf. François Houtart, " Les paroisses de Bruxelles 1803-1951," *Bulletin de l'Institut de recherches économiques et sociologiques,* Nov., 1953, pp. 761-784.

tries of a mixed or predominantly non-Catholic population the situation was better. For instance, the conditions were much more favorable in Holland. However, this statement is not wholly correct, for a pastor should not limit his care to Catholics.

There is one aspect of parish life of that time that we should not omit. At that time, namely the nineteenth century, when the masses began to slip away from the influence of the Church in many countries, she had recourse to the weapon of organizations. A great part of parochial work was transferred to activities in connection with those associations. These, certainly at the beginning, were principally organizations of defense and protection, and they accomplished most useful work. But it took the accent away from parochial activity, and in the long run this had inevitable harmful consequences for the properly ecclesial and strictly religious work. Moreover, the work of those organizations reached only a small percentage of parishioners; hence, there was no improvement of the situation in regard to the others. Thus the contact of the priests with the parishioners became an ever more difficult problem. We are well aware of this today, as we witness many efforts to make the parish a complete organ for pastoral care. It stands to reason, however, that responsible persons do not wish to discard the advantages obtained by social organizations. That is why the laity is now asked to take over much of that work.

The Present Juridical Structure of the Parish. In Canon Law the division into dioceses is the most important division of the universal Church. The diocese is *the* unit in the Church. According to Canon 216, the territory of the diocese must be divided into "clearly defined territorial parts." Each one of these parts has its own church with a "people" and its own administrator who is its shepherd, charged with the people's pastoral care. Hence the territorial division into parishes is the main rule. However, "personal parishes," in which the connection between the faithful is not based on the territory in which they live but has a different foundation, are permitted and even recommended for special situations.[51] There are in fact personal parishes for soldiers, students and, especially in the U.S.A., language minorities.

However, if we wish to get a proper concept of the parish, we may not content ourselves with that summary definition of the Code. If we wish to know the present structure of the parish, after so many centuries of development, we must also examine what the Church understands by a *pastor* and what is his task regarding pastoral care.

The pastor is the priest to whom the parish is entrusted and committed and who in it must exercise pastoral care under the authority of the bishop and as his cooperator.[52] The Church today strongly emphasizes the *pastoral* character of the parish priest's office, and, on that account, wants a *stability* of the pastoral function.[53] The pastors, and likewise the parishioners, must be assured that the pastor will remain for a long time in the parish, so that a bond of confidence will be able to grow between them. No pastor, however, is irremovable.[54] And today he is still taking care of the spiritual welfare of the faithful "from the cradle to the grave." It is his task to administer baptism, confirmation in danger of death, to officially witness marriages, to bless the homes on particular days, to anoint the sick and bury the dead.

---

[51]*Decree on the Pastoral Office of Bishops in the Church,* Ch. II, art. 23.

[52]*Ibid.,* Ch. II, art. 30.

[53]*Ibid.,* Ch. II, art. 30.

[54]*Ibid.,* Ch. II, art. 31. The Decree abolishes the distinction between "removable" and "irremovable" pastors.

Above all, "pastors should see to it that the celebration of the Eucharistic Sacrifice is the center and culmination of the whole life of the Christian community." They must promote the devout and frequent reception of the sacraments and an active participation in the liturgy. They must "take pains to know their flock," pay special attention to adolescents and youth, "devote themselves with a paternal love to the poor and the sick," have a "particular concern for workingmen," and "encourage the faithful to assist in the work of the apostolate."[55]

All this shows that there exists a very close spiritual bond between the shepherd and his flock.[56] As we have recalled in our historical survey, it was especially the Council of Trent that put a very strong emphasis on the relation of a shepherd to his flock. But the strict obligation of the faithful to go to the parish church on certain days has disappeared. Canon 467, No. 2, says that the "faithful must be urged to go frequently to their parish church, to attend there the divine services and hear the word of God, when this can easily be done." The irksome medieval concept of the parish has disappeared. The faithful are also free to determine themselves where their funeral service will be held and where they will be buried (Canon 1223).

Hence we can say that the present Church looks upon the parish as a community of faithful, who normally live within clearly-defined boundaries; it has at its head a priest who takes care of their spiritual welfare and who on that account is called to celebrate the Eucharist with them, to administer the sacraments, to proclaim the word of God and to do everything that will enable them to attain eternal sal-

[55]*Ibid.*, Ch. II, art. 30.
[56]See also the *Decree on the Ministry and Life of Priests* and Pius XII's allocution to Pastors and Lenten preachers of March 27, 1953, *A.A.S.*, vol. 45 (1953), pp. 238 ff.

vation. The parishioners have a right to expect these services of their pastor.[57]

On the basis of a survey of the whole history of the parish, we may be justified in drawing some prudent conclusions that may be important in our search for a solution to our modern problems:

1. The parish entered history as a help and support for the bishop's pastoral function. The connection with the bishop was very close at the beginning, and this sprang from the conviction that the bishop was *the* pastor in the Church. The Church has always opposed—for a long time with little success—a loosening of that bond.

2. The celebration of the Eucharist was held to be the high point of that unity with the bishop. The reason was that the bishop was considered to be Christ amidst the faithful in a particular way. The bond uniting all with one another in Christ was most strongly experienced in the celebration of the Eucharist in which Christ is present in our midst, and this celebration took place in communion with the bishop.

3. Throughout history the territoriality of the parish is considered as the matrix of the parish structure. Although there have always been exceptions, everything seems to point to the fact that the principle of territoriality is practically inviolable.

4. Excessively great parishes have proved calamitous in all periods of history.

5. Undoubtedly a fortunate development has taken place: whereas the medieval parish had a very pronounced juri-

---

[57]*Decree on the Pastoral Office of Bishops in the Church,* Ch. II, art. 29-30. See also Pius XII's allocution to the Sixth National Week on New Pastoral Methods, *A.A.S.,* vol. 40 (1956), pp. 699-711 (English text in *The Pope Speaks,* vol. 3 (1957), pp. 381 ff.); J. B. Montini (Pope Paul VI), Letter about the significance of the parish to the Canadian Week of Social Studies, August, 1953 (English text in *Osservatore Romano,* vol. XCIV, no. 215, p. 1.

dical character and served largely to maintain rights, the needs of the time have caused the parish, during the last centuries, to develop more into a true organ for the spiritual care of men. In consequence of this, the rights of the pastor have acquired a character that differs from those of olden times.

6. The principle that the parish *alone* is charged with the spiritual welfare of the faithful was abandoned already in the Middle Ages.

7. The fact that manifold changes occurred in the history of the parish shows that even today there remains a possibility of further changes.

The Term "Parish." If we wish to obtain a correct idea of the parish, it is most useful to find out the exact meaning of the term "parish," which comes from the Greek word *paroikia.* This word originally meant to live somewhere as a stranger, to live in foreign parts without a permanent domicile and without full citizen rights. In the Old Testament *paroikia* did not merely indicate that element of foreignness but it came to designate also a spiritual situation. The Jews were not permitted to consider themselves owners of the land that God had given them for their habitation. In the New Testament the *paroikia* is a characteristic of Christian life. The Christians were admonished, as sojourners and strangers in this world, to abstain from the carnal desires that war against the spirit. They must remember that they have here no lasting dwelling place; they must eagerly look forward to the future abode. Hence, the Christian idea of foreignness does not mean a sort of being alien to the world, but it means to exercise the Christian virtues which show that the Christian sojourns in this world without attaching himself to it.

It is clear, however, that the original means of *paroikia* has been practically lost and even forgotten in the Christian

148

manner of speaking. This has no doubt been promoted in particular by the christianization of the whole society. It is true that a christianized society and the *paroikia*-consciousness are not mutually exclusive, but it is very understandable that the sense of being-a-stranger precisely in the structure of a parish which was then becoming emphatically a juridical organization, was difficult to maintain in a society that had become totally Christian.

One could argue in favor of drawing the attention of parishioners to the original meaning of the *paroikia*. A particular reason for this can be seen in the present nature of parishes, especially those in large cities, but elsewhere also, though in a smaller measure. Wholesale and radical dechristianization has once more given a clear *paroikia* character to many parishes: the true and convinced Christian, the true community of faith and worship, constitutes a minority in society and is characterized by "foreignness" with respect to the world. As Christians we live in the world together with all other men, but we have our character and are conscious of our "foreignness." Hence, we must always keep in mind the danger that Christian life, even on the parish level, can be lowered to a matter of ordinary human relations.

Rahner's Theology of the Parish. Karl Rahner has made a special study of the theology of the parish.[58] How, one can ask, can there be a theology of the parish if the parish, at least at first sight, is only a juridical organization of pastoral care for the benefit of people who live within a definite territory? Of course, one can speak of a theology of all sorts of things, and, as Rahner tells us, there is now a kind of "theology" of clothing and of many other things. It is

---

[58]Karl Rahner, "Theology of the Parish," *The Parish, From Theology to Practice,* ed. by Hugo Rahner, Newman, 1958, pp. 23-25.

not in that very general sense that there is question of a theology of the parish. This term implies here that the parish has a special theological value which transcends the general thesis that everything was created by God and in one way or another plays a role in salvation. Similarly, it would not be a theology of the parish if we simply posited some general theses concerning the Church and then replaced the word "church" by "parish." The theology of the parish has, of course, many connections with ecclesiology, but it is necessary all the same that it say something about the parish as such.

We can speak of a theology of the parish when we find a theological relation between the Church and the parish; but only if this relation is something more than the juridical fact that the parish was founded by the Church, for in this case we would remain confined to the realm of Canon Law. As we shall see, the theological relation between the Church and the parish consists in this, that the parish as it *de facto* is, in a very definite sense represents the actuality of the Church, which finds expression in several central features of parochial life. At the same time, we will see that, *de facto*, according to the present Canon Law, only the parish represents the Church in that way, but that in one way or another, other communities of worship can also acquire this function. Hence, there are limits to the significance of the parish. Rahner divides his considerations concerning the parish in two parts: first, two positive theses concerning the significance of the parish; secondly, the limits of this significance.

The first of the two positive propositions states: *"The Church as 'event' is not necessarily a local community."* Although the Church evidently has also by divine right a static aspect and a historical continuity, it cannot be denied that where the Church acts, is actively engaged, "happens as an event," that is, preaches, witnesses, prays, offers the Sacrifice, etc., she attains a higher degree of actuality than by merely existing continuously. The Church is essentially visible; hence she must constantly and repeatedly become actuality, become an "event"; she must every time, become once more an "event" as community, for she *is* community. The Church is present whenever a person holding a hierarchical office acts as such; but it is undeniable that when the Church manifests herself as a community, there is a higher degree of the ecclesial "event" than when he acts in the name of the Church and the other members of the Church are not actively involved.

The Church in this sense as community is most intensively and actually an "event," when by the words of the Consecration Christ is present in His community as crucified and risen, as the cause of our salvation; salvation is then present in a palpable sacramental manner. The Church is most intensively an "event" when the Eucharist is celebrated for, not only is Christ present in this celebration as Savior and Lord of the Church, but the unity of the faithful with Christ and with one another is most visible in the Eucharist and is most intimately realized in Holy Communion. And to the extent that the Eucharist is the sacramental prefiguration of the nuptial banquet of heaven, we already get a glimpse of the eternal definitive form of the community of salvation, just as the origin of the Church, the Sacrifice of the Cross, is sacramentally present in the celebration of the Eucharist.

Now it is necessary that the Eucharist be celebrated *somewhere, in a definite place.* It can be celebrated only by a community that has come together in a particular place. Though preserving her universality, the Church, in virtue of

151

her most fundamental nature, is directed to become concrete somewhere. The Church becomes an "event" in the highest degree by the local celebration of the Eucharist. The local Church or community, then, is not a sort of subsidiary of the universal Church, but is the "event" of the universal Church herself: there does the world-church "come about as event," there is she actualized. Hence the proposition, "The Church as 'event' is necessarily a local community."

Rahner's second proposition reads: *The parish is the primary realization of the Church as 'event'.* Until now Rahner has spoken about "local communities." By this he does not simply mean parishes. Wherever the Eucharist is legitimately celebrated, it is the celebration of the Eucharist of a local community in the sense this term has in the first proposition. For example, this would apply to its celebration in a religious community or in a youth hostel. However, the parish is in fact and by law the primary, most normal and original form of local community, if only because the parish exists exclusively on the basis of "being there." For, if someone asks, "Why do those people go *there* to celebrate the Eucharist?" the only answer is: "Because those people also live together there in that one place." In all the other forms of Christian communities, such as monasteries, convents and associations, there are other elements besides the local factor. The Church is in the highest degree an actual "event" during the celebration of the Eucharist and this celebration is of necessity limited to a place. Hence the parish is the primary realization of the Church as actual "event." However, the term "parish" should not be taken in a narrow juridical sense; a "mission church" or a chapel where people of the vicinity gather, is in that sense already a "parish." But this point does not destroy the fundamental idea; moreover, says Rahner, we do not wish to maintain that all the elements of the parish as found in Canon Law can be given a genuine theological foundation.

Regarding the limits of the significance of the parish, Rahner points out that the parish and its celebration of the Eucharist are not the only form of the local Church in which "the" Church becomes an "event." That the Church and the celebration of the Eucharist are bound to a locality is a natural consequence of human nature: man looks for company in his surroundings. But there is more to social relations than merely dwelling together: there may be the same language, the same history, the same function or profession, etc. Therefore, a community can be formed on a different basis than mere locality; the celebration of the Eucharist need not of necessity be a parish celebration. To recognize only the parish and a parochial celebration of the Eucharist would be equivalent to denying the universal Church.

The importance of Karl Rahner's considerations lies principally in the fact that he reduces the matter to its fundamental proportions. Although the fruits that can be gathered from a theology of the parish appear rather limited, his considerations contain enough to permit a few prudent conclusions. Rahner notes that the Church is most Church, and hence community, when the Eucharist is celebrated. This is very true and offers an important starting point. He says further that the Eucharist is of necessity a local event and that, as a consequence, the most primary and natural realization of the Church as an actual "event" is present when people come together in a parish church or chapel solely for local reasons, i.e., because they live there. He thinks that the *local* aspect of the parish has a theological foundation. Whatever one may think about these two propositions, both the starting points and the limits to which they lead are very important. We may then be permitted to draw the following conclusions from them.[59]

We are most "one" and manifest our unity when we celebrate the Eucharist. It follows that the Eucharist is the proper community-forming element in actually existing parishes; hence this element should be cultivated as such. The fact that the parish is canonically established is of secondary importance, although this fact, by which the *Church* unites a number of faithful living within a definite territory into a parish, is not wholly without theological significance.

The celebration of the Eucharist has such a primary importance that the unity of the canonical parish should, if necessary, yield before better possibilities of celebrating the Eucharist within or without the parochial framework. We are "one" in the Eucharist. The parish bond is important but secondary; moreover, we must also keep in mind that we are above all "one" in the celebration of the Eucharist in communion with the bishop and with the pope.

The parish community that is based on a common dwelling-place and is constituted by the Church on this basis, is important but not exclusively so. A type of ecclesial community that is more directly centered on the bishop, as is

---

[59]For the problem of the parish, see, e.g., J. H. Fichter, *Southern Parish. The Dynamism of a City Church*, Chicago, 1951; H. A. Reinhold, *The American Parish and the Roman Liturgy*, Macmillan, 1958; M. Schurr, "The Parish as a Supernatural Reality," *Orate Fratres*, vol. 12 (1938), pp. 255 ff., 361 ff., 456 ff.; Hugo Rahner, ed., *The Parish, From Theology to Practice*, Newman, 1958; Andrew M. Greeley, *The Church and the Suburbs*, Sheed and Ward, 1959; Alex Blöchlinger, *The Modern Parish Community*, Kennedy, 1965; Casiano Floristan, *The Parish, Eucharistic Community*, Fides, 1964; L. A. Terrier, *Pour un renouveau paroissial*, Lyons, 1945, A. Rijckmans, *La paroisse vivante*, Paris, 1950; Viktor Schurr, *Seelsorge in einer neuen Welt*, 3rd ed., Salzburg, 1959; *Structures sociales et pastorale paroissiale* (Congress of Lille), Paris, 1949.

the case with certain other forms of pastoral care, or even a form of community that is more directly centered on the universal Church, is theologically unassailable.

Practical Considerations. From the practical standpoint of today's social situation, the following observations could be made.

People have increasingly less exclusive bonds with a definite locality. This fact diminishes the importance of the parish and makes it more imperative to rely on other bonds, all of which, however, have only a relative value. We must try to develop other forms of community and of pastoral care while always keeping in mind that, in the present "open" world, it is the Eucharist—the ultimate and most profound exercise and experience of unity—that will acquire more and more practical significance.

Parishes, however, will and must remain. Here it is well to keep sight of two things: the spiritual formation of a parish must take place more from within, through the Eucharist, the sacraments and the proclamation of the word, than on the basis of parish boundaries, parochial rights and all sorts of useful or even necessary associations. And since a parish is a union of people who live in the same place, more attention will have to be given to natural boundaries with respect to the parish.

This last point is a special source of difficulties in cities and large towns. Parishes have *always* been a problem in cities, particularly in large cities. It has never been possible to make them true communities. In some countries the history of such parishes has been one long story of failure. They continued to exist by virtue of their "rights." Those who happened to live near the parish church and fitted in with its ways of doing things went to its services; others did not. Moreover, there have always been excessively large

155

parishes. On the other hand, small parishes are not necessarily true communities.

Might it not be useful to organize a group of parishes, for instance, those of a particular section of a large city, as a unit which would take in all the churches and chapels of an area?[60] Baptisms, marriages and funerals could still take place in the different parish churches, but in other respects the area could be considered as a unity because it has a natural kind of coherence. This coherence remains relative, of course, because the bond arising from the same location of residence is not too absolute, especially in a large city. The formation of such a larger unit would require that the clergy of the various parishes cooperate closely, e.g., in establishing the general lines to be followed in the unit's pastoral activities, visiting of the families, and the merging of all kinds of groups that need not really be strictly along parochial lines. On the other hand, it might not be wise to divide a newly developed suburb of a city into several parishes, because that division is artificial. There it would seem preferable to organize one parish with a number of mission chapels for the celebration of the Eucharist.

In rural areas the division of one town into several parishes is often artificial and may be calamitous for the community life of the town. Perhaps here also it might be better to have one parish church with a number of mission chapels. This would provide for community life on a small scale without disrupting the larger unity that still exists there.

---

[60]The existing deaneries function largely as a system of supervision of the clergy, although there are tendencies to make them more meaningful for the faithful at large. Cf. M. Morillon, "Une expérience de doyenné missionnaire rural," Les Cahiers du clergé rural, 1950, pp. 341-358, 403-408, 443-446; 1951, pp. 161-164; "Deux initiatives concernant les doyennés," ibid., 1953, pp. 234-236; Msgr. Dupont, "Adaptation des doyennés au diocèse de Lille," La Maison-Dieu, 1953, pp. 119-121.

The Parish as a Community of Worship. Theological reflection upon the parish suggests also a closer consideration of worship in connection with parochial life. But before we speak about the parish as community of worship, we must prevent possible serious misunderstandings by considering the notion of "community" as it must be understood in this connection.

From the standpoint of sociology, we can ask ourselves whether or not the parish is an autonomous social unit. To which one can reply: "The question concerning the true nature of the parish as a social group comes down ultimately to the question about the intensity of the bond that exists between the individuals and the parish: to what extent are they 'parishioners,' that is, bound together in a unity, and integrated in the parish? Group solidarity presupposes that the members identify themselves with the aims of the group. To what extent is the parish, as a religious organ, successful in orientating itself to this goal?"[61] It follows from this description that there are parishes that are plainly not, or scarcely, a community; others fulfill that ideal to some extent or even very much. This question can also be applied to the Church herself, in her totality or in the diocese. Whether, from the sociological standpoint, the whole Church or the diocese is a community is a question that should be tested by the facts.

From the theological standpoint, the Church and the diocese, and also the parish, as an actualization and concretization of the Church, are undoubtedly a community; they are the body of which Christ is the Head. Hence, when we examine the relationship of worship to community and es-

---

[61]L. Egberink, "De sociologische aspecten van het parochieprobleem," *De nieuwe mens,* vol. 10 (1958-59), p. 186.

pecially to the parish community, we can also say here *a priori,* that is, on the basis of universally valid theological reasons, that the parish *is* a community of worship. When we are together for liturgical worship, we *are* a community.

Nevertheless, the sociological question always continues to play a role. On the one hand, it would be wrong to neglect the theological certainties and look at the parish only from the sociological standpoint. On the other, while accepting those theological reasons for recognizing the community character of the Church, diocese and parish, it is possible and even necessary to examine to what extent they *de facto* realize this community character by applying the criteria of sociology. At the same time, we must, of course, keep in mind that the Church is a supernatural community and as such remains largely, and even in her very nature, beyond the reach of sociological observation.

The term "worship" can easily be misunderstood. There is already a misunderstanding when it immediately brings up the idea of "church services." The term "church services" has a definite emotional tone that narrows down the meaning of the word "worship"; "church services" sounds too formal. We understand by "worship" first of all the interior attitude that is—necessarily—exteriorized, by which we give honor, thanks and propitiation to God. Worship is the attitude of Christ, by which He declared that He had come into the world "to give glory to the Father." Our salvation is harmoniously connected with, and flowing from that worship because Christ "for us men and for our salvation descended from heaven." When we speak of worship we want to emphasize first of all the honor that must be given to the Father. And this we do to prevent putting one-sided and therefore wrong emphasis on our salvation.

Those "services" are totally concerned with worship. But in reality the word "services" suggests more or less exclu-

158

sively our individual salvation. Nevertheless, the worship of the ecclesial community is fully present in church services. This is true in the first place of the celebration of the Eucharist and the other sacraments, but the official prayer of the Church, comprising scriptural readings and the recitation of psalms—the breviary or office—is also part of our worship. The concept of worship implies that of community. Of course "the Christian must also enter into his chamber to pray to the Father in secret," as the *Constitution on the Liturgy* says. But this is not liturgical worship. There is such a worship when the ecclesial community acts as such. That is why, in principle, it is correct to connect the idea of "worship" and that of "church services." But, unfortunately, the latter term is sometimes identified with a worship that is shrivelled and over-formalized.

The Church has an official juridically determined worship. The Instructions of the Congregation of Rites, issued on September 3, 1958, gave this summary of it: "The sacred Liturgy comprises the whole public worship of the Mystical Body of Jesus Christ, that is, of the Head and of His members (*Mediator Dei*). 'Liturgical services' (*actiones liturgicae*) are therefore those sacred actions which have been instituted by Jesus Christ or the Church and are performed in their name, according to liturgical books approved by the Holy See, in order to give divine worship to God, the Saints and the Blessed (cf. Canon 1256). Other sacred acts performed inside or outside the church, even if performed by a priest or in his presence, are called 'pious exercises' (*pia exercitia*)."[62]

According to the *Constitution on the Liturgy* (1963), "popular devotions of the Christian people are to be highly

---

[62]*De musica sacra,* Ch. I, no. 13; English text from *The Pope Speaks* reprint, p. 3.

commended, provided they accord with the laws and norms of the Church, above all when they are ordered by the Apostolic See. Devotions proper to individual Churches also have a special dignity if they are undertaken by mandate of the bishops according to customs or books lawfully approved."[63] Nevertheless, these devotions do not belong to the Church's official liturgy. It would be wrong, therefore, to minimize the importance of the official liturgical worship. For worship is of its very nature a communal action; hence it belongs to the authority in the community to determine in what that worship will consist. When, therefore, we study the parish as a community of worship, we use the term "worship" in its strict official sense, while not denying the value of "pious exercises" in the parish community. It is evident then that the celebration of the Eucharist and the other sacraments occupy the most important place in the parish as a community of worship.

A Christian cannot help being in and belonging to the Church. Whether he wants it or not, he belongs to Christ's community. He can, of course, tear himself away from it, but a return is always possible because an unbreakable bond remains in virtue of his baptism. There is also no moment in our life when we are not of the Church. We are always borne by the Church and we ourselves bear the Church whatever the circumstances of our life may be. This does not mean that all distinctions between "earthly" and "supernatural" realities are wiped out. We merely wish to point out that there can be no circumstance in which we do not belong to the Church, when we are not "of Christ."

From this standpoint our life is always ecclesial, and this ecclesial life is also always a life in community. It is

---

[63]*Constitution on the Liturgy*, Ch. I, art. 13.

160

impossible for us, for instance, to pray "individually," for we are not "individuals" but persons in an ecclesial community. We can pray either personally or socially. When we pray personally we remain connected with the community, and when we pray socially we remain a person with the proper value and significance of a person. Hence we are always the Church, and not only in our worship, however broad a meaning we may attach to that word. Similarly, the parish is always a realization, an explicit expression of the Church, for the parish can be called a community only on the basis of the fact that the Church is a community. In all its activity the parish is fundamentally the Church.

Nevertheless, we can rightly say that it is in liturgical worship that we act particularly in and by Christ as His community, for the glory of the Father and for the salvation of ourselves and all mankind. When we worship together under the direction of the hierarchy, we represent saved mankind in a primary manner. We are then in the most perfect way the authentic sign, the actual and efficacious symbol of saved mankind that is welded in unity by Christ, and in Christ is directed to the Father. With respect to mankind we are more than ever the actual and efficacious sign of God in this world. We are indeed never more the Church than in worship. Worship is the highest and most intense realization of ecclesial life. This the *Constitution on the Liturgy* brings out when it says: "Liturgical services . . . are celebrations of the Church, which is the 'sacrament of unity,' namely, the holy people united and ordered under their bishops. Therefore, liturgical services pertain to the whole body of the Church; they manifest it and have effects upon it."[64]

---

[64]*Ibid.*, Ch. I, art. 26.

161

Because liturgical worship is the highest actualization of the Church and a sign of God in this world, the administration of the sacraments is also by its very nature a proclamation, an efficacious symbol of God's plan of salvation for this world. If we pay no attention to the fact that this worship is a proclamation and a sign of salvation, the administration of the sacraments could easily degenerate into sacramental automatism.

On the other hand, the formal proclamation of the word must not be disconnected from worship. Even the proclamation that aims at winning converts is ultimately aimed at worship as the highest possible actualization. The proclamation of the word should not be divorced from its natural and necessary connection with worship. The proclamation of the word has always officially and formally retained its place in the celebration of the sacraments, but in reality it has been a formalism. When the sign character of the sacraments as such began to be left in the background, it was but natural that the formal proclamation of the word in the sacramental rite would cease to be a living reality. Hence, the evident connection between the proclamation of the word and worship will have to receive greater emphasis to the advantage of both proclamation and worship. The word element, the express proclamation, will have to regain its place in the administration of the sacraments. Only thus will the Church, will the worship of the Church, be the great sign of God in the world.

For this reason the *Constitution on the Liturgy* laid down the following norms:

> Although the sacred liturgy is above all things the worship of the divine Majesty, it likewise contains much instruction for the faithful. For in the liturgy God speaks to His people and Christ is still proclaiming His gospel . . . .

162

That the intimate connection between words and rites may be apparent in the liturgy: in sacred celebrations there is to be more reading from Holy Scripture and it is to be more varied and suitable . . . .

The rite of the Mass is to be revised in such a way that the intrinsic nature and purpose of its several parts, as also the connection between them, may be more clearly manifested . . . . For this purpose the rites are to be simplified . . . , the treasures of the Bible are to be opened up more lavishly, so that richer fare may be provided for the faithful at the table of God's word . . . . The two parts which, in a certain sense, go to make up the Mass, namely the *liturgy of the word* and the *Eucharistic liturgy,* are so closely connected with each other that they form but one single act of worship . . . .

The purpose of the sacraments is to sanctify men, to build up the body of Christ, and, finally, to give worship to God; because they are signs they also instruct . . . . It is therefore of the highest importance that the faithful should easily understand the sacramental signs.[65]

The conclusion to be drawn from what we have said is evident: it is primarily in worship that we are the Church, the community of Christ: concretely speaking, this means primarily in the celebration of the sacraments, the greatest of which, the Eucharist, is also the highest form of worship. Its eminence, however, must not mislead us and cause us to neglect the worshipful and communal character of all the other sacraments. Baptism, confirmation, marriage, the priesthood, penance and the anointing of the sick must also be, in their own ways, acts of worship in and through the ecclesial community. They should be withdrawn from the "individualism" into which those sacraments have fallen even more than the Eucharist.

All this has important consequences for our view of the parish, for our appreciation of the parish as a community

---

[65]*Ibid.,* Ch. I, art. 33, 35; Ch. II, art. 50, 51, 56; Ch. III, art. 59.

and of parochial pastoral care. The attention of the clergy and the faithful must be directed principally to worship. The parish derives its communal character from the fact that it is the local actualization and concretization of the Church. It is most community when it celebrates its worship because it is there that the highest concentration of ecclesial existence lies. Worship is not merely an important aspect of parish life; it is the basis and the climax of parochial life. "The liturgy is the summit toward which the activity of the Church is directed; at the same time it is the fount from which all her power flows."[66] When, therefore, we speak of the parish as a community of worship, we express that which is most essential in the parish.

Most of the time the ideal of the parish community is not approached from a proper standpoint. It is too often forgotten that the so ardently desired ideal of the parish community, to the extent that it is attainable, can only be realized in and by means of worship. When that ideal is pursued in any other way, a true parochial community will not be realized.

Although it is undeniable that the Church is a community and hence that the parish community, as the local representation of the Church, is a reality and makes present that community in the highest way possible in the liturgical celebration of worship, there are nevertheless reasons for speaking of the Church and the parish as a community-in-the-making. The reality of the Church is always a dynamic reality. And we must admit that there are still great deficiencies in the worshiping community. Through baptism we are members of the supernatural community of Christ, but this membership can co-exist with a high degree of individualism, even of egoism. The same phenomenon exists

---

[66]*Ibid.*, Ch. I, art. 10.

in the parish as the actual community of worship. Just as the existence of a supernatural community is a reality, so too the lack of living this community life is a reality. We do not conduct ourselves as a community and on that account there is also a deficiency in the reality of the community. This situation harmonizes perfectly with the actual situation of the Church in this world: the Church exists in it but, at the same time, is constantly in the making. We constantly build the Church; we constantly construct the ecclesial community. We are redeemed, but we continue to suffer under the weight of our sinfulness; there is in us a part that is unregenerated. But the Church is not built from without. It is self-construction; it is from within.

The celebration of worship presents a similar picture. Liturgical worship certainly makes a really existing community truly present: we who belong to the Church are a community in the most perfect manner when we are engaged in liturgical worship. But we are present there as a part of the Church in her actual reality, hence *also* with her shortcomings. The liturgical celebration works at the construction of the ecclesial community; by the celebration of the Eucharist and of the other sacraments, the ecclesial community as such becomes a greater reality. It is a construction from within.

Hence they are mistaken who reason that, in order to make a true community celebration of the Eucharist possible, the parish must first be a sociological community. They maintain that there should first exist a closely-knit community of families or of work. In short a *pre*requisite for such a community celebration would be the existence of an actual community in the sociological sense of the word. That kind of reasoning reverses the order of values; it wants to start from the outside in its attempt to build a community of worship. Where a number of Catholics who do not con-

stitute a community in any way from the sociological standpoint, celebrate the liturgy together, there *is* a community;
and it is precisely by that celebration that it will, or at least
can, become more truly a community.

We have purposively chosen an extreme example, namely,
of Christians who in no way form a society from the sociological standpoint. But this thing can happen, for instance,
on a boat or in an airport chapel. Our example serves to
show very clearly the difference between the theological and
the sociological concepts of community. On the other hand,
we should not completely divorce the supernatural and the
sociological realities. When the people who are present at
a celebration of worship meet one another in their daily
work or in any other way have much contact with one another, these circumstances can be advantageous for a true
community celebration of the liturgy in the complete supernatural sense of the word. That is also why the territoriality
of parishes—provided this is not determined too arbitrarily—
is meaningful for the construction of the ecclesial community
in its supernatural reality.

Reversely, the communal celebration of the liturgy in a way
that does full justice to the community also has value for
the construction of the community in a more sociological
sense. The liturgical celebration is, not only constructive
in the strictly supernatural sense, but also in the ordinary
and everyday sense: it binds men together. The bond that
arises from the common liturgical celebration demands that
it be prolonged in daily life, and it tends to this of its very
nature. That is why the liturgical celebration is also important for community consciousness in ordinary workaday
life. But this requires a framework within which the community can unfold; there must exist a concrete possibility
for the preservation of the bond. Hence from this side also
one sees the desirability of parishes in which a permanent

166

bond is possible even in the ordinary things of daily life. That is why it is desirable, as a rule, to base the parish on a meaningful territoriality. However, for the parish community, it is worship that is of primary importance; territoriality, and the parochial rights based on it, are of secondary importance.[67]

The liturgy of worship thus stands at the center of parochial life. But precisely because it is a source and a summit, other values also become important. To say that liturgical worship is the highest value is not a kind of supernaturalism that disregards sociological reality. On the contrary, it demands recognition of this reality which surrounds it and it fosters a community consciousness in the very broad sense of the word. One who lets the celebration of worship degenerate into the holding of "church services" and is content with that alone indulges in supernaturalism. This would not only be very harmful to the realm of supernatural values, but would also harm the ordinary workaday relations which should all be permeated with Christianity. Similarly it would be wrong to put the main emphasis on territoriality and on all sorts of bonds arising from it, while looking upon common worship as only one expression, though an important one, of the community spirit.

The Missionary Parish. Worship is the summit and the starting point of parochial life, but the parish may not be satisfied with celebrating the liturgy. Something important would be missing if the parish gave too little prominence to worship and if the liturgy were thus not at all the summit and the starting point; but it would likewise be wrong if liturgical worship were the only parish activity. A parish in which there is no truly living liturgy and which is not active

---

[67]Cf. also Alfons Kirchgässner, *Pfarrgemeinde und Pfarrgottesdienst,* Freiburg i. Br., 1949.

167

in any other way is almost equivalent to a dead body in the Church. Contemporaries speak of two kinds of parishes: the missionary parish which seeks converts and the "conservative" which tries to preserve the faith of its members. Others refer to these two as the "open" and "closed" parish. Parishes are generally "conservative," taking care of the faithful, and much less missionary. There are historical explanations for that fact; for instance, the history of the parish or, as often happened in the past, the weak position of the Church in Protestant or predominantly Protestant countries. There certainly is a measure of truth in the statement that parishes are conservative, although such a claim is not entirely free of too much generalization.

Insofar as the claim is true, the situation is obviously unacceptable. The parish as an ecclesial community and framework for pastoral care must not only be conservative but also seek converts. For the parish, too, represents the Church, which is missionary of her very nature and addresses herself to all men in all circumstances. It is true, of course, that conservation, the caring for what has already been won, finds greater expression in the parish than in the direct work of the apostolate; in any case, the apostolate is expressed in a different way in the parish. But this does not do away with the fact that the parish must be, not only "conservative," but also apostolic and missionary: it must reach out "to everyone living within the parish boundaries."[68] There is, of course, a limit to the possibilities open to a parish. The care of the community of the faithful demands so much attention that little time and possibility remain for actual apostolic work. Hence the parish can only partially fulfill the total task of the Church. This is a sec-

------

[68]*Decree on the Pastoral Office of Bishops in the Church*, Ch. II, art. 30.

ond limitation of the parish, added to the first limitation coming from its restriction to a definite locality.

If we speak, nevertheless, about the "missionary parish," it is for two interconnected reasons:

First, the parish *mentality* must be apostolic, missionary. How can the care of the faithful be combined with this missionary mentality? To take care means to preserve and foster a Christian way of living and a Christian community spirit in those who are already believers. To spread the faith, to witness, is an essential aspect of Christian life, without which no flourishing faith is possible. A Christian must witness in his nearby and more distant environment. Hence an apostolic mentality is necessary to insure the preservation of Christian life. From this it follows that the Church, hence also the parish as the concrete Christian community, must be open and hospitable; she must let outsiders see what Christianity is, namely, a potential home for all. In short, it comes down to this that parish life must be as good as possible and that it must always take into account the impression the parish is making on those who stand outside, viz., those who no longer practice their faith, non-Catholic Christians, and those who do not belong to any Church.

Secondly, the parish, in spite of its natural limitations, must *do what it can* in the matter of missionary activity. The parish as such is spiritually responsible for all who live within its territory; this is a responsibility it has before God and before men. No one may be "written off." A very important task of the parish is the formation of its parishioners into apostolic-minded Christians. For in the parish are formed those who will become cooperators in institutions and associations that apply themselves in a special way to the apostolate, and their activity will, at the same time, be a blessing for the parish.

There is also a close connection between the apostolic mentality and liturgical worship. It is the worship that makes the Church really present and makes her the witnessing sign of salvation in the most perfect way. In the liturgy we pray to God, we ask Him to pardon and reconcile us, to give us strength. Here it is not primarily a question of psychological influence of the liturgy upon non-Catholics who may be present, but it is a question of the power of the liturgy itself. In liturgical worship we acknowledge fully that it is God who gives the increase to anything we undertake for the spreading of Christ's kingdom on earth. It is precisely in the liturgy that the priests of the parish and all parishioners find the energy for bearing witness to their faith, the power to be missionary, apostolic, in the very best sense of the word and in the way that is most adjusted to the circumstances.[69]

Relationship Between the Pastor and the Parishioners and Attitude of the Parishioners Toward the Parish. This problem turns principally around two questions, viz., Is the pastorate to be regarded as a task or as a right? Are the parishioners bound to slavish obedience or do they have freedom and responsibility?

Regarding the first question, the crucial point is, How must we approach the parish? Is it from the side of the pastor's *rights* or from that of the *task* which the pastor and his assistants have with respect to their parishioners? Task and rights are not incompatible, of course, but the faithful

---

[69]For the description of a parish with a strong liturgical and apostolic orientation, see Michonneau, *Paroisse, communauté missionnaire,* Paris, 1945; Jean de Féligonde, *L'Hay des Roses,* Bruges, 1953; *Paroisse, chrétienté communautaire et missionnaire* (Congress of Besançon), Paris, 1946; Werner Schöllgen, "Der Ruf nach der missionarischen Methode," *Wort und Wahrheit,* vol. 7 (1952), pp. 729-737. See also Joseph P. Fitzpatrick, "Parish of the Future," *America,* 1965, pp. 521 ff.

can easily get a wrong idea of the pastoral task if the pastor's rights are emphasized too much.

The pastor has rights with respect to baptisms, marriages, the anointing of the sick, funerals and many other important events in the life of a Christian. The historical background of those rights is not very pleasant, but it had a pastoral reason all the same: it was meant to safeguard pastoral care and put it into good hands. Many rights have gradually lost their strict exclusiveness and this, too, has taken place in order to improve the spiritual care of the faithful. At present the situation is such that it depends largely upon the pastor whether he will be rigid or flexible with respect to his rights. However, the pastor cannot be so supple as to be indifferent whether or not the parishioners keep contact with the parish and its clergy. And it is quite natural for a pastor to think in this respect also about the means to maintain the parish church and support the clergy of the parish.

The parish priest has, in the first place, a pastoral task, and its exercise is guaranteed as much as possible by definite rights. Those rights should never become an obstacle to pastoral work. It belongs to the essence of parochial life that, first of all, a possibility be created for ecclesial life and that there be, at the same time, a certain delimitation guaranteeing that one or more priests assume the care for a group of concretely designated faithful. To offer a possibility of ecclesial life means to bring Christ nearer in the way He lives in His Church and desires to encounter men with His salvation by taking them up in Himself in the structure of the Church. The Church acquires that structure, first and foremost, in and around the figure of the bishop, who lives in union with the pope as the universal head of the Church, and, secondly, also in the pastor and the parish.

171

The parish is the Church in her concrete actuality, but parish and Church are not identical. To live as a member of the Church is possible also outside one's parish. The parish creates a concrete obvious possibility, but not the only one. The possibilities vary according to time and place. In places and at times where transportation facilities are limited, the faithful are actually restricted in their ecclesial life to the local parish church. But the situation is different in countries and times where travel is easy. In cities with several parish churches, the parishes have always had a less exclusive character and the *rights* of pastors could never be severely insisted upon. The faithful there took the liberty to go to Mass in the church they found most convenient. In spite of the strong emphasis on the parish which binds the faithful juridically to the parish, for example, for baptism, marriage and funerals, a great deal of freedom is left to them. They have always had the freedom to go to confession where they pleased, and the obligation of celebrating the Eucharist in the parish church was abolished long ago. Moreover, the pastors can grant permission to the faithful to have their children baptized in another church, to marry and to have their funeral in the church of their choice.

Hence, although the faithful are not free in their choice of their parish—their place of residence generally assigns them to a particular parish—and although the parish priest has some rights that are derived from its circumscription, it would be incorrect to look at the parish principally from the standpoint of those rights. The main point is the spiritual welfare of the parishioners who are entrusted to the pastor. And precisely for the sake of that spiritual welfare, he must respect the freedom of the parishioners and be moderate in exercising his rights. Juridical severity can manifest itself, for instance, in refusing to grant parishioners permission to eat meat on days of abstinence on the occasion of a family feast, or the refusal to grant permission to celebrate a marriage or have a funeral in another church. Such acts are harmful to the spirit of mutual understanding that should exist between the pastor and the parishioners. In such cases the parishioners look upon the pastor as an obstacle that has to be overcome, as a difficult functionary.

Even when the pastor has reasonable objections against the custom of some individuals who always go to other churches, or the custom of others who have their marriages celebrated in another church, it is preferable that he insist less on his rights in order that he may appear more as a shepherd inspiring confidence and love. He should recall that the parish is an actualization of the Church, but not the only one.

Regarding the question of slavish obedience or freedom and responsibility, let us keep in mind that the pastor's rights are rather his *duties*: the pastor must know who are entrusted to his care and what his primary duty is. And, ultimately, the pastor's specific duties are only salient points of particular importance which are included in the entire pastoral attitude of the parish priest and his assistants. He must be a father in Christ, but not one who wants to settle everything. As the *Constitution on the Church* emphasizes, "Let the spiritual shepherds recognize and promote the dignity as well as the responsibility of the laity in the Church."[70] In order to fulfill his task properly he must leave a great measure of freedom to the faithful.

While enjoying this freedom, the faithful should on their part keep equally in mind the aim pursued by the parochial system of spiritual care. One who faithfully goes to Mass in the parish church, who would not even think of getting

---

[70]Ch. IV, art. 37.

married in any other church and who lets his children be
baptized in the parish, is not automatically a good parishion-
er, for he might think merely in juridical terms. On the
other hand, one who knows the freedom that has to be
granted to him, and who in season and out of season makes
use of that liberty to go elsewhere and avoid his parish, is
likewise thinking too much in juridical terms.

There should be responsibility within freedom; a freedom
that also recognizes and accepts the decision of the bishop
and corresponds to it by a proper attitude in a spirit of
freely accepted responsibility. When the bishop establishes
a parish he wishes to bring the Church closer to the people
who live in a definite territory. Naturally it is the interest
of the faithful that should be decisive in the making of
such a decision.[71] The faithful must not only consider that
decision lawful and valid, but should do more than that.
The bishop and the pastor can make an appeal to the responsibility of the laypeople to help them realize the aims
of that decision. Obedience is implied in the response to
the bishop's decision but it is no longer slavish obedience.
The faithful must accept the decision: they belong to a particular parish. In practice, the faithful understand rather well
the necessity of that obedience as an integral part of their
responsibility.

However, in order that a parish may function as the
"Church-near-them," the faithful should, as much as possible, be given the opportunity to accept that decision with
free responsibility. The parish as community is called to accomplish a task. The more their freedom is respected, the
more the faithful will experience that they are a community. An inexorable absolute norm that everybody *must*

---

[71]*Decree on the Pastoral Office of Bishops in the Church,* Ch. II,
art. 32.

come to Mass here, every one *must* have his marriage cele-brated here, etc., spoils wholesome relations. This is cer-tainly the case in our time when there is everywhere a greater call for personal responsibility. To exclude every free decision is to exclude responsibility. We cannot ex-clude all "obligations" but obligations should be imposed only when it concerns important matters that cannot be attained in any other way. And in that case the pastor must make it clear why there can be no choice in the matter.

The bond between parishioners and parish must begin with the pastor and his assistants. Through their openness and genuinely pastoral attitude, they must make it easy for the faithful to become real parishioners. The priests must seek contact with them without imposing themselves. They must be friendly and full of interest; and the rectory must really be open to their flock. When the faithful need to speak with the pastor, they must know that they are welcome in the rectory. This openness and accessibility impose their demands on the pastor; they require a certain atmosphere. The fact alone that someone goes to the rectory to discuss a serious matter is a sign of a confidence demanding accessi-bility and empathy on the part of the priest. The faithful themselves, on their side, should understand that they must accept the parish as a part of their own responsibility, i.e., their attitude must not be dependent on that of the pastor. However, if a pastor were to take advantage of the fact that the faithful have to accept him regardless of his own attitude, he would make a mockery of all normal human relationships.

Obviously, something has to be done on both sides. The parish does not prosper through decrees and ordinances but through the loving exercise of the pastoral task and the free but responsible response to this task. This total responsi-bility of the faithful with respect to their parish is the basis of what contemporaries call the "layman's role" in the work of the parish.[72] Strictly speaking, the laymen always have a role in the parish. They belong to it and have a responsibility in it. Lay apostolate is possible only on the the basis of the layman's awareness of this responsibility. Every layman has responsibility with respect to the Church and with respect to the parish, for all of us together constitute the ecclesial community. Whether a particular layman engages in certain activities because of this responsibility is a matter that depends on circumstances. But total responsibility is always present.

Contact between priest and faithful is a fundamental factor by which the faithful realize that they are parishioners. It is a matter of creating and developing a bond between men, so that the priests know they are called to walk before lay people, to guide and sustain them in living a Christian life, while the layman who realizes what the Church is, is ready to accept that leadership.[73] Hence, on the one hand, there is contact between men who encounter one another as men, knowing that nothing that is human is absent from either side and that, precisely because they are Christians, they must endeavor to live according to the loving human relationship that is willed by Christ and by which they are brothers and sisters. On the other hand, there is the specific human relation in virtue of which one group leads and has authority over the other group.

It is most difficult in practice to maintain fully and specifically this relationship between priest and layman. The priest as well as the layman may feel inclined to experience a relation of authority. When there is an excessive accent

---

[72]For a brief description of a parish with a lively involvement of lay people in parish affairs, see C. J. McNaspy "The Total Parish" (St. Richard's, Jackson, Miss.), *America*, Oct. 23, 1965, p. 465.

[73]Cf. *Constitution on the Church*, Ch. IV, art. 37.

upon authority, there may come about a reaction—also on both sides—that expresses itself in a disproportionate emphasis on purely human relations. Consequently, the specific character of the relation between priest and faithful is lost sight of too much. Today in many places Catholic communities are earnestly seeking for a better harmony. Mistakes will be made in the process but we may expect fruitful results if the right principles are kept in mind.

Lay people sometimes accurately point to the right road in that matter when they say: we want to be able to recognize the priest in all circumstances and in all our contacts with him. This does not mean that they want him to be expressly "occupied with their spiritual welfare" in all circumstances. Far from it! Nevertheless they want always to be able to feel that this man is their priest. Priests, on the other hand, are looking for a less authoritarian attitude. In this search they must always remind themselves that they are priests, which, however, does not in any way exclude their being fellow-men. Priests should keep in mind that not every easygoing, being-a-regular-fellow behavior is acceptable. They are always "the priest," the minister of Sacrifice and sacraments, the shepherd and the teacher. The layman expects, for instance, that the priest should preach the word of God, but as man to man. A layman, a psychologist, made the remark that "there are priests who keep announcing the word but understand nothing of the present situation; but —what is even worse—there are others who understand everything, but have no longer anything to announce."

There is contact between priest and people wherever they meet, in worship, in preaching, in pastoral guidance as well as in daily life. It would be fundamentally wrong to think that there is contact only in pastoral guidance and in social intercourse. There is contact whenever priest and layman meet. It follows from this that every effort must be

177

made to make the celebration of the Eucharist, of the other sacraments and also the preaching of God's word such that it is possible to look upon them as an encounter, a genuine contact between priest and people. If this is neglected, the pastoral and social contact between priest and lay people lacks the necessary foundation.

Moreover, every contact that is not directly connected with the sacraments or preaching must still reflect the specific relation of priest and faithful. The priest remains always someone who is "set apart"—however burdensome this may be to many priests—precisely because his contact is that of a *priest* with the people. This does not mean that the priests should be a separate social caste, but that the priest, because he must lead, stands in this life as a special sign of God. Every Christian is such a sign, because the Church is the sign of God; but the priest is that in a special manner. The layman stands in a special way in the earthly reality which he is called to sanctify. The priest does not stand outside the earthly reality but he stands indeed in a special way "in the things that belong to God." There he must stand. And mankind has a right to it. The priest may never lose his own specific character.

Actual parochial life has many problems. We have called attention to only a few. All those problems appear to point in one direction, to the fact that there is, in line with the total social situation of our time, a movement from a juridically closed parochial community to a more free and open community. There is a tendency to an inner openness both in the relations between priest and lay people and in the wider and freer contact with churches, priests and faithful who do not belong to the parish. This wider outlook, this greater openness, can also serve as a foundation for a greater outward openness toward non-Catholics, so that the parish does not make a forbidding impression but rather invites outsiders in the village, town or city. In this way the parish must be the Church in her concrete actuality, for the Church is the sign of God in the world, the efficacious sign of God's salvation.

OTHER FORMS OF PASTORAL CARE

A Survey of Their Historical Development. When we take the diocese as the historical starting point, it is evident that there is at least a theoretical openness in respect to other forms of pastoral care besides that of the parish. In particular there is a possibility to develop new structures of pastoral care that are adapted to the needs of the present time. This development has been going on since the Middle Ages. Fortunately there have always been movements for renewal in the Church. Movements like those of St. Bernard of Clairvaux (1090-1153) and St. Norbert of Xanten (1080-1134) were still totally adapted to the feudal system of their time and the corresponding system of pastoral care. In their time there took place a great flowering of religious life in abbeys. And in the case of St. Norbert, with his strong orientation to pastoral care, many parishes were taken over by his Canons Regular. Both these men were at the same time great popular preachers.

With the change of society and the partial modification of the feudal system through the rise of cities, great changes occurred also in the system of pastoral care. There developed an intensive spiritual ministry outside the parish system, especially among the burghers in the rising cities. One of the greatest needs of that time was that of a proper preaching of the word of God, which had been neglected for so long a time in the churches. In this movement, which has continued even to our own days in constantly changing forms, we can discern two characteristics.

179

First of all, in contrast with our modern tendencies, this pastoral work was not seen as centered on the diocese, that is the bishop, but rather on the pope. This was wholly in keeping with the medieval situation and also that of the Counter Reformation. Secondly, at least until the seventeenth century, hence until a strong emphasis was placed on national states, that form of pastoral care had a strongly international, that is, European character. The great preachers of those days traveled all over Europe; they preached everywhere, whatever their origin might be.

The origin of those forms of pastoral work lies in the rise of the great mendicant orders, the Friars Minor and the Order of Preachers. In complete contrast with existing monastic traditions they established their houses preferably in cities. They scrupulously avoided calling their establishments "monasteries" or "abbeys"; they likewise had no abbot but a "guardian" or "prior." The pope gave them the right to attach a public church to their houses, where they celebrated the Eucharist with the people and administered the other sacraments, in particular confession, and primarily preached the word of God. They traveled all over Europe as preachers. Their work was looked upon as a violation of the parochial system, which indeed it was. This gave rise to great and rather disgusting controversies, because of the *rights* of the parishes. But the "preachers" won the battle with the help of the pope, for the sake of the pastoral care that had to be given to the spiritual needs of the people. As we know from the history of the parish, the Council of Trent upheld those forms of pastoral care and freedom to exercise them.

Those orders and their pastoral activity, especially of preaching, flourished throughout the Middle Ages. Already St. Francis of Assisi (1182-1226) and St. Dominic (1170-1221) travelled personally through large sections of Europe to give the necessary support to the people by their example and their preaching. St. Anthony of Padua (1195-1231), a Portuguese by birth and one of the first followers of Francis, preached not only in Italy where he won his greatest fame and died, but also in France.

In this respect we note a great activity in the fifteenth century. The pacemaker of that activity was no doubt St. Bernardine of Siena (1380-1444) who together with his pupils and collaborators, St. John of Capistrano (1386-1456) and Jacob van de Marken (1393-1476), sounded a spiritual reawakening throughout Europe. This was a true movement of renewal in the full meaning of the word. While laboring among the people, they also successfully renewed their own order of Mendicant Friars by their reform of "Observance." It is typical that they placed their work among the people, as it were, under an emblem, the famous sign IHS. Even today we still find that sign placed everywhere on houses in Italy, particularly in Siena. It was not their intention at all to spread a particular devotion to the Name of Jesus by that means. But they wanted to keep before the eyes of the people a sign that was easy to remember and that would remind them that our Lord Jesus Christ should dominate life in all things. Using this eloquent and simple letter-symbol, they sought to renew the life of faith and the morals of all the people.

In Holland there was at that time a gifted preacher who labored for the same purpose, and was also a zealous promoter of the "Observance" among the Friars Minor, the famous Jan Brugman (1400-1473) whose memory is still preserved in the Dutch expression "to talk like Brugman." He did the same kind of work in the Netherlands that was done by his fellow preachers in the rest of Europe. It was St. John of Capistrano, however, who undertook the greatest journeys. He was also the pope's envoy to various rulers on particular occasions; he took part in the war against the Turks and gave spiritual elan to that struggle; he went throughout France and visited the Low Countries.

In the sixteenth century the great movement of the Counter Reformation began, of which St. Ignatius of Loyola (1493-1556) was no doubt the most impressive figure. However, his ideas did not drop from the blue sky, for he began by taking over the sign IHS and even adopting it as an emblem for his society, which he founded after he had traveled around for a while with his companions preaching the word. But his movement was of a totally different nature. It was more systematic and was especially aimed at the instruction of the faithful, particularly of the elite and of youth, for the purpose of creating a new mentality. By his famous "Spiritual Exercises" he gave a great impetus to the work of retreats which exists to this day. He did much for the instruction of the people, especially through his diciple St. Peter Canisius (1521-1597) of Nijmegen, and he exercised great influence in the field of education.

Other figures of that time are the Capuchin St. Lawrence of Brindisi (1559-1619), who can be considered as having had as much importance for southern Europe as Peter Canisius had in Germany. There was also the universally known St. Vincent de Paul (1581-1660). All these men did much to improve the education of the clergy which was particularly recommended by the Council of Trent.

Especially during the sixteenth century there arose also all sorts of "pious exercises." There is, for instance, the "Forty Hours Devotion" that began in Italy and was very strongly recommended by Pope Clement XI. It was originally aimed at counteracting the debauchery of *Mardi gras;* that is why in many places in Europe that devotion still coincides with those days. Then there came "Days of Adoration," the already named "Retreats," and especially the "Missions" in which preachers tried to renew a parish by every spiritual means at their disposal. At the beginning these missions often aimed at purifying the faithful from Reformational influences.

In the eighteenth century we meet another group of three great figures. There is the Friar Minor St. Leonard of Portu Mauritio (1676-1751), then St. Paul of the Cross (1694-1775) the founder of the Passionists, and St. Alphonsus of Liguori (1696-1787), the founder of the Redemptorists. We note that in that century great emphasis was placed, especially by the first two men, on the passion of our Lord. St. Leonard of Portu Mauritio introduced the "Stations of the Cross," which he intended not as a devotional exercise for the purpose of gaining indulgences, but as a way of preaching the Cross by going from station to station, while meditating on Christ's passion as the central point of our Redemption. This great emphasis on the passion of Christ, stressing also the human aspects of that suffering, is indeed typical of the eighteenth century, especially when we recall that this was also the case in Protestant circles. It suffices to recall here Johann Sebastian Bach's two "Passions." This century saw also the beginning of the "meditations on the passion" or Lenten sermons which reached their apex in the nineteenth century. Both St. Leonard and St. Paul labored prodigiously as missionaries for the people. The eighteenth century saw also the great work of St. Alphonsus who put full emphasis on the religious renewal of the people.

All these men, who worked between the Middle Ages and the end of the eighteenth century, have exercised enormous influence precisely because each of them enlisted a legion of followers and began a mighty movement.

This work continued in the nineteenth and the beginning of the twentieth century. But it is notable that the devotional character of life also put its stamp on it; and, in re-

183

verse, this form of pastoral work began to foster devotional life. This was the time when congregations arose on the basis of some devotion or even for the principal purpose of spreading a particular devotion. This form of pastoral care has had a very great influence in the nineteenth and the beginning of the twentieth century. Then, too, there were great preachers, such as the Dominican Père Lacordaire. Presently, however, there is a crisis in that type of work. One reason is, certainly, a change of mentality in the faithful. Those devout exercises were marked by a particular atmosphere that is no longer ours. In Europe the Forty Hours Devotion is definitely on the wane; in the U.S.A. it is still practiced as a quasi-obligation for every parish at a determined time of the year. Rarely now do we have sermons on that occasion, but usually there is an impressive gathering of priests at the final exercises. More vernacular in the recitation of the litanies and other prayers will perhaps enable people to appreciate better what all those long prayers are about. In all probability, however, that devotion born in other times will never regain the popularity it once had.

Coupled with this change in mentality of the people, is the general desire to find forms of "exercises" that will replace the old structures which have lost their appeal. There is often little time on Sundays,, however, to give proper instruction and inspiration to the faithful. That is why efforts are made for giving some groups particular instruction, away from the parish for those who can leave their homes, and in the parish for others. There are thus "weeks" or "days" for Cana groups, for young married couples, for youths of various ages, for students, etc. These quasi-retreats are taking the place of popular missions where the latter have ceased to have sufficient attraction. Those exercises are performed in an atmosphere of recollection; they do not rely solely on sermons but also on discussion. Moreover, they are aimed at producing a more lasting effect, not only on the individuals concerned, but for the spiritual renewal of the parish.

Add to this that realms of life are constantly being discovered that are either new or have undergone great changes, areas that, in any case, have not received pastoral attention. Means are sought for cultivating them, but the need is also felt to give an institutional character to that work in order to guarantee lasting results and enduring operation.

Specialization in Pastoral Care. Especially since World War II there has been a remarkable tendency toward a well-ordered and constant specialization of pastoral work. It is an *ordered* specialization; everything that comes into consideration in that respect is approached from the special standpoint of pastoral care. Efforts are made to avoid overlapping of the pastoral work done by a variety of priests and a collaborating laity through concerted planning. But in fact there is still much to be done in this respect to prevent some groups from being almost neglected, while others are served by a multiplicity of priests and their helpers.

It is a *constant* specialization: efforts are made to give, as much as possible, a permanent character to that sort of pastoral care, so that it does not depend on more or less casual circumstances and occasions.

There are various principles of specialization; there is, at least, specialization with respect to *objects, persons, forms* and *environment.*

As is evident from history, the specialization of personal care in a simpler form has existed for centuries and, let it be noted, independently of circumstances and occasions. There has also existed for a long time a more orderly and constant specialization concerning particular persons, viz., the spiritual care of religious, of youth and the sick. Nevertheless, recent developments are such that we may speak of a new and very important phenomenon.

With respect to objects, as we have already mentioned above, this specialization is becoming more and more structural in character. The number and kind of special "weeks" or "days" for engaged couples, for married couples, for families with their children, for professional groups, for vocations, etc., is constantly growing in many countries. These weeks or days do not merely deal with some important aspect of Christian life nor is there merely an attempt to adjust the exercises to the needs of a particular group, but they are also becoming better organized from within. Not only priests, but also lay people are particularly engaged in organizing such weeks; and a system has been developed for the proper way to give those weeks, e.g., in the Cursillos.

In all these the aim is not to hold some exercises of devotion in the church and give a few sermons, but there is an endeavor to involve or influence the whole parish by means of those weeks or days. The goal is to reach the great mass of the faithful, but by concentrating on certain basic groups, on members of the Legion of Mary, the Holy Name Society, groups of students, etc. Provision is also made for following up such weeks, for, as was already well-known in the past by the Redemptorists who preached missions for the people, a single exercise often has no lasting results.

The distinction of various groups of persons is another very important principle of specialization. In most European countries and also in the United States there exists already a special spiritual care for priests and religious of both sexes, for the young, for youth organizations, for students in colleges and universities, for soldiers, seamen, laborers and employees. There are retreats and meetings for reformed alcoholics, for the sick and the aged, for converts and non-Catholics; retreats also for prisoners, etc. This incomplete enumeration gives sufficient evidence of the importance that is rightly attached to the specialization that is based on the diversity of *persons*.

*The form of pastoral ca*re is also a principle of specialization. We have merely to consider the constantly growing branch of pastoral activity called *religious instruction*. Religious instruction is playing an increasing role in the work of the Church; not only priests and Sisters, but lay people, especially members of the Confraternity of Christian Doctrine, are asked to labor in that all-important task. There is the problem of instructing those who are unable or unwilling to go to Catholic schools; the problem also of giving suitable advanced instruction to college and university students.

Another form is that of *instructing non-Catholics* who have expressed the desire to learn more about the Catholic Church and perhaps eventually to enter it. To instruct all prospective converts separately is often an impossibility. Because of the vastness of that work, organizations have been formed for that purpose and there are even secular institutes that devote themselves wholly to that task.

An older form of special spiritual care is the *work of retreats*. It was strongly specialized from the very beginning, and it was developed according to a particular method which now has become the subject of a re-examination. Special retreat houses were built, and sometimes congregations of Sisters were formed to take care of them. Priests, usually belonging to a religious order, are put in charge of these houses, and are exclusively employed in that work.

A very ancient form, perhaps the oldest, is the *parish mission*. In many countries, parochial missions are now in a

187

critical stage, for the ways that promise to be efficacious for the spiritual renewal of a large group of parishioners, and especially of the whole parish, depend greatly on cultural and social factors of a particular time and country. Hence it is necessary to re-examine the manner in which parochial missions are usually conducted and try to find to what extent they fit the rapidly-changing mentality of our time. Many priests are still engaged in that work; in some countries they hold conventions to discuss problems connected with that work and publish the conclusions of their investigations.

Formation centers are another form of special pastoral care. This form, which is mixed with very many other activities in the cultural and social field, has developed rapidly in the last decade. Because of the rapid evolution of society in many countries of Europe and America, and also in those that have recently won their independence, there is a great need of instructing and guiding the people so that they will be able to deal properly with their new situation. Here also, of course, there is a special task.

The environment also makes us distinguish various types of pastoral care. There is pastoral care for the employees of factories, offices, stores, in colleges and universities, in prisons, in military barracks, for circus personnel, etc.

Usefulness of Specialization. The tendency toward specialization in pastoral care is wholly in accord with the development of modern society, at least in countries that are sufficiently developed. We witness the same phenomenon in modern society. Society is becoming increasingly complex, and more and more specialized attention is given to various aspects of life and all sorts of groups and social milieus. Starting from the incontrovertible fact that life has unity, hence that being-a-Christian plays a role in every respect and aspect and circumstance of life in some way, there arises a need for religious guidance in all those situations. But precisely because of the proper character of specialization, the way and the extent to which this guidance must be exercised will differ according to the diverse situations.

We have summed up a few principles of specialization: object, persons, form and milieu. There may be more, and others may arise in the future. Moreover, there are all sorts of gradations within those four principles we have named; hence there is always a need for care and study on the part of the persons concerned to find out in what way and to what extent there can be spiritual care proper to the situation. This requires much time, competence and labor; it also makes the work of the Church more burdensome. But, unless it becomes specialization without rime or reason, we may feel confident that it will make the work of the Church more fruitful because it will then be more firmly and realistically integrated into the social pattern of our time.

Role of the Layman in This Specialization. It is both noteworthy and pleasant to record that, in general, the laity have a share in those special forms of pastoral work. Two reasons can be given to explain that phenomenon. In the first place, those forms of pastoral work for the most part do not yet have a history. It is precisely here that the best opportunities are found for the laity's involvement in the work of the Church. This is a new type of work; its form has not yet become crystallized; it is still unhampered by canonical regulations and "vested rights."

Another, and probably the most important reason for the great role that lay people are playing in most forms of specialized pastoral work, lies in the very nature of that

189

work. Those forms are so intimately woven into the fabric of modern society that it is practically never a question of mere pastoral care. Most of the time it is a very complex work that involves so many aspects of life that it is really necessary that expert laymen be engaged in it.[74]

Add to this—and here there is again a connection with the first reason—that today's clergy realize more and more that they cannot be experts in all those fields. Even when pastoral care in those fields calls for the priest in person, he will most often be able to act only after lay people have prepared the way for him. In this way he remains more or less in the background.

Specialization Is Not an Emergency Measure. We are not permitted to look at those special forms of pastoral care as emergency measures. They are a permanent phenomenon in our changed society. It is totally incorrect to speak about the parochial structure of pastoral care as "normal" and to call all other forms of pastoral care "auxiliary." The expression "extraordinary" pastoral care dates from earlier times, as we have briefly recalled in our historical sketch. It is also wrong to speak of them as "extra-parochial" pastoral care, in the sense that these activities infringe on parochial (by which they mean "normal") pastoral work. In reality there is here no trespassing but merely a juxtaposition or a mingling of several forms of pastoral care. The tendency to make things a little less complicated by incorporating everything into the simple territorial divisions of parishes must be looked upon as a dangerous temptation, even if one is ready to accept certain things for the time being as "emergency measures." The ideal of the other forms of pastoral work need not be "to bring people back to

---

[74]Cf. Vatican Council II's *Decree on the Apostolate of the Laity,* Ch. III, art. 13.

the parishes." In particular cases it may indeed be necessary to do precisely that; for example, in the pastoral care of those who are socially maladjusted. An attempt is then made—and this might take generations—to lead such people gradually to a normal social life. It is then a question of trying to incorporate such people into the ordinary life of the parish.

However, many other forms of pastoral care have their own importance *alongside* the parish. Hence the faithful involved are cared for both by the pastor and by others: by their pastor insofar as they belong to a parish by reason of their place of residence; by other priests and laymen with respect to other dimensions of their lives. As we have mentioned before, there exists a real danger that some people receive too much and a too specialized attention whereas others are neglected. However, this phenomenon is not due to the fact that there is too much specialization but rather to the fact that there is not yet enough concerted planning of these modern developments. It is a very good thing, on the other hand, that there is no immediate desire to lay down strict rules regarding those works, because the picture is still far from clear. Ultimately, however, a better division of labor and a clearer demarcation will have to be achieved.

In any case those who talk about "ordinary" as against "extraordinary" pastoral care and speak of "encroaching upon the parish," show that they have a wrong idea of the organizational life of the Church. They proceed from the thought that the parish is both the starting point and the center; which is wrong. On the contrary, it is the diocese that is the starting point, the heart and core of the organizational life of the Church. This statement is not only more exact from a theological standpoint but also more in keeping with sociological trends: society is now approached in different ways and by different methods and in terms of units that are neither too large nor too small. In this development of the human community, then, the diocese gains in prominence.

The nature and content of specialized pastoral care is also very important. Many forms of this care are active in the field of formation, education and direct pastoral work. In practice, however, all sorts of special groups do not confine themselves to their specialized work but try to include in it also the administration of the sacraments, particularly the celebration of the Eucharist.

Must we consider it to be an evil and a modern form of the abuse of "private churches," when those who engage in those special works occasionally celebrate Mass and administer the sacraments to the people who are entrusted to them? Of course, there are sometimes priests who try to form a sort of private parish around some association, even around a religious organization. And this is certainly not right. But when we look at it from the standpoint of the essence of pastoral concern, which certainly has as its first and principal element the administration of the sacraments, it is not unavoidable and hence perfectly acceptable that the administration of the sacraments and the celebration of the Eucharist are involved even in specialized forms of pastoral work?

Industrial Apostolate. We should like now to add something concerning a special form of pastoral work, the industrial apostolate. This work is obviously connected with the problem of industrialization which, particularly in continental Europe, was the occasion for a mass dechristianization of the workers. We recall the expression "the workers have been lost to the Church." What were the reasons? Two kinds of causes can be offered as an explanation.

192

First of all, the role that the Church played in the "old" society. Social conditions, especially in the last century when industrialization began, were very bad for the workers who were then still called proletarians. The Church that had only recently freed itself more or less from the bonds of feudalism was still strongly connected with the ruling class of society in many parts of Europe. It is understandable then that the workers, who justly rose up against the evils of the social situation, identified the Church with the society that was so unjust toward them. This identification was not wholly right but it is perfectly understandable that such an identification was made. Moreover, real faults were committed by the Church, by its clergy and by men who called themselves Catholics and in a sense also lived as such. But it would be unjust to claim unqualifiedly that the workers turned their backs to the Church because of the bad social conditions for which the Church was partly responsible. It is especially the identification of the Church with the "old" society that was in fact a reason why the workers did leave the Church.

A second reason for the mass dechristianization of the workers is seen especially in the fact that the labor milieu of the workers was not christianized. By "christianized" we understand here not so much outward signs of Christian faith and Christian profession of faith but rather an atmosphere and circumstances that are truly permeated by Christian thought. In the older agricultural form of society work was fully christianized. This does not mean that all situations and especially those of farm workers were very Christian, but work as such was interwoven with Christian life. This bond found expression also in a variety of external facets, such as Christian harvest festivals, "Rogation Days," and Christian feasts connected with agricultural work. Hence that kind of work was situated within the totality of Christian life. Industrial labor, on the contrary, did not have that kind of atmosphere and it does not have it even today; and this separation of work and its environment from the life of faith is another important cause of the dechristianization of the workers.

It is from such considerations that there developed an awareness of the need of organizing an industrial apostolate. Added to that was the consideration that the milieu in which the laborer works no longer coincides with the milieu of the home in which he lives. The pastor of a parish must care principally for everything that is connected with the home milieu of the workers and others who are engaged in industry. In contrast with the former situation in earlier times, the workers spend a very great part or even most of their waking hours outside their home environment. This fact also demands spiritual attention, even apart from the fact that the work environment in which they spend it is in no way christianized.

When we now ask ourselves what forms that kind of apostolate takes, we see that there are a number of factors of which one or the other is predominant according to countries and other circumstances. The following factors can be named with respect to that industrial apostolate: christianization of the milieu, the rechristianization of the workers or employees, and positive support to Catholic workers, or to Protestant workers on the part of Protestant Churches, in their work. To these must be added from a negative standpoint, the protection of Catholics (and Protestants) against evil influences, and, last but not least, making the Church present among the workers precisely in order to make it clear that at least today it is unreasonable to identify the Church with an unjust society.

The form of the industrial apostolate is still very much in the process of evolution, but very evident in that apostolate is the strong influence of lay people who really must do the direct work. This apostolate is successful when lay people have become so interested and involved in it that they actually form cores of ardent Christians. The priest is in charge of the general spiritual guidance and formation. Generally speaking, the industrial apostolate has not yet found a stable form. No doubt, several forms will be needed and it will be necessary to preserve great flexibility. We note also that there is now a tendency to make the industrial apostolate independent from the social organizations with which it was at first connected and whose help and support were greatly appreciated.

In the United States the industrial apostolate is much less developed than in Europe. The main reason lies undoubtedly in the fact that in the States the Catholic Church, throughout the nineteenth century and until World War II, was largely a church of immigrant workers and in no way identifiable with capitalistic owners of industry. Priests and bishops alike were practically always sons of workers or at most of lower middle class people. They formed a kind of natural rallying point for the working man, so that in the States the worker as such did not become estranged from the Church.

Pastoral Care and the Mobility of the Population. Of great importance also are the questions concerning pastoral work in connection with the mobility of the population. Apart from people who permanently move to foreign countries or to distant territories, there are others who go away for a shorter or longer period to live or work elsewhere.

In a certain sense, emigration to a foreign country presents in this respect the least difficulties. These emigrants go and fix themselves permanently elsewhere. We do not mean, of course, that emigration presents no pastoral prob-

195

lems. Entering another milieu can bring with it great difficulties for the life of faith. We see this clearly in the United
States where many descendants of Catholic immigrants have
been lost either because they went to parts having no priests
or because they did not feel "at home" in the local Catholic
parish. And in cities like New York there are major problems involving, for instance, the giving of necessary spiritual
care to immigrant Puerto Ricans. The pastoral care of immigrants is of necessity connected with the problem of ad-
justing those people to their new surroundings. Here is a
great field of activity for laymen as well as priests.

Foreign workers who come for a shorter or longer period
to labor in industry or agriculture constitute a kind of temporary "immigration." Many Spanish, Italian and Portuguese
workers go north in Europe to labor for indefinite periods
of time. The only solution then is that priests of their own
nationality, aided by others who know their language, take
care of the spiritual needs of those workers. For it is obviously impossible for those workers to be helped by the local
parishes. There are similar problems in the United States,
for instance, with respect to Mexican workers and other mi-
grant laborers who come to California, although sometimes
they can be properly cared for there in the parishes.[75]

Asian and African students who go for studies to Europe,
Russia and America are another major and even world problem. It is evident that when they study in Russia, Czecho-
slovakia and any other satellite country at special universities, this can be more dangerous for the whole development of Asiatic and African countries; in fact, we have

---

[75]Cf. Vatican Council II's *Decree on the Pastoral Office of Bishops
in the Church*, Ch. II, art. 18, which wants the episcopal conferences
to pay special attention to the spiritual care of such people.

already witnessed the evil results in some countries. Many thousands of others study in Europe and in America. It is of the utmost importance that proper contact be maintained with those students, many of whom, particularly from Africa, are Catholics. These must be helped to live a Christian life within the framework of the local Christian community; everything should be done to make them feel at home in their new surroundings. These students as well as their hosts are given an excellent opportunity for knowing one another's ideas and values and for benefiting from those contacts. This most important form of pastoral care is still poorly organized.[76]

The many international organs which have arisen since World War II also introduce problems in the field of pastoral care. Regarding Europe, the Common Market and NATO have concentrated in Luxemburg, Strassburg, Brussels, and Paris; many higher and lower functionaries of various nationalities, of whom a great number are Catholics, reside there. These people, who are mostly intellectuals, are in need of special spiritual care. In Luxemburg there exists a "European parish." This organization of parishes that are more or less separate from the surroundings and perhaps of a special "European diocese," will have to be given special attention.[76a] In the States there is a similar problem with respect to the headquarters of the United Nations. The major difficulties concern not so much those who remain only a few months or weeks—although they must be taken care of—but especially those who will re-

---

[76]The Overseas Students Coordination tries to organize pastoral work among them.

[76a]Vatican Council II speaks explicitly about the possibility of "personal dioceses" in the *Decree on the Life and Ministry of Priests,* Ch. II, art. 10.

main there more or less permanently and do not want to be integrated into American life, because they feel that in all probability they will eventually return to their own countries.

Migration within a country belongs more to the field of parochial work. Means must be found to facilitate the transition of people from one city to another and especially from the country to the city. In Europe the latter has been catastrophic for many in the last century and the beginning of the present. In the United States we have the problems of urban redevelopment which forces people to move from their old environments; large-scale migration to the suburbs which often necessitates the division and subdivision of parishes; and frequent moving from one city to another because of changing industrial patterns.

In connection with migration we realize how necessary it is to give a solid spiritual formation to all so that they become less dependent on their environment and more autonomous in the profession of their faith. The Confraternity of Christian Doctrine can play a great role in this matter. The parishes that receive those newcomers should have services that will facilitate their integration. It is not enough for a pastor to register them and give them collection envelopes. It is necessary to establish contact with those people and to introduce them to parishioners however much time this might take—for this task belongs to the parochial office of the parish priest. It is precisely when those people still feel strangers in their new parish that they may not feel inclined to seek contact with the pastor and the parish. Some will become negligent with respect to going to Mass and approaching the sacraments; they gradually become indifferent and lose all contact with the Church. They did not start with ill will. An immediate contact with those people on the part of the parish will not do wonders but it can accomplish much.

Tourists and vacationers constitute another field of pastoral care that is largely untended. Not so many years ago, only wealthy people could afford spending their vacation in foreign countries. Today, however, many go abroad or at least to distant places spending several weeks away from home. On that account Sunday services in a number of parishes during summer months have a different character than at other times of the year. Many strangers may be present at the parish Masses and many parishioners may be absent. This, of course, must be taken into consideration. It is for the priests an opportunity of making friendly contact with the strangers, and this may help them to remain faithful to Mass and the reception of the sacraments.

In vacation resorts, special services should be organized to take care of the needs of tourists and vacationers. What is fundamental is that vacationers and tourists should be made to feel that the priests are always ready to help them in their spiritual needs. Of course, sufficient publicity must be given regarding the hours of liturgical services and the administration of sacraments. Parish priests in such areas should not take their own vacation at the time when vacationers flock to these places, and would do well to provide extra services for the convenience of those visitors. Immediate spiritual assistance in case of accident or illness should be available, of course, and its availability should be made known in hotels and other places.

It is almost impossible not to talk in vague generalities concerning this kind of pastoral work. In any case, tourism is a phenomenon that is not likely to disappear. It is desirable that everything possible be done so that tourists and vacationers be able to maintain a living contact with the

Church wherever they may happen to be in their journeys and voyages.[77]

4. The Supranational Character of the Church and the Missionary Spirit

AN EVIL EFFECT OF TOO MUCH CENTRALIZATION: EXPORT OF LATINISM

One of the characteristics of the present change and renewal in the Church is that it is now evident why the Latin Church with all her concrete regulations and practices should no longer be handled as an "article of export." Hence we can foresee the rise of greater diversity within the Church's unity.

It is rather strange, when we reflect upon it, that the whole situation of the Latin Church with her language, law, liturgy, art, architecture, etc. has been simply transplanted to Africa, America and Asia. Although it is not correct to call the Latin Church an Italian Church, because the German element has exercised an enormous influence upon it, she is certainly a West European Church. That idea of "exportation" suited well the colonial expansion of European nations; but now that the period of colonialism is past, our eyes are opened and we wonder how such an exportation could ever be considered normal. In reality that sort of thing has taken place especially during the last four centuries, i.e., since the time of the Counter Reformation. The missionary élan was admirable and is a clear proof that the Counter Reformation has, in many respects, been a blessing for the Church. But that same excessive centralization, that not infrequently

---

[77]Cf. *Decree on the Pastoral Office of Bishops in the Church*, Ch. II, art. 18. See also the collective articles "Fremdenverkehr und missionarischen Seelsorge," *Zeitschrift für missionarische Seelsorge*, vol. 33 (1961), pp. 69-100.

led to rigidity and which was *also* characteristic of the Counter Reformation, was the cause of that strange and perhaps fatal situation on the mission front.

However, we must be on guard against exaggerations: there have always been men who felt that it was necessary to adapt oneself to the particular character of the peoples to be evangelized. In particular, fifty, sixty and even more than one hundred years ago there were missionaries who made every effort to penetrate into the language, customs and mentality of the people among whom they labored. In 1847 for example, Francis Libermann wrote to his missionaries in Africa: "Divest yourselves from Europe, its customs and mentality. . . . Become Negroes with the Negroes, to train them as they should be trained, not in the European fashion but retaining what is proper to them. . . . Adapt yourselves to them . . . in order to transform them slowly and gradually into a people of God."[78] Nevertheless, it remains true that, generally speaking, "exportation" was a characteristic of missionary activity.

It is a striking fact that the Church used totally different methods in her evangelization of the Germanic peoples. There she came to peoples who had their own character though they had already had some contact with Roman culture. This contact greatly facilitated the Church's access to those peoples. Latin was the language of all who were somewhat civilized; it was the language of law and government. Nevertheless, the character of the Germanic peoples had an enormous influence on the further development of the Church. This is evident, for instance, in the transformation of the Roman liturgy into the Roman-German liturgy that has existed until now. The result, all along

---

[78]*Notes et documents relatifs à la vie et l'oeuvre de F. M. P. Libermann*, Paris, 1926 ff., vol. 9, p. 330.

the line, was a commingling which, among other things, still characterizes present Church law, liturgy and popular devotions. Similarly, when the Slavs were converted by Saints Cyril and Methodius, their own language was explicitly accepted for use in the liturgy, although there was already an increasing current of opposition to such a policy. Even in the late Middle Ages, in the thirteenth and fourteenth centuries, the Friars Minor took very much into account the particular culture of the people of Asia, particularly in China. In the missionary period of the sixteenth century, however, there arose a severe struggle over that matter and adaptation was no longer possible.

Today we realize how wrong this was. Much, almost everything, has still to be done to correct the situation. But many Christians now consider it perfectly natural that the Church in Africa should have its own African character as regards, for instance, the liturgy, laws and the way of preaching the Gospel. The same applies to Asia in all its colorful variety, and wherever in the world there exist people with a culture of their own. Unfortunately, the idea of the Church's universality has become so intimately connected with the faulty concept of the universality of the *Latin* Church that it is now sometimes difficult to convince the native clergy of mission countries, who were educated in a Western manner, that their own culture has value for Christianity.

THE NECESSITY AND EVOLUTION OF THE MISSIONARY SPIRIT

A missionary spirit is not a luxury item but belongs to the necessities of Christian life. Of course, it is possible to have some sort of Christian life without a noticeable missionary spirit, but it will then be defective. Evidently our concept of Christian life should not be governed by such a minimal and deficient notion. That is why it is not an exaggeration to say that without a missionary spirit there is no Christian life. By this we mean that no completely evangelical, Christian life is possible for a person or a community, when the missionary spirit and the missionary impulse have no essential place in them.

It is not our intention to lecture on the missionary *obligation* and to determine to what extent the Church must evangelize and what obligation every Christian has to give some kind of support to the missionary apostolate. This does not mean that what we are going to say here has nothing to do with this missionary obligation. This obligation undoubtedly rests on the fact that the Church is the mystical body of Christ, is Christ continuing to live on earth. This fact is also the foundation of the thesis that no Christian life is possible without a missionary spirit. To that extent, then, we will not speak here directly about the missionary obligation.

In fact, however, we touch here essentially the same question but we look at it from another standpoint. We do not say here: if we wish to fulfill our obligation as Catholics, if the Church wishes to fulfill her God-given task, we must support the missions and the Church must tackle her missionary task with zeal and energy and with confidence in God. But we declare: if the Church desires to be fully the Church, the mystical body of Christ, the living Christ on earth; if we wish to live fully as Christians in all our expressions of Christian life, then the missionary spirit and the missionary endeavor must be present in our actions. The distinction made here might seem subtle, and in reality the two aspects cannot be separated, but the point is that one can and should throw light on the various sides of one and the same question. It seems imperative to us not to neglect this distinct approach, for in connection with our considerations regarding the structural changes of the Church it is necessary to point out how the missionary apostolate also is more and more seen from within, from the standpoint of a new view of the Church.

We read in the Encyclical "The Mystical Body" (1943):

> As He hung upon the Cross, Christ Jesus not only avenged the justice of the Eternal Father that had been flouted, but He also won for us, His brothers, an unending flow of graces. It was possible for Him personally, immediately to impart these graces to men; but He wished to do so only through a visible Church that would be formed by the union of men, and thus through that Church every man would perform a work of collaboration with Him in dispensing the graces of Redemption. The Word of God willed to make use of our nature, when in excruciating agony He would redeem mankind; in much the same way throughout the centuries He makes use of the Church that the work begun might endure.[79]

Thus does the Church stand, and so do we stand before God: as collaborators of Christ in restoring honor to the Father and as cooperators in the distribution of the fruits of salvation. This we are as community and as persons. The hierarchy has a special place in the Church, but all of us are the Church. In this, for the whole Church and for all the members of the Church, lies the foundation, the core of our life of faith: we are collaborators of Christ in our own life and in the life of our fellowmen. Only a life that recognizes and is lived according to this foundation can rightly be called a Christian life. In all our deeds and omissions we must remain conscious of our particular and purposive connection with Christ. A spiritual life that is

---

[79]English text, *The Mystical Body*, America Press, 1943, art. 16. Cf. Vatican Council II's *Decree on the Church's Missionary Activity*, Ch. I, art. 7.

concerned only with one's own salvation is wanting in a true Christian spirit.

In the Encyclical *Fidei Donum* regarding the situation of the Catholic missions, especially in Africa, we read:

> The missionary spirit and the Catholic spirit, we have said before, are one and the same thing. Catholicity is an essential note of the true Church. This is so to such an extent that a Christian is not fully faithful and devoted to the Church if he is not equally attached and devoted to her universality, to desiring that she take root and flourish in all parts of the earth. Nothing is more foreign to the Church of Jesus Christ than division. Nothing is more harmful to her life than isolation, retiring into oneself, and all forms of collective egoism which induce a particular Christian community, whatever it may be, to close itself up within itself.[80]

The realization that we are cooperators with the whole Church in Christ's work of salvation, is essential to the spiritual life of the Christian. This can be done in many ways. John a Montecorvino, who in the Middle Ages went on foot to China, and a few centuries later St. Francis Xavier, were as much convinced of that as St. Therese in her solitude of the Carmel. We shall find that characteristic in all great Christians of whom we say that they lead a profound spiritual life, for "the Christian vocation by its very nature is also a vocation to the apostolate."[81]

When we study history it is striking that the great spiritual movements arising in Christianity were in many cases directly missionary movements. This does not mean that they were founded precisely for the missionary apostolate; but

---

[80]English text, *The Future of Africa,* Sword of the Spirit, 1957, p. 13. See also the *Decree on the Church's Missionary Activity,* Ch. VI, art. 35 ff.

[81]Vatican Council II's *Decree on the Apostolate of the Laity,* Ch. I, art. 2.

the spiritual power, the spiritual character and the spiritual union with Christ of those movements drove them by necessity to apostolic and, in particular, to missionary activity. Their spirit was unable to avoid it; it had a need for such activity. An example is the missionary movement among the Benedictines in the early Middle Ages. Very typical in this respect is also the Franciscan movement of the thirteenth century. St. Francis himself went for some time to Palestine and North Africa. When some of his brothers were martyred in Morocco, he reacted to the news saying: "Brethren, let us rejoice, for they are true Friars Minor." St. Francis was seized with a love for God and men and he realized that those brothers had understood and lived according to the ideal. Hence it is not to be wondered at that the Friars Minor together with the other Mendicants, especially the Dominicans, gave a new élan to the missionary activity of the Church.

A few centuries later we meet a figure and a movement in which the intermingling of spiritual life and missionary activity is particularly evident—St. Ignatius of Loyola and his Society. A very strong impetus was given by St. Ignatius personally for the renewal of Christian life and, at the same time, he sent St. Francis Xavier to the Far East, thus inaugurating a new missionary movement in the Church. It is also worth noting that he did this in spit of the fact that an enormous amount of work had to be done in sixteenth century Europe, and that this work was the first reason for the founding of the Society of Jesus. He was not tricked by any false reasoning such as: let us first take care of our own countries; then the rest will follow. Although St. Ignatius was not a stranger to carefully calculated considerations, it was the spiritual impulse that was the decisive factor.

In all these movements we find a clear-cut connection between the spiritual life and the missionary apostolate. Not only did the spiritual life inspire missionary activity but this spiritual life was in need of missionary activity and was ennobled and deepened by this activity. Reversely, the lack of missionary élan is not only a bad sign pointing to a low degree of spiritual life, but the want of missionary spirit and missionary activity lowers the religious level. Catholic life always remains essentially missionary and apostolic whatever the circumstances of the Church may be; but when those essential traits grow dim, evil consequences are unavoidable. When we say that the missionary spirit is a vital necessity for the spiritual life of the Church and of every Christian, we do not, of course, refer merely to "foreign" missions, but we take the term "mission" in a wider sense.

Nevertheless, the missionary apostolate in the strict sense —the establishment and implantation of Christ's Church— continues to have an important and special place in the Church's whole apostolic endeavor and activity in the broad sense; and it has been so from the very beginning.

Because the missionary spirit is so very important for the life of the Church, great care must be taken to educate Christians in that spirit and inspire them with missionary zeal. A large place must be given in religious education to the missionary idea because we have a missionary obligation, because Christ's Kingdom must be extended, because the missionary work is the task of the mystical body of Christ.[82] But the mission must also be explained from the other side; that is, educators should always keep in mind that, for the development of the life of faith in the young people entrusted to their care, it is necessary that they be filled with the missionary idea. In order to do this well, the idea of the "mission," in the strict sense of the word, namely, the estab-

---

[82]Cf. Vatican Council II's *Decree on the Pastoral Office of Bishops in the Church*, Ch. I, art. 6; Ch. II, art. 30.

lishment and implantation of the Church, must never be separated from the idea of apostleship in the broad and the complete sense of the word. Youth must be educated in the missionary, the apostolic spirit. This will be one of the most important contributions toward the renewal of the life of faith.[83]

[83]For the missionary task of the Church see the recent works, D. J. Hatton, ed., *Missiology in Africa Today,* Dublin, 1961; Gerald H. Anderson, ed., *The Theology of the Christian Mission,* C.S.M. Press, London, 1962; Eugene Hillman, *The Church as Mission,* Herder and Herder, 1965.

CHAPTER THREE

Structural Changes in the Life of Faith

There is a very close connection between the changes in the organizational structure of the Church of which we have spoken in the preceding chapter and the changes in the life of faith with which we intend to deal here.

The changes in the relations between hierarchy and laity, the changes within the hierarchy, the changes in the structures of pastoral care and the greater emphasis on the supernatural structure of the Church, are all based on *one* profound foundation: a growing consciousness on the part of believers that the Church is a community. This is the foundation, as well as the background, of all the changes in the Church that are outwardly perceptible. There is a spiritual background that influences the life of the Church and brings about in her the changes which one can unhesitatingly call "structural changes." There are changes in our attitude toward sacrament and word, hence changes in our life of faith, changes in our attitude toward the Christians who are separated from us.

1. From an Individualistic Devotional Life to the Liturgical Movement

As an introduction to the whole chapter, we wish to give here a brief sketch of the development of the Church's life of faith, especially with respect to the sacraments and the word, during the last fifty years. This development, which is still going on, has not been the same in all countries and continents. In order to understand the development during those fifty years, it is necessary to delve further into history. This will enable us to understand the gradual changes, which met with many obstacles and have only slowly affected the faithful.

We can provisionally indicate the objective of the liturgical movement in the following words: it is the *positive* reaction against liturgical decay, against individualistic and devotional-moralistic piety; or, to pay more attention to content: it is the effort to make the Eucharist and the other sacraments become more central in the practice of ecclesial life. The liturgical movement wants to make present the reality of Redemption, especially the Eucharist, in the ecclesial community. The Eucharist, as the social memorial banquet of our Lord Jesus Christ, is always present; but its reality also lives in the consciousness of the faithful so that from it may develop a new biblical-liturgical piety appropriate to our time.

A Survey of the History of the Eucharistic Liturgy

If we wish to understand the liturgical movement we must first recall the principal historical data concerning the celebration of the Eucharist. When we study those data in the light of the present liturgical tendencies, we note a remarkable development. (We shall confine ourselves to the Western, and especially the Roman liturgy.)

Ancient and Medieval Development of the Liturgy. We are probably justified in saying that the Roman liturgy reached its first peak around the year 500, as the result of the following process of development.

210

In apostolic times there was a very simple supper liturgy which was or was not connected with an "ordinary" supper. The first development took place in the time of St. Justin and St. Hippolyte (second and third century); the service of the word, which came from the service of the Synagogue, had developed further. In large services, the "ordinary" supper of brotherly love (*Agape*) had certainly disappeared; there were more evident signs of a sacrificial supper than formerly; we see also the first traces of an offertory, namely, in the form of a common offering of the gifts (offertory procession); but the eucharistic prayer (Preface and Canon) remained the high point and was one continuous prayer.

Pope Gelasius (492-496), as is commonly believed, put the finishing touches to that liturgy. Pope Gregory the Great (590-604) regulated it more closely and made certain corrections. This liturgy of around the year 500 is described in a document that dates from about 700, namely the *Ordo Romanus I*. The document, however, contains only the papal Mass, which was mixed with the papal court ceremonial that, to a great extent, was derived from the imperial court ceremonial. We have no data concerning an ordinary bishop's or priest's Mass of those days; but in all probability these were much more simple.

Gaul did not follow the Roman liturgy but had its own "Gallic" liturgy, which was much more exuberant than the Roman liturgy. Pepin (714-768) desired, in part but not wholly for political reasons, to have liturgical uniformity with Rome. It was he, and not the bishops, who decreed that the Roman liturgy should be taken over. This decree was officially executed; but, as was to be expected, it met with much opposition and, since there were not yet printed books, the process of change was slow and incomplete. What really evolved from the situation was a Roman-Frankish liturgy. This new "Roman" liturgy took over many Gallic elements

211

and was evidently influenced also by Germanic and Eastern factors, manifesting themselves, for instance, in a great abundance of gestures and prayers. This liturgy was introduced into Rome and Italy around the year 1000 and it replaced there the original Roman liturgy which had greatly deteriorated. It is this Roman-Frankish liturgy which is essentially our present "Roman Liturgy." We say "essentially," for there was not yet any rigid uniformity in the Church; there existed many variants of the one official liturgy in different dioceses, abbeys and orders. Especially through the influence of the Friars Minor, who experienced great difficulties in liturgical matters in their ambulant apostolate, the liturgy of the Roman *Curia* (hence *one* of the variants of the official liturgy) was introduced almost everywhere.[1] But there remained variations in the liturgies of the Dominicans, Carmelites, Carthusians and others. The liturgy of the Roman Curia developed and was finally fixed by Pope Pius V after the Council of Trent.

A very important point in that development was the fact that through German influence there occurred a shift in emphasis: complete and one-sided attention was given to the real presence of Christ under the species of bread and wine and too little attention was paid to the common sacrificial meal. Especially in the Middle Ages very great attention was given to the Eucharist (and the other sacraments) as *means* of grace rather than as praise and honor of the Father and, through them, man's salvation. Moreover, increasing emphasis was placed on the *individual* salvation of the recipient.

The liturgy proper became more clericalized. The faithful were ignorant of the content of the liturgical texts because they no longer understood Latin. Unlike the Jewish and pagan

---

[1]Cf. S. J. van Dijk and J. H. Walker, *The Origins of the Modern Liturgy*, London, 1960.

religions, the Church had always agreed to use the language of the people. In Rome she first used Greek, then Latin, because Latin had again become the language of the people. When the Germans became Christians, Latin was introduced because it was the official language of Europe and it was impossible to use the numerous German dialects. However, when the great European languages had been formed, the Church stuck to Latin. The people had already lost contact with the liturgy, and in turn they became even more estranged from it by the maintenance of Latin. In this way the people's piety had to find outlets outside the unintelligible clerical liturgy.

Grave abuses arose in the late Middle Ages, particularly in the century before the Reformation: superstitious attention was given to seeing the Sacred Host; there was a multiplication of Masses to which "infallible" effects were ascribed; the system of Mass stipends became corrupt; and people hardly ever received Holy Communion.

Trent abolished the most flagrant abuses and, in order to prevent such things in the future, made everything subject to the Holy See, prescribing a great uniformity, with the exception of such variants as that of the Dominicans and the remnants of the ancient Western non-Roman rites known as the Ambrosian and the Mozarabic liturgies. But Trent did not bring about a change of mentality. The mentality of the Counter Reformation with respect to the liturgy was the purified mentality of the late Middle Ages.

That mentality continued to exist until our own time: a strong individualistic accent was placed on the real presence under the two species and on gaining merits. In reality that emphasis became even greater during the Counter Reformation. The people nourished themselves with devotions and learned how to spend "usefully," that is, meritoriously, the time during which priests celebrated the liturgy. The clergy and religious had two kinds of pious exercises: the official liturgy (Mass and Office) and a very devotional "breviary" which meant much more to them. However, there were always tendencies in the Church to counteract that mentality. They gave rise to efforts of renewal and finally lead to "the liturgical movement" of our time.

The Seventeenth and Eighteenth Centuries. In the seventeenth and also in the eighteenth century the historico-critical study of the liturgy was pursued on a high level.[2] It suffices to name Jean Mabillon (d. 1707), Cardinal Bona (d. 1674), J. M. Thomasius (d. 1713), L. Muratori (d. 1750), Edmond Marten (d. 1739), and Prosper Lambertini (Benedict XIV, d. 1758).

This scientific study of the liturgy turned away from the purely allegorical explanations of the Middle Ages. Excellent as this was, it remained almost wholly a scholarly undertaking of the theoretical kind; it did not aim at bringing the liturgy closer to the people and educating the faithful to make them really participate in the liturgy. There were people, especially in France, who tried to make use of those scientific findings for practical purposes, but little was effected for reasons that will be discussed later. Hence we should not see in those scholarly endeavors the origin, but at most a distant preparation for the liturgical movement.

Added to that is the fact that the eighteenth century Enlightenment brought about a decline and even a interruption of that strictly scholarly work, so that later a new beginning had to be made. For this new beginning in the nineteenth

---

[2]For the history of the liturgical movement see, e.g., *The Liturgical Movement,* by priests of St. Severin and St. Joseph, Hawthorn, 1964; Olivier Rousseau, *The Progress of the Liturgy,* Newman, 1951, and *Histoire du movement liturgigue, Paris, 1945;* Waldemar Trapp, *Vorgeschichte und Ursprung der liturgischen Bewegung, Regensburg, 1940.*

century, however, the results of seventeenth and eighteenth century studies, of course, were not without significance.

The renewal of the scholarly historical study of the liturgy in the thirties and forties of the last century can be called a preparation for the liturgical movement, with the reservation that there was then little, if any, consideration of the pastoral side of the problem. This study, nevertheless, is historically connected with the rise of the liturgical movement; and this cannot be said about the scholarly studies of the seventeenth and eighteenth centuries.

In the realm of practical liturgical publications, relatively few appeared during these two centuries, and the few that did, show how little connection they had with the present liturgical movement. This is particularly true of German-speaking countries. For example, in 1702 the famous Capuchin Martin von Cochem (1634-1712) published his *German Mass Prayer Book Sweeter Than Honey,*[3] in which he says: "As often as you devoutly look at the Sacred Host, you merit great reward in Heaven. As often as you humbly beat your breast, so often do you obtain forgiveness of a few sins." According to this influential author, these are only two of "the seventy-seven graces and benefits that flow from the devout hearing of the Mass." Typical is his admonition to hear several Masses at the same time, for one gets more grace this way. The author also urges the faithful to say, from the beginning of the Mass until the Consecration, ordinary daily prayers, such as the Rosary and the prayers of confraternities. After the Consecration one is advised to offer Christ constantly to the heavenly Father and to repeat the oblation prayer as frequently as possible. That book appeared in a Latin edition in 1700 under the title "The Marrow of the Mass"

---

[3]*Teutsch Messbuch über Honig süss,* 1702. See also Cochem's *Explanation of the Holy Sacrifice of the Mass,* Benziger, 1896.

(*Medulla Missae*) and, from 1702 on, in many German editions until far into the nineteenth century. The influence it exercised in German-speaking countries was great. All his writings abound in tales of the most unlikely miracles. These did real harm to genuine piety, the more so because he had many followers. His books were rarely printed during the Enlightenment and were even forbidden in Austria; but, during the period of Romanticism in the first half of the nineteenth century, they appeared once more.

The situation was somewhat different in France. Two bishops both named François de Harlay, an uncle and his nephew, of Rouen and Paris respectively, published important pastoral-liturgical works. The one of Rouen published in 1651 *The True Way of Hearing Properly the Parish Mass.*[4] His nephew published in 1680 a *Parisian Breviary* and in 1684 a *Parisian Missal;* in 1685 he had his uncle's book reprinted in Paris. Both these authors stand much closer to the present liturgical movement than Martin von Cochem. Very important was Nicolas Letourneux who, in 1680, published *The Best Way to Hear Holy Mass.*[5] In this work he tells us, for example, that the Christian cannot say, think and do anything better during Mass than what the Church guided infallibly by the Holy Spirit says, thinks and does .All other prayers must cease when the priest prays and celebrates the Sacrifice for you. Most people communicate outside Mass; but when they communicate during Mass they must first repeat the *Confiteor* and "*Lord I am not worthy,*" a rite that originated outside the Mass. We must not only "hear" Mass but offer it together with the celebrant. Letourneux also translated the complete breviary into French. He published a *Christian Year* (*Année chrétienne*), which in 1686 had six parts but was later com-

---

[4]*La vraie manière de bien entendre la Messe de Paroisse*, 1651.
[5]*La meilleure manière d'entendre la sainte Messe*, Paris, 1680.

pleted in thirteen parts by M. de Ruth d'Ans. In this work the Masses of every day were translated and, at the beginning of every part, there was a translation of the Ordinary of the Mass.

The Jesuit Jean Croiset also published a kind of "Christian Year" designed to counteract and offset Letourneux's work. Its lengthy title was *Exercises of Devotion for All the Days of the Year, with an Explanation of the Mystery or of the Life of the Saint for Every Day.*[6] It was in twelve parts, the first appearing in 1712. This work, which was nothing but a series of legends about the saints, went through sixty-six editions and many translations. Its last edition appeared in 1852-1866, when there already existed *The Liturgical Year* (*L'Année liturgique*) of the famous Benedictine restorer of the abbey Solesmes, Prosper Guéranger (1805-1875), about whom we shall say more later on.

With the work of Croiset we are in the midst of the Jansenist controversy involving liturgical activity. The translation of the Mass, and especially of the Canon, caused scandal; to invite the faithful to actively offer the Mass with the celebrant was considered an expression of Jansenism. Joseph de Voisin's complete translation of the missal was forbidden by Pope Alexander VII (1655-1667):[7] "Certain sons of perdition . . . have lately come to such madness as to dare to translate the Roman missal . . . and to hand it over to persons of every rank and sex. . . . By their rash action they have attempted to degrade the most sacred rites . . . and to expose the divine mysteries to the common gaze." Letourneux's *Christian Year* was also placed on the

---

[6]*Exercises de pieté pour tous les jours de l'année contenant l'explication du mystère, ou la vie du saint de chaque jour,* 1712 ff.

[7]Prosper Guéranger, *Institutions liturgiques,* Paris 2nd ed., 1883, vol. 2, pp. 54 ff.

Index in 1695. The missal of the Diocese of Meaux caused a storm of indignation in 1709 because in the Ordinary of the Mass the letter R (*Respondetur*) stood before "Amen," indicating that the people were asked to make that response. It was against these and similar tendencies that Father Croiset published his work to defend "orthodox" piety. This book unfortunately had great success, a success comparable to that of Martin Von Cochem in German terirtory. The representatives of the two great Counter Reformation orders, then, appear to have played an influential role also in this matter.

Another important phenomenon in France at that time was the publication of diocesan missals and diocesan breviaries. Many bishops made use of the rule of Pope Pius V permitting missals and breviaries to be retained if they had been in use for more than two hundred years—the basis on which the Dominicans and Carmelites also kept their own missals. The bishops thought that the same rule also gave them a right to make changes and additions to their missals. Thus there appeared new editions in which the results of the liturgico-historical studies were partly applied. This was done, for instance, by the already named François de Harlay, Archbishop of Paris. Gradually other bishops, who could not base their action on that rule of Pius V and, in whose diocese Pius V's edition of the Missal and Breviary should have been followed, began to publish missals and breviaries in accordance with their own Gallic mentality. In this way, at the time of the French Revolution, most French dioceses had their own missal and breviary.

The general tendency in both official and unofficial editions and declarations was that the adoration of God should stand at the center and that the veneration of saints should be kept more in the background. That is why there should not be too many feasts of saints, and Sundays and the feasts of Our Lord should not yield to feasts of saints. Greater

218

emphasis should be placed on the ecclesial year. Holy Scripture should make up the primary content of the liturgy and should be diffused more widely among the people outside the liturgy also. Christian antiquity should serve as the model. The new critical examination of the traditional texts should be taken into account and whatever was purely legendary or even superstitious in the liturgy should be eliminated. The laity should take a more active part in the liturgy and they should be given more opportunity for doing so. Attempts were made in this direction partly by having the Latin liturgy prayed aloud, partly by translations or a limited use of the vernacular.

Although Jansenistic and Gallic influences undoubtedly played a role in the French liturgical movement, this does not alter the fact that it contained valuable elements. It would be wrong to adopt the view of Guéranger who, in his struggle against everything Jansenistic and especially Gallicanistic, branded the whole movement as heretical.[8] We can, on the contrary, point to three valuable characteristics in that seventeenth-century movement: 1) the development of liturgical studies; 2) efforts to reform the missal and the breviary; 3) attempts to bring the liturgy nearer to the people. That these features are not Jansenistic or Gallicanistic is evident also from the fact that the Encyclical *On the Sacred Liturgy* (*Mediator Dei*) and the *Constitution on the Liturgy* of 1963 manifest the same spirit. Although these features were accompanied by Jansenistic and Gallicanistic tendencies, it was very unfortunate that the whole movement was combated as unorthodox and, consequently, did not have any success. Insofar as the movement managed to prolong its existence, the opposition continued to make it suspect of heresy and thus drive it to greater extremes.

---

[8]*Ibid.*, p. 178.

We repeat that those French tendencies had no direct bearing on today's Liturgical Movement but they did influence the Enlightenment in Germany. It is at the time of the Enlightenment that the first practical liturgical tendencies appeared in Germany. Before, Germany had been rich only in writers like Martin von Cochem.

The Enlightenment, which manifested itself first in philosophy, exercised influence on almost all mental sciences and also on theology, especially Protestant theology. The origin of the Enlightenment must be sought principally in England and France. From these countries it spread to Protestant Northern Germany, but there it did not acquire the sharp features that appeared in the English Deists and the French Encyclopedists. From Northern Germany, the Enlightenment spread to the Catholic South, where its Protestant origin remained plainly visible. At the same time there was a direct French influence in the Rhineland, Bavaria and Austria. The whole of Europe, large sections of Italy and Spain, stood under the influence of the Enlightenment.

The Enlightenment was characterized by a very great emphasis on reason and a very earthly-minded, even pragmatic, attitude of life in which man is placed at the center. These characteristics were particularly evident in theology. In some cases it led to a loss of faith. Yet when there was nothing more than a certain amount of influence, it is true that it still brought with it dangers; but, on the other hand, it inspired renewal and revitalization as a reaction against an antiquated mentality and antiquated forms.

Although its influence was not so great on Catholic theology as on Protestant theology, nevertheless those two chief elements were present there, though more moderately. On the one hand, we may say that all the Catholic movements of those days, namely, Gallicanism, Febronianism, Josephinism

220

and liturgical tendencies, were influenced by the Enlightenment. On the other hand, it would be wrong to brand all those movements with the stamp of "rationalism." It remains true, however, that the liturgical tendencies in particular were influenced by those two main ideas of the Enlightenment. Here a distinction must be made between an extreme influence of the Enlightenment and a more moderate one.

The extreme influence of the Enlightenment on the liturgical field showed a strong external resemblance to the modern liturgical movement. There was a desire for a general active participation of the faithful; great emphasis was placed on the community spirit. To attain that end, it wanted the vernacular in the liturgy. More emphasis was placed on the liturgy than on private prayers and devotions. Sloppiness and formalism in rites and ceremonies was opposed. There was a return to ancient sources; greater attention was given to Holy Scriptures; it also wanted to reform and simplify the breviary, a desire of Benedict XIV's which did not come to completion.

Some of the particular points desired by this movement may serve to clarify that picture: no saying of the rosary during Mass; only one altar in the church; celebration of the Mass facing the people; a strong emphasis on community Masses as against "private" Masses; more preaching and fewer confraternities; tendency toward making Confession a community celebration; fewer statues in the churches; less frequent exposition of the Blessed Sacrament; fewer processions and fewer feasts of saints. From that time also date the great German aversion for Latin in the liturgy; local revisions (diocese by diocese) of missal and ritual; greater attention paid to the laity in the Church; publication of a lay breviary; and theology courses for lay people. Very important was the eighteenth century introduction of the German Mass and

Vesper chants. Enormous attention was given to German church hymns. It was then also that the *Singmesse* came into vogue.

The advocates of the Enlightenment found fellow-combatants and leaders in Jansenism, Gallicanism and Febronianism who constantly appealed to "early Christianity." In the Netherlands there were, from about the year 1700, priests who administered baptism, marriages and the sacraments of the sick in the vernacular; the same happened also in Germany and France—not, however, with respect to the Mass. Summing up the essentials in the liturgical efforts of renewal at the time of the Enlightenment, we can distinguish three aims: 1) simplification; 2) community worship; 3) more understanding and edification and, for that purpose, use of the vernacular.

The men of the Enlightenment of whom we have spoken above made use, as we do, of the terms *Gottesdienst* (divine service) or worship but gave a different meaning to those words. A few quotations will show this clearly. Vitus Anton Winter (1750-1814) the author of a "Mass Book," wrote: "Religion according to reason and faith is the same as worship, and worship is a good moral life with proper attention to God."[9] On the very first page he spoke about God as the "Moral and World Ruler," who must be honored as such and not so much as Lord and King. Thus public worship was viewed as an incentive for the exercise of virtue, and instruction was seen as an important purpose of the liturgy. The whole of pastoral theology, which arose at that time, was moralistic. The sermons too were almost exclusively moralistic. The existing liturgy, they said, is not sufficiently instructive; hence it should be simplified and made understandable. The same Vitus Winter said in his book on liturgy: "There was

---

[9]Winter, *Messbuch*, p. 31.

a time when public worship was thought of as a service to be rendered to the Deity," but now "religious moral enlightenment of the mind is the first purpose of the liturgy; amendment of the heart or edification is the second purpose of external worship"; "purposiveness is the third principle of the liturgy."[10]

There were a good number of authors who under Protestant influence made the sermon the principal matter of the liturgy. There existed also a kind of ecumenism aimed at emphasizing in our worship only what Catholics and Protestants had in common. A hymn that became the vogue began: "O Father of all minds" (*O Vater aller Geister*); it was entitled "General Hymn of Tolerance" (*Allgemeines Toleranzlied*). From the same source also came an opposition to the veneration of saints, processions, devotion to the Sacred Heart, novenas, etc.

There was a desire to change and transform the whole liturgy in accordance with those standpoints. The era's desire to "go back to the sources," however, did not try to rediscover the essence of worship or liturgy. It was rather a movement that started from the assumption that the liturgy should be adapted to the "enlightened mind" of those days; and it was thought that more possibilities would be found for that purpose in the ancient, more simple liturgy than in the later, and especially the medieval, liturgy. One thing that was absent from all those liturgical tendencies was the awareness that the Christian is a child of God and that the life of communion with God must be lived in joy. On the contrary, what was prominent everywhere in them was the moralistic and instructional character. The ecumenical tendencies did not flow so much from an awareness that the dividedness of Christ's Church is sinful but rather from a rationalistic tendency toward uniformity and standardization.

---

[10]Winter, *Liturgie*, pp. 33, 67, 70.

The whole movement was more against the Church than in the Church.

In spite of all this, we must ask ourselves if the Enlightenment was really totally worthless for our liturgical movement. The Enlightenment was, both theologically and liturgically, very one-sided; but we must not forget that it was a reaction against the evil conditions then existing. The religious situation was bad and, as this was attributed principally to the liturgy, great attention was paid to the renovation of liturgical worship.

In our evaluation of the Enlightenment we must neither abstract from the fact that it was a reaction nor be blind to its wholesome tendencies which might eventually have produced good fruit. It cannot be denied that in the Church of those days there existed an excessive attention to the saints, miraculous statues and all sorts of peripheral devotions. The convents and monasteries played a sorry role in this. It is to the credit of the Enlightenment that it fought against such abuses. The Enlightenment has also been beneficial for religious instruction, as well as for the pastoral education of the clergy. Further we must not forget that those who opposed the Enlightenment not infrequently were motivated by an attachment to the old ways, that is, conservatism. In the liturgical field almost everything gained by the Enlightenment was lost once more. Only the German church hymns were preserved and have survived, a thing that has proved very advantageous to the German liturgical movement of today.

The more moderate Catholic representatives of the Enlightenment had, in general, the same concrete desires with respect to the liturgy; but they were less extreme in expressing those desires and, above all, their desires were based on a better foundation. It is true that their concept of the liturgy and of pastoral care was not entirely correct, but neither was it as wrong as that of the extreme advocates of the Enlightenment. Nevertheless, even these moderates must be counted among the disciples of the Enlightenment, for they also adhered to the two principal elements of the Enlightenment, viz., the emphasis on reason and an earthly-minded mentality. Fortunately, it was the moderate tendencies and not the extreme ones that were diffused among the clergy and people in all sorts of pastoral publications.

The Nineteenth Century Catholic Revival. The Enlightenment lost power and gradually disappeared. At the same time there was a quickening of Catholic life. Was this a direct consequence of the Romanticism that arose in this century? It was certainly not a direct result, for man remained central in Romanticism. In the Enlightenment man with his *reason* was the focal point and, hence, his tendency was directed toward a good moral life. In Romanticism it was rather *sentiment* and a life animated by feeling that was predominant. The Romanticist, like the disciple of the Enlightenment, loved to look back to ancient times, but for the Romanticist this meant rather the Middle Ages. To realize this we have merely to recall his love for neo-Gothic style. Hence, although Romanticism did not directly cause a Catholic revival, the latter was nevertheless connected with it. The general sphere became more favorable for the Church because of the Romanticist's loving approach to the Middle Ages, even though it is true that this return to medieval times also had great disadvantages for the Church.

The entire atmosphere after the French Revolution and Napoleon was favorable to a Catholic restoration. People were tired of all they had undergone in connection with the Enlightenment. They felt the need for authority, and Romanticism shed light, from its standpoint, on many parts of the old Catholic heritage.

During the decades of the nineteenth century there was, within the framework of a general development of science and scholarship, also a powerful flourishing of theology. France led the way in the renewal. The prominent men were mostly converts: François de Chateaubriand (1768-1849), Hugo de Lamennais (1782-1854), Joseph de Maistre (1754-1821), Louis G. de Bonald (1754-1840), Louis Bautin (1796-1867), Henri Lacordaire (1802-1861), Charles R. de Montalembert (1810-1870). De Lamennais, Bautin and Lacordaire later became priests.

Faith, and by some extremists even fideism, was held to be the only source of certitude opposing unbelief. In opposition to the democratic principle, great importance was attached to authority; and, in this respect, the pope's central position of power received particular emphasis.

This movement had great influence in Germany, especially among laymen; for instance, Count von Strolberg (1750-1819), Clemens Brentano (1778-1842), Adam Müller (1779-1829), Joseph von Görres (1776-1848). In German countries there were several centers of spiritual renewal. The first of these, since 1805, was in Vienna under the direction of St. Clemens Hofbauer, C.Ss.R., Adam Müller, Friedrich Schlegel and Zacharias Werner; these men worked by means of lectures, reviews and popular almanacs. Another center existed in Münster with Prince Gallitzin and Count von Stolberg, a convert. There was also the Bavarian group of Johann Sailer and his collaborators and, finally, the School of Tübingen. In general they produced many publications and did much scientific work. In Germany a sharp division grew once more between the Catholic and Protestant confessions; and the Catholics assumed a more militant attitude. This whole development exercised an influence also on the liturgical tendencies.

In Germany there was a gradual transition from the moderate Enlightenment to a deepening of Catholic life, including the field of liturgy.

In this respect the principal figure is that of Johann M. Sailer (1751-1832). He began as a Jesuit but, after the suppression of the Order, was ordained a secular priest and became professor of the new pastoral theology. He always remained a faithful and devout Catholic. Although he belonged to the moderate Enlightenment, his later development was fully in harmony with the true nature of the Church. But, he always preserved the freshness and zeal for renewal of his younger years. In 1829 he was appointed bishop of Regensburg at the age of seventy-nine, after his nomination had been held up for years because of his past association with the Enlightenment. He died in 1832.

According to his view—and this is true of all the periods of his life—the liturgy is the center of ecclesial piety; and the more he recognized the faults of the Enlightenment, the more also did this piety find its center in a sound and fundamental concept of the Church. He put great stress on the active participation of the faithful and also on a reverent and tranquil celebration of the Mass. He strove for the reformation of the liturgy and also dealt with the question of the vernacular, although he did not see the use of the people's language as *the* solution. Important figures similar to Sailer were Hirscher and Johann A. Möhler (1796-1832).

After them came men who belonged to the nineteenth century; they were typical representatives of the Catholic restoration and firmly rejected the Enlightenment even in liturgical matters. Among others there was Joseph A. Binterim (1779-1855) who began as a Franciscan and became a secular priest after the abolition of the monasteries in 1805. He was very interested in the liturgy, but remained conservative in his views and opposed the use of the vernacular; he was also interested in the ecclesial year, opposed the recitation of the rosary during Mass, and stressed the importance of the parochial Mass. Another figure with similar interests was Edward Herzog (1801-1867). At this time there appeared, once more, translations of the breviary and the missal, and more attention was also given to the beauty of the liturgy.

In France, too, both Romanticism and a Catholic restoration took place. The reaction against the ideas of the eighteenth century was more violent in France than in Germany; that is, at least there were no transitional figures as prominent and as constructive as Sailer. Movements arose in every field against the tendencies of the eighteenth century. We notice that in the first half of the nineteenth century there was literally a question of a "liturgical movement." In France the great man of this movement was Prosper Guéranger, O.S.B. (1805-1875). He is very important and we may perhaps place him in history alongside Binterim in Germany, although Guéranger was the more important of the two.

Guéranger re-established and restored the Benedictine abbey of Solesmes that dated from the—romantic—past. He was fascinated by tradition as well as by mystery. Hence his violent reaction against Rationalism as well as a Gallicanism that was not very fond of the pope's power. He favored a strong papal authority—which was so greatly scorned in the eighteenth century and downtrodden in the time of Napoleon —and advocated a far-reaching unity which in reality was closer to uniformity. It is within this larger perspective that his liturgical interest must be appreciated.

Guéranger was opposed to the regional variation of the liturgy which had been preserved or reintroduced—with at least the tacit approval of the Church—in the eighteenth century. These still existed in the beginning of the nineteenth century and had obtained explicit approval of Rome, in spite of the severe rules established by Pius V. Guéranger was against these variations because, according to him, they affected the unity of the Church. He was in favor of one, uniform Roman liturgy as a means of Church unity. He did not like the Eastern liturgies or, for that matter, the Ambrosian rite of Milan. It did not enter his mind to adapt the liturgy to time and place. The liturgy, as it had developed, was good, holy and would no longer change; to the extent that it was not celebrated properly, it was necessary to strictly enforce all the rubrics. This mentality has had great influence during the first period of our own liturgical movement of the twentieth century, and traces of it can be seen even in our own day. This liturgical movement, of course, could not directly lead to a pastoral adaptation of the liturgy but remained restricted mostly to large monasteries.

Nevertheless, Guéranger was a great liturgist and made valuable contributions to the cause of the liturgy. Because of the popular interest during his time in the ecclesial year, he wrote his book, *The Liturgical Year* (*Année liturgique*). Also very important for the liturgy is Guéranger's *Institutions liturgiques*. In spite of typical shortcomings, his works are animated by a wholesome liturgical spirit that has produced salutary effects.

In England also there grew a stronger liturgical consciousness almost at the same time as in France and Germany; but it developed there at first in Anglican rather than in Catholic circles. Romanticism and the study of the Fathers of the Church brought the Anglican into contact with Catholic piety and Catholic ideals of life. This took place in the High Church which had arisen from the Oxford Movement (around 1840). As is well known, John Henry Newman was the most prominent advocate of this tendency and the liturgy played

229

a considerable role in that movement. After Newman had become a Catholic, together with one hundred and fifty Anglican clergymen, Pusey went even further. There was an increased borrowing from the Catholic liturgy which led to a split in the High Church during the decade from 1860 to 1870 and to the formation of the distinct group of Anglo-Catholics. On the Catholic side Cardinal Wiseman (1802-1865), Archbishop of Westminster, established contact with that movement and tried to arouse more liturgical life among Catholics. In England the liturgical movement showed a clear esthetic character.

Concluding Remarks. This movement in the nineteenth century Church was particularly significant at the beginning of that century and was coupled with the study of the liturgy and the Fathers. It was spiritually sound but, unfortunately, meant too little in the actual life of the Church. Devotionalism flourished as before. In the second half of the nineteenth century, although there was a further deepening of the liturgical tendencies, there was also a luxuriant overgrowth of all sorts of devotions. Consequently, at the end of the nineteenth century the situation was theoretically and practically rather worse than in the first half.

The great difference between the tendencies of the seventeenth, eighteenth and nineteenth centuries and the present-day liturgical movement can perhaps be summarized in the following points:

1. The idea that it is from the liturgy that the whole of Christian life and Christian piety must receive its form was still very weak, although there was a slowly increasing attention to this point.

2. All sorts of extreme ideas concerning the liturgy were given expression, especially during the period of the Enlightenment.

3. Church authorities showed no practical interest in liturgical tendencies, certainly not in a positive sense.

4. Those liturgical efforts had little influence on the Church as a whole.

THE ORIGIN AND DEVELOPMENT OF THE MODERN LITURGICAL MOVEMENT

Origin. We place the start of the present liturgical movement at the beginning of the twentieth century. We notice, in the first place, that in France the Congregation of Solesmes, as heir of Guéranger's ideas, continued his work. It was also continued by a few abbeys that were forcefully exiled from France in 1900. A similar role was played in Germany by the Benedictine Congregation of Beuron and especially by the Abbey of Beuron itself.

Abbot Maurus Wolter, who founded Beuron in 1863, was in personal contact with Guéranger. The foundation of Beuron was made in the spirit of Solesmes; here also did the *"Opus Dei"* (the work of God, the Liturgy) take the central place. Beuron has, not only a remarkable place in the history of sacred and especially liturgical art, but also has done much in Germany for Gregorian chant and, in general, for the diffusion and strengthening of the liturgical spirit.[11] The man who exercised the greatest influence was Dom Anselm Schott, with his popular missal and vesper book. Before Schott there already existed translations of the missal in Germany and also in Belgium (in French). The difference between Schott's missal and the older translations was that Schott put explanations in his missal. During the *Kulturkampf*

---

[11]Important books that came out of Beuron were Benedict Sauter's *Choral und Liturgie,* Schaffhausen, 1865; his *Das heilige Messopfer,* Paderborn, 1894; and Maurus Wolter's *Psallite sapienter,* Freiburg, 1869.

Schott resided in Maredsous (Belgium) and found an incentive for his own work in the French edition of the missal by Dom Gerard van Caloen, who later founded the Abbey of St. Andrew in Belgium. Schott's missal enjoyed enormous diffusion in Germany so that Schott became practically synonymous with missal.

Of considerable importance was Maria-Laach, an early medieval abbey which had been secularized during the French Revolution. It was later occupied by the Jesuits, but in 1893 it became once more a Benedictine abbey. It actually assumed the leadership of the liturgical movement in Germany, especially under the Abbot Ildefons Herwegen and through the work of Dom Odo Casel.[12] Of great importance for his direct influence on the faithful and for his part in the biblico-liturgical movement was the Augustinian Canon Pius Parsch of Klosterneuburg near Vienna. His works are well-known and popular in the United States.[13]

From Beuron, two more Benedictine abbeys were founded in Belgium at Maredsous in 1872 and at Mont-César, near Louvain, in 1899. It was in Belgium that the liturgical movement first began to function as such in congresses, study days, liturgical weeks, liturgical associations, etc. It was there that the liturgical tendencies and activities developed into

---

[12]Born in 1886, he entered Maria-Laach in 1905 and was ordained a priest in 1911. He received his doctorate in theology at Rome on a dissertation concerning the Eucharistic doctrine of St. Justin, and in 1918 he earned a second doctorate in classical philology at Bonn. From 1922 until his death in 1948 he was chaplain of the Benedictine convent at Herstelle. He exercised great influence on the liturgical movement and also on sacramental theology in general through his theory of the mystery. His numerous writings provoked opposition, but were very stimulating for both liturgy and theology. He was the founder of the *Archiv für Liturgiewissenschaft.*

[13]Born in 1884, he entered Klosterneuburg in 1904 and founded there the Liturgical Apostolate for the People. Works in English translations are *The Liturgy of the Mass,* 3rd ed., Herder, 1957; *The Year of Grace,* 5 vols., Liturgical Press, 1962.

a true "movement," and it was there also that the name "liturgical movement" was born.

The birth of the "liturgical movement" in the strict sense can be placed around the year 1909. Monsignor Callewaert, professor of liturgy at the Senior Seminary of Brugge, Belgium, established there a "Liturgical Association" which, however, had a strictly scholarly character. The great impulse came from the large congress of Catholic "works" held in Malines in 1909. It was at this general congress that Dom Lambert Beauduin, O.S.B. (1873-1959),[14] gave a liturgical lecture, centering primarily on the Mass. It received little attention at first; but the historian of Liège, Godfroid Kurth, called attention to its importance. His intervention led to the adoption of certain resolutions that were the inauguration of the movement on a larger scale. Still in the same year, Beauduin, in collaboration with his confreres of Mont-César Abbey, published *La vie liturgique,* a monthly for High Mass and Vespers that was also meant to serve as an introduction to the liturgy. This monthly quickly spread far and wide. In 1910 Beauduin founded the review *Les questions paroissiales et liturgiques.* Maredsous, in the same year, began its *Revue liturgique et bénédictine.*

On June 7 and 8, 1910, the first liturgical congress was held at Mont-César under the presidency of Cardinal Mercier. From 1911 on, there were two yearly congresses, one French and one Flemish. The Abbey of Affligem began to prepare a popular missal in Dutch, and the first edition appeared in 1916. There were also several Flemish liturgical reviews which, after World War II, merged into one review for Holland and Belgium.

---

[14]Ordained in 1897, he entered Mont-César in 1906, where he subsequently taught dogmatic theology. In 1922 he went to San Anselmo Abbey in Rome, where he devoted himself to the work of Church unity. He died in 1959 at the house of his order in Chèvetogne.

In those days there were many factors favoring the rist of the liturgical movement, although, leaving aside the diffusion of the popular missal, it remained restricted to a small select group. One of the major favorable factors was a new attitude of life that manifested itself especially in the youth movement. Great influence was exercised in this by Romano Guardini (b. 1885).[15] Particular emphasis was put on the totality of man's body and soul, on the idea of community and on man's bond with nature. Moreover, a new Catholic attitude developed that was less defensive in character. There was also a change in religiousness which now became more directed to fundamental truths. A new concept of the layman arose, granting him recognition as an active member of the ecclesial community. On the part of Church authority, St. Pius X in 1903 issued his famous *Motu proprio* on sacred music.[16]

Development. With respect to the further development of the liturgical movement, we will say more about its content and nature later on, when we deal with the increasing attention that is now given to sacrament and word. We mention here only a few of the most important events in the liturgical movement.

On December 20, 1928, Pope Pius XI published the constitution *Divini Cultus* on the occasion of the twenty-fifth anniversary of the *Motu proprio*. This constitution marked a further progress and placed particular emphasis on the active participation of the faithful; in it appeared the well-known

---

[15]He was born in Italy but raised in Germany, where his father was Italian consul in Mainz. Ordained in 1910, he subsequently became a doctor of theology. He taught at the universities of Bonn, Berlin, Breslau and, since 1948, at Munich. Through his numerous publications he continues to exercise great influence.

[16]For papal documents about the liturgy see R. Kevin Seasoltz, *The New Liturgy, a Documentation, 1903-1965*, Herder and Herder, 1965. Text of forty major pontifical documents and addresses.

phrase that "the faithful should no longer be present as silent spectators."

Pius XII in 1943 issued the already mentioned encyclical *Mystici Corporis Christi* (The Mystical Body of Christ), which should be studied in connection with the great encyclical of 1947 on the liturgy, *Mediator Dei*. The latter dealt explicitly with the liturgical movement and spoke very positively about it, although it also contained a number of warnings concerning certain liturgical tendencies that had arisen during World War II and its aftermath, especially in Germany.

The same Pope gave us the new Holy Week Liturgy. At first this was only the Easter Vigil liturgy, which was optional in 1953 and became definitive in 1955. In 1956 there was a simplication of the rubrics. Under Pope John XXIII, new rubrics were published January 1, 1961. In the meantime the Congregation of Rites had already issued directives for the active participation of the faithful (September 3, 1958); these were of great practical significance and very progressive for the Church as a whole. The ritual for the administration of the other sacraments has also come in for consideration, and great concessions were made by Rome for the use of the vernacular in that administration. *Mediator Dei* alluded to that possibility, and an increasing number of applications have been made of it, although there were many restrictions, especially with respect to the so-called essential parts of the rite. Several countries now have beautiful, sometimes new, rites for marriage and baptism with considerable use of the vernacular. Also of great importance is the encyclical *Musicae sacrae disciplina* of 1955. However, there are still parishes in the United States where those liturgical activities have found few echoes.

A great incentive for the active participation in the present liturgical renewal was the *Constitution on the Liturgy* of

235

1963 which showed that such a renewal was part of the Church's general spiritual renewal desired by Pope John XXIII. It can no longer be said that the liturgical movement is an activity restricted to a number of priests and lay people who have fallen in love with the liturgy. Vatican Council II has given official approval to the reformation and re-creation of a liturgy better adapted to our times and which would facilitate intelligent and active participation in it. The first stage of this reformation is now being carried out everywhere in the Church, in such a way that its results are in Pope Paul VI's words "a cause of profound consolation and joy" (Encyclical *Mysterium Fidei*).

The history of the movement shows that private initiative, when undertaken in the right spirit and with due obedience to authority, can spread powerfully until the highest authorities in the Church are affected and act upon it. Liturgical conventions and publications showed how strong public opinion in the Church was in favor of a far-reaching liturgical reform. Their efforts finally produced the desired results.

2. A Stronger Orientation of Christian Life to Word and Sacrament

The tendencies we have just recalled were often misunderstood and not infrequently bitterly opposed. But their development not only affects the liturgy, but also influences the whole structure of Christian life. They do indeed affect first of all our liturgical life, that is, worship and prayer in all its forms; but they also affect marriage and family life, charity, work, social relations and all other forms and situations of life.

A structural change is going on in the *whole* of Christian life. When we start from the conviction that our whole existence is worship of God, lived in the *Ecclesia,* the ecclesial community, a different and more explicit emphasis falls on

236

the liturgical life of word and sacrament. But this in no way detracts from our sanctification through work and family life. On the contrary, in a view of the general structure of Christian life, all this results from one and the same tendency.

We exercise the universal priesthood at all times, but not always in a liturgical manner, in accordance with the words of St. Peter: "Unto whom coming, as to a living stone, rejected indeed by men, but chosen and made honorable by God: Be you also as living stones built up, a spiritual house, a holy priesthood, to offer up spiritual sacrifices, acceptable to God by Jesus Christ. Wherefore it is said in the scripture: Behold, I lay in Sion a chief cornerstone, elect, precious. And he that shall believe in him, shall not be confounded."[17] Peter here alludes to the whole of life; we share always in Christ's priesthood.

Hence we must speak about liturgical worship as well as about the sanctification of daily life. In this second section we will deal with the liturgical celebration. In the third section we shall consider the sanctification of daily life. In the fourth, we shall speak about the characterization of *both* and the slow and painful growth of a new Christian pattern of life.

During the half century since the birth of the modern liturgical movement, it has undergone a strong development. We can discern in that movement a twofold concern: 1) a *deepening* in the sense that there is a tendency to make worship once more the center of religious life, to go from peripheral questions to the heart of the matter; 2) a *widening* of the field of endeavor; for at first the liturgical movement was almost exclusively concerned with the Mass, but in later years it extended its interests to the other sacraments and the whole realm of worship.

---

[17] 1 Pet. 2:4-6.

THE EUCHARIST

The Situation at the Beginning of the Present Century. At that time a small select group of priests and lay people cherished many fundamental desires with respect to the Eucharist. The conditions here were such that anyone who had a certain amount of dogmatic, historical and pastoral insight felt that something should be done about it. On the other hand, these conditions were so deeply rooted and so widespread that only the most courageous dared to tackle that problem.

The Mass was, in the eyes of most priests, religious, and lay people, not much more than one among many devotional exercises. They realized, of course, that it was the most important; but there was nevertheless too little appreciation of the fundamental distinction between, for instance, Holy Mass and Benediction of the Blessed Sacrament. During Mass people occupied themselves, very piously, with litanies, the rosary, acts of faith and adoration and some occasionally beat their breast like the publican. We may feel certain that many people got to heaven in this way, but that is not the point here. In the best cases the faithful let themselves be directed in their devotions by what was taking place at the altar; at the Consecration and Communion most of them spontaneously expressed their devotion in acts of faith and adoration. But it was less than ideal when they were busy saying the rosary—though Pope Leo XIII had recommended the practice for the month of October—or when some even walked from station to station making the Way of the Cross. We have not even mentioned the great number who really were merely "present" at Mass, perhaps with a rosary in their hand, standing or seated in the same place where their parents had been before them. Mass with exposition of the Blessed Sacrament was the most normal thing in the world;

in fact, in many places one could not imagine a solemn Mass without exposition.

Of great importance for the liturgical movement was the activity of the pastoral pope, St. Pius X. This is true not only of his *Motu proprio* on Church music (1903), but also of his decrees concerning frequent communion (1905) and the communion of children (1910). Participation through communion is the most important and highest form of participation in the Mass. Yet that participation had been reduced to a minimum; most Catholics communicated only once or, at the most, only a few times a year. Even then it generally took place outside of Mass. At this time, communion was not sufficiently seen as connected with the Mass, as the making-present of Christ's sacrifice of the Cross. Communion was seen rather as a coming of Christ to the individual believer. It was looked upon as a good, a meritorious action, a reward, and an exercise of devotion. It is well-known that, since the period of Jansenism with its over-emphasis on one's unworthiness, people did not dare to receive frequently. In line with an earlier eucharistic movement, which, among other things, led to international Eucharistic congresses, Pius X gave a mighty impetus to frequent communion and the communion of children. This served as a foundation for genuinely liturgical participation through communion.

However, at the beginning, frequent communion developed outside the context of the Mass and remained mostly a private devotion. The then flourishing eucharistic movement was in no way integrated with the liturgical movement. People began to go to communion more often, and there were more opportunities to receive communion: on Sundays and even weekdays, every quarter of an hour. While there was little desire to be present at the celebration of the Mass as such during the week, there was a growing devotion to daily communion; hence we can understand the pastoral advice to spend at lease five minutes in preparation and fifteen in thanksgiving after communion. This whole question of a quarter of an hour thanksigiving is to a great extent based on the custom of communicating outside of Mass, and was proposed to insure some time for meditation and prayer after communion. The fact that the liturgical movement and the Eucharistic movement were not integrated was harmful to both. The Eucharistic movement remained too one-sidedly orientated to the adoration of the Eucharist and frequent communion had failed to integrate them sufficiently into the whole Eucharistic celebration. On the other hand, as a reaction to that, the liturgical movement has undoubtedly pushed that adoration too much into the background, and it has not always sufficiently remembered that communion outside of Mass always retains a connection with the Mass and that, in some circumstances, it is the only possible solution. But the liturgical movement has rightly fought for a proper hierarchy of values in eucharistic piety.

St. Pius X published his *Motu proprio* on Church music shortly after becoming pope; in it he tried to banish from the churches the theatrical and orchestral music he had learned to dislike while he was Bishop of Mantua and Patriarch of Venice, and which he had condemned in his pastoral letters. In their stead he wished to give primacy to Gregorian Chant and classical polyphony. But his decree did not say anything about singing. These activities of Pius X arose also from tendencies that existed in the Church at that time and which became the foundation for a genuine liturgical movement. But we cannot say that Pius X took the lead in the liturgical movement, for this was not the content or intention of his decrees. This movement was to come later when, as we have already mentioned, the "Congress of Catholic Works" held in Antwerp in 1909 became the more or less accidental cradle of the liturgical movement. This congress gave rise to a movement that gradually influenced many countries. The wishes formulated in that congress are typical for the situation at that time and they long served as directives of the liturgical movement:

To each of those wishes expressed over fifty years ago, we can attach some marginal notes:

1. The popularization of the missal became a great success. Missals that contained both the Latin and the vernacular or only the vernacular were placed in many hands. Thus in our own day a missal belongs to the ordinary prayer books of the laity. There were complete missals, Sunday missals, leaflet missals, missals for children, with or without introductions and explanations; and this "giving the altar missal to the people" proved highly beneficial for true Catholic piety. In this way also the faithful became more familiar with Scripture.

However, with the passing of the years, we have come to the realization that, advantageous as the use of the missal is, it does not solve the problem of the celebration of the Eucharist. "Following the priest" with the help of a missal does not yet make the Mass a community celebration. Even with missals in the hands of the faithful and even though these texts speak constantly of the community, the piety of the faithful can remain very individualistic. In fact many people shut themselves up, as it were, in their missal and resented any "disturbance" such as community singing. Some continue to do so even today.

However, we are now developing new ideas in that respect, precisely because we look differently upon the celebration of the Eucharist. It is not enough to wish to offer the Mass "together with the priest." We must offer it *with one another, as community*. Here, then, a new step has been made in the right direction. "Guidance" during the celebration of the Mass,

241

for instance, is not aimed merely at helping the faithful find their way through their missal. Such guidance would be useless and even annoying now that people are familiar with the missal. In the future the old use of the missal will become superfluous. After having been necessary to enable the faithful to follow the priest, it will now have to become a useful means to celebrate the Eucharist together with the priest and one's fellow-Christians, that is, as a community. But the missal's purpose is not to enable the faithful to read what is taking place at the altar, but to enable them to participate actively in that community action.

2. *The Solemn High Mass* was greatly stressed at the beginning of the liturgical movement. The High Mass is indeed the highest form of the celebration of the Eucharist; but it had been overshadowed by the many "low" Masses and, on the other hand, had been spoiled by its own orchestral and theatre music. This strong emphasis on the High Mass lasted for a few decades, in Europe at least, almost until World War II.

The Low Mass, however, gradually began to receive greater attention. For a long time there existed an official fiction that all non-solemn or unsung Masses were "private" Masses, even though genuinely private Masses had already existed for a long time. This was based on the fact that formerly all public Masses were solemn or sung Masses. But this custom gradually disappeared. In some countries, like Ireland, a sung Mass was very rare. The High Mass remained popular on Sundays, for example in Belgium and in the United States; but there was a series of low Masses, which not infrequently were best attended. On weekdays, in most dioceses of Europe, nearly all Masses were low and officially "private." Some of those Masses were really "low," almost silent, inspite of rubrics calling for audibility in some parts.

242

On September 3, 1959, the Instruction of the Congregation of Rites condemned the further use of the term "private" Mass since every Mass is really public worship. The growing liturgical movement and a better idea of the nature of the Church also lead to a better understanding of the social character of the celebration of the Eucharist. An attempt was thus made to give a better form to the so-called low Masses, within the framework of the rubrics. For, generally speaking, it was not possible to replace all of them with High Masses. Further, there was no desire at all to do this because, at the present stage, a modified low Mass offers more possibilities to many faithful than the High Mass which, however, remains the highest form of eucharistic celebration.

The so-called "community Mass" arose from these efforts. By "community Mass" is meant here a particular concrete form of the low Mass that aims at making possible and stimulating the active participation of the faithful. A distinction is often made between community Mass and "dialogue" Mass. This distinction is justified for, in the community Mass in the strict sense of the term, there is also singing of songs or parts of the ordinary of the Mass in the vernacular, and there may also be an offertory procession and an offertory litany. But both types have in common the most important factor: the possibility of a true community celebration of the Mass by active participation of all those present through responses, common prayers, and readings in the vernacular. Because there are so many varieties in the celebration of the low Mass, it is often difficult to make a clear distinction between these two types. The earliest form in several countries was the "dialogue" Mass, and at the beginning an attempt was made to have the people make all or most of the responses to the priest in Latin. Later it was felt that "explanations" were necessary; thus large sections—especially the Canon—were read in the vernacular by a "commentator" or "reader."

This had the disadvantage of placing the priest, as the true leader of the celebration, in the background; moreover, there was also much opposition by the faithful to this form of participation.

Following World War II, other forms were devised that avoided such disadvantages. A more attractive and real participation was desired, for instance, by letting the people's singing correspond with the various parts of the liturgical action. In this way there came about various forms of "community Mass" in a stricter sense of the word: it is in a certain sense something midway between the High Mass and the dialogue Mass. The term "community Mass" is rather strange, for every celebration of the Eucharist really has a social or community character. Thus the use of that term shows that this community character had become a problem.

It is pleasant to record that, especially since 1952, many particular, episcopal and finally also papal directives were given with respect to those low Masses. Rome at first showed hesitancy toward any attempt to enliven the low Mass. As late as 1922, the Congregation of Rites published a decree on the dialogue Mass, which said that, while permissible, it is not to be recommended since that kind of Mass easily distracts the faithful in their devotion and also brings with it difficulties concerning the rubrics; consequently the bishops should not easily grant that permission. In 1928, however, Pope Pius XI's constitution *Divini Cultus* was more positive regarding that form of participation. Much, of course, had happened since that time.

In Germany, since 1942, there were three distinct forms of low Mass: 1) German dialogue Mass (*Gemeinschaftsmesse*); 2) "Pray-sing-Mass (*Betsingmesse*); 3) Latin dialogue Mass (*Missa recitata*). The Pray-sing-Mass is particularly attractive and it was, with important modifications, adopted in many countries, including the United States.

244

The search is still going on for a form that, from the pastoral standpoint, presents the best possibilities (use of the vernacular, dialogue, song) for establishing contact with the people. This is a very good attitude. In general, interest in the High Mass has not disappeared. In some American dioceses people still want High Masses on weekdays, although this is perhaps merely the result of long-established customs. It would not be right to undervalue the High Mass as celebrated on Sundays. The High Mass offers more possibilities than a Mass with people's songs; it is not only the most solemn but, when properly performed, the most inspiring celebration. For a public that is more fully educated, as in schools and convents, the High Mass is the only form that ultimately corresponds with their aspirations.

On the other hand, precisely because the congregation consists of such widely differing types of people, attention must be given to the ordinary *dialogue Mass* as a more simple form of worship than the High Mass. In spite of the fact that evening Masses are now permitted, parishes still have many Masses on Sunday mornings; and there will have to be devised some form of dialogue Mass that will help the people who flock to those Masses take a "living" part in the celebration. As the *Constitution on the Liturgy* (1963) says: "Pastors of souls must . . . realize that, when the liturgy is celebrated, something more is required than the mere observation of the laws governing valid and licit celebration; it is their duty also to ensure that the faithful take part, fully aware of what they are doing, actively engaged in the rite, and enriched by its effects."[18]

In 1958 the Instructions on Sacred Music and the Sacred Liturgy stressed that the faithful should be as actively involved as possible in low Masses. Four ways were offered, with increasing degrees of active participation, including

---

[18]Ch. I, art. 10.

dialogue; however, the official prayers and responses were still required to take place in Latin. The new *Constitution on the Liturgy* puts great stress on the communal character of the Mass, which it wants to be a truly participated liturgical celebration; the whole congregation must take part in it by means of responses, gestures, etc. Large parts of the Mass are now in the vernacular, so that they can be recited conveniently by priest and people together. The rites are revised to make them more simple and easy to understand. They should, moreover, be adapted to the cultures and traditions existing in various parts of the world.

Communion during Mass was one of the major aims of the liturgical movement. This was especially desired so that the unity between "sacrifice" and "sacrament" might be more fully realized. This point has always been a difficulty, for there existed ingrained habits, based on allegedly practical reasons, of distributing communion to the faithful outside of Mass. In this matter the liturgical movement can take legitimate pride in its success. Moreover, it will be difficult to maintain those unliturgical customs in view of the rubrics of January 1, 1961, in conformity with the Directives of 1958, in which the distribution of communion during Mass is categorically prescribed. In line with this, Pius XII even recommended that hosts for the faithful be consecrated in each Mass, so that the people could receive the hosts consecrated in the Mass at which they had assisted. Of course, there is nothing wrong, theologically speaking, in receiving hosts that were consecrated in another Mass. Yet this new custom is not without theological significance, for it points to a more direct participation of the faithful in the Holy Sacrifice of the Mass. This use of hosts consecrated at the same Mass is even strictly prescribed for Holy Thursday. In this way there has been an endeavor to bring eucharistic piety back to what constitutes its core.

Regarding exposition of the Blessed Sacrament, this custom has been reduced to more reasonable proportions and the practice of celebrating Mass in the presence of the exposed Blessed Sacrament has been abolished. The Code of Canon Law of 1918 was already rather severe on this point. The exposition during Mass was permitted only on the Feast of Corpus Christi. In spite of that, many European countries, especially the typically Counter-Reformation regions of Southern Germany and Austria, continued to have numerous Masses with exposition of the Blessed Sacrament and to have at least a brief Benediction every day.

Regarding the strictly eucharistic practice of communion during Mass and adoration of the Blessed Sacrament, one can say that the eucharistic and the liturgical movements have become integrated. Very important in this respect was the International Eucharistic Congress of Munich of 1960.[19] This congress differed considerably from the previous eucharistic congresses, for the influence of the liturgical movement was clearly manifest in it.

3. *The reform of Church music and the renewal of the liturgy* went hand in hand at the beginning of the liturgical movement. Gregorian chant that had been neglected and had deteriorated enjoyed a new flowering and it signified, for a good number, a true religious experience. Classical polyphony came into its own again. New polyphonic compositions that were genuine Church music made their appearance. While Pius X did not yet mention community singing in his *Motu proprio,* Pius XI spoke of it in the Constitution *Divini Cultus* of 1928 on the occasion of the twenty-fifth anniversary of the former.

---

[19]Cf. Rudolf von Moreau, *Die Eucharistischen Weltkongresse; Werden Wachsen, Wirken,* Rotweil, 1960; *Statio orbis. Eucharistischer Weltkongress 1960 in München,* 2 vols., Munich, 1961; Roger Aubert, "Eucharistic Congresses from Leo XIII to Paul VI," *Concilium, vol. 1* (1965), pp. 155-167.

The introduction of community singing was one of the principal activities of the liturgical movement. This activity was a source of disagreement with the movement for Church music; for the latter wished to retain the cultural values inherited from the past. The liturgical movement also desired this; it was and is fully in favor of cultural excellence in church buildings, vestments and especially the eucharistic celebration. In this respect song and music stand in the front line, for they play an important role in all worship, even in non-Christian religious services. Through song and music a man is freed from isolation, becomes united with other men and is lifted Godwards. However, a difficulty arises when polyphonic music is introduced in the celebration of the Mass; for the polyphonic parts available for a choir interfere with community singing and the community celebration. Polyphonic repertoires are primarily derived from a period when there existed another religious mentality and another attitude toward the Eucharist. The difficulties become even greater now that Gregorian chant is losing some of its popularity—many people never had much liking for it—and there is a growing desire for good Church community songs in the vernacular as is acknowledged in the encyclical *Sacred Music and Sacred Liturgy* of 1958 and the *Constitution on the Liturgy* of 1963.

All this led to a kind of estrangement between the Church music movement and the liturgical movement, which is only very gradually being overcome. It is to be hoped that, when, the use of Latin and the vernacular in sung Masses is finally determined, a balance will also be attained in the use of Latin and vernacular chants. The two movements should be united, for music is too important to be allowed to go its own individual way. Church music is a subdivision of the liturgy and there should be marital harmony between those two movements. In fact they should be *one* movement.

248

Active participation of the faithful has become more and more the heart of the matter. Since Pius XI this term is used increasingly in papal documents, and Pius XII spoke at length about it in *Mediator Dei*. The question, however, is whether the expression "active participation of the faithful in the Holy Mass" is still satisfactory. For, as ideas have developed, objections arise against that terminology: is it right to speak that way, at least, if it implies that now the faithful can also participate in a reality which is already there, because it is made present by the priest? Ought we not rather speak of the Eucharistic celebration as an "event" brought about, as a whole, by the community, the community that is present? In this community there are various functionaries. The celebrating priest presides over the gathering of the faithful and is the most important and indispensable leader of that assembly. Yet, although without the priest no celebration of the Eucharist is possible, others are also obviously active: the servers and all those who are present. These three categories, the priest, the servers and the faithful, together form *one* community; this community, that is, the local Church, celebrates the Eucharist.

The faithful obviously have an active role in that community event. Hence it should not be said that they, as it were, *join themselves to* the priest who offers the Sacrifice. We must not start from the distinction between priest and faithful and then attempt to bridge the seperation by speaking about the way they should join together and the way the faithful can take an active part in the work of the priest. What we should begin with is the *Church*, that is, the present assembly. Starting from this basis we can then ask what is the task and place of the various functionaries who together form the ecclesial community. When we start in this way, we have not robbed the priest of anything that dogmatically belongs to him in the Eucharistic celebration; we have merely become

249

explicitly aware that only in this way can one truly speak of a community celebration.

Joseph Jungmann, in dealing with the active participation of the faithful, starts from the true fundamental structure of the liturgical celebration of the Eucharist. How truly the celebration of the Mass is the sacrifice of the Church, of the community, he says, "is specially striking when we examine the basic plan of our Mass-liturgy as it was devised in the earliest days of the Church. One of the oldest names used to describe the celebration is *Eucharistia,* Thanksgiving. This name was given precisely because the liturgy of the Mass, since its origins in the first century, took the form of thanksgiving. In those days there was no Fore-mass; the preparation of the gifts took place without any particular formalities. The celebration began with the summons: *Gratias agamus Domino Deo Nostro,* 'Let us give thanks to the Lord our God.' Then followed immediately the prayer of thanksgiving, as described to us by Justin the Martyr—that which was called the *Eucharistia . . . .* Then follows the account of the Last Supper; the words of consecration are spoken; the expression of thanks is transformed into the act of offering. *Gratias agamus* becomes *offerimus* ['we offer']. The Church offers sacrifice and Communion follows . . . . This ground plan of the Mass . . . [is] still underlying the Mass-liturgy of today . . . . The real Eucharist begins with a formal speech of thanks, a thanksgiving prayer. And from this prayer of thanksgiving there originates the offering: *Te igitur rogamus ac petimus uti accepta habeas,* 'We pray and beseech thee graciously to accept . . . .*

"This central element of the celebration . . . is completely surrounded by prayers and ceremonies which all serve to express the praying and sacrificing of the Church. They constitute an ascent of many steps which the Church mounts until the heights of the consecration are attained. There is . . .

the hearing of God's word in the Scripture readings, the preparation of the gifts which, even in their natural condition, show forth homage to the Creator; then there is the great prayer of thanksgiving and the triple *Sanctus* in which the praises of heaven are united with those of earth. Thus does the Church climb up towards her Lord . . . . And here [in the consecration] she meets her Lord who now offers his own sacrifice with her. For the priest who at that moment stands at the altar as the representative of Christ does not thereby cease to be also the representative of the Church . . . . After the consecration it is once more the Church's sacrifice—and this alone—which is brought into the foreground. '*We* offer.' . . .

"What exactly is this 'Church' who is offering? Does the word always mean the Universal Church? . . . Or does it mean just the priest who is here and now her representative? —and that the faithful are merely called on to be present as witnesses who follow the course of the Mass with devotion? We can be certain that this is far too narrow a view . . . . At each individual celebration of the Mass there stands in the foreground the particular community which here and now is gathered about the celebrating priest. That is very clearly expressed in the liturgy of the Mass. The priest speaks in the plural not as the spokesman of any indeterminate group of people or even as the spokesman of the entire Church. Before any of the prayers he explicitly call on the community which is here and now gathered together to join him in communal prayer: *Oremus,* 'Let us pray.' He even . . . speaks to or at them, he extends to them a specific greeting; a greeting, moreover, which they are expected to answer. Even that does not suffice: it is envisaged that all those present should cry out *Amen.*

"And when he comes to the very sacrificial prayer, the eucharistic prayer, the priest expresses his invitation even more emphatically. He says *Sursum Corda* ['Let us raise our hearts'], and follow with *Gratias agimus,* [We give thanks] . . . . [In the solemn offering after the consecration, he says:] *Nos servi tui sed et plebs tua sancta,* ['We your ministers and also your holy people']. In addition to all this, . . . the Offertory procession which flourished for more than a thousand years in the Western Church . . . expressed very clearly: this is our sacrifice which we are now offering . . . . That the assembled faithful are all invited to Communion within the Mass in direct connection with their sacrifice follows naturally from what has been described. . . .

"The Mass is, then, the sacrifice of the Church and, indeed, of that congregation of the faithful here and now gathered about the priest . . . . For that reason it is right that they should make the answers to the priest's prayers, and join with him in saying aloud the *Gloria, Credo, Sanctus* and so forth . . . . It is clear that only in this way can the concept of the Church become really alive in the minds of the faithful, and that the liturgy can effectively exert its great power to renew pastoral work. 'The Church' is thus no more a merely nebulous idea referring only to the Pope, bishops and priests as responsible for the salvation of our souls. The Church means ourselves; the Church means 'God's holy people,' the community of the redeemed, those who have been incorporated into the holy unity of the Body of Christ, who thus can glorify God *per Christum Dominum nostrum,* ['Through Christ our Lord'], and who with him can offer the great sacrifice by which his name is glorified from the rising of the sun even until the going down thereof."[20]

---

[20]Jungmann, *The Sacrifice of the Church,* Challoner Publications, 1956, pp. 6 ff. See also John J. Jankauskas, *Our Tongues Were Loosed. Parish Experiences in Liturgical Renewal,* Newman, 1965; Auguste François, *Participation active à la Messe,* Louvain, 1935; L. Agostini and J. Wagner, *Participazione attiva alla liturgia,* Como, 1954. Also to be recommended is Jungmann's *The Place of Christ in Liturgical Prayer,* Alba House, 1966.

THE OTHER SACRAMENTS

It was natural that attention would first be given to the Eucharist, the "sacrament of sacraments." Although attention to the other sacraments was never wanting—as is evident from the many publications, especially those of a practical-pastoral nature—a more profound interest in them is of recent date, primarily since World War II. Great attention has been given to all the other sacraments during the past few years, namely to baptism, confirmation, marriage, confession, the sacrament of the anointing of the sick and, to some extent, the priesthood.

In this re-orientation of those sacraments, the central idea is also the fact that worship is a community celebration. These sacraments also must be seen from the standpoint of a more thorough ecclesial consciousness, with respect to both the way they are celebrated and the way they are "lived."

Baptism and confirmation were the first to receive renewed consideration. Leaving aside all sorts of problems regarding details—some of which will be dealt with later—we want to stress a point of immense interest within the framework of the greater attention paid to the Church as community, namely, the fact that those sacraments are once more seen primarily as an *incorporation into the ecclesial community.* This community is not seen, of course, as a purely human organization but as the community of Christ, so that one's personal entering into relationship with the Father—as a child of the Father—in and by and with Christ, in the loving power of the Holy Spirit, and the concomitant removal of one's sinful situation are integrally realized in that reception into the Church community.

When baptism and confirmation are approached from this perspective, we see not merely the close connection existing between these two sacraments, but also their obvious bond with the recipient's first complete participation in the Eu-

253

charist. We thus come to realize once more the inseparable trinity of the so-called "initiation sacraments," by which the new Christian, as child or adult, is taken up into the community of the believers in Christ and becomes an active member of it, one who shares in the general priesthood.

There are many consequences flowing from this view of baptism and confirmation culminating in the first complete participation in the celebration of the Eucharist. One obvious consequence is the tendency to celebrate those sacraments preferably during gatherings of the faithful, since we realize better how great a role the faith of the Church plays in the administration of baptism. There are, however, many practical difficulties. One results from the custom of strictly interpreting the rule of baptizing the child "as soon as possible." Thus, soon after birth, every child is brought to a deserted corner of the Church to be baptized in isolation, in a simple and hidden ceremony. Further, many children are baptized, not in the parochial church, but in the hospital. Then there is the mentality, shared by most of the faithful and priests, which visualizes baptism almost exclusively on the personal level as a removal of original sin. Again, there is the difficulty of introducing the celebration of baptism into the actual life of the parish and making it somewhat a community celebration. There are also difficulties in the structure of the liturgical rite of baptism which was born of a mentality that differed from the modern outlook. It is to be hoped, nevertheless, that with the growth of community consciousness in the parish, more of the same consciousness will also develop with respect to the administration of baptism. As a matter of fact, this is already taking place in a number of parishes.[21]

---

[21]See Charles Davis, *Sacraments of Initiation,* Sheed and Ward, 1963; Joseph Jungmann, *Pastoral Liturgy,* Herder and Herder, 1962; and the special baptismal issue no. 32, 1952, of *La Maison-Dieu.* For the modern emphasis on the sacraments in general in the spiritual life see Bernard Häring, *Sacramental Spirituality,* Sheed and Ward, 1965.

A special consequence is the desire to introduce a real liturgical catechumenate for adults who desire baptism. Regarding these adults, not only in mission countries but also in places where the Church has been established for centuries, a strange situation existed: months were spent in preparing baptismal candidates and then, as a disappointing climax, generally in a "private" baptism, they went through all the stages of the catechumenate in a ceremony lasting, at most, half an hour. The many proposals made in this respect have now been crowned with success. For the *Constitution on the Liturgy* says: "The catechumenate for adults, comprising several distinct steps, is to be restored and to be taken into use at the discretion of the local ordinary. By this means the time of the catechumenate, which is intended as a period of suitable instruction, may be sanctified by sacred rites to be celebrated at successive intervals of time."[22]

A special difficulty occurs in connection with the reception into the Church of *baptized non-Catholic Christians*. There is a growing dissatisfaction with the still prevailing practice of baptizing those persons conditionally, that is, "unless the baptism was valid." Confidence in the validity of the baptism administered by a number of Protestant churches has grown considerably so that this "conditional baptism" has become repugnant to both Protestants and Catholics. Moreover, the profession of faith required on that occasion is too emphatically apologetic and not enough a positive confession of faith. Added to this has been—for safety's sake—an absolution from excommunication, that is, from an ecclesiastical punishment inflicted upon those who knowingly and sinfully adhere to a "heretical sect," a thing which, after so many centuries of separation, is a gratuitous insult, for it assumes guilt in people who are generally in good faith.

---

[22]*Constitution on the Liturgy,* art. 64. Issue no. 58, 1958, of *La Maison-Dieu* is devoted to the topic, "Du catéchumenat à la Confirmation."

A further consequence is the increasing difficulties with respect to the *bond between baptism and confirmation*. More and more emphasis is placed on the close bond that exists between these two intrinsically related sacraments. Here we note two tendencies. Some emphasize particularly the initiation character of baptism and confirmation (together with the Eucharist); that is why they would like the following order: baptism, confirmation, first complete participation in the Eucharist (that is, first Communion). This means that confirmation would be received at a very early age, as is the case in Spain and in other countries that have undergone Spanish influence and also in the Eastern Churches, in which the priest confirms directly after baptism.

The Roman and German tradition, on the other hand, stresses the administration of confirmation by the bishop, and this practically excludes the administration of confirmation directly after baptism. Moreover, there are now theologians urging that confirmation, as a completion of baptism, should be administered at a later age, so that the young Christian can accept his being a Christian and his task in the Church with proper awareness of those obligations. The difficulty in this proposal, at least with respect to large dioceses, is that, if the right to confirm remains reserved to the bishop, it will be almost impossible to prevent the administration of this sacrament from becoming a kind of "assembly line" performance instead of a truly meaningful ceremony.[23]

The sacrament of penance has been the latest to be examined from the standpoint of community. The idea of its social character, however, is steadily gaining ground. A more profound study of this sacrament has reawakened the realiza-

---

[23]Cf. Marian Bohen, *The Mystery of Confirmation*, Herder and Herder, 1963; issue no. 54 on confirmation of *La Maison-Dieu;* Louis Bouyer, "La signification de la confirmation," supplement of *La vie spirituelle,* no. 29, 1954, pp. 162-180.

tion that the penitent Christian approaches God in the *Church* and that this Church is not merely the hierarchical Church in the person of the priest but the whole Church: we confess our guilt to the ecclesial community. This, however, in no way, excludes secrecy concerning the penitent's concrete sins. This new vision is made possible because the concept of the Church has been freed from one-sided emphasis on the hierarchical and organizational structure of the Church. There is no question here of the "Church" invading the realm of one's personal relationship to God, especially with respect to guilt, but it is rather a question of a broadened and deepened concept of the Church.

For this reason there is now a search for ways of having a real *liturgical* celebration of this sacrament.[24] By this is not meant a public confession of concrete personal sins, but a gathering of the ecclesial community, in which the faithful read the Scriptures, sing Psalms and listen to a sermon in order to examine their shortcomings in living a truly Christian life. After that, each one personally confesses his sins in the confessional, and receives forgiveness by the absolution of the priest in the name of the Church and hence in the name of Christ. The personal confession of each one's sins should never be replaced by that common acknowledgment of guilt.

The sacrament of marriage has for a much longer time been emphasized as having a particular bond with the community, especially with respect to the procreation and education of the children. Typical of this perspective is the fact that for several decades the emphasis was placed particularly on the expression: "We will administer the holy sacrament of matrimony to each other." The role of the Church commu-

---

[24]Bernard Pochmann, *Penance and the Anointing of the Sick,* Herder and Herder, 1964; issue no. 56, 1958 of *La Maison-Dieu,* which is devoted to "La pénitence dans la liturgie."

nity, acting as a whole and under the presidency of the ecclesial authority, was thus strongly de-emphasized.

There is a growing awareness that the Church has a much
greater role with respect to marriage than is usually assumed.
It is not true that two human beings, although they are members living in the ecclesial community, contract marriage as
a personal concern in which the priest is only a kind of con-
trolling witness of the Church. The liturgical celebration of
the sacrament of marriage means much more than that. Just
as in the Eucharist, baptism, confirmation and penance, here
too, the whole community is involved. The sacrament of marriage is a concern of the whole ecclesial community. This
idea fostered endeavors to make the liturgical celebration
correspond to the social reality. This has been emphasized
more strongly than before in the German, Dutch and Flemish
rites of marriage; in contrast with the very sober and reserved
Roman rite, they signify a great enrichment.[25]

The anointing of the sick may seem to be a strict personal
concern; yet the sick person should not be seen apart from
the community: "Is any among you sick? Let him bring in
the presbyters of the Church and let them pray over him,
anointing him with oil in the name of the Lord. And the
prayer of faith will save the sick man, and the Lord will
raise him up, and if he be in sins, they shall be forgiven
him. Confess, therefore, your sins to one another, and pray
for one another, that you may be saved."[26]

This well-known passage from the letter of St. James not
only shows the soundness of the modern tendency not to
postpone the anointing until the sick person is almost uncon-
scious and there is, humanly speaking, almost no more hope

---

[25]Cf. issue no. 50, 1957, of *La Maison-Dieu*, devoted to "Liturgie
et pastorale du mariage."
[26]James 5:14-16.

of recovery, but we see from it also how greatly this sacrament concerns the community. What is true of all the others is true also of this sacrament, namely, we no longer wish to look upon the sacrament as almost exclusively a kind of "thing," and we refuse to pay a too one-sided attention to the sacramental action. We now give attention to the totality of the sacramental reality in which the faith and prayer, not only of the minister of the sacrament, but of the whole community play a considerable role.

The text of St. James can be understood only from the standpoint of a living community. The very first words are significant: "Is any one *among you* sick?" "Let him bring in the presbyters *of the Church*," i.e., the community. "Confess, therefore, yours sins *to one another* and pray *for one another*, that you may be saved." It is this idea of bringing out the important role played by Christ's ecclesial community that has prompted the formation of the new rites for the administration of this sacrament in several countries.

The sacrament of the priesthood occupies a special and central place in the life of the community. The sacramental conferring of the hierarchical office directly and primarily concerns the community. The priesthood, however, has not escaped the influence of the individualistic mentality of former ages. More attention was given to the otherwise undeniable fact that the priestly ordination is a grace for the recipient, than to the foundation and the reason for the giving of that grace: the giving of an *office* to be exercised in and for the benefit of the community. There is presently a tendency to focus greater attention on that office and it is from this standpoint that we look at the solemnity of the priestly ordination. The whole structure of the rite of ordination presupposes a community that is present, that prays with and judges with the ordaining bishop. At the time of the ordination the bishop still asks the community of the faithful that is present to express its judgment. He must then wait for a moment and even look around to see if anyone wants to say something. But this again, due to the use of Latin, has become a pure formality. Thus it has been suggested that there are certain elements in the rite of ordination that demand adjustment; for instance, there are many formalized allocutions and exhortations of the bishop that are expressed in unintelligible Latin. The Roman *Pontificale* which is used in the rite of ordination has been in need of reform for a long time.

EMPHASIS ON THE READING OF HOLY SCRIPTURE

In recent years there have been more efforts to encourage the faithful to read the Holy Scriptures. In some places so much publicity has been given to the invitation that many people have become psychologically deaf to it. Nevertheless, there are still many Catholics who practically never read any part of the Scripture. There are even some who still consider "reading the Bible" a Protestant activity; they may also believe that this whole biblical movement is born of the desire to enter into contact with non-Catholic Christians. The introduction of "Bible Services" may have confirmed these Catholics in that idea. Many Catholics do not yet realize that the real meaning of reading Sacred Scripture is letting God's word act upon us and give us grace; God not only *speaks about* His saving action, but His word is itself a saving action. The reading of Scripture attains its apex in liturgical celebrations. The liturgy is totally biblical from beginning to end, and the modern liturgical movement would be impossible without the modern biblical movement. But, reversely, without a liturgical movement, the bible movement would not be possible either. It is in the liturgy that Holy Scripture most authentically reaches us. It is in worship that God's saving word and our believing acceptance find their highest expression. God's word must be experienced and lived first of all as worship. His word must be accepted by the assembled ecclesial community with faith and self-commitment. This does not exclude the value of personal reading and meditation of Scripture, any more than community prayer excludes private prayer.

It would be wrong, however, if we were to establish a sort of intellectual biblical movement which would emphasize personal *study* of Scripture. This intellectualistic tendency undoubtedly exists. Until recent years it found expression, for instance, in calling the "liturgy of the word" the "instructional part" of the Eucharistic celebration. This tendency manifested itself also in the desire to do away with the solemn reading of the Holy Scripture to the people in our liturgical assemblies, under the pretext that every one could "just as well" read those texts in his Missal or Bible. There were even some who proposed a renewed liturgy in which the priest would say "Read now this or that section of Holy Scripture." Each one would then privately read those parts, after which the celebrant would give a commentary.

Concerning the reading of Holy Scripture, the same question comes up as in community prayer versus personal prayer. Both have great value, but the community prayer of the assembled people of God has a special value, precisely as worship by this people of God. The same applies to the official reading and the prayerful listening to Holy Scripture in a Christian assembly. This is a liturgical worship, in which we are united with God and with one another by bonds of grace; it is liturgical worship, hence an action of the community. Holy Scripture is an operation of our salvation within the whole of the liturgy. As the presiding choir member says before the reading of the Gospel in Matins: "May the reading of the Gospel serve for our salvation and protection."

There is still much to be done in this field. In particular we need a new mentality. For a good number of years Catholics have been urged to read the Bible. The meager result has been that a small number of Catholics, mostly priests and religious, privately read the Scriptures. Even in the liturgical movement emphasis on Bible reading dates only from recent years. Particular credit for this emphasis must be given to Pius Parsch of Klosterneuburg and his Bible movement and also to the third national congress of the French "Center of Liturgical Pastoral Care" (July 25-28, 1958), which was devoted to the Bible and the liturgy.

Nevertheless, there presently exists a general interest in Holy Scripture as an integral part of worship. While many efforts have been made in the right direction, there is still much room for initiatives. Also, from the practical standpoint, it is only by way of the liturgy that the faithful will come to a mature appreciation of the Scriptures. Consequently it is regrettable that some would like, as they say to "celebrate the liturgy in a language and in symbols that are immediate-understood and are like those that are used by people to-day." This sounds very attractive and is praiseworthy insofar as a modern and intelligible translation of Scripture is very much desired. But, on the other hand, the Bible continues to speak its own language and it has its own imagery and particular modes of expression. If we were to celebrate the liturgy in the language of the "common man," this would mean, beside other drawbacks, that the Bible would have to practically disappear from the liturgy. And this is not only undesirable but absolutely impossible because the liturgy would thereby lose its character of Christian worship.

This is why we must take up the opposite approach: the faithful must become familiar with Sacred Scripture. There are various ways to attain that end. In the first place Holy Scripture must be heard frequently in the liturgy, "heard" and not merely followed in a missal. It is not a major inconvenience if presently the vernacular translation of the popular missals does not coincide with the vernacular in the altar missal or lectionary used by the priest. Sermons or homilies have to be strongly based upon Sacred Scripture. The younger generation and possibly even older people will simply have to be made familiar with the Bible by way of instruction. Familiarity with the Bible must not remain the privilege and characteristic of our Protestant brethren.

At present, and particularly on account of the introduction of the vernacular in the celebration of Mass, more attention is given to the question of scriptural reading during liturgical celebrations. In this connection it is desired that the liturgy contain a richer scriptural content; there could be a cycle of several years so that a greater number and variety of Scripture pericopes are read in the liturgical services. In line with this the *Constitution of the Liturgy* states that "in sacred celebrations there is to be more reading from holy Scripture and it is to be more varied and suitable . . . . The sermon, moreover, should draw its content mainly from the scriptural and liturgical sources and its character should be that of a proclamation of God's wonderful works in the history of salvation."[27]

Furthermore, it is also desirable to restore the ancient custom of having two readings, one from the Old and one from the New Testament, before the reading of the Gospel. This would not only make people better acquainted with the Old Testament, but they would appreciate again the fact that the Old Testament is a part of God's total salvific activity for men, of which the New Testament is the completion. In many countries Scripture has been given a larger role in the new liturgy of marriage and in that of the anointing of the sick.

---

[27]Ch. I, art. 35.

Bible Vigils. Of great practical importance are the "Bible vigils" that are gaining in popularity. In some places that sort of evening devotion has proven more attractive that the traditional Benedictions. Of course, we cannot expect a huge turnout for those Bible vigils; but, for those who attend, they will certainly have a great religious and liturgcial value. Though we may not call them liturgical services in the strict juridical sense, they are worship in the more general sense of the term. The *Constitution on the Liturgy* says that "Bible services should be encouraged, especially on the vigils of the more solemn feasts, on some weekdays in Advent and Lent, and on Sundays and feast days. They are particularly to be commended in places where no priest is available; when this is so, a deacon or some other person authorized by the bishop should preside over the celebration."[28]

In a certain way we can be glad that they are not strictly liturgical, for on that account we have much more freedom in the establishment and organization of these biblical devotions. There is no need here to obtain permission from Rome; the bishop's permission suffices and he can allow much freedom. For a number of years now there have been Advent exercises, Lenten exercises, and here and there Bible vigils. It is certainly desirable that in parishes and especially in religious communities, where the possibilities might be greater, there be an increasing use of such exercises. The introduction of such Bible vigils, for instance, during Lent would make the faithful better appreciate the Church's desire to recall the history of God's total salvific activity for sinful mankind which culminates in the passion, death and resurrection of His Son. There is thus a broadened scope which in former Lenten sermons seemed to be riveted almost exclusively on the Passion of Christ. Both the Old and the New Testament

---

[28]*Ibid.*

reveal how full of love and mercy is God's work for and with man.

Singing of Psalms. In recent years particular attention has been given to the singing of the psalms. The modern liturgical movement has encouraged a more widespread use of the psalter; a readily understandable development in view of what has been said above. Scriptural reading and the singing of psalms are inseparable. When we examine the liturgy of the Eucharistic celebration, we see that it is full of psalms. Holy Mass begins with an entrance psalm of which, unfortunately, only one antiphon and a single verse have been preserved; most people do not even know that a psalm is sung at that time. The same is true of the offertory and the Communion psalms. Also, between the reading of the epistle and the gospel, some psalm verses are sung in the gradual, the alleluia and especially the tract. This psalm-song between the two readings became very ornamental and rich in melodic accompaniment in the course of centuries. But the heart of the matter lies in the psalm-song and not in its musical ornament; hence a more simple way of singing it is perfectly in order and even the simple chanting of those verses by the assembly in the vernacular is most appropriate when it is authorized.

Before the publication of the *Constitution on the Liturgy,* psalms were already being sung in the "community Mass" at all or some of the following parts: at the entrance of the priest, between the two readings of Scripture, at the offertory and the Communion and often also at the end of the service. During the last years there have appeared many compositions for psalms in the vernacular. Of course, they are not all of equal value and musicians have expressed their oppositions to some of them, sometimes, perhaps, through personal prejudice, but not infrequently for objectively valid reasons. But we may hope and trust that other compositions will be made so that eventually we can choose a good "repertory" of psalms in the vernacular.

The honor of being the first to spread the singing of psalms widely among the people belongs undoubtedly to the French Jesuit Joseph Gelineau. His psalms[29] are sung not only in France but they are used, with proper adaptations to the particular vernacular, in Holland, Germany and America. They seem to have a fine musical quality; in fact, people like to sing them and find no particular difficulty in their use. Another composer of psalms is the Spiritan Lucien Deiss. His psalms are very beautiful but more difficult to use in community singing.[30]

Now that the introit, gradual, offertory and communion psalms are in the vernacular, there is a great demand for compositions that will permit the proper singing of those psalm verses by the people. Every language has its own characteristics; hence it is not possible to take a Gelineau or a Deiss melody and apply it to English words. Moreover, some translations, like those of the Confraternity, are not written to be sung. Texts will have to be made that combine fidelity to the meaning of the original words with rhythmical well-balanced phrases for which a proper melody can then be composed. Much can be learned in this respect from the Anglicans and Episcopalians who have sung the psalms in English for many years and have attained great refinement in that singing.

---

[29]Published by Editions de Cerf, Paris; gramophone records by Studio Monastère, Paris. *The Psalms,* Paulist Press, 1965, are arranged for singing to Gelineau's psalmody. For the role of music in the liturgy see Gelineau's article, "The Role of Sacred Music," *Concilium,* vol. 2 (1965), pp. 59-65; Gelineau, *Voices and Instruments in Christian Worship,* Liturgical Press 1964; the proceedings of the liturgical conference of Fribourg, 1964, *Le Chant liturgique après Vatican II,* Fleurus, Paris, 1965.

[30]Published in four parts "Psaume et Githare"; records by Studio Monastère.

Holy Scripture, in the musical field, receives attention not only in the singing of psalms and in modern psalm-compositions, but we can now listen to it also in contemporary "chansons," like those of Père Aimé Duval, S.J., Père Coconac, O.P., and Marie-Claire Pichaud.

PRESENT-DAY TENDENCIES OF THE LITURGICAL MOVEMENT

The liturgical movement, which already had a long and excellent record, underwent a strong development after World War II. The two principal and interconnected characteristics of this evolution appear to be the following:

A Pastoral Character. The liturgical movement has become predominantly pastoral. Its first phase during the nineteenth century was strongly monastic in character. The reason for this was, not only the origin of that movement in the work of Dom Guéranger and his followers, but also the urge to arrive at a perfect execution of the Roman liturgy which was thought to be immutable. These two factors made it practically impossible for the liturgical movement to penetrate into the parishes.

The liturgical movement in the proper sense, which started at the beginning of the twentieth century, was certainly animated by a pastoral intention. True, Benedictine monks still exercised great influence at that time; but some of them, for example, Dom Lambert Beauduin, were very much pastorally minded. However, parochial priests desiring to introduce changes in their parishes in accordance with the new liturgical mentality were sometimes considered "nuts" by their clerical confreres, for conservatism is powerful even in "young" countries like the United States. That the liturgical movement was less pastoral during the first decades of its existence than now was due to the enduring influence of the direction given it by Dom Guéranger. But it was equally due to the lack of understanding and the opposition of the majority of the clergy who spoke bluntly of "liturgitis," labeled priests and laymen interested in the new liturgical tendencies "litnics" and prevented the movement from entering into their parishes. Nevertheless, the zeal and perseverance of the pioneers in the liturgical movement, activities such as liturgical confrences and liturgical weeks, and publications like *Worship* forced, as it were, a breakthrough toward pastoral care. Today, especially following the impetus of the "pastoral" Pope John XXIII, the work of Vatican Council II and the prominence given to the "pastoral" *Constitution on the Liturgy,* a growing number of priests have come to recognize the pastoral value of the liturgical movement.

Adaptation of the Liturgy. A second characteristic of the liturgical movement after World War II was the desire for an adaptation of the liturgy; this was corroborated by Pope John's *aggiornamento.* The origin of this tendency lies in a greater knowledge of history and in the present pastoral character of the movement. Further, there was a growing realization that the liturgy is so essential for the life of the Church that a dead, formalistic liturgy which is no longer meaningful is disastrous. That is why the liturgical movement passed through a period of *"Sturm und Drang,"* of feverish search for a way out from a blind alley. Everybody wanted to make a contribution to the discussion. This was a good sign, for it showed that the liturgical question was of vital interest for the entire Church community. Leaving everything to the "experts" would be very dangerous, if not disastrous, for the liturgical renewal.

This general interest runs parallel with a development in the whole of theology: professional theologians are absolutely necessary but theology is something that concerns the whole community. Expert liturgists are indispensable, but the liturgical movement remains a dynamic *movement* precisely by the lively interest and sometimes impetuous proposals by the whole community of the faithful. The great decision of Vatican Council II expressed in the *Constitution on the Liturgy* has crowned the liturgical movement with a formal success. Now is the time of application and adaptation. And on this level that document, and the decrees of national groups of bishops, will remain ineffective if the people do not realize the importance of becoming fully engaged in the liturgical renewal. The people need much instruction, a thorough education, so that they may learn to worship as a community in spirit and in truth. The liturgical reform, however, needs fresh ideas and proposals. Most of them will have to come from below, from the non-experts who are vitally interested in their Church. Occasionally such proposals and ideas will be immature or even preposterous. That does not matter much as long as the stream of ideas helps to keep the renewal in touch with the real life of the Church.

A Living Liturgy. Sometimes the question is heard: Has the liturgical movement reached a deadlock? But the preliminary question to be answered is what exactly do those words mean. Precisely because the present liturgical movement is strongly pastoral and many lay people are now interested in it, there are a number of things which were formerly considered essential to the liturgy and which have now been discarded. Many no longer look on Latin as *the* liturgical language to be preserved at any cost; nor do we still maintain that the existing liturgy should remain unchanged. For pastoral reasons there is a search for a liturgy that will be really alive in the ecclesial community. In this the dominant factor is the ecclesial community itself. It is not principally for psychological reasons that we look for an adapted liturgy, but we realize that the liturgy of the word and the sacrament must occupy the center of our ecclesial life.

This is not possible with the liturgy we had until recently. In a common effort of the whole Church community—priests, religious and laypeople—experts and the hierarchical authority are looking for a liturgy that once more will be the highest concentration of pastoral care and Christian life.

Consequently, it is easily understandable why cries arose for the introduction of the *vernacular* into the liturgy. However, it would be foolish to expect that the recent introduction of the language of the people into the liturgy will solve all problems and, in particular, that it will fill the now empty churches of many parishes, for instance, in France and South America. We have merely to visit some non-Catholic churches, for example in England, where the vernacular has been in use for centuries and where there is an almost perfect liturgical singing of English psalms and hymns, to realize that more than the vernacular is needed to bring people back to the Church.

Yet, on the other hand, when the celebrant, be he the bishop or a priest, comes in direct contact with the Christian assembly or when they proclaim God's word in the reading of Holy Scripture, a living liturgical celebration evidently demands that the language used be one that the people understand. The vernacular thus used should retain its natural characteristics and should not be a mere transliteration of ancient languages. At the same time, however, there should be a difference between the language used in the liturgy and ordinary colloquial language.

For the same reason there is also a demand for greater *simplicity* and intelligibility in liturgical celebrations. Until recently, our liturgy often impressed people as an inextricable multiplicity of successive prayers and actions. Too much historical knowledge, hence also too much instruction, was needed to make people understand symbolic actions that seemed meaningless. Of course, history has its rights and initiation in Christian worship will remain a necessity, but greater clarity and simplicity are certainly more desirable. Fortunately, much is being done in this direction in the new liturgies that are now being introduced, as directed by the *Constitution on the Liturgy.* Simplicity in no way excludes good style and aesthetic care. On the contrary, cult and culture are closely related. In cult or worship the whole man comes into action and, indeed, man at his best. All human characteristics and qualities must be permitted to play a role. It would be wrong to strive for a non-cultural liturgy.

However, cultural elements, especially those that belong to earlier periods, must not be allowed to remain predominant and overshadowing. Song and music must play an important role in the liturgy. Although "the musical tradition of the universal Church is a treasure of inestimable value," the liturgy must be a living liturgy of the people of God, hence the culture of a particular time and place has a definite function in worship. As the *Constitution on the Liturgy* also says: "In certain parts of the world . . . there are peoples who have their own musical traditions, and these play a great part in their religious and social life. For this reason due importance is to be attached to their music, and a suitable place is to be given to it, not only in forming their attitude toward religion, but also in adapting worship to their native genius."[31]

Precisely because we now have a deeper insight into the nature of the liturgy as the worship of the living Church and, consequently, see the necessity of freeing ourselves from an antiquated and too rigid framework, it can be said that in some sense we have reached an impasse. We are not too sure about the best way of making a good adaptation of the liturgy.

---

[31]Ch. VI, art, 119.

The liturgy, after all, is a delicate matter. We will not solve our problems by wrecking the whole structure with a bulldozer and then raising an entirely new edifice on the ruins. One thing we must avoid is liturgical iconoclasm. We need, on the contrary, a prudently and carefully planned reconstruction that preserves the good parts of the liturgical structure while making the proper changes and additions. This, of course, requires the help of experts. We may also feel that, even though generous concessions have been made by the *Constitution on the Liturgy*, a thorough renewal of the liturgy can still be hampered by diocesan or regional rules, for instance, regarding the use of the vernacular.

While it is true that too much liberty to introduce a great variety of local practices could lead to chaos, on the other hand, a certain *pluralism* with respect to the form of the liturgy seems greatly desirable if we wish the people to participate readily and with more understanding in the rites. "Pluriformity" especially in "mission lands" is foreseen by the *Constitution on the Liturgy*, and it is expected that such variety will find expression in the young Churches of Africa and Asia. But it will be useful to take into account the needs of various groups of faithful in the same region and to make provisions even for special situations in one and the same locality.

As we attain deeper insight into the ecclesial character of the liturgy, we realize more than ever that the liturgy is not something that may be left to the whims and arbitrary decisions of individuals; on the contrary, it must be governed by the final word emanating from the Church's authorities. However, before making its decisions, the hierarchy should listen attentively to what the living ecclesial community has to say.

Liturgical Experiments. What role does experiment play in all this? At the present stage of the liturgical movement there is a need for experimentation and, in virtue of the *Constitution on the Liturgy*, experiment is particularily necessary during the present period of change. That is why the question has often been heard, How far may we go? While this generally means "How far are we permitted to go within the law?", the question concerning experiments must not be approached only from the juridical standpoint. We should also add the liturgical question: Is this experiment justified liturgically?, that is, Does it agree with a sound concept of worship? Of course, it is always necessary to keep the juridical question in mind also.

Worship possesses a potentiality for development, hence it leaves the way open for experiments. The whole liturgy grew by means of experiments at a time when the bishops had great freedom of action in liturgical matters. This was the case with the Mass and the other sacraments. However, from the beginning there was—to speak only of the Eucharist —one inviolable datum, viz., Christ's mandate of the Last Supper. But we note that very soon and in spite of a great measure of freedom, some particular and *per se* not indispensable structures were considered inviolable. This is particularly true with respect to the liturgical structure of the Eucharistic celebration. Thus, from early times, there consistently took place: an opening ceremony which was concluded by the official prayer (oration) of the bishop or priest; after this followed readings from Sacred Scripture; then came the celebration of the Eucharist which began with a preparation, the offertory, which had a variety of structures; next the great Eucharistic prayer of thanksgiving, which was followed by the rite of Communion and a short final ceremony. This we find in all the rites of East and West.

Certain special parts were also present everywhere: the greeting of the assembly by the celebrant, the dialogue at the preface, the triple "Holy," the Our Father, litany prayers and the singing of psalms. Within this practically inviolable framework there remained possibilities for a good number of

273

variations and nuances, as is evident when we recall the formation of diverse liturgies. Hence those possibilities still remain in principle, for instance, if it is desired to have Chinese or African liturgies. But the fundamental frame will be preserved, and this must always be kept in mind with respect to liturgical experimentation. (We abstract here from the juridical question.)

We will also be obliged to take into account the social character of public worship, the fact that it is not primarily instituted for individual devotions and actions. Here and there, there have been "wild" experiments which showed a want of proper sensitivity to "style." The general style of worship cannot be broken up with impunity. This is not merely an aesthetical matter but it affects the whole of worship; without style it becomes a disorganized jumble and is weakened in its spiritual efficaciousness. We must therefore, always keep those factors in mind. Hence, while experimentation is possible and in many respects desirable, it must be done in an expert way, while keeping especially in mind the true nature of the liturgy.

DEVOTIONS

A ticklish question is that of devotions. They have a bad name especially among "liturgists." The very term has acquired a particular emotional value that no longer corresponds to its true meaning. By "devotions" we now understand prayers and actions which, although they arise from the central religious experience, lie more or less at the periphery of Christian life, either as one's personal experience or in connection with a group. Such are, for example, the adoration of the Blessed Sacrament in the tabernacle, the many devotions in honor of Our Lady, praying to a particular saint, lighting a symbolic candle or votive light, the veneration and respectful kissing of relics of saints, and pilgrimages to places where God, directly or through His mother or some other saint, manifested Himself to man in a particular way.

The difficulty with these devotions lies in their tendency to "absolutize" themselves, that is, they tend to divorce themselves from their starting point and take on so much significance that they become for many people the core of their religious life. Not infrequently there are deformations in particular devotions that bring them close to superstition.

This situation still exists in many countries, but in other sections of the Church, notably in Western Europe, there is a strong reaction against these. Reactions usually go too far, and this is true also in this case. It is certainly a good thing that abuses be done away with and that there be a growing opposition to the harmful propagation of devotions that are praised far beyond their spiritual value. On the other hand, however, we must admit that certain religious experiences arising from the fundamental truths of Christianity can acquire a form of their own adapted to time, place and persons. Although devotions should be very flexible, they have, unfortunately, a tendency to outlive their usefulness.

The liturgy itself provides a foundation for the adoration of the Blessed Sacrament, the most beautiful of all devotions, and also for the veneration of the Mother of God and other saints. The idea of pilgrimage is as old as Christianity and is present already in the Old Testament: man is always on the way. However, a fundamental purification and reorientation of devotions is necessary. We must also take account of the fact that some devotions present a wrong image of the Church to non-Catholics and therefore are not worth preserving. Nevertheless, some of these more or less free forms of religious life continue to have a function in the Church. That is why the *Constitution of the Liturgy* insists that "popular devotions of the Christian people are to be highly commended, provided they accord with the laws and norms of the

275

Church, above all when they are ordered by the Apostolic See. Devotions proper to individual Churches also have a special dignity if they are undertaken by mandate of the bishops according to customs or books lawfully approved. But these devotions should be drawn up so that they harmonize with the liturgical seasons, accord with the sacred liturgy, are in some fashion derived from it, and lead the people to it, since, in fact, the liturgy by its very nature far surpasses any of them."[32]

RELIGIOUSNESS AND BEING A "PRACTICING" CHRISTIAN

At the end of our considerations of the changes that are taking place in Christian life, the question naturally arises concerning the relationship between religiousness and being a "practicing" Catholic in the sense of being a churchgoer, especially since there are actual problems connected with this matter.

Both in novels and in religous periodicals, it has become a popular pastime to denounce faithful churchgoers who in their daily life are anything but models of true Christianity. It is now perhaps trite to point to the modern pharisee who never fails to attend church but at home and at his work is mean, unjust, unchristian as a worker or employer. Yet the fact that this theme constantly recurs shows that there is a problem. On the other hand, the absence of any qualification and the fierceness with which those "pharisees" are judged and condemned seem to indicate that the problem is still far from solved. People whom we have good reason to believe are faithful churchgoers sometimes criticize those "pharisees" in such a vituperative way that did we not know better, we

---

[32]Ch. I, art. 13. See also Joseph A. Jungmann, "Liturgy, Devotions, and Bishop," *Concilium*, vol. 2 (1965), pp. 51-58.

would suspect that they themselves never set foot in the church.

The famous Abbé Pierre said in one of his sermons: "When we stand before God's tribunal and loudly protest: 'But I never missed Mass on Sunday nor did I fail to be present at any religious function . . .,' the Lord will answer: 'What! you dare to tell Me, as an excuse that you have been a 'practicing' Catholic? If that is so, then depart from Me, twice cursed, for you practiced these things without love and without hunger or thirst for justice; you have caused Me to be cursed by your brethren . . . . All my commandments, my sacraments, the Mass, prayer, all this I have given you only for one purpose: in order that you might love. And when all this has not made you love more, I don't want to hear any more about your prayers; all this I loathe.' God vomits forth all your Masses and your virtues . . . ."[33]

We intuitively feel that it is necessary to go to church but, at the same time, that more than that is required which in some way or other is not done. We began by mentioning what is most obvious, "going to church." But this is still vague, very general, even if we take it to include a number of things which have a direct connection with membership in the Church and especially with public worship. Protestants speak of a more or less "active" or "living" member in contrast with one who has membership merely because he was baptized. Catholics mean by "practicing" to be present at least on Sundays at the celebration of the Eucharist, to receive Communion at least once a year around Easter time and, if necessary, to go to confession before it. To this one could add a lesser or greater number of other "church practices."

The heart of the problem lies in our increasing realization of the necessity that those "church practices" have an inner

---

[33]Quoted in *Action catholica,* April, 1956, p. 158.

foundation and that their influence permeate the believer's daily life. This, not infrequently, even in Catholic circles, leads to doubts about the value of "practicing." This is a problem which we are not permitted to put aside. Are those doubts in conflict with the changes we have recorded regarding word and sacrament and a life inspired by them? Does this problem also exist among non-Catholics? Why? Was this so formerly? What conclusions must we draw for our own time?

Distinction Between Religiousness and Active Church Membership. According to the *Yearbook of American Churches* for 1964, published by the National Council of Churches of Christ in the U.S.A., the religious bodies reporting claimed a total membership of 117,946,002, of whom around 43 million were Catholics; the reports from 223 bodies showed a total Sunday or Sabbath school enrollment of around 44 million. We can safely say that the remaining seventy million Americans who do not claim any Church affiliation are not "practicing" Catholics or "active" Christians, although they sometimes come to services, for instance, at Christmas, Palm Sunday or Easter. But can we call all those people "irreligious"? Some, including many Catholics, are inclined to identify irreligiousness and lack of church affiliation. It is true that in this respect we should not be too optimistic. Yet facts seem to indicate, although this is hard to determine exactly, that among people without church affiliation there are, in addition to true unbelievers, many who are indifferent in religious matters but not complete unbelievers. But it is then a faith that is non-living; it does not affect their lives; it is not a believing commitment but merely a willingness to admit that "I guess that religion is right."

There is another phenomenon which, in this respect, is very important: we find that a rather good percentage of those who do not belong to any church, or practically never attend services, explicitly or implicitly protest against what they call "systematic, empty, formalistic, pharisaic religiousness." This "protest" in one way or another is also found in many people who are indifferent. Among those who officially belong to no church, there are certainly people who pray, even call themselves explicitly religious, and yet never enter a church. This phenomenon is even more predominant among people who still belong officially to a church communion but have lost all real connection with it.

In any case, we find a theoretical and factual discrepancy between religiousness and attending church. But there is, as is to be expected, a great difference between Catholics and Protestants in this matter:

Regarding non-Catholic Christians, since the Church as manifesting herself visibly is of less significance in many Protestant circles than in Catholic thought, the understanding of the difference between religiousness and "practicing" expresses itself more sharply and spontaneously among Protestants. This is true of practically all Protestant communions. The large Protestant groups, however, such as Lutherans and Calvinists, do attach value to active membership in the Church as expressed in church activities and attendance of services. But the fact that the proliferation of Protestant sects, taking the term in its widest sense, has assumed such enormous proportions gives one cause for thought. This phenomenon, no doubt, has a variety of causes; but one of them is a dissatisfaction with, if not a protest against, official ecclesiasticism, that is, against the organized church. Here we may mention the Jehovah's Witnesses (founded at Allegheny, Pa., in 1872 by Charles Taze Russell, 1852-1916), who manifest a strong adventist character and claim that the kingdom of the millenium has already begun. They are very zealous and stongly opposed to any church whether Protestant or Catholic. In 1963 there were around 989,000 Witnesses in over 22,000 congregations in eighty-one countries. Each witness is considered an ordained minister charged with the duty of spreading the message of Jehovah. There are, in addition, other sects or groups that do not want to be known as churches and who have a strong biblical and adventist orientation, for instance, the Seventh-Day Adventists. Remarkable has been the success of Billy Graham who each year reaches an average of two and a half million people. He desires to proclaim the faith in a very simple way and thereby lead people to an immediate commitment to God. His audience is composed primarily of non-practicing Christians and people who do not belong to any church, although he himself maintains good relations with Protestant churches and is ready to entrust his followers to the pastoral care of the various communions. One thing is certain: there are many people who are indifferent, dislike and even hate churches or, in some cases, are even opposed to Christianity, and yet who want to be religious. In their religiousness they do not simply avoid the churches but blame them because they feel the churches betray man's religiousness.

Among Catholics the problem is quite different. So long as a Catholic wants to be recognized as such, he also "practices" in the sense that he in some way takes part in church activities. particularly public worship. And yet there are phenomena among Catholics that are similar to those we have noted among Protestants. There certainly exist definite groups in the Church that are dissatisfied with official ecclesial life. The displeasure finds expression in a variety of ways.

Father I. Rosier deals with that problem in his book *I Sought the Absence of God*.[34] He shows that a certain measure

---

[34]*Ik zocht Gods afwezigheid*, The Hague, 2 vols., 1956 f.

of religiousness, that wants to call itself Catholic, can go hand in hand with a profound dislike for the Church. But this often involves extreme cases in which several question marks can be put after the so-called "Catholicity" of such people. In less extreme cases we find a similar dislike in people who are baptized and want their children to be likewise baptized and even married in church but who, for the rest of their lives, do not want to participate in any ecclesial life. This attitude can have many causes, but one of them is an explicit or implicit protest against what they call the formalism, pharisaism or even hypocrisy of institutionalized church life.

That dislike and protest are also found in some degree in people who, as they say, "were regular churchgoers" but gradually stayed away "because with all that running to church we are not getting any better." There exists among Catholics a doubt, of a less theoretical and more a practical nature, concerning the value of being a "practicing" (church-going) Catholic. For this reason one may question the value of dividing parishioners into such classes as "fulfilling Easter duty," "coming to Church on Sundays," and "communicants."

This dislike of official "practice" also finds expression in a totally different way in our Catholic milieu, especially among people who feel that their pious aspirations are not fulfilled by the Church's official services. Although they do not become practically indifferent toward the Church, they seek contact with God more or less outside the ordinary ways. This trait, too, has a variety of causes; but it is our opinion that one of them is that such persons are dissatisfied with what they actually find in Church life. This dissatisfaction may seek relief in certain varieties of the devotion to Our Lady, in a kind of fanaticism with respect to certain apparitions, particularly when the Church hesitates or refuses to consider them authentic. Exorbitant and unfounded faith in private revelations belongs also to these phenomena.

281

In summation, we must say that in both Catholic and non-Catholic circles—though the phenomena are differently structured—there is a definite tendency to a religiousness that partly, or even wholly, draws away from official and actual "practices." Once again we confront here a complex phenomenon; we believe, nevertheless, that this is a matter demanding serious attention. We can also look on these sects and sectarian phenomena as "unpaid bills" of the Church. That tendency is a bad sign. Why do people who seek an outlet for their sometimes impetuous religousness turn away from the churches and, in particular, find difficulties regarding that point within the Catholic Church? No doubt the particular people involved are part of the reason, but we must ask ourselves if the Church herself is not partially responsible for this situation.

Being a "Practicing" Catholic in the Past. There is no period in her history during which the leaders of the Church did not attach some importance to "practicing," in the sense we have explained. The people also have always kept alive the idea that taking part in worship and listening to the proclamation of the Gospel are characteristic features of Christian life. But history also reveals aberrations and laxity. St. Augustine complained that his Christians on some Sundays and holidays preferred to go to the theatre—which, moreover, was rather immoral in those days—instead of participating in the celebration of the Eucharist with the bishop. Although at that time there was as yet no formal precept to attend Mass on Sundays, such participation was, nevertheless, considered a sign that one was a Christian, a necessary expression of being a Christian.

When the new peoples of Europe gradually became members of the Church, the problem of poor attendance at services grew increasingly greater. Consequently, a formal precept was promulgated in the thirteenth century for the whole Western Church ordering assistance at Mass on Sundays, Communion at Easter time and, if necessary, preliminary confession. This precept was not a bolt from the blue. Before that time it was certainly not thought that participation in the basic Church celebrations was unimportant or that one had perfect freedom to assist or not to assist. The Church authorities had always insisted that participation in such activities was necessary and a moral obligation, but they finally saw themselves forced to introduce a formal obligation because there was such poor response.

It was certainly not an individualistic moral basis that inspired the moral pressure and, later, the juridical precept of the Church to take part in certain liturgical activities. That pressure and precept were not originally motivated by the thought that "this would be good for the people," in other words, by concern for their individual salvation. On the contrary, it was considered self-evident that the members of the eccesial community should all take part on certain days in community activities that would give honor to God.

In that period when the formal precept was promulgated, there existed sectarian currents in the Church which, no doubt, sprang from a certain religious élan. They came into conflict with the official Church which was passing through difficult times and had to cope with much spiritual decadence. As is well known, it is due especially to the Franciscan and Dominican orders, each working in its particular way, that that religious élan was finally met and saved for the Church, to the extent that this was still possible. In any case, those religious orders were successful in their appeal to the dormant religious consciousness of the masses and brought about a rich development of spiritual life.

Later in the Middle Ages no special complaints had to be made regarding a lack of participation in liturgical celebrations. In fact, just before the Reformation participation was even particularly good, although its value was very relative. People faithfully went to church on Sunday, but the reception of the sacrament, except once a year, was very infrequent. "Practicing" in the late Middle Ages, the whole piety of the people at that time, showed clear aberrations. The preachers had so strongly insisted on the importance of attending services that the churches, just before the Reformation, were usually crowded. However, the ordinary faithful were firmly convinced that their mere presence would be productive of most wonderful spiritual, corporal and material fruits. In the light of those aberrations in church practice, in which there was so much stress on externals, we can understand the cry of the Reformers for worshipping the Lord "in spirit and in truth," although we must be on guard against looking upon the Reformation as nothing more than a reaction.

The entire practice of the late Middle Ages proved to be diseased and totally incapable of withstanding the stormy religious élan of the Reformation. The Counter Reformation undoubtedly brought about a restoration, a religious revival which produced great spiritual benefits. But, in general, it did not result in a reception of the sacraments. The Reformers also desired such a participation at the beginning and this is certainly true of the Lutherans, but they, too, were unsuccessful in their efforts to make people participate more frequently in the Lord's Supper. Nor did the Counter Reformation counteract the individualism of the late Middle Ages. The ancient and in fact original idea of ecclesial services as acts of the community had been lost for a long time, and the Counter Reformation did not manage to restore it. No doubt medieval society had certain collectivist traits that needed correction; nevertheless, the medieval era in its period of bloom cannot be called collectivistic. In the later Middle Ages there were praiseworthy efforts to let the person attain his rights. These efforts certainly proved fruitful, but both that time and the era that followed were in reality more individualistic than personalistic, because too little attention was paid to the community.

There was increasing evidence, moreover, of a phenomenon which began to manifest itself already in the late Middle Ages, namely the separation of liturgy and piety. The liturgy had become incomprehensible to the ordinary faithful; hence, piety sought other outlets that often lay at the fringe of ecclesial life. The Counter Reformation was less than unsuccessful in restoring the unity of liturgy and piety; that split remained and, in a certain sense, became even greater. For, the Counter Reformation had a certain antithesis to the formalization of the late Middle Ages and desired to serve the Lord "in spirit and in truth" in a Catholic way. It is noticeable that the books dealing with "the spiritual life" showed a strong spiritualistic one-sidedness and stood entirely outside the liturgy. This phenomenon also had its roots in the late Middle Ages themselves. There thus arose a dangerous tension between religiousness and piety, on the one hand, and church attendance, on the other. In the eyes of the many people the official church functions came to stand outside real religiousness and piety.

In the eighteenth century a new danger was added by the dissemination of the mentality of the Enlightenment. For the official liturgical actions came to be seen exclusively from the standpoint of a one-sided moralistic mentality.

In the nineteenth century there was at first an impetuous reaction that brought about a totally different concept of norms. We notice, however, that the earlier formalism of participation in church functions continued to exist while life and conduct became ever farther removed from the liturgy. Thus the tension between "practicing" and daily life, and also between religiousness and "practicing," continued to grow.

When we survey that whole situation we must be on guard against assuming too pessimistic a view. Throughout all ages there has always existed an authentic Christian piety and religiousness, and the Church has always been the people of God and the sign of God in this world. Nevertheless, what we have sketched is correct in its broad lines; and, when we keep the background in mind, we are better able to understand the actual problem of religiousness and "practicing."

Our Task in the Present Situation. We in our time have an urgent task to fulfill in that matter. Things are evidently developing more rapidly and more thoroughly now than formerly; hence our time is also a critical one for man's religious life and for the Church. This is one reason for giving special attention to the problem of religiousness and being a "practicing" Catholic. On the other hand, a time like ours also offers particular opportunities. We who at this moment are the Church have a definite task to fulfill with respect to that problem. That is why the question forces itself more insistently upon us: What, properly speaking, is Christian religiousness? What is being a "practicing" Catholic?

At the beginning of these considerations we gave a general description of "practicing," explaining that it means going regularly to church and receiving the sacraments regularly, to which one can add observing the holidays and the laws of fast and abstinence. And this, in fact, is what people mean when they speak of being a practicing Catholic. But we must ask ourselves whether that idea is correct. For, if we wanted to equate this "practice" with "practicing one's religion," with "practicing one's faith," doubts might arise.

True, for some people, all these expressions mean the same thing. but there are also others for whom these expressions evoke something different. For example, "to practice one's faith" might mean to practice brotherly love in

286

Christ, to be just, prudent, chaste. Those "practices" are even indispensable when we wish to call a man "religious," or to say that he is a good living member of the Church, as the mystical body of Christ. But, reversely, must we say that whether or not someone is a "practicing" Catholic, in the ordinary sense of the word, is not so very important or even unimportant? It is readily admitted that one should try to establish harmony in this matter. According to Catholic thinking, there can be no "religiousness" that does not include also practicing one's religion by attending church. This attendance, understood again in the ordinary sense of participating in the celebration of the Eucharist and in the other sacraments and hearing the word of God, is both the starting point and the apex of religious life in the full and widest sense of that word. Here we cannot do better than recall the words of Father E. Schillebeeckx. Speaking about the approach to be used with people who have lost all contact with faith, religion and the Church, he points out that Christianity's power to enlist people lies in the tangible presence of grace, that is, in the concrete way we treat men, thus translating the way we treat God. This is not a question of tactics or a new method of apologetics, but of authentic, non-fictitious love of men. Our existence and our deeds *as* Christians in the world must make visible and tangible a life that is redeemed in Christ. "It is precisely in this that the true 'belonging to the Church' of the Catholic layman and of all the faithful consists. By merely going to church and abstaining from meat on Fridays we have not yet placed holiness in the world; thus we obscure the sign which the Church is called to be in this world."[35]

Religiousness, therefore, always means "belonging to the Church" for us, but this term must then be understood in a

---

[35]*Tijdschrift voor geestelijk leven*, Feb. 1959, pp. 108 ff.

broader sense than that which is usually attached to the term "a practicing Catholic." What, then, is the true significance of that "practice," of participating in the sacraments, the liturgy, the proclamation of the word? Schillebeeckx answers: "In the administration of the sacraments and in preaching, that human encounter, as manifesting the encounter with God, merely receives a salient, hierarchical expression, in which the divine gift is present in a concentrated form. The true 'belonging to the Church' that is present in a genuine Christian life and in a Christian dealing with our fellow-men is present in the sacraments, as it were, in a prominent way. But the structure is really the same."[36]

We must therefore reject that fatal one-sidedness which would limit ecclesial life to being a "practicing" Catholic in the above-described narrow sense. It is very true that worship, the celebration of sacrament and word, is the apex of ecclesial life and finds its supreme concentration in the celebration of the Eucharist. Hence religiousness and "belonging to the Church," in the fullest sense, lie on the same level, although this "belonging" and observing church practices, in the narrow sense, do not lie on the same level. But it is not possible to belong to the Church without those highpoints which we prosaically call "church observances" or "being a practicing Catholic."

All this has important consequences. Catholic religiousness must, not only in theory but also in fact, be truly permeated with ecclesial consciousness. This consciousness is a community consciousness but, at the same time, contains the realization that this community is an effective sign of grace for the world. In that ecclesial religiousness, the sacrifice and sacraments and the proclamation of the word should, as points of concentration, play a greater role than they have had up to

---

[36]*Ibid.*

now. Ecclesial practice (sacrament and word) must be orientated much more to total "ecclesiality"; it must be aimed much more at the Church as "sign" of God in the world; and it should *de facto* also more fully possess the character of such a sign. Once that ecclesial practice is less isolated from the Christian's actual life of faith and better integrated in his total "ecclesiality," it will also be easier to liberate the sacrament and the word from the oppressive rigidity in which they have been fettered and imprisoned in the course of the centuries.

The whole of ecclesial life will benefit by that renovation. The Catholic renewal, which was begun very hesitantly and under heavy pressure at the end of the Middle Ages and was only partially realized in the Counter Reformation, will then finally have a greater chance of success. But this renewal will take place in a world that has totally changed in the meantime; and, on that account, the changes that will take place in the Church will be greater than could have been imagined by past generations.

It is necessary to develop somewhat fuller the sketch we have just drawn. The most notable and central point in the changing Christian life and in the changing pastoral care is, as we have already indicated, an increasing and developing ecclesial consciousness, the consciousness that the Church is the people of God of the New Covenant and as such stands in the world "as a sign for all peoples." This ecclesial consciousness is the central point in the new developing pattern of Christian life and pastoral care. This realization that we belong to the Church, that we have been taken up into Christ's community, is the indispensable condition for being able to live a life of personal relation with the Triune God. We are persons in the ecclesial community. A Christian cannot help being of and in the Church; even if he does not will it, he belongs to Christ's community. Of course, he can tear himself away, but a return is always possible, because baptism creates an unbreakable and lasting bond with the Church. There is no single moment in life when we do not belong to the Church. Mother Church carries us at all times and we ourselves carry the Church with us in all circumstances of life. This does not mean that all distinction between "earthly" and "supernatural" realities is thereby wiped out. It merely illuminates the truth that there can be no circumstances in which we do not belong to the Church, to Christ, when we are not members of the People of God, are not a sign in the world. When looked at from this standpoint, our life is always an ecclesial life.

The explanation above shows that that ecclesial consciousness, as the starting point of the spiritual life and pastoral care, stands in sharp contrast with the individualistically orientated mentality of the period that is now coming to a close. However, in spite of its sharpness, it is not a black-and-white contrast. This sort of "color-combination" never occurs in the life of the Church. There exists a continuity in spite of everything, but there is a difference in mentality. Moreover, there is a fluid boundary line between the various eras; periods gradually merge. Nevertheless, one cannot help noticing that, at present, there is an evident change in mentality. This we must consciously foster. We shall have to work consciously in the direction which Schillebeeckx calls "the Church as the visible presence of grace in this world," so that men, in their profound desire for religiousness, will no longer by-pass the Church or even abandon her.

In this growing ecclesial consciousness, a new and different emphasis must be put on sacrament and word in the Christian life and pastoral care: the People of God of the New Covenant which together listens to the proclamation of God's word and knows itself responsible for the whole of mankind in the celebration of the Eucharist and the other sacraments.

In this worship we act in a very special way in and through Christ as the community of Christ, for the glory the Father, by which we attain our salvation and the salvation of all mankind.

United with one another in worship under the guidance of the hierarchy, we represent redeemed humanity in a primary way. We are, then, in the most perfect way the authentic sign, the real and efficacious symbol of redeemed mankind that is welded into unity by Christ and in Him is turned toward the Father. As turned toward mankind, we are more than ever the real and efficacious sign of God in this world; we are indeed never more the Church than in worship. Worship is the highest and most intense realization of ecclesial life.

With this in mind we see clearly how unsuitable the usual narrow sense of the term "to practice" is to designate what we have just now called "worship," which includes proclamation. It sounds too individualistic and too one-sidedly moralistic, although this should not necessarily be so.

In this connection it is necessary to reconsider what value can be attached to terms such as "communicant," "Sunday Catholic," "Easter-duty Catholic," "non-Sunday Catholic," "non-Easter-duty Catholic." Of old attention was directed to acts of worship as a sign of a Christian life and the various degrees of such a life. A "communicant" is an adult believer, that is, one who can participate fully in the official life of the Church; he is not merely baptized but may partake fully in the Eucharist (strictly speaking, confirmation should also be included here). To express that communicants are good Church members, people who earnestly try to live as Catholics, we speak of "Sunday Catholics": they are faithful in attending Mass on Sunday, in contrast with "non-Sunday Catholics." To indicate those who receive Holy Communion at least once a year, we speak of "Easter-duty Catholics," and those who no longer do this we call "non-Easter-duty Catholics." We also attach value to the fact that some of the faithful participate not merely in liturgical celebrations on Sundays and holydays of obligation but freely take part in them also on other days.

These standards can be used in a one-sided and formalistic way both by the clergy and by the faithful themselves. When attention is directed to attendance and presence alone, without regard for the way the liturgy is celebrated and participated in and without regard also to the way that worship affects daily life, we are then using a formalistic yardstick. Those standards, however, are correct in themselves although they can be refined.

"Practicing" as it expresses itself in baptism, confirmation, participation in the Eucharist at least on days of obligation, going to confession regularly, having one's marriage celebrated sacramentally in the church, receiving the sacraments when one is ill and going to die, and the desire to be buried from the church—all these are a good standard for evaluating a Christian, an ecclesial life, provided this "practice" be properly understood in the sense we have described above. In one way or another, the statement is frequently heard: "that man never comes to church but he is, neverthless, an exemplary Christian." This idea rests on a misunderstanding; it is based on a one-sided moralistic view of Christianity. Because of that man's baptism, we cannot say that he is not a Catholic at all or that he stands entirely outside real ecclesial life; nevertheless, an essential element is absent from his being-a-Catholic, from his belonging to the Church. "Going to church"— a deficient term for participation in sacrament and word—is not "a mere expression" of only secondary importance. Christian religiousness is always ecclesial and this "ecclesiality" necessarily tends to its high point through participation in worship.

We would be guilty of gross misunderstanding and irresponsible exaggeration if we call the norm itself formalistic because there exists a formalistic interpretation of it.

Hence that which is most weighty and important in ecclesial life must also dominate it; we must put the accent where it belongs. Liturgical worship will have to take first place, but this worship must be understood as the apex and point of concentration of ecclesial life. As we read in the *Constitution on the Liturgy*: "The liturgy 'through which the work of our redemption is accomplished,' most of all in the divine sacrifice of the Eucharist, is the outstanding means whereby the faithful may express in their lives and manifest to others, the mystery of Christ and the real nature of the true Church."[37]

3. Sanctification in Work and in One's State of Life

GROWING AWARENESS OF THE UNITY OF FAITH AND LIFE

Christian life does not consist of some more or less isolated actions but is a co-existing with one another in God. This co-existence necessarily demands a certain number of actions, of which the liturgical acts of worship are by their very nature the highest; but Christian life is primarily an active *state* encompassing the whole of life. As the catechism used to express it, "We are on earth to serve God and thereby to be happy here and hereafter." Our whole life is a worship. This is the starting point which we find, not only in the above quoted epistle of St. Peter, but also and with particular clarity in St. Paul's letters. Our life is sanctified by Christ, is sanctified interiorly by redemption, in spite of the fact that we can remove that character from our lives through our own

---

[37]Introduction, art. 2.

freely-willed sinfulness or at least obscure it. For God respects the freedom He has given us.

The idea of the holiness of our entire life is an ancient and ineradicable conviction of the Church, and it has, as such, never been absent. But there have always been tensions in the Church with respect to the realization of that total holiness of our life. There were and are tensions that naturally arise from the disorderly situation in which we live on account of sin, whether it be personal sinfulness or the sinfulness embodied in many relationships in the world. This fact prevents an unqualified and unconcerned acceptance of "life in the world." As Christians we always maintain a certain reserve toward the world, although the measure of this reserve may vary according to one's personal attitude as well as circumstances of time and place.

It follows that variations in the attitude toward the world are a permanent phenomenon in the Church.[38] St. Paul already had to inveigh against the faithful of Thessalonica because they "abstained" from all work in expectation of the Lord's second coming. A few centuries later, the monks looked with disapproval at Christian people because they felt that the "ordinary" people no longed had any esteem for prayer. Gregory the Great, the monk who had become pope, reproved the monks in this respect. St. Thomas Aquinas strongly defended the primacy of contemplative life over active life but expressed his own preference for a life mixing contemplation and activity. This goes to show that there were discussions and disagreements in the Church as well as a tendency to swing from one extreme to the other. But it is also evident

---

[38]Cf., e.g., Henri Sanson, *Leben mit Gott in der Welt,* Freiburg i. Br., 1961; Dennis Geaney, *Christians in a Changing World,* Fides, 1960; Arthur Mirgeler, *Mutations of Western Christianity,* Herder and Herder, 1964; Bernard Häring, *Christian Renewal in a Changing World,* Desclee, 3rd impr., 1965.

that there was no desire to give up the sanctity of the "ordinary" life. This is variously, yet clearly, expressed by St. Paul, Gregory and Thomas.

Nevertheless, we find a certain one-sidedness in many spiritual writers. Most of them put particular stress on the necessity of prayer, a thing against which no one has any objection; but they warn, at the same time, against the dangers of activity. Others do indeed emphasize fidelity to the obligations of one's state of life, but they immediately start moralizing and pointing out what we have to give up in order to avoid sin. Positive explanations of the Christian attitude toward work and one's state of life are mostly wanting in such authors. And yet a positive appreciation of work continued to live in the Church; for example, St. Francis of Assisi speaks emphatically about "the brothers to whom God has given the *grace* of being permitted to work." St. Francis de Sales also represents clearly the more positive attitude.

During the last part of the decadence of the Greco-Roman Empire, the fathers of the desert withdrew from the "wicked world." Similarly in the sixteenth, seventeenth and especially the eighteenth century, there was a narrowing of ideas. Catholics lived once more in what was evidently an inimically "evil" world. And in fact there was, for the believing Catholic, a divorce between faith and life, a divorce which was also explicitly propagated by another attitude which proclaimed that religion is a private affair, that in the Church we make acts of faith but elsewhere business is business. Freedom of religion was guaranteed; but this meant freedom of worship, which clearly shows that religion was taken to mean to engage in acts of worship or to be present at them. Notably in the nineteenth century, at the time of the industrial revolution, there also developed a world of work divorced from Christianity. Acts of worship were emphasized as almost the only thing necessary, and this was fostered by an increasing emphasis on the quantity of these acts. Perhaps that emphasis also resulted from the existing practical and even theoretical divorce between faith and life.

At the present moment there exists in the Church a very strong tendency to restore the unity of faith and life. Vatican Council II has attached its seal of approval to this tendency: "This split between the faith which many profess and their daily lives deserves to be counted among the more serious errors of our age."[38a] Life is once more seen as a unity. This goes hand in hand with the conviction that it is not necessary to attach the label "Christian" or "Catholic" to all expressions of life. In no case is it considered necessary that everything should outwardly manifest certain Christian facets. In other words, the restoration of the unity between faith and life goes hand in hand with the recognition of a certain "independence" of the "earthly values," an independence within the one Christian view of life.

The times when everything, outwardly and socially, presented a Christian appearance are no more. But it has been necessary to accustom ourselves to this fact. Something can be Christian or more Christian in character without being called or appearing to be Christian; and, as Christians, we can live according to, and take up into our total life of faith, these same values which others embrace from the standpoint of another view of life.

We have also had to become accustomed to the idea that the homogeneity of "Christendom" has been broken, not for a short time, but in a relatively permanent way; and moreover, besides that divided "Christendom" there exists in this world a vast and steadily increasing majority of non-Christians. There are signs that we now, though in a different way, are developing again toward a unified view of life and do not

----

[38a]*Constitution on the Church in the Modern World*, art. 55.

feel spiritually divided, although we must live in two worlds. It is already bad enough that we behold a cleavage from within because of our sinfulness, which, in many ways, has penetrated into the life of the world.

It would indeed be strange if that development were not accompanied by growing pains. These can be trying and the phenomena themselves cannot possibly be called good, but they are inevitable and have a positive function in the whole of life.

Activism. One of those phenomena has been called "activism," a term repeatedly used by Pius XII in his discourses and writings. It means that an exaggerated value is attached to "doing." The activist says or thinks: "Something must be 'done'! All that talking and all that praying is of no avail if we do not translate them into deeds, into deeds that bring grist to the mill, deeds which make men feel tangibly what Christian charity toward our neighbor really is. God does not expect us to withdraw into solitude to pray, while our fellow men are dying of wretchedness."

This passion for activity is particularly directed to socio-charitable work. There is question here of a typical phenomenon of reaction, in the sense that one can endorse almost everything the activist promotes and, at the same time, precisely not endorse it. Everyone will agree that an enormous task lies before the Church in the socio-charitable field. But when the Church impresses non-Christians in mission countries as a kind of Red Cross institution, we feel that something is not right. In principle, all those "deeds" come forth and are contained in the religious life and the work of the Church. But the phenomenon called "activism" reacts so strongly against an earlier inertia of the Church in many fields in which man happened to be in distress, that the organic connection with the whole of Church life is broken.

It is most difficult to determine concretely in what that activist mentality consists, but we sometimes meet with facts which clearly show that something of the sort does exist.

For instance, when we hear it said that contemplative cloistered life is no longer justified in our time, and when it is even called unsocial because a number of priests and laypeople are thereby withdrawn from the work of the Church, we are indeed in the presence of an "activist" mentality. This is also the case when priests are busy the whole day long with "pastoral work," but fail to see that their prayer and meditation are an essential part of their pastoral task. Sometimes the faithful get the feeling that it is no longer possible to have a quiet conversation with many priests, "for they are always so busy." This "busyness" is not always due to a wrong mentality but may be caused by the present system of pastoral care. We have to admit, nevertheless, that there are many priests who relish all that hustle and bustle and who are profoundly unhappy when they are called to themselves for some time to prayer, meditation and study—things which, after all, provide them with the most necessary "material" for their "active" pursuits.

Sacramental Piety Versus Personal Piety. Another growing pain, one less crude and more fully deliberate, sets up the false dichotomy in which we have to choose between the ancient sacramental piety within the organized framework of the Church and a personal piety that is more adapted to our times. Here we have a reaction both against a legalistic mentality which put too great a stress on observing the precepts, on "doing one's duty," and against an emphasis on quantity with respect to the sacraments.

This is a false dilemma. It is deceiving as long as the problem is looked at as one where: instead of people going in a body to church and there receiving the sacraments because

298

of a precept, from now on let there be a personal, that is, individual, and free service of God, especially in work and in fidelity to the duties of one's state of life. In this way, then, the latter type of piety comes to be considered a higher form of spiritual life. This dilemma is conceived from the standpoint of an old schema, and it somewhat parallels the so-called dilemma of the socio-economic field: *either* socialist *or* liberal, in other words, either collectivist or individualistic. This "either/or" is both insufficient and antiquated. It is not possible to posit the alternative: either personal piety or sacramental-organized piety. For Christian piety is ecclesial piety, is sacramental piety. When we proceed from a sound concept of the Church we do not have to face that dilemma.

The general theological tendency is founded on the realization that the Church is a *community*. We are a community and this governs our whole life. The juridical obligation of community actions, for example, the participation in the celebration of the Eucharist, is secondary in relation to that; this duty and precept arose because there existed not enough community-consciousness. The celebration of the Eucharist is the most important meeting of the faithful. And an ecclesial consciousness will bring with it an interior desire to take part in those assemblies if this is at all possible. That consciousness is certainly lacking if we wish to "free" ourselves from the duty, so as to practice a "higher" and "better" kind of piety that is more personal, free and more engaged in life.

It is true, of course, that the juridical precept should not constitute the basis of our life. In reality there should be no need to impose an "obligation" to worship. We should feel an interior necessity to come together with others for the celebration of the Eucharist and the other sacraments; this is the ideal at which we should aim. But in practice we must look upon the precept and duty as psychological incentives that help us to overcome our natural sloth. As we have already pointed out, the tendency to community celebrations that springs from a proper ecclesial consciousness has been present in the Church in every century.

But this does not mean that those who are unable to assist frequently at those community celebrations live outside, or at the fringe, of Christian and ecclesial life. Abstracting from the canonical precept, we should strive for a regularly recurring gathering of the faithful; yet those who are unable to come do not stand outside ecclesial life or outside the sacramental life. Our life is always ecclesial and sacramental. This is true, not only of sick and old people, but equally of those who on account of their family or work are less able to take part in the community activities of the Church. In other words, the proposition that consciousness of being a church tends to make people assemble does not imply that it is necessary to attain the greatest frequency of attendance, so that a person who cannot attend with a certain frequency should be considered to be in a bad state. On the contrary, it is normal for true community celebrations to be merely high points that recur at regular intervals. But one who reacts against wrong emphases must avoid going to the other extreme, making a sort of ideal of non-attendance.

The fundamental fault in this matter lies in the fact that the ecclesial dimension of our life is too much neglected while too much emphasis is placed on man's direct relation to God. Man has a relation to God, but in and through and with Christ and with one another. It is not right to say, "I can find and serve God better by personally addressing myself to Him and in my work and my marriage than by means of compulsory organized actions." Wanting to develop oneself spiritually to such an extent that one no longer needs the "prescribed" community actions is certainly a false ideal.

300

WORK

Today special attention is given to the Christian appreciation of work.[39] It is not very difficult—at least theoretically speaking—to place work within God's universal plan and order. It is not difficult to integrate work into our total Christian view of life, a view that sees life on earth, with which work is necessarily connected, and eternal life as one great unit. Nevertheless, for a variety of reasons, we had to a great extent forgotten to develop a Christian view of work.

For it was difficult to look upon *work* as belonging to our Christian life, as belonging to our life as free redeemed men, when work was slave-labor, when men, especially at the beginning of industrialization, saw themselves obliged to labor in inhuman conditions, for most of their waking hours, at wages that did not respect their human dignity.

It is particularly difficult to look upon culture, understood here as the higher forms of work, as being Christian, when that culture is, in many respects, directed against the Christian view of life. It is then possible—and this is what actually has happened—that cultural expressions are seen primarily as dangerous. The idea may then develop that Christian culture should bear an evident and explicit Christian label. In such a situation it almost necessarily happens, especially when social factors begin to play a role, that Catholics finally live outside cultural life and come to be considered, more or less rightly, as a cultureless part of a nation.

---

[39]Cf., e.g., E. G. Kaiser, *Theology of Work*, Newman, 1966; Peter Schoonenberg, *God's World in the Making*, Duquesne University Press, 1964, pp. 135-184; A. du Bovis, "Le sens catholique du travail et de la civilization," *Nouvelle revue théologigue*, vol. 72 (1950), pp. 357-371; M. D. Chenu, *Pour une théologie du travail*, Paris, 1953; E. Rideau, "Teaching the Christian Attitude to Work and Suffering," *Lumen vitae*, vol. 9 (1954), pp. 303-314; Remy C. Kwant, *Philosophy of Labor*, Duquesne University Press, 1960. See also *Constitution on the Church in the Modern World*, art. 33 ff.

It has been exceedingly difficult to develop a Christian appreciation of *science*—which is a highly refined and very important form of human work—because that science rubbed so strongly against allegedly Christian ideas. This can easily lead to the idea that only a theology and a philosophy sanctioned by the Church can be considered safe and reliable. Consequently, it might then be considered preferable that those disciplines be taught in the old familiar form and under the constant watchful eyes of Church authority, lest they be contaminated by "modern ideas."

There is presently a growing appreciation of work in all its forms, an appreciation that is both different and positive. It is, first of all, positive. Of course, there are dangers in work, but every human situation has its dangers. And must we not admit that the fact that work, culture, and science have to a high degree become un-Christian is due in part to our aloofness? The dangers involved must not constitute the basis of our approach to the value of work. On that account there is now a more optimistic and hence Christian appreciation of work, culture, and science. This we do not find everywhere in the same way in the Church, and its development is laborious. Nevertheless, the idea that we can be good Christians merely *in spite* of work, culture and science is gradually disappearing.

Particularly, there is a growing appreciation of *intellectuals*. There was a time, now gone, when Catholics were less interested in the quality of someone's scholarship than in the astounding fact that in spite of his learning, he was a believer. Gone also—let us hope—is the time when pastors looked upon intellectuals as, by definition, troublesome parishioners. Today we ask intellectuals to be good intellectuals as a realization of their being-Christians.

It is not easy, however, to say exactly what an intellectual is. Could we say that he is a person who reflects upon the sense, the meaning, of being-man, even though this is done from a particular point of view? He is someone, then, who is not content with superficial knowledge but looks for the deepest core of the matter; from there he makes applications in various fields, but he has, of course, to limit himself and therefore has to specialize. Thus he is called to the role of a leader in human society. One cannot be an intellectual if one does not reflect upon the deepest meaning of being-man. He can specialize in theology, physics, medicine, philosophy, in the history of art or in politics only when he continues to look at the whole ensemble of relations. When a man goes to work in this way, he deserves to be called an intellectual.

The Catholic intellectual can and must, therefore, render great service to the Church and to the entire human community. He does not have the right to cloister himself into an ivory tower, and still less has anyone the right to isolate the intellectuals from society. The intellectual is not called to peacefully enjoy the insight he has acquired, while abandoning his fellow-men to their fate. He must help to foster the proper course and development of society. Each one has his own scientific or scholarly field but he must never lose sight of the whole. A Catholic physician renders his greatest service to mankind by being a good doctor; but if he does not want to be merely a "body technician," it is his duty to also be of service in other relations according to his possibilities. We are therefore justified in saying that the intellectual has a vocation, especially at a time when a revaluation of work, culture and science is taking place among Catholics.

MARRIED AND FAMILY LIFE

If there is one realm of Christian life that is in a state of fermentation, it is surely that of married and family life. The urgent problem of the regulation and limitation of births is but one of the ways in which this ferment manifests itself. However important that question may be, and however much that precise problem is of primary concern in the practical life of many convinced Christians, it is neverthless but one aspect of our present-day total view of marriage. The proper, though not absolute, value of sexual intercourse in marriage also receives more attention than formerly. This change is closely connected with the changing general view of life of which we spoke above. The greater appreciation of the "earthly" values of marriage is not contrary to but rather in complete harmony with the higher appreciation of marriage as a sacramental state of life. A complete appreciation of marriage implies that we value in a Christian way all the aspects of that state of life, just as we do for the whole of life.

For a long time we who are in the Church have not been able to fully appreciate marriage, or at least we have had difficulties about it. Sexuality was, in fact, *the* source of difficulties. To realize this it is not necessary to go back far in history nor far from home. Sexuality in marriage was looked upon, more or less, as "permissible unchastity." As a reaction against that and within the larger framework of the sexual overemphasis in literature, films, plays, and advertisements, sexuality has reached such proportions that one can now almost say that sex has become an absolute.

In view of this background, the present tendency in the Church to accept marriage fully as a sacramental state of life and to place it unhesitatingly in the totality of the Christian life, the tendency as well as to give full value to sexuality, must constitute the foundation on which a renewed ethics of marriage will be built. It would certainly be wrong to give our exclusive attention to the problem of sexuality and the regulation of births, for we would again have too one-sided a view of marriage. We shall not reach a solution from either extreme.

304

The Sacramental Character of Marriage. The Church has found it difficult to recognize marriage as a sacramental state of life.[40] In the early days of the Church, a religious character was certainly attributed to marriage and it was seen as a kind of sacrament in the nonspecific sense of the term; but there was no express recognition of marriage as one of the seven sacraments. The Church Fathers pointed to the symbolic value of marriage and of becoming one in the flesh, in connection with the love between God and man. Married love had its sublime model in the love between Christ and the Church, and was an image of that love. The Church Fathers, for the rest, confined themselves mainly to practical, moral questions; hence their frequent pessimistic utterances concerning marriage.

In the twelfth century, at the time when the first systematic theological works were written, marriage presented a number of difficulties: 1. Marriage has existed since creation; how then can it be a Christian institution of the New Testament? 2. Marriage is indeed a Christian remedy against the consequences of sin, but what grace does it give? In the thirteenth century the difficulties were gradually overcome by a better understanding of the relationship between the sacrament in general and divine institutions of the natural order: sacraments are natural human realities that have been integrated by Christ into the new order of salvation; they are thus brought to completion and blessed with a new fruitfulness. The sacraments of penance and marriage, in particular, received their true value in those perspectives. They are human activities and institutions, established in man's nature by God Himself, which were raised by Christ to a sacramental efficacy. This doctrine was repeatedly and solemnly confirmed

---

[40]Cf. J. de Baciocchi, "Sturture sacramentaire du mariage," *Nouvelle revue théologique*, vol. 74 (1952), pp. 919-929; E. H. Schillebeeckx, *Le mariage est un sacrament*, La pensée catholique, Brussels, 1961.

by the Church in the course of centuries, although primarily on the occasion of errors.

The Church sees the passion, death and resurrection of Christ, the incarnation of God's salvific love for men, as the foundation of the proper value and efficacy of Christian marriage. The efficacious and sanctifying bond between Christ and marriage is established in and by the Church. Marriage, on the one hand, is sacramental in virtue of the baptismal character of the married couple; this makes them members of the Church, authorizing them to take part in and perform salutary sacramental acts. On the other hand, the sacramental character of marriage is borne by the faith of the Church and the spouses. By that faith and on the basis of the baptismal character of the partners, marriage has an actual bond with Christ. Christian marriage is a true encounter with Christ in the ecclesial community. The *Constitution on the Church* speaks of the family as "the domestic Church."[41] Christian marriage establishes and consecrates a community of love between two of the Church's members who are appointed and, as it were, "consecrated" for a proper function in the Church and the whole human community. Hence marriage is a particular form of incorporation into the Church, by which the married partners are given the power and vocation to cooperate in the mission of the Church by their married life. By this they attain to a new similarity with Christ and are brought into intimate communion with the Triune God. The *Constitution on the Church* of Vatican Council II connects married and family life "with the prophetic function" of Christ because "husbands and wives find their proper vocation in being witnesses of the faith and love of Christ to one another and to their children."[42]

---

[41]Ch. II, art. 11.
[42]Ch. IV, art. 35.

The marriage of the baptized, then, is really a sacrament, a salvific action of Christ and His Church. The sacrament of marriage as a "consecration" for a particular state of life has a permanent efficacy. Married life is a special sacramental form of Christian life. It places the spouses in a particular state of life in the Church, by which their human and Chrisian vocation is more closely determined. In and through their wedded community in all its aspects, the partners must strive for and realize the holiness and fulfillment of Christian life, the perfection of love.

If we wish our people to arrive at a real genuine revaluation of marriage, we must imprint on the minds of the adolescents the primary meaning of life as directed toward God. Our whole life is directed to God in love; we are children of the Father and in this lies our happiness. Our whole life here on earth, in all its manifestations, such as work, culture, science, marriage, is an interaction of love for God and to one another.

Married life and the family life that is built on it stand in a sacramental way within the whole of that Christian life. It is therefore a matter of sanctification *through* married life, not *in spite* of it. "By virtue of this sacrament, as spouses fulfill their conjugal and family obligation, they are penetrated with the spirit of Christ, which suffuses their whole lives with faith, hope and charity."[43] The sanctification of Christian life does not come exclusively "from outside," from prayer, frequent attendance of church services and the reception of the sacraments, but it is also a sanctification from within; but then this sanctification from within, of course, demands personal and community prayer and participation in the Eucharist and the use of the sacrament of penance. In addition, life in sacramental union with Christ implies having a share

---

[43]*Constitution on the Church in the Modern World,* art. 48.

in His passion. This is true with respect to all Christians in all circumstances; but for those who are living in the special sacramental state of marriage, the cares, illnesses, sufferings, and trials of married life will acquire also a special Christian meaning.

By putting this special emphasis on the sacramental character of marriage, seen in the ensemble of Christian life, we avoid placing too great a stress upon the juridical aspects of marriage, and giving too much attention to marriage as an institution. We can then harmoniously place the accent on the personal bond of love within our greater theological appreciation of marriage, just as a general emphasis on personality can be harmonized with a greater emphasis on our life in the ecclesial community. Husband and wife are not isolated in their love; they are not abandoned to themselves, but they are borne by the great community of love which is the Church. By and in their mutual love they encounter the Savior Jesus Christ in a special sacramental way and, in and with Him, the Father and the Holy Spirit and the whole community of the faithful.

Family Life. Today's tendency to attach greater value to marriage is directed to the totality of that state of life.[44] This tendency affects not only a few theologians but is at work precisely among married people themselves. In what follows here we shall try to give an orderly sketch of the efforts that are being made in some countries for the purpose of realizing the new ideas concerning married and family life.

---

[44]Cf. Alphonse Clemens, *Design for Successful Marriage,* Prentice-Hall, 1964; Bernard Häring, *Marriage in the Modern World,* Newman, 1966; F. X. von Hornstein and A. Faller, *Sex, Love, Marriage, Guide for Catholics,* Herder and Herder, 1964; and *Ehe, Familie und Seelsorge,* the work book of three Swiss pastoral workshops in Luzern, Luzern, 1942. See also Aimée Carey, *A Bibliography for Christian Formation in the Family,* Deus Books, 1964. For a listing of various Catholic family movements, see the *Catholic Almanac.*

In France a leading place belongs to "The Golden Ring" movement.[45] The movement known as "The Golden Ring" appears in two forms: 1) "Teams of Our Lady," which are small in number and rather tightly organized; and 2) "Christian Homes" which have a more flexible structure and leave more to local initiatives. Both groups aim at deepening spiritual life and union with God.[46]

There are other family groups in France. There first arose, between the two world wars, a movement organized among younger people. It developed out of an association with the Scout movement, which in Europe appeals also to boys in their late teens and to young men. The original name of "Scout Friendships" (*Amitiés Scoutes*) was changed to "New Life" (*Vie Nouvelle*), in 1947, to emphasize the movement's independence of the scout organizations. This "group" is principally composed of married couples but single persons are also admitted. It tries to approach all the problems of modern man from a Christian standpoint.

"New Life" is made up of a great number of groups. A group is composed of a number of "brotherhoods," each consisting of from four to eight families or single persons. These "brotherhoods" aim at and practice: 1) friendship, which expresses itself in the form of neighborliness and mutual assistance; and 2) a common task, e.g., the study and discussion of a particular article of faith or some form of activity. Every year one married couple is chosen and made responsible for the proper functioning of the group. A couple who are called to act as directors spend some time in preparing themselves for their task together with other selected couples in their

---

[45]The *L'Anneau-d'Or*. There exists also a periodical of the same name, but it is not an organ of that movement. The data for this survey have been taken from *Bulletin des foyers,* Oct.-Dec., 1953.

[46]Their French names are *Les Equipes Notre Dame* and *Les Foyers de Chrétienté*. Their members keep in touch, respectively, through *Lettres mensuelles* and the above-mentioned *Bulletin des foyers*.

district, and they exercise their function in cooperation with a priest.

There is an effort to insure the autonomy of the particular groups of "brotherhoods," while trying to establish a certain coordination among them. That is why annual general meetings are held in which as many groups as possible are represented. In those meetings the participants try to penetrate more deeply into the idea of the "new life." In this way the idea acquires a more concrete form; and there develops a sort of fundamental law which, however, is not imposed, although each group tries to live according to the spirit of this fundamental "law." Every year each group tries to determine how it has grown toward the ideal. A certain order is thereby insured while the danger of rigidity is also avoided. The groups of "New Life" are found mainly in the cities of France. Their periodical is called "Earth and Heaven" (*Terre et Ciel*).

In the country the work for the spiritual formation of the family is done principally by the teams of the "Rural Family Movement" (*Mouvement familial rural*). These teams, composed of couples as well as single persons, have no official character. The outside world is often unaware of their existence. They reject every characteristic of a group in the sense of constituting a strict bond; in this way they hope to avoid becoming isolated from the rural community. For this reason they make use mainly of normal contacts with one another in order to exchange ideas, so that special meetings are reduced to a minimum. The priest likewise rarely comes to the meetings, although the members have individual contact with him. They are truly militant teams who constantly ask themselves the question: what can be done in our locality to improve things? After plans have been devised, efforts are made to execute them by means of existing institutions. The chief purpose of the teams always remains the same, namely, to stimulate family life in the country. The movement endeavors to deepen a Christian style of life in rural areas among the masses, especially with respect to family life. Their journal is called "The Rural Home" (*Foyer Rural*).

There is also a movement called "The Fellow Wayfarers of St. Francis," founded by Joseph Folliet in 1927. It tries to create bonds of friendship between people who belong to different milieus and nations by bringing together Christians who are ready for "the spirituality of the journey." While physically journeying, its members meditate on man's great spiritual journey to God. The movement contains a special group for families. Every year its members go on a journey together with their children. Meditation is made while walking. During the journey they meet for reflection and exchange of ideas; and in the evening there is a campfire to which they they invite the people of the village where they want to pass the night. The families are grouped together into "bands," of which there are a dozen in France. Each "band" is directed by a group of four married couples, each with its own particular task. The movement's national direction is likewise formed by four married couples. Among the members of those groups there exists great mutual helpfulness and solidarity.

In addition to these groups, there are various others in which spirituality plays a major role, such as the "Tertiary Families of St. Francis" and the "Marian Teams" of sodalities of Mary. Furthermore, there are groups based on particular contacts and concerns, for example the "Teaching Teams.[46a]

Besides all these associations there is also an official Family Movement organized by the bishops of France. It is called the "Association of Christian Marriage" (*L'Association du Mariage Chrétien*). In 1932, this Association, as an official

---

[46a]Their French names are, respectively, *Foyers Tertiaires de S. François, Equipes Mariales,* and *Equipes Enseignantes.*

branch of Catholic Action, received from the episcopate the mandate to serve all the interests of the family. Hence the Association is engaged in the following activities:

1. Promotion of the sciences that deal with the family. At the request of the episcopate, the Association founded the Institute of Higher Family Studies. In this Institute, philosophers, moralists, sociologists, theologians and medical doctors study the fundamental problems of the family.[47]

2. Preparation of young people for marriage. For this purpose the Association publishes, among other things, the periodical "Girls and Boys" (*Filles et Garçons*).

3. Formation of married couples. The periodical "Homes" (*Foyers*) is published for this purpose. In a number of parishes the Association has directly organized groups of married couples; these groups are characterized by great flexibility in their structure. As a rule, the Association addresses itself to the parish and not to a particular social group.

4. Instruction for the priest concerning marriage and family. To do this the Association also publishes a special periodical "The Priest and the Family" (*Le prêtre et la famille*). For all its periodicals, and other publications, the Association has its own printing establishment.[48]

In Germany, the family movement was strongly influenced by the chaotic conditions of family life after the war. The most fundamental interests of the family were in danger. The

---

[47]A number of reports of this *Institut des hautes études familiales* have been published; e.g., *Essai sur l'être familial; Limitation des naissances et conscience chrétienne; Morale sexuelle et difficultés contemporaines.*

[48]It is called *Editions Familiales* and has published, e.g., Gabriel Marcel, Biot and others, *Recherches de la famille*, Paris, 1949; Jean Viollet and others, *Orientations de pastorale familiale*, Paris, 1955.

desperate housing situation made even simple family living a serious problem. The spiritual distress of the family was so great that even the most elementary Christian values were in danger. Consequently, in Germany, great emphasis was put on working for the family on the economic and social level.[49] Nevertheless, voices were raised in Germany for a more direct religiously-orientated family movement, and for the development of a "Catholic Family Movement." But this movement is not an organization and it functions properly only when it makes the families realize what their own place and task are in the Church and in the nation. The movement operates above and through organizations and individual families.

In the United States, the *National Catholic Welfare Conference* has an agency called the *Family Life Bureau,* which was founded by the bishops of the United States in 1931. It serves as a center for the distribution of study material, organizes exhibitions, courses of study and conventions, and coordinates family life program throughout the nation. Almost all the dioceses have "Family Life" directors who are associated with the Bureau. It periodical publications are *The Family Apostolate* and *Catholic Family Leader.*

The Family Life Bureau operates principally in three areas: the first two are concerned with the life of faith and education for a good family life; the third area of interest is termed "inspirational activities."

The religious program aims at counteracting the secularization of family life. Means promoted for that purpose are family prayer ("The family that prays together stays together"),

---

49August Sahm, "Die Familie. Ihr Recht und ihre Sicherung," *Werkhefte für Katholische Laienarbeit,* no. 6 (1952), pp. 121-129; "Familien-Bildungswerk in Frankfurt a.M.," *Herder Korrespondenz,* vol. 8 (1953-54), pp. 206 f.; "Fortschritte der Familienbewegung in Oesterreich," *ibid.,* vol. 8 (1953-54), pp. 378-381.

the enshrinement of the Sacred Heart, family celebration of holydays, the preservation of old Christian family customs, the celebration of one's patron saint, day of baptism and the wedding anniversary of parents, attendance at Mass and reception of the Eucharist.

For the education to good family life, every means of publicity is used, radio, television, lectures, public discussions, discussion clubs, etc. The following points are discussed or explained on such occasions: preparation for marriage, principles of Christian marriage, relations of the partners in marriage, family virtues, the various phases of child education, rights of families, family ethics, civil and church laws concerning marriage, economic family problems, marriage instruction and advice, etc.

The inspirational activities form the third group. These appeal more to the heart than to the mind. Their purpose is to inculcate a sense of responsibility for the family, to lead the people back to an appreciation and love of the family. To give a few examples of that work: the choice and honoring of the "Catholic Mother of the Year," granting rewards to people who have rendered particular service for the well-being of the family, the "Family Hour," the renewal of marriage vows in a Church ceremony and, since 1961, the annual selection of the "Catholic Family of the Year."

The Family Life Bureau follows carefully the developments that affect the economic and moral security of the family; but in this area it sometimes contents itself with promoting other organizations which work in those fields, for example the Christian Family Movement, Holy Family Guilds, and Holy Family Retreat Associations. There are also other organizations of the N.C.W.C., like the Social Action Department, the Legion of Decency and the National Organization for Decent Literature, that give valuable assistance to the Family Movement.

314

Besides that official work there are also excellent organizations such as the Cana Conference (for married people) and the Pre-Cana Conference (for those who are engaged). The Cana Conference Movement was begun by Father John Delaney, S.J., in 1943 under the name of "Family Renewal Days." It was changed to "Cana Conference" by Father Dowling, S.J. Married couples are brought together for the purpose of giving them inspiration and encouragement and enabling them to find the happiness which God destines for them in and by means of their married life. The bishops of the United States have given their warm recommendation to those Conferences and these play an important role in the program of the Family Life Bureau. Pre-Cana Conferences for engaged couples serve to prepare young people spiritually, intellectually and emotionally for a truly Christian marriage. Most useful is the "Together in Christ" course that is used in more that seventy dioceses of the States.

Finally there is the Christian Family Movement, organized in 1947. It is truly a Catholic Action movement, aiming not only at the spiritual formation of the members but at fostering a community spirit of Christian charity. The movement organizes groups of five of six couples who regularly exchange ideas about those problems and activities. In Chicago the Movement has created a permanent local council which tries to prevent and cure both juvenile delinquency and parental misbehavior.

We are "one world" more than ever before and what takes place in France or the United States can strongly affect Christian life in many other countries. The Church, standing amid the world and the life of mankind, feels the repercussions of what is taking place in the world. This is so, not only with respect to difficulties and weaknesses, but also regarding more pleasant phenomena. In many countries—of which we have given only a few examples—there is a growing appreciation of the family and a realization that we must meet the evils that afflict marriage and the family in a positive way.

The way in which this is done varies greatly. The French put the accent on *"esprit"* and "dialogue." So much so that some wonder whether they are not talking too much. And yet they certainly have a sense of reality which manifests itself, for instance, in the wonderful way members of various groups help one another even to the extent of giving up part of their income. The movement bears the marked character of being that of an elite; this is so almost inevitably everywhere, but in France it is connected with the way the Church endeavors to overcome the dechristianization of the people.

In the United States, as we should expect, there is a strong emphasis on organization and on practical measures. However, here also there is a special accent on the spiritual care and the spiritual growth of the family, although the Americans very quickly develop a practical and concrete program, such as the Family Life Bureau and the Christian Family Movement. The "organization man" is not wanting in France, but he is more evidently present in the United States. It is worth noting that the economic and social family movement is closely connected with the spiritual movement but, nevertheless, functions apart from the latter.

This whole movement of organizing groups of families is closely connected with present tendencies to bring small numbers of people together for religous conversations and discussions. The latter idea was certainly not absent from the minds of those organizers of family groups which had as their primary object married and family life; but some groups have gradually broadened the objects of their conversations so as to embrace whatever belongs to the whole realm of Christian living.

These group discussions and conversations are encouraged by Vatican Council II,[49a] for they appear to answer a growing need. Experience has already shown that many formal and informal group discussions and conversations make a most valuable contribution to the formation of a sound opinion in the Church and that they also lead to a better understanding between priest and laity. A type of group existing in Holland deserves special mention here because it could serve as a model in other countries.

We are referring to the so-called *"Ecclesia* groups." In Holland Catholic Action considers the formation and guidance of such groups as the special task of today's lay apostolate. In nearly all the dioceses there are many such groups that have chosen the subject of living one's faith in the modern world as the general topic of their discussions. The *Ecclesia* groups are not too large and are methodically well-ordered, but there is no rigid organization. In a periodical bearing the same name, schemes for discussions and some well-chosen questions are presented to the various groups. No priest is present at the first meetings of the discussion groups. But he comes to later ones so that theological and pastoral questions that have come up may be discussed with the priest. In this way lay people get accustomed to discussing religous questions with one another and there is also a regular contact with the priest.

THE PRACTICE OF THE EVANGELICAL COUNSELS

In the whole of the Church, life according to the evangelical counsels occupies a special and important place with respect to sanctification through fulfilling the duties of one's

---

[49a]*Decree on the Ministry and Life of Priests,* Ch. II, art. 6: "It is desirable that these [married people and parents] join together in friendly meetings for mutual aid in leading more easily and fully and in a Christian manner a life that is often difficult."

state of life and work. From the very beginning there have been Christians who, on the basis of their Christian commitment, chose celibacy, detachment from earthly possessions and from the freedom to make their own decisions. This way of life may never be absent from the whole of the Church community, for it accents the things that are essentially Christian and that are inherent in the life of every Christian. As Vatican Council II's *Constitution on the Church* expresses it: "The religious state, whose purpose is to free its members from earthly cares, more fully manifests to all believers the presence of heavenly good already possessed here below . . . . It not only witnesses to the fact that a new and eternal life acquired by the redemption of Christ, but it pretells the future resurrection and the glory of the heavenly kingdom."[50] Life according to the evangelical counsels stresses the fact that this earthly life is not the final phase but the way to it. It witnesses in the Church to the eventual fulfillment which is destined for all men and for the entire Church. Not every man on earth can or is required to lead that life, but all must constantly keep their final goal before their eyes.

That is why life according to the evangelical counsels has a special function of witnessing in the Church. The nature of this witness implies that those who live that state of life practice its detachment honestly and without paltering; but this does not mean that that state of life is merely negative or that it implies the denial of the earthly values. One who accepts that state of life aims directly at the goal of the whole Church. This he does without separating himself from the Church. For this he cannot do; without an express and conscious connection with the Church, his life is meaningless.[51]

---

[50]Ch. VI, art. 44.

[51]Cf. Vatican Council II's *Decree on the Adaptation and Renewal of the Religious Life,* art. 5.

Neither does he have a negative attitude toward earthly values. "Let no one think that religious have become strangers to their fellow-men or useless citizens of this earthly city by their consecration."[52] The religious separates himself from the earthly values in order to experience already now something of that which is destined for all and bears witness to it before his fellow Christians.

Historical Forms. The manner of following the evangelical counsels can express itself in a great variety of forms, and this is what has actually taken place in the course of history. This is true not only with respect to the forms themselves but also regarding the accents placed on one aspect or another within that common type of life. The fathers of the desert were true solitaries; they withdrew from the turmoil and corruption of a decadent civilization and, in this way, gave compelling witness in the young Church and the whole society of those days, for their existence was not at all unknown. They witnessed for a life in Christ.

Not all religious communities that arose later expressed so strikingly their rejection of the world. A certain withdrawal from the world, nevertheless, remained proper to all who in a more or less organized form desired to live according to the counsels which they also confirmed by vows. The life of hermits likewise continued to exist for many centuries.

But this "leaving the world" underwent an important change in the Middle Ages. The great founders of orders in the thirteenth century, such as St. Francis and St. Dominic, "left the world" but at the same time desired to live and work in its midst. St. Francis spoke explicitly about "leaving the world" but, though he occasionally hesitated and regularly withdrew to the Carceri near Assisi or to the Alverna mountain, he continued to live and work among his fellow-men. He purposive-

[52]*Constitution on the Church*, Ch. VI, art. 46.

ly shunned the term "monastery" to designate the houses of his Brothers. He did not want to be a monk in the popular and canonical sense of the word. His followers established themselves by preference in the cities, the new population centers of that time, and not on a mountain or in some remote area. The vocation of St. Francis lay among his fellow-men. And this has remained the tradition of his order. Somewhat different in this respect, and yet parallel with it, were the ideas and development of the Order of Preachers.

It is unfortunate that a similar development among women was still impossible at that time. During the first centuries of the Church women lived at home with their families; later, and largely because of the unsafe conditions of society, there arose the custom that women should lead their lives safely behind closed doors. A woman had practically no other choice than to be under the safekeeping of a man or within the walls of a cloister. The desires of Clare and her sister Agnes and their first disciples constituted a great problem for Francis. The final result was a real cloistered life according to the customary style, and even under the authority of an abbess, though lived in extreme poverty.

The "third orders" of the Middle Ages are worthy of note. They must not be looked upon as an attempt to live a "cloistered life" in the world, for Francis did not even desire a strict "cloistered life" for his first order, but as an attempt to attain a higher degree of sanctification of family life and work. The first and third orders stood much closer to each other in those days than we can now imagine.

Religious life, at least among men, continued to develop toward a more "active" life in the Church. Meanwhile, the older forms were maintained, so that there flourished a rich variety of life according to the evangelical counsels. We have merely to think, for instance, of the great man of the sixteenth century, St. Ignatius of Loyola. He, as is well-known, did not intend his Society to live in monasteries or to seek withdrawal from the world and local isolation. He, too, paid great attention to a more perfect life "in the world." This we find very emphatically also in St. Francis de Sales; but the latter's efforts to found a community of women who would be apostolically and charitably active failed and he had to adopt, once more, the old pattern of cloistered convents.

Beside the ancient orders of monks and the societies of canons regular such as the Premonstratensians of St. Norbert, who existed before the Franciscans and Dominicans, and beside the great medieval orders, there were now the Society of Jesus and many congregations that were founded according to the same pattern. Finally, in the nineteenth century, active congregations of women were given a chance and came to flourish vigorously.

Yet there always remained a tendency to return to the original monastic ideal of spatially withdrawing from the "wicked world" or to approach this ideal as integrally as possible. This we find not only in those religious communities to which that tendency rightly belongs, but also in other orders and even in congregations. The whole development in the Church, since the sixteenth century and especially since the French Revolution, had strongly reawakened the idea of withdrawing from the "wicked world." This idea was strengthed further by the Romanticism of the first half of the nineteenth century. It became almost an ideal to flee from the world and to abandon one's family, leaving them to cope with the dangers to soul and salvation as best as they could. The tension between the cloister and the world, between religious life and secular life reached a high point.

This tension had many consequences for the mentality as well as the structure of all religious institutes. This applies particularly to the active religious congregations for women whose mentality and structure clearly vacillates between the two poles. It has also affected the active congregations of men and the so-called "mixed" orders, that is, those that are both contemplative and active. They usually have the difficulty of being fully engaged in pastoral care, education and charitable works, while they are hemmed in by all kinds of obstacles, at least officially, because their society *de facto* prescribes a kind of cloistered existence for its members. This situation causes many difficulties in our time.

Meanwhile, there has been a further development through the official recognition of the "secular institutes" of priests and lay people, men or women, who live according to the evangelical counsels but do not differ outwardly in their type of work or clothing from other Christians. At one time there was some fear that these would absorb a good number of the vocations that formerly went to the regular religious communities. However, they do not, or at least not yet, appear to attract many candidates. According to the *National Catholic Almanac* (1964) the members of such Institutes make a vow or promise to observe the evangelical counsels and to carry on apostolic works according to their talents and opportunities. Pope Pius XII approved the pattern of the secular institute in 1947.[53] Sixteen secular institutes are listed as having establishments in the U.S.A., although most of these were founded in Europe. There has been much talk these last years, and more particularly since Cardinal Suenens' book *The Nun in the World,* about religious life for the "active" congregations of women that is more adjusted to modern social conditions and needs. A proper *aggiornamento* to enable Sisters to exercise greater spiritual influence in the world, while insuring a true religious life according to the spirit of their so-

---

[53]Apostolic Constitution *Provida mater ecclesia,* A.A.S. vol. 39 (1947), pp. 114 ff. For a general study of the secular institutes, see *De institutis secularibus,* Rome, 1951 (papal documents, dogmatic, canonical, historical and practical studies).

cieties, is a major problem of our time. The same can be said
of the congregations of men. It would be most unfortunate if
there were a levelling down of all the forms of life according
to the evangelical counsels. It is important for the Church
that the contemplative, the "mixed" and the active institutes
preserve their own distinct characters, as is stressed by the
Vatican Council's *Decree on the Adaption and Renewal of the
Religious Life*.[54] Still, we ask ourselves what will happen to
the secular institutes? Will the active congregations develop
in the direction of the secular institutes or will the secular
institutes gradually become more like the active religious congregations or even be absorbed by them?

One almost universal problem is the decrease in religious
vocations. One of the reasons, no doubt, is the present atmosphere of life. But a number of questions must be raised with
respect to the actual structure of religious life itself. This
structure, too, is an obstacle that prevents many groups from
getting sufficient vocations. The situation of these organizations needs to be clarified. For a situation in which, because
of his vague status, a religious lives more or less in constant
conflict with the rules and the official "image" of his society,
is hardly beneficial for the formation of a sound spiritual life.
When this happens great harm is suffered by the Church, and
many of the faithful are beginning to realize this.

Religious life is presently in a state of transition. In all societies there is a development parallel with the general tendency in the Church, toward a more positive appreciation of
the "world." And this new attitude need not at all be out of
harmony with living strictly according to the evangelical counsels. On the contrary, this ideal is thereby purified. The tendency toward greater differentiation—as against a levelling
down—has begun to appear more clearly during the past few

---

[54]Art. 2.

years. The old monastic orders, which all, in one way or another, live according to the rule of St. Benedict, are asking
themselves how in our time they can embody the pure monastic ideal; they are thus faced with the problem of the priest-
monk. The great medieval orders desire to free themselves
from the more or less monastic mold that they have acquired
in the course of centuries, and they are reflecting upon their
own proper character, which certainly differs greatly from
that of later congregations. They wish to live and labor as
priests or laymen amidst their fellow-Christians, in complete
conformity to their ideal and with good conscience. The same
is taking place, though in a different way, in many congregations of priests and lay religious, whether men or women.
Particularly in some active congregations of women there is
an evident movement toward profound renewal and reorientation.[55]

In its *Decree on the Adaptation and Renewal of Religious
Life*, Vatican Council II has laid down the general norms governing this reorientation. The ultimate norm, the Decree says,
"is the following of Christ set forth in the Gospels." But "their
founders' spirit and the special aims they set before them as
well as their sound traditions" must be faithfully held in
honor."[56] Adaptation must be in harmony with the Church's

---

[55]M. O'Keefe, *The Convent in the Modern world*, Regnery, 1963;
Bertrande Meyers, *Sisters for the Twenty-first Century*, Sheed and
Ward, 1965; Gertrude Donnelly, *The Sister Apostle*, Fides, 1964. See
also Gerard Huyghe, *Tension and Change. The Problems of Religious
Orders Today*, Newman, 1965; Leon Suenens, *The Nun in the World*,
Newman, 1963; Jacques Leclercq, *The Life of Perfection*, Liturgical
Press, 1960; Jean Leclercq, *The Love of Learning and the Desire for
God*, Fordham University Press, 1961; Louis Bouyer, *The Meaning of
the Monastic Life*, Kenedy, n.d.; Adrian L. van Kaam, *Religion and
Personality*, Prentice-Hall, 1964, and *Personality Fulfillment in Religious
Life*, Dimension Books, 1966; Sister M. Charles B. Murkenhirn, *The
Changing Sister*, Fides, 1966.
[56]*Decree on the Adaptation and Renewal of the Religious Life*, art.
2 a and b.

life of today, with "the modern physical and psychological circumstances of the members," the "necessities of the apostolate, the demands of culture, and social and economic circumstances."[57] Religious poverty implies not only that individual members be "poor both in fact and in spirit," but also that the religious institutes themselves "avoid every appearance of luxury, excessive wealth and the accumulation of goods."[58] Religious chastity is and remains "an outstanding gifts of grace," to be protected by "mortification and the custody of the senses" and especially by the spirit of "brotherly love in the common life of the community." Religious candidates should not be admitted to the vow of chastity until they have been sufficiently tested and "have been shown to possess the required psychological and emotional maturity . . . . They should be so instructed as to be able to undertake the celibacy which binds them to God in a way which will benefit their entire personality."[59] With respect to obedience, the *Decree* specifies that Superiors "should exercise their authority out of a spirit of service" and with "due respect for the human dignity" of his subjects. The latter's "full surrender of their own will as a sacrifice of themselves to God" does not mean the passive obedience of a puppet, but is "an active and responsible obedience." As such it implies that superiors "should gladly listen to their subjects," even though they alone retain the authority to decide.[60]

The *Decree,* moreover, favors abolition of class distinction among religious. All must be "on an equal footing and with equal rights and obligations excepting those which flow from sacred orders."[61] Proper education, not only in spirituality but also in "secular" subjects, including preparation for appropriate degrees in the arts and sciences, must be given to all

[57]*Ibid.*, art. 2c and 3.
[58]*Ibid.*, art. 12.
[59]*Ibid.*, art. 13.
[60]*Ibid.*, art. 14.
[61]*Ibid.*, art. 15.

young religious as required by their future functions. And "religious should strive during the whole course of their lives to perfect the culture they have received in matters spiritual and in arts and sciences."[62] The religious habit should be adapted to modern times, and the religious works must be relevant to today's needs of the Church.[63] Non-viable communities will be suppressed or urged to merge with others whose scope and spirit is similar.[64] Finally, the *Decree* favors the establishment of conferences of major superiors "to encourage effective cooperation," to "encourage a more just distribution of ministers of the Gospel in a given area," and to "conduct affairs of interest to all Religious."[65]

These general norms of renewal will be supplemented by more detailed instructions to be issued by the Holy See. Each religious institute will then undertake its own renewal program keeping in mind that "an effective renewal and adaptation demands the cooperation of all the members of the institute." Superiors therefore should "hear the members in those things which concern the future well-being of the whole institute." However, the power to embody the renewal "in legislation as well as to make allowance for adequate and prudent experimentation belongs only to the proper authorities, especially to general chapters."[66]

4. The Bible and the Liturgy as Sources of a New Spirituality

In the second section of this chapter we indicated that Christian life is increasingly orientated to word and sacrament. In the third section we tried to show how the chang-

---

[62]*Ibid.*, art. 18.
[63]*Ibid.*, art. 17 and 20.
[64]*Ibid.*, art. 21 and 22.
[65]*Ibid.*, art. 23.
[66]*Ibid.*, art. 4.

ing attitude toward the sanctification of one's state of life and work is also connected with the liturgical renewal. Here we want to point out that a new spirituality will develop from these changes.

"Spirituality" is a dynamic and variable concept. By calling it "dynamic" we want to stress that there are diverse forms of living an authentic Christian life. "Form" is not the right word, at least if it makes us think of a rigid structure and the concomitant danger of formalism and fixity. Some people speak of particular "ways" or "patterns" of Christian life.

DIFFERENT PATTERNS OF SPIRITUALITY

One can speak of spirituality in diverse ways. The term can be used in reference to the great movement in the Church, for instance, of the Benedictine, Franciscan, Dominican, or Ignatian spirituality. Each of these is a realization of integral Christian living; but, at the same time, they are clearly distinguished from one another. It is very difficult to express in words in what that distinction consists, so that the best way to realize the difference is to study the lives of those who follow those particular types of spirituality. The term "spirituality" is also used in reference to the diverse patterns of Christian life that have existed in various periods of history. These two uses appear closely connected but they are not identical.

The royal sovereignty of the risen Lord was predominant in early Christian spirituality and especially in the Christian form of life prevailing at the time of the great Church Fathers. This idea of the Lord's sovereignty undoubtedly exercised a great influence on Benedictine spirituality. St. Benedict grew up and was educated in that Christian atmosphere. For example, the figure of the Abbot (father), who is seated among and yet principally above his spiritual sons, is in com-

327

plete accord with the spirituality of this period; but it would be totally wrong to say that the spirituality prevalent in the time of the great Church Fathers was a "Benedictine" spirituality. On the contrary, the latter is a particular pattern of the former. It would also be wrong to claim that the Benedictine type of spirituality was valuable only for the patristic era; and this is true also of the other spiritualities.

The humanity of our Lord Jesus Christ received special attention in the Middle Ages, as early as the time of St. Bernard of Clairvaux, but especially and most evidently in St. Francis of Assisi. The Lord entered fully into human existence, living our life, dwelling in our midst and from the motive of a most pure love. He suffered for us and died for us on the Cross. It is in this way that Man entered into His glory. The Bible and the liturgy served also as the foundation and source for this emphasis.

When we examine the medieval liturgical texts and the pious and mystical literature of that time, it is perfectly evident that a different kind of spirituality was then alive in the Church. St. Francis and his movement can be understood only against the background of that general medieval spirituality, although they are at the same time a specialization and sublimation of it.[67] The Franciscan and the medieval spirituality are not at all identical; this is made clear by the fact that there existed several medieval spiritual movements which perfectly harmonized with the spiritual image of those days and yet were quite distinct from the Franciscan movement. This is true, for instance, of the movement and spirituality of St. Dominic. In the later Middle Ages a strong emphasis was put on the person in general and particularly in the spiritual life. The personal, loving and intimate connection of every

---

[67]Cf. S. Verhey, *Der Mensch unter der Herrschaft Gottes,* Düsseldorf, 1960.

Christian with the incarnate God Jesus Christ was given particular prominence in the "Modern Devotion." Although Thomas a Kempis and his associates were its unmistakable representatives, again, this Devotion also had its own characteristics.

The spirituality of the Counter Reformation is most difficult to characterize. Although we rightly maintain that developments in the Church are not abrupt but gradual, it must also be said that there exists a sharper distinction between the patristic spirituality and that of the Middle Ages than between the medieval—especially late medieval—spirituality and that of the Counter Reformation. One may characterize the Counter Reformation by saying that it is a late-medieval mentality purified of its abuses. By this we do not wish to imply that the Counter Reformation, especially at the beginning, did not produce a great spiritual élan, the clear proof of which is the great number of saints contemporary with that period. We must keep this in mind, too, when we describe the spirituality of the Counter Reformation. The personalistic tendency, with its inclination toward individualism, received new impetus in the Counter Reformation. Piety became more and more concentrated upon a personal, intimate and interior bond with the incarnate God Jesus Christ and His Mother Mary.

The reaction against late-medieval externalism caused—certainly at the beginning—a dislike of all exuberant liturgical, and, especially formalized, practices. Understandably, the polemical situation of that time brought about a one-sided accentuation of certain practices which the Reformation opposed, but which were originally quite orthdodox and Catholic. On that account a number of medieval devotions, particularly those concerned with the Eucharist and the Mother of God, were given new life and flourished with great vigor. The movement and spirituality of St. Ignatius of Loyola bear evident marks of the Counter Reformation; but this is true also, though in a different way, of other spiritual movements of that time, for instance of the Capuchins.

It must be said, therefore, that changes and modifications in spirituality are a normal phenomenon in the Church. But change does not mean that an earlier spirituality simply disappears from the scene; the change is essentially an enrichment. The great values of a "previous" spirituality are preserved when there is a gradual transition to another pattern of spirituality. Hence there is never any need to return to an earlier spirituality nor is that possible. But it is possible that certain things, formally pushed too much in the background, are put forward once more in the process of change. This is almost inevitable. The earlier emphasis, however, expresses itself again in a different way, in another context, and together with new emphases that, as such, were not present before, at least not in the same degree.

Rise of a Biblical-Liturgical Spirituality

Many signs point to the fact that the spirituality of the Counter Reformation has come to an end. Because of the totally changed situation in the Church and the world, a different Christian pattern of life is developing. For us who are in the midst of this transition, it is difficult to specify in what this new spirituality consists. It is certain, however, that the new piety is as yet only in its early stages. It is a growth that is also a contribution of the existing spirituality and it is especially a positive reaction against the decay of the piety that has been with us until now.

Not without good reason have we called the present section "The Bible and the Liturgy as Sources of a New Spirituality." This new spirituality is still "at the sources"; it is yet a search and there is still hesitation. Both Scripture and liturgy are "accents" which were very weak in the late Middle Ages and in the Counter Reformation. But now, in our reaction against an almost outworn way of leading a Christian life, those accents are becoming particularly strong.

However, it is never a mere question of reaction, however strong the reaction might be. It is at the same time an enrichment. There is presently a dislike for all sorts of precisely defined religious practices, many of which belong in reality to the fringe of Christian life. In contrast, there is now a desire to "go back to the sources, to the fundamental values." But this going back is not really a "return" to the past but a new reflection upon the true values of Christian life. The occasion for this new reflection is a dissatisfaction with the old moldering spirituality; hence it is a reaction that positively seeks something different. It is not an attempt to resurrect what existed in olden days; it is a seeking further. That is why this search brings with it an enrichment, and why we hope that in this way we shall attain to a truly modern spirituality. There is no desire to "return," let us say, to a patristic spirituality. But we look into and search the two great sources of Christian life, Scripture and the liturgy, for a pattern of Christian life suitable for our time.

Both Scripture and the liturgy had, for many centuries, been greatly left in the background as sources of inspiration for the spiritual life. We no longer lived by God's word and by liturgical worship. This statement seems particularly bold. It is difficult to maintain such a proposition because Christian life is possible *only* on the basis of Scripture and sacramental celebrations, which, together as a unit, animate the life of Christians in the living Church. However, we must confess that we have been living only more or less *indirectly* by those sources. Holy Scripture and the liturgy did not animate our life of faith as an immediate source. Scripture, in particular, was used by theologians, preachers and spiritual

331

writers rather as an arsenal of texts to affirm and illustrate their argumentation. Liturgical worship was exercised more at the fringe than at the core of Christian life; it was strongly pietistic. Further, the approach to Scripture as well as the liturgy was very individualistic.

Theology, biblical science, the liturgical movement and the religious feeling of many Christians grew dissatisfied with that situation. They sought and are still seeking a pattern of life in which God's word and liturgical worship are the immediate determinants. In this connection Scripture and the liturgy are looked on as one connected whole, that is, it is natural that in liturgical worship the proclamation of the word finds its highest expression.

Ecclesial Character of the New Piety. A spirituality based on Scripture and the liturgy is still free to develop in various directions; hence we must look for a further determination of biblical-liturgical piety.

The liturgical worship that is based on Scripture and wholly orientated to the Bible is the worship of the Church, the community of Christ. A biblical-liturgical piety is naturally and necessarily an ecclesial piety; consequently it is one in which belonging-to-the-community-of-Christ is the predominant and determining factor for our pattern of life. Here, of course, we must apply what has been said above about the liturgy and the Bible as a foundation of the spiritual life: there has never been any real Christian piety that was not ecclesial.[68] No true Christian piety is possible if it does not rest on belonging-to-the-community-of-Christ.

---

[68]A particularly important publication about this question is *Sentire Ecclesiam. Das Bewusstsein von der Kirche als gestaltende Kraft der Frömmigkeit,* ed. by Jean Daniélou and Herbert Vorgrimmler, Freiburg i. Br., 1962. Contributions by de Lubac, Daniélou, Bouyer, Jungmann, Congar, Karl Rahner, Urs von Balthasar, and others.

However, whether one pays direct and express attention to that is another matter. For we are concerned with spirituality, that is, a particular form of piety. We can say that today there is slowly developing a biblical-liturgical piety which pays special attention to the ecclesial aspect. It is a piety that is neither distracted by nor does it lose itself in all sorts of more or less separate exercises of piety. In the spirituality that now begins to disappear, there were, at most, some efforts to leave the periphery and penetrate to the core, to envision everything as one great whole; but this could be done only with very great difficulty. Most of the time, the "ordinary" Christian did not rise above a disorderly and even chaotic tangle of all sorts of religious practices, in which an unreasonable predominance was given to marginal devotions.

In such a framework it was most difficult to see life as a unit so that the whole of life could be looked at from the perspective of Christian existence. If, on the contrary, we start from the fundamental values, if we begin with human existence in the community of Christ as the basis of our Christian pattern of life, we can at one glance see our whole existence in a Christian perspective, as worship in which the liturgical expression of this worship takes the highest place.

A Negative Reaction Only or Something Positive? We must ask ourselves if such a spirituality actually exists in the Church or if it is at least incipient?[69] Is it not a pipedream? Should we not speak of a rejection of the old pattern, so that the question is rather that of reaction *against* something than a positive construction? Certainly the first thing we notice is the sharp reaction against individualistic devotionalism. But we

---

[69]Cf., e.g., W. Grossouw, *Spirituality of the New Testament,* Herder, 1961; Louis Bouyer, *Liturgical Piety,* University of Notre Dame Press, 1955; Joseph Grispino, ed., *Foundations of Biblical Spirituality,* Dimension Books, 1965.

can also see the broad lines of a positive new spirituality that is beginning to unfold. Highly determinative for today's spiritual life is what we should like to express in the following two paragraphs:

We know that we have been taken up into the stream of God's loving salvific action; we have been taken up and carried in God's plan of creation and redemption from the beginning of mankind. God's promise after the Fall, expressed with increasing intensity in the Old Testament, has been fulfilled in us. We live in and through the risen Lord Jesus Christ. We are redeemed, saved men, God's People of the New Covenant. But we are God's People *on the way* to the final fulfillment by the return of the Lord. We are still, also as a community, as Church, impeded by our sinfulness and imperfection; but we have been saved from our fundamental situation of sin and have become children of the Father, brothers and sisters of the incarnate God, heirs of the Kingdom. As God's People, we are lovingly united with one another in the saving community of the Church.

However much we appreciate and must appreciate the recognition of our personality and the possibilities of its development, we in no way wish to be left to our own resources; but we are glad that we are borne by God and our fellow-men in Christ, in His body which is the Church. The bond that binds us with God, with Christ and with one another is *love*, and not, in the first and principal place, a hard and inexorable obligation. In the proclamation of God's word and the celebration of worship, as these are living in the Church, we encounter, through Christ and in the highest possible way, that God of love who especially then binds us together in love, so that our whole life, whatever we might do or be, must and can be a loving attitude toward God and our fellow-men.

This general line of spirituality is certainly present today; but more is necessary before one can say that it really constitutes a modern pattern of Christian life. The Church herself and, in the Church, Scripture and the liturgy, are explicitly accepted by us as the principal source of our spiritual life. The Church, however, remains too vague a datum for us; the Bible and the liturgy, too, are still to a great extent a closed book. We do speak and write about Scripture and liturgical worship as the sources of the present-day spiritual life, but are they really *the* sources for us?

Holy Scripture does not primarily demand great intellectual knowledge and erudition but rather a proper attitude of faith. We are now experiencing a change of attitude regarding Scripture. This is all for the good, of course, but this change does not take place without hesitations and difficulties. Our former preference for "Bible history" led us astray; we thought we knew Holy Scripture when we had become thoroughly familiar with the *historical sequence* of events. Today it is becoming clear that the heart of the biblical message lies rather in God's *message of salvation* to us as it is expressed in the Bible. When we have fully assimilated this changed view of Scripture, the Bible will again be the living word of God for us. But most of us have not yet reached that point, and in this sense the Bible remains a closed book for us. This source of spiritual life, of our spirituality, still has real significance as such only for the very few.

The *liturgy* presents, of itself, enormous possibilities for the development of a new spirituality but, at the same time, poses enormous difficulties. We do not refer merely to the capital difficulty that the core of it is still celebrated in a foreign language; the structure and actual celebration itself, in many cases, is also more of an obstacle than a help for the formation of a new Christian pattern of life. Moreover, we must add to that, with respect to content, the intermingling of diverse currents in the liturgy. While we have no reasonable objections to elements in the liturgy which echo the faith and

335

the life of various centuries, it must be considered unfortunate that the devotional pattern still has too much influence in the liturgy. Fortunately, the new rubrics of January 1961, which de-emphasize the sanctoral part of the liturgical year, are a development in the right direction. And the new liturgy of the Mass, introduced in 1964, with its stress on a service of the word and the Eucharistic banquet and with its many simplifications, shows how earnestly the Church is trying to make it possible for Scripture and liturgical worship to become the sources of contemporary piety. It is to be expected that further changes will be made in line with these developments.

THE CONTEMPORARY CRISIS
IN THE SPIRITUAL LIFE

It cannot be denied that there presently exists a serious crisis in the spiritual life. This crisis affects every strata of the Church: the educated as well as the uneducated, priests and religious as well as lay people. It is stronger in some countries that in others but is beginning to make itself felt everywhere. A genuine, living concrete modern spirituality has not yet taken shape or, in any case, its form is very fragile. Because the new spirituality is still embryonic and, on the other hand, the earlier spirituality is disappearing, there arises a very real and most dangerous spiritual vacuum.

The individualistic and devotionalistic piety is passing away more and more, but there is too little that comes to take its place. That a certain tension should occur, as a result of the more rapid disappearance of the old and the slower development of the new, is not a matter for concern. However, at the present moment, the difference in tempo between the two is of disturbing proportions. There is too little awareness of the fact that, whereas the negative side of the change in spirituality will unavoidably occur of itself and needs no prompting, the positive part of the change will *not* come about of itself and will certainly not automatically acquire a concrete and viable shape.

The decay of the old-fashioned mentality goes on ceaselessly. No special efforts are needed in this direction. We may ask whether it is justifiable to foster that process of decay, and if so, determine how it must be done. There are, unfortunately, too many who are convinced that renewal consists in doing away quickly and abruptly as possible with the existing situation. In some parishes there exists a strange sort of proclamation of the word that exhausts itself in red-hot sermons *against* the rosary, *against* frequent communion, *against* going to Mass during the week, *against* thanksgiving after Holy Communion, confessions of devotion, all sorts of novenas and prayers, indulgences, pilgrimages, medals and what not. Those "sermons" often make no attempt to separate the chaff from the wheat in those religious practices but are simply "against it." Too often our Christians hear: "You don't have to believe this any more"; "That didn't really happen"; "That law must not be understood so strictly." And when the proclamation of the Gospel in this negative way has given the preacher the chance to release his overburdened heart, he has nothing positive to add and finishes his sermon with "Amen: So be it." Most positively, may it *not* be so!

This is certainly not the way to start a new spiritual élan among the faithful. It is, on the contrary, a totally useless and even dangerous chatter. This method will not form the faithful for our own times; it will result, rather, in making them nihilists. Many of the faithful draw their own conclusion from such harangues: "No need to take things so seriously any more." And then, particularly when they meet with difficulties in their lives, there are often regrettable consequences that can trace their origin to those "sermons." This is perfectly understandable, for the faithful have lost their bearings and very often it is not they who are responsible for that loss. Others feel somewhat riduculous if they still clin to the "old" ways, regardless of whether this "old" way concerns the celebration of the Eucharist or a novena in honor of the Miraculous Medal; for they no longer know where they stand. Only one thing is clear to them: "Lots of things have been abolished."

Practices which are really outworn we had best quietly remove or just let them die peacefully. What is still alive but weakened should be studied thoroughly to ferret out the valueless elements. This valuation must be made concretely with respect to the people of the country or region with which we are concerned. At the same time, we must also try to discern those things of permanent value among the many that are threatened with extinction in the general chaotic upheaval; and these we must endeavor to save.

Moreover, we must always ask ourselves the question: What will come to take the place of the things that disappear? Of course, it is not necessary to replace every concrete "devotion" with a new one. But we must keep in mind that a number of religious practices form a part of a *whole*. There exists a very real danger that many people will lose their religious anchorage through the disappearance of fixed customs, and by that fact their whole religousness might be lost, or, at least, suffer great damage.

It is therefore of the utmost importance that we gradually prepare the way for a new piety. We must facilitate access to the sources, to Scripture and the liturgy. This can be done in a number of ways. *The* great means is a good proclamation in sermon and catechesis. It was also chiefly by those means that the older mentality was formed. This will be a difficult and burdensome task. Thundering tirades against "all those old-fashioned ways" is a sham renewal and has nothing to do with a genuine modern piety. We must become thoroughly familiar with the main lines of the new mentality as it is present in the life of the Church, in the decisions and recommendations of Vatican Council II and of the Holy See, and as it comes to light in study, reflection and practice. On that basis we must construct or reform our life, our personal life, our family life, the life of the ecclesial community.

Where there exists a truly good Catholic life, as is the case in much of the English-speaking world, even if this life is based on an aging pattern, a spiritual renewal will be easier. That which is antiquated will eventually show its deficiences, when seen within the general framework of our changing times; and we shall be able to *transform* it gradually, in line with the present-day mentality. We will then discover that a number of customs really ought to disappear and that a number of new ideas should find expression in a concrete form, for example, the reading of Holy Scripture; we will also realize that a shift will occur with respect to many other things. For instance, sanctification through one's work, family life, and state of life will acquire greater significance. Celebration of the Eucharist will possibly become less frequent but this will be the result of the fact that this "Sacrament of Sacraments" will acquire a much more fundamental significance. Confession will become much more the sacrament of penance than a regular cleansing of the soul. "Devotions" will continue to exist but then really on the fringe; they will have less influence on the general image of religiousness yet will flow from the central religious experiences of Christ's community.

Much thoughtfulness and prudence will be required during that process of change. Where a vacuum already exists, one faces a much more difficult situation. Ultimately the only fruitful soil on which a new spirituality can flourish is true piety, whatever its nature might be. Where that piety is dead or has been extirpated, the introduction and development of a new piety will be an almost hopeless undertaking.

Perhaps an example will best clarify this thought. In several countries, as a justified reaction against the constant stress formerly put on the *frequency* of receiving the sacraments, there has been a marked decline in the frequency of confession (This phenomenon is also connected with a more discerning concept of sinfulness). More or less constantly hammered in has been the idea that "it is not at all necessary to go so frequently to confession." Thus, in a good many Catholics the idea has slowly developed that confession is meaningful *only* when one is certain to have committed moral sin. But new study of the meaning of the sacrament of penance shows that this sacrament is a special sacramental encounter with Christ in the ecclesial community, by which we become aware, in penitential love, of that aspect of our life that must be called the sinful and unredeemed aspect. As human beings, we "always fall short." Of this we must from time to time remind ourselves and, therefore, in penitential love seek contact with Christ in the ecclesial community. We do this precisely in the sacrament of penance, by which we acknowledge ourselves as sinful men, regardless of whether the sinfulness be mortal or not, and in which we are strengthened to become more truly redeemed men.

Looked at from this standpoint, going regularly to confession, though not with forced frequency, is very meaningful. But once people have given up frequent confession on the basis that "it is not necessary," it is almost impossible to bring them back to a better and more wholesome practice.[70]

---

[70]Cf. P. Anciaux, *The Sacrament of Penance,* Sheed and Ward, 1962; Claude Jean-Nesmy, *Conscience and Confession,* Franciscan Herald Press, 1965.

5. The Ecumenical Tendency

The ecumenical tendency has become an important factor in Christian life. However divided Christians still remain, they are presently united in the uneasiness about their lack of unity. Catholics have decidedly not been leaders in the early ecumenical movement. Looking at ourselves as living in the one true Church of Christ, we considered other Christians as "children who had run away from their Father's house." From our safe fortress we peered eagery for signs of movement in "the Protestant camp." The military terminology used in that connection is a particularly interesting phenomenon. We felt that we were right and therefore had merely to wait until the prodigal sons would eventually return to their Father's house.

This attitude did not necessarily imply any pharisaism. It simply meant that we knew that we were within the safe haven of Christ's Church and that we did not see what else we could do except making the others change their minds or attacking them in polemical disputes. Fortunately, both sides had already given up recourse to violence to settle the issue as they did in former times. It never dawned upon us that we could meet others with understanding and that we could modify *our* attitude toward them. Further, the hope for a return to the fold, however slight it may have been, was almost exclusively concerned with Protestants. The great body of the Eastern Orthodox, who are so close to us in faith and Christian life, stood practically outside our field of interest.

The Basis of Today's Ecumenism in Greater Church Consciousness

During the last decades a change began to occur in some parts of the Church, and this change has been made universal by Vatican Council II. The uneasiness concerning the dividedness of Christians has become an integral part of Catholic

341

life. The motives for that uneasiness are of the utmost importance. It is natural, of course, at the beginning, for any movement to remain at the periphery of the question rather that penetrating to its core. This was so with respect to the liturgical movement, the biblical movement, the lay apostolate and the question of the diaconate. And the same applies to the ecumenical movement. The ecumenical movement began among the chaotically divided Reformed Christians and later, strengthened by the Eastern Orthodox, received its first major impetus when Christians realized how scandalous their lack of unity was in mission countries. A high point in that movement was the meeting of the World Council of Churches at New Delhi in November 1961.[71]

In a certain sense it is an advantage for Catholics that the ecumenic endeavor was so late in becoming significant in their circles. The development of the ecumenical movement teaches us not to pay too much attention to various practical, organizational and opportunistic motives for attaining reunion and to go to the root of the question, namely, the realization that it is contrary to Christ's explicit will that we are divided. The nature of the Church demands that all those who have died and risen in Christ by baptism, should belong to the one community of Christ. But it is not only the study of the ecumenical movement that leads us to that conviction. The internal development itself of the Church was bound to convince us that division is against the nature of the Church. It is this which particularly interests us here. That conviction may be expressed in the following words: The development of the biblical-theological concept of the Church as the one community of Christ, necessarily brings with it that we will feel ever more keenly the wretched condition of dividedness,

---

[71]Cf. W. H. van de Pol, *The Christian Dilemma*, New York, 1952; Georges Tavard, *Two Centuries of Ecumenism*, New American Library, 1962; *The Church and Ecumenism (Concilium)*, vol. 4 (1965).

especially when we celebrate the Eucharist in which we are most "one" as the community of Christ. The ecumenical tendency in Catholic circles is indissolubly connected with the growing awareness that the Church is the one community of salvation for all.[72]

FORMER ECUMENICAL TENDENCIES

It is true that there have been ecumenical tendencies in the Church before our time but they had totally different foundations; they were based on a weakened ecclesial consciousness. This, for instance, was the case in the eighteenth century. At the time of the Enlightenment, the consciousness of the sacramental community of salvation became very vague and was largely reduced to the idea of an organizational framework. At that time people tended individually to live decent moral lives in obedience to the one God of all men, and in their efforts they increasingly experienced this organizational framework as a useless burden. Above all, the Enlightenment stressed that all men should feel united as *rational* beings. Thus they sought something that transcended annoying ecclesiastical bonds. In the search for something that binds men together, especially on rational-ethical grounds, dogmatic differences were looked upon as relatively unimportant. The "tolerance" of those days differed from the present ecumenical mentality. The tendency toward tolerance permeated the whole of Christendom of that time, though in varying degrees and forms; but it was nevertheless almost universal. It served as a kind of bond between Catholics, Protestants and Orthodox.

It was especially in German-speaking countries, and most strongly among Reformed Christians, that the attitude of tol-

---

[72]Cf. Augustine Card. Bea, *The Unity of Christians*, Herder and Herder, 1963.

erance became more and more pronounced at that time. This resulted in a far-reaching "fraternization" between Catholics and Protestants; but the real question is whether it was a fellowship in Christ, the Christ of Revelation, or a fellowship of rational human beings. The French Revolution even more accentuated that human fellowship (*fraternité*) and marked its apocalyptic high point. Typical are the more or less humorous stories about Catholic pastors and Protestant ministers who frequently strolled together in towns and villages of Holland, pulling at their long clay pipes. Certainly this was a revolutionary phenomenon for the Netherlands, but the question remains whether we can look upon that as a truly *Christian* phenomenon.

It is perhaps less well known that this tolerant attitude spread to the Eastern Orthodox where, of course, it had a more fertile soil.[73] In the seventeenth and eighteenth centuries there were rather close connections betweenCatholics and Orthodox; in those days they lived together as if the schism that became definitive in the eleventh century had lost much of its acuteness. This is shown by the fact that the problem of intercommunion (*communicatio in sacris*) was then by far not so rigorous as it has been until recently in our own days (i.e., until the recent decree on the Eastern Church).

There were wide breaches in the barricades on both sides and Rome was very tolerant with respect to those practices. In Constantinople relations were so good that the patriarch gladly accepted the activities of the Catholic missionaries in that city. Many Orthodox, including priests and bishops, assisted at Catholic ceremonies and even asked for sacramental absolution from Roman missionaries. The Orthodox

---

[73]These data are based on a publication of P. Grigouriou, editor of the weekly *Katholiki*, Athens, as summarized in *La Croix*, Feb. 4, 1960. See also Wilhelm de Vries, "Communicatio in Sacris," *Concilium*, vol. 4 (1965), pp. 18-40.

pupils of the St. Benedict College followed the course of religion based on the catechism of St. Bellarmine. Patriarch Cyril Contaris was an alumnus of that college. Patriarch Parthenios did not hesitate to write to Cardinal Barberini, the Prefect of Propaganda, giving the highest praise to the preaching of a Catholic missionary who counted many Orthodox among his audience. There are already clear examples of intercommunion in the seventeenth century; Latin bishops and priests celebrated Mass in Orthodox churches and the Orthodox received Holy Communion at those services. The Jesuits absolved Orthodox believers with the consent of the patriarch. Orthodox deacons assisted Catholic priests. There are even cases where Catholic and Orthodox bishops and priests concelebrated. The monks of Mount Athos entertained excellent relations with the Holy See.

Whatever secondary and perhaps political motives may have played a role in all this, those remain extraordinary facts. The religious foundation common to both groups was very strong, and their relationship of mutual tolerance was certainly of a noble nature. In any case the tolerance possessed much higher qualities than the vague tolerance that existed between Catholics and Protestants. We may even doubt whether these phenomena had a direct connection with the Enlightenment, especially since they were already fully present in the seventeenth century. In any case they merit our attention.

In Holland we meet with extraordinary happenings in the eighteenth century among the "old episcopal cleresy" which, after 1870, assumed the name "old Catholics."[74] Of great importance in ths connection is the so-called Council of Utrecht of 1763, a gathering of the three bishops and the priests of

---

[74]See Bertrand van Bilsen, *Het schisma van Utrecht,* Utrecht, 1949, pp. 104-112.

this separated group of Catholics. That Council was an intense endeavor to come to an agreement with Rome. In the time of the French occupation and especially under King Louis Napoleon, these efforts toward reunion were renewed, in perfect agreement with the spirit of that time. But after the restoration of independence, there was a return to the former antagonism.

NINETEENTH CENTURY REACTION

There was a violent reaction to all this at the beginning of the nineteenth century. As a result of the "restoration," at least of a seeming restoration, of the old situation the ranks were closed once more. A typical example of that reaction is found in a Dutch translation of a two-volume book entitled: *The Banquet of Theodulus, or Conversations Concerning the Reunion of Divers Christian Religious Societies.*[75] It was written by baron Dr. Johann August von Starck, a German Evangelical preacher. The Catholic translator was of the opinion that the publication of this book would present a mirror to his "Protestant brethren" and would make them see clearly "what fate the highly praised Enlightment had in store for them." The reactionary spirit is quite manifest in the Preface appended by the translator:

> The German Enlightment was until now, in our fatherland, no more than a dawn. There was still respect for the Formulae and the Confessions of Faith. Their authority was still recognized as binding. And, however much this was contrary to the fundamental Protestant principle [of free examination], there was still found in them a safeguard against the flood of the Antichrist which in Germany totally destroyed the Faith

---

[75]*Theoduls Gastmahl oder über die Vereinigung der verschiedenen christlichen Religionsozietäten,* Frankfurt a.M., 1809. Dutch translation, Amsterdam, 1819.

in a Savior. But now contempt for the Formulae and the declaration of the Reformed Synod to the effect that *they are no longer needed,* open the way here also for the Doctrine of the Antichrist. Hence it is now the opportune time to show our Protestant compatriots, by the example of our neighbors, what fate the so highly praised Enlightenment will bring them, in the hope that they may escape from the stream of unbelief into the one safe ark of preservation. For here they will see clearly that the degeneration of Protestantism into Antichristianity is an inevitable result of its fundamental principle and structure which, on that account, are not of divine origin.

May our Protestant Brethren not despise this warning; but consider it a hint of Providence. Here they hear the truth from the mouth of a Protestant teacher. May this make an impression on their heart and help their return to the bosom of the one true Church of salvation.[76]

Baron von Starck, the author of this book, was ecumenically minded with respect to the Catholic Church but was greatly opposed to the vague tolerance of the Enlightenment, which, according to his firm conviction, would completely destroy the Faith. He was certainly not one who swung with the prevailing wind. In the Preface of the first (1809 and second editions, he tells us:

In all periods of sacred and profane history we find a great number of proofs and examples of the harmful results for religion and the state which have flowed from all the cleavage of minds especially in the matter of religion. It is perhaps originally and especially that source to which must be traced the ever deeper downfall of Germany in the last three centuries from its former greatness and power, and its present misfortune. On account of the religious division which has been so very sad for France in the past and also for our own days, several proposals toward a reunion have been made recently; and these have found friends, not only in France but also in Germany.

---

[76]*Ibid.,* Preface.

In others, however, they have raised all sorts of anxious questions. Have those proposals been made on the basis of a sufficient knowledge of affairs? Will a reunion in our own days not meet with greater difficulties than ever? Will this reunion nevertheless be easy and even, ultimately, entirely necessary? All this is examined in this small book, and perhaps these things are not unworthy of serious consideration; that is why I do not object to a wide diffusion of this book. It is the wish of the author that the book be read, pondered and judged without passion, with impartiality and love of truth, and that one may remember that the purpose of the mission of the Lord, Mediator and Teacher of all is "to gather into one the children of God who were scattered abroad" (John 11:52).[77]

We must ask ourselves whether this book by a sincere believing Protestant, in which there is a clear reaction against the destructive influence the Enlightenment had on the faith, is not misused by the Catholic translator, who seems to handle it as a club with which to strike the Protestants and to make them return quickly to the Church in whom alone is salvation. But that was then the new atmosphere; the French Revolution's escapades with freedom had left a severe hangover and people no longer wanted to hear anything about "Liberty, Equality, Fraternity."

In the first half of the nineteenth century the theology concerning the Church underwent an evident revival in more serious Catholic circles, especially in Germany and particularly in the circle of the already mentioned Johann Sailer. However, this movement later subsided. The same revival occurred also in France; but there it was strongly aimed at stressing the power of the pope and his infallibility, as a guarantee of Church orthodoxy and unity. The climate of the second half of the nineteenth century became less and less suited for ecumenical tendencies.

---

[77]*Ibid.*, author's Preface to first and second editions.

DISTINGUISHING CHARACTERISTICS OF TODAY'S ECUMENICAL MOVEMENT

The contemporary movement can in no way be called a revival of the ecumenical tendencies of the eighteenth century. It is true that some people speak of the ever recurrent "waves" of efforts toward reunion. But it is important to realize that we would do great injustice to the present Catholic and Protestant endeavors by depreciating them in that manner. Today's ecumenical efforts have a character that differs entirely from the mentality we have described above. What gives us confidence in the present situation is the fact that the longing for unity does not spring from a dilution or obscuring of the concept of the Church; rather it is founded precisely on a better consciousness of the Church. This, at the same time, makes us realize more keenly how great the difficulties are that present themselves in the way of ecumenism, for it is precisely the concept of the Church that creates the great gulf existing at least between Catholics and Protestants. Hence, we do not base our efforts on a vague feeling of "let us deal with one another as rational human beings." But their foundation lies precisely in Scripture and particularly in Christ's own pressing call for unity.

Consequently, we are permitted to say that today's ecumenical tendencies are on the track that can ultimately lead to unity. But this does not mean that we are already able to see how and when unity will actually be achieved.

Inner Growth Toward Unity. There is in the Church an inner growth toward unity. We of today no longer accept Christian dividedness as a deplorable fate, as an accomplished fact, but we see it as the greatest calamity that has befallen Christianity. This calamity, however, was not a natural catastrophe that befell us like an earthquake, beyond our control. Nor was it a calamity that is to be attributed solely to

349

the ill will of those who broke away from the unity with Peter. It is not even sufficient to recognize that the Orthodox, Protestants and others were possibly not in bad faith or that they surely may now no longer be branded as such.

It has taken the Church centuries to recognize that good faith, just as those who were on the other side had the greatest difficulty in accepting the good faith of Catholics. This was wholly in accord with the spirit of the time. This idea about the good faith of the other party could mature only very slowly. The absolution from excommunication, given "for safety's sake" to Protestants and others who join the Catholic Church is a remnant of the earlier mentality; for a real absolution from excommunication presupposes that there exists personal guilt. A general rule prescribing such an absolution in our own day is unjust, for only rarely does someone guiltily leave the Church, thus incurring excommunication, and afterwards ask for reconciliation and reunion. Converts are nearly always people who have grown up outside the Church without any personal guilt.

But it is not enough to recognize the good faith of such people, because it is still possible for us to stand aloof, conscious of our righteous position but oblivious to our own faults. Christian dividedness is not merely a calamity; it is also a *sin,* a sin of the whole of Christianity: both Catholics and other Christians were and are guilty of that division and discord. While acknowledging the good faith of others, we must not go to the other extreme of completely excusing those who separated themselves from the Church. Such an absolution from all guilt, in combination with a total absolution of ourselves, would indeed make of the lack of unity a sort of natural calamity for which no one would have any responsibility; then we could stand before it in perfect helplessness. It is, on the contrary, a *human* tragedy in which both parties are guilty. God certainly gives us His grace to overcome that tragedy, but it belongs to us to cooperate with that grace.

Catholics do not have a proper ecumenical attitude when they think they must be full of criticism of their own Church while, at the same time, having almost nothing but praise for Reformational Christianity. Protestants will naturally be inclined to consider such an attitude insincere and incredible. By the very nature of things we have to consider it fundamentally wrong when many finally severed their relations with the Church, whoever may have been responsible for it; and we cannot do otherwise than consider it right to be and remain in the Church. But the question concerning the guilt must be addressed to *both* sides.

We are, then, all of us, *responsible* for the restoration of unity through our combined work and prayer. Although we may start from different standpoints, we aim at the same goal, a goal that might not yet be very clear to us but that, in any case, should be the attainment of true unity. But precisely because the dividedness is not a natural calamity but a human tragedy, there exists the prospect of a solution, however distant the time for its fulfilment may be. The endeavor to reach and restore unity, to attain greater unity, is an enduring aspect of the Church. This tendency is not something occasionally present on account of particular circumstances that affect the Church. The human character of the Church is the reason why there have been, are, and will be constant difficulties about unity; but this is also the reason why we must constantly strive for the restoration of complete unity.

However, for centuries, the situation has, as it were, remained frozen. Fortunately the ice is presently broken or at least breaking up. We are living in a time of the Church's history when more attention is paid to unity than to the defense and struggle against new divisions, because the danger of the latter, though not absent, is less acute.

351

The character of the present ecumenical effort, that is so intimately connected with a deeper insight into the nature of the Church, brings with it a greater differentiation in the ideas regarding the *future unity*. For a long time we have envisioned the "return" of non-Catholic Christians in a particularly simplistic way: they should return "into the bosom of Mother Church," with a complete acceptance of that Church as it has developed in the course of centuries, embracing all her customs and habits and abandoning everything that has been meaningful to them until now. But is such a "return" really necessary?

To begin with the latter, in the supposition of an eventual "reunion," is it necessary for the Orthodox, for Reformational Christians and others to relinquish everything that is dear to them? For all of us, it is not so much a matter of relinquishing old values as of coming to the fullness of Christian faith and life. This naturally implies that one-sided attitudes of faith must be corrected and completed. Thus what is wanted is not the acceptance of partial truths but the whole truth. This full acceptance, of course, contains a great many practical consequences for Christian life. But, we must ask, does this also necessitate the rejection of particular accents and even forms of living the faith that are authentically Christian?

This problem is considerably easier with respect to Eastern Christians desirous to return to unity with the Bishop of Rome, than is the case with Protestants. The Church does not disturb their whole community with their own bishops, their own liturgies and laws nor does she touch the married state of the priests. The question is certainly more difficult in regard to Reformational Christians because the break is much deeper and more fundamental. But in case of an eventual reunion with Protestant groups, would it be necessary for them to enter into the Catholic Church as she is actually structured, or could they remain more or less distinct groups within the unity of the Church, with their own bishops, their own married or celibate clergy, their own liturgy and rules that are adapted to them? The unity of the Church does not require unformity, as is evident from the fact that Eastern Christians united with Rome remain distinct communities, even if they exist in the West, e.g., in the United States.

On the other hand, must the present Catholic Church remain totally unperturbed by the eventual return of the other Christians? We do not mean this solely from the external standpoint. We can say, no doubt, without tampering with the complete Catholicity of the present Church, that particular values that now are more or less hidden or neglected in the Church could be brought to new life by the contribution of Orthodox and Reformational Christians. This could also serve to eliminate the excessive emphasis now put on other values. In any case, if there were objections against retaining distinct communities of former Reformational Christians, at least the Church should make herself more attractive to them, more a community in which they can feel "at home." Unity most certainly does not require that they give up values which are "Catholic" in themselves but which in fact are more stressed by Reformational Christians, such as their respect for and love of the Bible.

The United Church of the future will in all probability be totally different from anything we now try to imagine. It will be the one Church of Christ, but a Church that will have different features and a great variety in liturgical and other forms of Christian life. The question of the decentralization of Church government is not a mere matter of organization but is of great significance in respect to ecumenism.

External Manifestations of a Catholic Ecumenical Mentality. The inner growth toward unity on the Catholic side goes hand in hand with external signs that manifest an ecumenical

353

mentality. For obvious reasons, attention was first directed to the *Eastern Orthodox.* Pope Leo XIII, who in many ways opened new perspectives to the Church, had a particular interest in that problem and published three encyclicals on the Eastern Church. He tried by means of certain regulations to safeguard the position of the Eastern Churches united with the Holy See. This line of conduct was continued by the popes who followed. But there were and still are difficulties, especially on account of the centralized system of the Roman Curia. The position of the patriarch remains a thorny question. In our own days Maximos IV Saigh, the Melchite Patriarch has ardently defended the rights and freedoms of the Eastern Churches. This merely shows that allegiance to the Holy See does not, as many Orthodox believe, lead *per se* to servility toward Rome, nor does it make the Eastern Churches lose their own character. Universally known is the great interest Pope John XXIII had in the Eastern Churches in relation to Vatican Council II. This attention is also manifested by his successor, Pope Paul VI, especially in his spectacularly friendly meeting with Patriarch Athenagoras in Palestine, and the recent disavowal of the mutual excommunications pronounced in 1054.[77a]

Vatican Council II's *Decree on Ecumenism,* which was promulgated by Pope Paul VI on November 21, 1964, explicitly declares "that the Churches of the East . . . have the power and the duty to govern themselves according to the disciplines proper to them" and recognizes that the "perfect observance of this principle which, for all its periodical neglect, is sanctioned by longstanding tradition, is one of the essential prerequisites for any restoration of unity."[78] More-

---

[77a]See the joint Catholic-Orthodox Declaration of December 7, 1965.

[78]A.A.S., vol. 57 (1965), pp. 98 ff. English text, N.C.W.C. translation, Ch. III, art. 16. Also Cardinal Lercaro's article "The Decree on Ecumenism and the Dialogue with non-Catholic Eastern Churches," *Concilium,* vol. 5 (1965), pp. 156-174.

over, the *Decree on the Eastern Churches* now permits Catholic and Orthodox Christians to receive the sacraments of Penance, the Eucharist and the Anointing of the Sick from each other's priests when access to their own clergy is physically or morally impossible.[79] This decree shows how deeply the ecumenical attitude has penetrated into the decisions emanating from the highest authorities in the Church. It is left to the local bishops to regulate the details of this decision in consultation with the bishops of the Orthodox Churches. This decision is important, not only for Eastern lands, but also for America where many Orthodox often live far away from their own churches. As a matter of fact, the *Decree on Ecumenism* had already specifically commended "to the pastors and faithful of the Catholic Church to develop closer relations with those who are no longer living in the East but are far from their home."[80]

Regarding the Reformation, interest in it increased considerably after World War II. This took place especially on the lower level and, quite naturally, in the countries where Catholics and Protestants live together. The mutual relations between them have greatly improved in most places. Good human relations are, after all, the first condition for eventually achieving unity. We, human beings, must know how to act in a Christian way in our mutual relations and try to understand one another. All sorts of contacts have developed both in Europe and in America. There have been conversations, study meetings, retreats, invitations to various councils and assemblies, joint visits to the Holy Land, etc. All this presents problems to us and to non-Catholics. What is the way we should follow in this matter in obedience to Christ?

---

[79]A.A.S., vol. 57 (1965), pp. 76 f.
[80]Ch. III, art. 18.

We desire to arrive at unity, but we are not yet united. We would be insincere and would not show respect for our faith, if we acted "as if" we were one, when actually we are not. Every "make-believe" in this respect, simply because it is presently "fashionable" to "do something ecumenical," is misguided.

In America, as well as in Europe, it is becoming a sign of being ecumenically minded for Catholic groups to occasionally invite Protestant ministers as speakers. This in itself may be good if there is a real need for such things, but it must not be thought that this is demanded by ecumenism. What is to be regarded as more ecumenical: to substitute a minister for a priest in the preaching of a Lenten sermon to Catholics, or to have Catholics and Protestants come together to meditate on the passion, death and resurrection of Our Lord, under the guidance—alternating if necessary—of a priest and a minister? Undoubtedly the latter.

Common liturgical worship is not yet feasible and, specifically, the common celebration of the Eucharist does not yet appear possible. As long as we are not really united in our faith, especially with respect to the Church and the Holy Eucharist itself, a common celebration seems to be a lie. For the same reason "Masses for non-Catholics" must be rejected as a contradiction in terms, for in such a celebration there is no possibility for a genuine community. It would at the most inspire vague religious and Christian feelings. We are not speaking here of occasionally inviting Protestants to be present at our services, for this might be the occasion for them to become acquainted with the Catholic Church. The same can be said of so-called "demonstrations" of the liturgy. The real celebration of the Eucharist demands the intimacy of one's community: Karl Rahner is so strong on this point that he is opposed to the televising of the Mass, an opinion that is not shared by many.[81] In any case the common celebration of worship is the *final goal* of our strivings for unity; it is not a *means*.

The official attitude of Church authorities also has very positively developed in an ecumenical direction. As late as 1948 the Holy Office issued a *Monitum*[82] recalling the Canon Law prohibition against direct participation in non-Catholic religious services and public discussion of the faith with non-Catholics; it added that Catholics were forbidden even to be present at so-called "ecumenical" gatherings without explicit permission of the Holy See. And no such permission was given for the meeting of the World Council of Churches held in Amsterdam in the same year. But in 1950 this prohibition was superseded by an Instruction concerning the ecumenical movement,[83] which was much more positive. It spoke with great respect of the ecumenical tendencies and stated clearly that this is *par excellence* a work of the Church in which the bishops have a task. They received faculties for three years to authorize ecumenical meetings of a diocesan nature, so that permission from the Holy See was needed only for interdiocesan, national and international gatherings.

Pope John XXIII's open attitude is well known. He founded the Secretariat for Church Unity under the direction of Augustin Cardinal Bea; received the Anglican Archbishop of Canterbury and several Protestant leaders; welcomed Orthodox and Protestant observers at Vatican Council II; and sent official observers to the meeting of the World Council of Churches at New Delhi in 1961.

Since then Pope Paul VI has officially promulgated the Council's *Decree on Ecumenism*. It states that the Council

---

[81]Cf. *Orientierung*, vol. 18 (1953), no. 17.
[82]*A.A.S.*, vol. 40 (1948), p. 257.
[83]*A.A.S.*, vol. 42 (1950), pp. 142-147.

is gratified to note that the participation by the Catholic faithful in ecumenical work is growing daily. It recomends this work to the bishops everywhere in the world to be vigorously stimulated by them and guided with prudence."[84] It call "the attainment of union . . . the concern of the whole Church, faithful and clergy alike." Acknowledging that Catholics bear part of the guilt for the division of Christianity, the Council "humbly begs pardon of God and or our seperated brethren" for our sins against unity. After stating that it is "allowable, indeed desirable," that in special circumstances, such as ecumenical gatherings, "Catholics should join in prayer with their separated brethren," the Decree says: "Worship in common is not to be considered as a means to be used indiscriminately for the restoration of unity." "Witness to the unity of the Church," it adds, "very generally forbids common worship to Christians, but the grace to be had from it sometimes commends this practice." Hence the Decree leaves the course to be adopted with respect to common worship to the "local episcopal authority, unless otherwise provided for by the Bishops' Conference according to its statutes, or by the Holy See."[85]

We have already indicated above that, with respect to the Eastern Churches, Orthodox and Catholic Christians are now permitted to receive certain sacraments from each other's clergy in case it is physically or morally impossible to have recourse to their clergy. It would seem that Church authorities could without difficulty extend this permission to other ecclesial communities which are more or less in a similar doctrinal situation as the Eastern Church. We are thinking here, for example, of the Old Catholic Church in Holland, the Polish National Church in the U.S.A. and even Anglican

---

[84]Ch. I, art. 4.
[85]Ch. II, art. 8.

and Episcopalian Churches. With respect to others fully based on Reformational principles, however, it is not yet possible, it seems, to suggest any such steps. The disagreement with them, especially about the Eucharist, the Church and the Ministry, is still too profound to permit even the limited communion now authorized with the Orthodox. However, even with respect to the Reformational Churches, we need not despair. The important point is that on both sides there is now a new willingness to remove the obstacles preventing the unity desired by Christ. It this willingness is genuine, as we have every reason to believe, then the desired goal will eventually be reached, for then no obstacles will be "set to the future inspirations of the Holy Spirit" (*Decree on Ecumenism*).

RELATIONS WITH NON-CHRISTIAN RELIGIONS; RELIGIOUS FREEDOM

Now that mankind is gradually being drawn together the Church also re-examines her relationship to non-Christian religions. She wants to reject "nothing that is true and holy in these religions," but "regards with sincere reverence those ways of conduct and of life, those precepts and teachings which, though different in many aspects from the one she holds and sets forth, nonetheless often reflect a ray of that Truth which enlightens all men." For this reason the Church desires her children prudently to engage in dialogue and collaboration with men of non-Christian religions in order to "preserve and promote the good things, spiritual and moral, as well as the socio-cultural values found among these men."[86] She regards with esteem not only Hindus and Buddhists but also Moslems and Jews. She wishes Christian and Moslems

---

[86]Vatican Council II's *Declaration on the Relation of the Church to non-Christian Religions*, art. 2.

to forget their former antagonisms, "to work sincerely for mutual understanding and to preserve as well as promote together to the benefit of all mankind social justice and moral welfare, as well as peace and freedom."[87] Mindful of "the spiritual patrimony common Christians and Jews," the Church "wants to foster and recommend that mutual understanding and respect which is the fruit, above all, of biblical and theological studies as well as of fraternal dialogues." Rejecting every form of persecution against any man, the Church decries especially any display of "Anti-Semitism, directed against Jews at any time and by anyone." Declaring that what happened to Christ "cannot be charged against all the Jews, without distinction, then alive, nor against the Jews of today," she forbids her children to present the Jews "as rejected or accursed by God."[88]

Christ's death on the cross is "the sign of God's all-embracing love" of the whole of mankind. We cannot truly call on God as our loving Father, "if we refuse to treat in a brotherly way any man created as he is the image of God. Man's relation to God the Father and his relation to men his brothers are so linked together that Scripture says: 'He who does not love does not know God.'" No one, therefore, should be discriminated against "because of race, color, condition of life or religion."[89]

Regarding religious freedom, the Council declares that man's dignity as a person gives him "a right to religious freedom . . ., to be immune from coercion on the part of individuals, of social groups or of any human power." Man is bound to follow his conscience and "he is not to be forced to act against his conscience." This human freedom in reli-

---

[87] *Ibid.*, art. 3.
[88] *Ibid.*, art. 4.
[89] *Ibid.*, art. 5. Cf. *Constitution on the Church in the Modern World*, art. 29.

gious matters is also to be recognized when individuals "act in community." Hence, provided the just demands of public order are observed, religious communities of any kind have the right to govern themselves in freedom, to erect places of worship and to publicly teach their faith. This universal human right must effectively be recognized even if in a particular country one religion receives special recognition. These statements are not inspired by opportunistic motives but the Church "recognizes and gives support to the principle of religious freedom as befitting the dignity of man and as being in accord with divine revelation."[90]

Man's fundamental right to religious freedom is a right also to reject any form of religion and to profess atheism. But even then, the Council declares his right has to be respected: "The Church protests against the distinction which some state authorities make between believers and unbelievers, with prejudice to the fundamental rights of the human person."[91]

---

[90]*Declaration on Religious Freedom*, art. 2, 3, 4, 6 and 12.
[91]*Constitution on the Church in the Modern World*, art. 21. For this whole matter see also Louis Janssens, *Freedom of Conscience and Religious Freedom*, Alba House, 1966.

361

CHAPTER FOUR

Pastoral Consequences

The changes in the organizational and spiritual structures of the Church necessarily imply certain consequences with respect to pastoral care. Before we can consider these consequences, we must first determine accurately what is meant by "pastoral care," for otherwise we would be beating around the bush. This is further necessitated because our thinking about pastoral care itself is undergoing a renewal and a number of distinctions have been introduced which were not made formerly, at least not in that manner.

Changes in the ecclesial and social structures have inevitable consequences for pastoral care as a whole; there are shifts of emphasis in pastoral work that result from shifts of emphasis in life and thought. Pastoral care is a most difficult task in this time, that is not incorrectly compared to a rapid in the stream of ideas, the consequences of which are almost wholly beyond our power of foresight. It is not at all surprising that many priests no longer know in what direction their efforts ought to tend or that they lack a proper idea of their pastoral task. But is there no answer? Does not precisely our present time present several important perspectives for pastoral care?

Not all pastoral care has a priestly character, but the priest is, in virtue of his office, particularly called to engage in the Church's pastoral mission. The fulfillment of the priestly office can and must be the pursuit and fulfillment of an ideal of life. As a result of the seemingly disorderly movement that is taking place in the Church of today, the priestly ideal itself is also under discussion. In close connection with the changing view concerning the Church herself, concerning pastoral care and the meaning of the office in the Church, much thought is being given to the ideal of the priesthood for our time. Doubts have also arisen concerning particular existing forms of priestly life and activity. New forms of priestly existence are sought and efforts are made to put them into practice. Uncertainties concerning priestly existence in our time also have a repercussion on the problem of vocations to the priesthood. We must also ask to what extent, in connection with the changing structure of the Church, we can speak of an actual shortage of priests.

1. What is Pastoral Care?

THE TERM "CARE OF SOULS"

One could question the very term "care of souls" which often serves to express what we have called "pastoral care." For that term implies too much a splitting of man into two more or less independent and mutually opposed entities, the "soul" and the "body." We are becoming increasingly aware of the fact that the pastor is not so much concerned with "souls" as with undivided human beings. A medical doctor must also pay attention to the undivided man and not merely to his body. Yet there is a striking difference between the attention of the physician and that of the pastor of "souls." The focus of attention of the psychologist and the psychiatrist —like that of the pastor—is also not primarily directed to the body; but there is an evident difference in viewpoint. The pastor, moreover, has something in common with the social worker, namely, he approaches a man, not only as an individual person, but also as one who belongs to a particular milieu, for the undivided human person can only be approached within his milieu. Nevertheless, we must avoid confusing social work and pastoral care.

While the study of pastoral care has never been entirely absent from the Church, the present situation was bound to lead to a more intense interest in it. This study has already had good consequences for a proper definition of pastoral care; it has especially established a greater awareness of the necessity of widening the concept of pastoral care in connection with the development of the concept of the Church. In this widened concept the lay apostolate acquires an organic place in the whole of pastoral care. The present social and religious situation also necessitates distinguishing more clearly the various forms of pastoral care than was the custom in the past.

Pastoral Science, Theology of Pastoral Care and Pastoral Theology

Pastoral study has received increased attention during the last decades. German authors like to speak of "pastoral science" (*Seelsorgewissenschaft*) to indicate that pastoral care must be studied scientifically but, especially—and this is the main reason for using the term "science"—that it must be studied on a wider basis that that of theology alone. Notably sociology and psychology must be involved in that study, and, in regard to sociology, remarkable results have already been obtained. Institutes for religious sociology are very active.

For obvious reasons, however, the scientific approach to pastoral care has its starting point and foundation in a theological reflection upon Revelation. For in pastoral care it is ultimately Christ's Church with which we are concerned; it is the Church which through her activities constantly incorporates herself into the life of mankind. Some authors prefer to speak about a "theology of pastoral care." And the term "pastoral theology" is also applied to the theological aspects of the total body of knowledge concerned with pastoral care. However, we should not simply make the theology of pastoral care identical with pastoral theology. By "theology of pastoral care" one could mean the endeavor to reply properly to the questions: What does Revelation teach us about pastoral care? What is pastoral care when viewed from the theological standpoint? What are its fundamental points? What is essential and what is accidental? What, therefore, is a pastor? However, starting with such a theology of pastoral care, we must then determine a standpoint with regard to many practical questions. This practical side of pastoral theology makes this branch of theology broader than a strictly theological reflection on the nature of pastoral care. On the other hand, these practical considerations should not be divorced from the theoretical; otherwise they could easily lose their theological anchorage.

Consequently, we prefer to call the whole body of these studies "pastoral theology" and to regard the "theology of pastoral care" as its essential core. Then, together with sociology, psychology and the history of pastoral care, we obtain the whole body of knowledge devoted to the study of pastoral care.

HISTORICAL ORIGIN OF PASTORAL THEOLOGY

Pastoral theology has had a peculiar origin and a difficult development.[1] It is the youngest among the branches of theology. Although the terms "pastoral theology" and "pastoral-

---

[1]Cf. F. Schubert, *Pastoraltheologie,* Part 3, 3rd ed., Graz, 1935, pp. 3-6; L. Bopp, *Zwischen Pastoraltheologie und Seelsorgewissenschaft,* Freiburg i. Br., 1938; F. X. Arnold, *Grundsätzliches und Geschichtliches zur Theologie der Seelsorge,* Freiburg i. Br., 1949; P. A. Stonner, "Die Pastoraltheologie als theologische Disziplin," *Anima,* vol. 13 (1958), pp. 195-204; Heinz Schuster, "The Nature and Function of Pastoral Theology," *Concilium,* vol. 3 (1965), pp. 4-14; F. X. Arnold, K. Rahner and L. M. Weber, *Handbuch der Pastoraltheologie,* vol. 1, Freiburg i.Br., 1964.

theological" are older, we find pastoral theology as a separate branch of theology only at the end of the eighteenth century, and then in a very unfortunate connection. On October 3, 1774, Empress Maria Theresa, mother of Joseph II, promulgated a new regulation for the theological faculties in her realm. The fact that this was done by the State is itself worth noting. In this regulation there appeared, as far as is known, for the first time the distinct branch of "Pastoral Theology" besides Dogma, Canon Law and Moral Theology. This regulation was put into practice despite objections from the Church, for the spirit of that pastoral theology was that of the Enlightenment, with its erroneous mentality regarding the nature and task of the Church. However, we should not be too severe in our judgment regarding the intentions that inspired that decree. No doubt, the education of the clergy left much to be desired with respect to direct pastoral care. As a result, the State considered it its duty to intervene. This, of course, was wrong especially since the reform was made on the basis of a mentality that was theologically unacceptable.

However, as a happy result of that unacceptable introduction of a pastoral theology, against which many objections could be raised, great efforts were made by the Church to develop a sound pastoral theology. This took place especially in South-German countries at the beginning of the nineteenth century. It was most fortunate that on account of the historical situation the central place of the Church was emphasized in that young pastoral theology.

One of the trailblazers who deserved great credit for this was Johann Michael Sailer, an outstanding and progressive man in that critical period of transition from the eighteenth to the nineteenth century.

Although the Church received special attention in Sailer's thought, he nevertheless considered the pastor, in his pastoral

366

activity, too much in isolation from the Church.[2] Around 1840, in the writings of Anton Graf, the Church appears still more in the foreground; and for Graf the pastor is an organ of the Church.[3] About fifteen years later Joseph Amberger gave the following definition: "Pastoral theology is the science of divine-human activity for the construction and development of the Kingdom of God upon earth."[4] A definition that sounds very much like what is heard nowadays. Many years later, in 1904, Johann Prunner carried that line of thought even further by stressing the fact that it is Christ who works in the Church: "The object of pastoral theology is Christ's permanent pastoral activity for the salvation of souls, as this is fulfilled in the Church, His mystical body, under the guidance of the Holy Spirit, by the priests as her organs."[5]

It is worth noting that when these authors limited pastoral care to that exercised by priests, they did not—with only one exception—deny that the activity of the laity also belongs in principle to pastoral care. Their restriction was due rather to a practical consideration, namely, that they were writing for priests about the priestly pastoral ministry. Moreover, at that time little attention was paid to the lay apostolate. However, the definitions we have quoted leave open the possibility of including the apostolate of religious and lay people in pastoral care.

Unfortunately pastoral theology did not attain everywhere the excellence that is found in those German authors, and in later years a decline set in also in Germany. If a distinct "theology of pastoral care" was present in those authors, hardly any theological reflection is contained in the following defini-

---

[2]*Vorlesungen aus der Pastoraltheologie,* Munich, 5th ed., 1835.

[3]*Kritische Darstellung des gegenwartigen Zustandes der praktischen Theologie,* Tubingen, 1841.

[4]*Pastoraltheologie,* Regensburg, 2nd ed., 1855.

[5]*Lehrbuch der Pastoraltheologie.*

tion written in 1912: "Pastoral theology is a treatise in which the tasks and occupations of shepherds of souls are dealt with *ex professo*, and which is specially aimed at forming above all good pastors for the diocese."[6] In this book, everything is concerned with the diocese and especially with the parish, a very questionable restriction. The author is in fact so restrictive that when he asks himself if pastoral theology is concerned with pastoral care in general, he answers in the negative. Moreover, he and many others classified pastoral theology under moral theology as a sort of professional ethics of priests. And in the twenties of this century a widely-used definition was even poorer in content: "Pastoral theology is the theological science which gives practical rules for the care of souls."

At present pastoral theology is developing once more. Some of the important authors in this field are Franz Xaver Arnold of Tübingen[7] and Franz Xaver von Hornstein of Fribourg[8] with their staff of collaborators and former students. Although it is not a question of life or death whether one has at his disposal a good definition, the authors do their best to make clear what they are talking about; and it is particularly important for us to know how the various authors look upon pastoral theology. Thus we read, for instance, in Constantin Noppel: "Pastoral theology is the doctrine about the pastoral function of the Church."[9] This he means in the strict sense for he accepts, in the total priesthood of Christ, the usual distinction between priesthood as such (worship), the office of prophet or teaching, and the pastoral function. According

---

[6]A. Berardi, *Theologia pastoralis*, Favenza, 3rd ed., 1912.

[7]Cf., e.g., his works, *Dienst am Glauben*, Freiburg i.Br., 1948; *Glaubensverkündigung und Glaubensgemeinschaft*, Düsseldorf, 1955; *Seelsorge aus der Mitte der Heilsgeschichte*, Freiburg i.Br., 1956.

[8]His largest work is *Wesentliche Seelsorge*, Luzern, 1945, 608 pages.

[9]*Aedificatio corporis Christi*, Freiburg i.Br., 1937.

to him, therefore, pastoral theology is related to this pastoral function.

Viktor Schurr follows the same line of thought in his recent excellent book about pastoral care,[10] where he states: "We take 'pastoral [theology]' in the narrow sense, as the science of the ecclesial pastoral office." But the author feels obliged to add: "However, we also desire to offer some timely orientations for the proclamation of the faith (office of teaching) and for the administration of the sacraments (priestly function), particularly for the Eucharist and the sacrament of penance."[11] This restriction to the pastoral office is neither correct nor tenable. We must, on the contrary, bring in all three aspects of the total priesthood of Christ; after that we may be able to evaluate the significance of that threefold division.

THE PLACE OF PASTORAL THEOLOGY
IN THE WHOLE OF THEOLOGY

Even if the aim of pastoral theology is already clear, in broad provisional lines, and even if we recognize that it is truly a theological science, this does not in the least mean that we have thereby solved the question whether pastoral theology is rightly called a special branch of theology. May we say that pastoral theology has its own "formal object," or must we—as has generally been the case until now—continue to classify it under moral theology, with all the dangers of bringing one-sidedly moralizing tendencies into pastoral care? Or is it preferable to say with Noppel that pastoral theology is "essentially to be classified under dogmatic theology"?

Although dogmatic theology is an important foundation for the specialization of pastoral theology, it is nevertheless im-

---

[10]*Seelsorge in einer neuer Welt*, Salzburg, 1957.
[11]*Ibid.*, p. 12.

possible, or at least not desirable, to make pastoral theology a sort of subdivision of dogmatic theology. But we are justified in claiming that pastoral theology has its own "formal object" alongside Dogma, Moral Theology, etc. We must then begin with the idea that the whole of theology must be seen as a unity, as having one object which, however, can be approached from various standpoints. The "object," the datum to be studied by the whole of theology, is the total datum of Revelation. This we consider from various sides, and a dogmatic consideration differs from that of moral theology, however much the two may be related. While a good exegesis of Scripture is an indispensable condition for all theologians, pastoral theology, in close connection with dogmatic and moral theology, is directly interested in the activity by which the Church guides the ecclesial community and accompanies its members in the service of God and their striving for personal salvation. Pastoral theology gives its direct attention to the establishment, consolidation and the expansion of the Kingdom of God. Of course, that attention is essentially the interest of the whole Church and hence of the whole of theology. But it makes a difference whether, in that total theology, one pays particular attention to the mystery of the Holy Trinity, the divinity of Christ, *or* to the significance and execution of Christ's command: "Go and teach all nations."

To specify this further, we must ask ourselves whether pastoral theology considers the Kingdom of God primarily under the aspect of God's honor or principally under that of salvation. Although these aspects can never be separated in a universal theology, and although even a specialized theology may never lose sight of their inner connection, we are, nevertheless, justified in asking that question. We could answer it in this way: pastoral theology and hence pastoral care sees everything under the aspect of procuring man's *salvation*. The glorification of God is most intimately connected with this, but it is not the primary point of view from which pastoral theology approaches Revelation.

In pastoral theology our first attention is directed to the salvation of men, but through and beyond it we see the totality and therefore the glorification of God. In reality, this ultimate end, the glory of God, coincides with the salvation of man. It is most important to keep particularly in mind this ultimate end, namely, God's glorification. For, it often happens that in pastoral work everything is looked at exclusively, and therefore wrongly, from the standpoint of "what is good for man." This exclusiveness contains the danger that this "good" may be seen too much from the standpoint of "what is agreeable to man" or, at least, that man's primary orientation toward God fades too much into the background. This could lead to a restriction of pastoral care, in the sense of making it an activity in which values are reversed, as if man were not made for God but God for man. Or it could transform the work of the Church into a purely social, humanitarian activity. The question "what is good for man?" is aimed at man's salvation and must be seen in the proper perspective within the total reality, viz., God's glorification is the salvation of man.

However, the fact that there is a danger of taking too narrow a view of pastoral theology and pastoral care must not make us forget that it is man's salvation that is the true formal object of pastoral theology. It is the spiritual salvation, the salvation by Christ, of the human beings who are living on earth as embodied spirits and in definite concrete circumstances. To illustrate this we can take as an example the celebration of the Eucharist. In this celebration, glory is given to God in the most perfect way but, at the same time and precisely by it, this celebration tends to the salvation of man. We must say that the celebration of the Eucharist is a pastoral work insofar as it procures salvation. Yet this does not mean

371

that pastoral care looks upon the Mass solely from the standpoint of "how do men draw from it the means to become better?" The Mass as *worship* is pastoral care, which means: the bishop or priest presides as "minister of the people's worship" (*leitourgos*); he goes to stand before God in the name of, and with, his fellow-believers in order to procure the salvation of men by the glorification of God.

Since a new development of pastoral theology is taking place at a time when the value of specialization in a branch of theology has greatly diminished, it is to be expected that pastoral theology will not develop into so distinct a branch as has been the case with "Dogma" and "Morals." The specialization of pastoral theology means rather a special attention, a particular orientation, within the whole of theology toward the Church who incorporates herself into the whole of human existence, for the salvation of men.

The organization of the study of pastoral care is also, like pastoral theology itself, in a process of construction and development. With respect to the philosophical and theological training of all priests, whether diocesan or religous, the explicit directive of the Holy See in the Constitution *Sedes Sapientiae* of May 31, 1956, and in the *Decree on Priestly Training* of Vatican Council II aim at procuring a suitable pastoral formation. It is worth noting that the Church authorities insist that in this pastoral study an important place be given to catechetics, pedagogy, psychology and sociology.[12] In theological faculties which offer several years of post-seminary study leading to a doctorate, there exists, as yet, no possibility of specializing in pastoral theology as such. But in German universities particular attention is given to pastoral theology, because the basic seminary training is also offered at the universities. It would be desirable, however,

---

[12]*Decree on Priestly Training*, VI, art. 20.

if advanced study of pastoral care would be offered at the university level. There exist, however, several important institutes for pastoral study that are more or less directly geared to pastoral care.[13] Also important are the various liturgical institutes.[14] In addition many good periodicals are published that deal with those matters. Besides a number of catechetical periodicals and reviews that are principally concerned with homiletics, the following that deal with general pastoral science deserve special mention: *Anima,*[15] *Evangéliser,*[16] *La Maison-Dieu,*[17] *Der Seelsorger,*[18] and *Lebendige Seelsorge.*[19] To these we may add the bi-monthly *Pastoral Life.*[20]

NEW AND RECURRENT PROBLEMS OF PASTORAL CARE

Already in the thirties, Pius XI declared that the pastoral theology and methods of former years were no longer ade-

---

[13]For example, at the University of Fribourg (Sw.) the *Institut für Seelsorgewissenschaft und Seelsorgearbeit;* at the University of Freiburg i.Br. the *Arbeitsstelle für Seelsorgewissenschaft,* which since 1937 publishes the series *Neue Seelsorge* and undertakes many practical activities such as the training of *Seelsorgehelferinnen;* at Tübingen, whose best-known representative is F. X. Arnold; in Vienna the *Oesterreichisches Seelsorgeinstitut;* at Antwerp the *Studiecentrum voor predicatie en zielzorg,* conducted by the Dominicans.

[14]For example, the *Centre de Pastorale Liturgique* of Paris and the *Liturgisches Institut* of Trier.

[15]Published by the above-mentioned Institute of Fribourg.

[16]Published by the Belgian Dominicans of Sarte.

[17]Published by the above-mentioned Institute of Paris.

[18]Published by the Vienna Institute.

[19]Published eight times a year at Freiburg i.Br. Also important for pastoral theology are Konrad Metzger, *Katholische Seelsorge der Gegenwart,* Innsbruck, 1935; *Seelsorgsfragen unserer Zeit* (study topics of the 1st and 2nd Swiss "Seelsorgtagungen" in Luzern, 1935-36), Luzern, 1939; E. Kleinedam and others, *Amt und Sendung,* Freiburg i.Br., 1950; A. Fischer and others, *Seelsorge zwischen gestern und morgen,* Freiburg i.Br., 1961; Karl Rahner and Heinz Schuster, ed., "The Pastoral Mission of the Church," *Concilium,* vol. 3, 1965. See *ibid.* also the articles about sociology and pastoral work.

[20]Published by St. Paul's Monastery, Canfield, Ohio.

quate. Pastoral care in our present time demands something different; the circumstances of the Church, society and men have changed.

Change is an ever recurring phenomenon in the history of the Church and mankind, though it does not always have the intensity that it has at present. The constant cycle of changes presents a twofold aspect: on the one hand, there is a circular process in history in the sense that, after some time, the same problems recur but in a different guise; on the other hand, there also arise new problems and situations. This may be illustrated by means of the already mentioned Johann Michael Sailer. This author, who was born in 1751 and died in 1832, lived his mature years during the time of the Enlightenment and the French Revolution. He was always very progressive and was also very positive toward those points in the Enlightenment which he, along with many others, considered acceptable. But, when the reaction triumphed, this acceptance caused him much trouble. Nevertheless, he was at the same time one of the leaders against the Enlightenment and rationalism; and, at the beginning of the nineteenth century, he was one of the men who were very influential in the revival of the Church and of theology, without being either reactionary or conservative.

The first edition of his manual of pastoral theology[21] came out around 1780. Speaking about the changes that had happened since then in the preface to the third edition of 1811, he says: "God, Christ, Religion—these still exist . . . and no hour will ever strike when it can be said 'They are no more,' for they exist forever." He continues, saying that we face the following facts:

1. Holy Scripture is divested of its old truth and a "new truth" is put into it.

---

[21]*Vorlesungen aus der Pastoraltheologie.*

374

2. Virtue is conceived as something purely human: without God, without eternity, without religion.

3. Consequently, our time now has an image of the "ideal man"—that is why in the process of education youth is now flooded with sciences of nature, of man and of the world. But what really makes man a man, namely, his relation to God, is left out of consideration; Church and priest are appreciated, at the most, as being still useful for public morality.

This he wrote in 1811. What is peculiar in this is the fact that the particular situation he describes is strange to us while, at the same time, we find in it a similarity with our present state. The problems he mentions are once more most actual, but the manner in which they present themselves is greatly if not essentially different. We must keep well in mind that—and this we wish to stress particularly—old situations never return. A situation is never exactly like the previous one, however striking the resemblance might seem to be. Hence, it would be very dangerous to return to earlier methods of pastoral care on the basis of such a similarity.

New facts and situations, however, that in no way existed previously also present themselves. Telling examples of this are industrialization and the unification of the whole world as a consequence of the enormous developments in the means of communication.

These considerations should make us realize that there will always be changes in pastoral care, that there are many contingent elements in it. These have only a relative value. Many forms of pastoral care are now losing their value either in whole or in part. For a proper evaluation of the possibility of change and, at the same time, in order not to become too attached to the new present-day forms which are also contingent, it is of the utmost importance that we learn to know what pastoral care is, what its foundations are, and what un-

375

changeable characteristics it shares with the nature of the Church.

What is Pastoral Care?

When we ask ourselves what pastoral care really is, we may omit the care for our own personal salvation as something that goes without saying. But we face a modern distinction that was not known in former times: we distinguish the task of every baptized person, of every member of the Church, in regard to the eternal salvation of his fellow-men, from the commission of the official minister who is "ordained" by the Church to go before his fellow-believers and all men to help, serve, direct and guide them in the service of God and on the road to salvation. Formerly the idea of putting pastoral care and the lay apostolate under a common denominator would not even have arisen. But when, at present, we make an explicit distinction for theological reasons and, for practical reasons, continue to keep the two terms apart, we are aware, at the same time, that the two have their roots in the same soil: Christ's priesthood, as it is exercised by Him in the Church.[22] Just as the official (ordained) priesthood is a special participation in the general priesthood of Christ, so too, pastoral care attached to an office, a function, is a specialization of pastoral care taken in a general sense.

When in the following pages we speak of the essential characteristics of pastoral care, we refer to pastoral care in its totality, to the pastoral care of the Church. From the context it should be clear when in certain cases there is a question of pastoral care as attached to the office in the Church.

Christ was and is the pastor par excellence. God's Son became man to glorify the Father and lead men to salvation.

---

[22]Cf. Vatican Council II's *Decree on the Apostolate of the Laity,* Ch. I, art. 2.

This work of Christ is both the *model* and the *source* of all pastoral care. Thus all pastoral care is *supernatural,* precisely because it is fundamentally the work of Christ himself, though by means of men. However, the supernatural and the natural are not separate elements; this is true also with respect to pastoral care. We have to deal with a concrete redeemed world and concrete individual men whom Christ has redeemed. Hence we are not permitted to neglect natural means and must take proper account of the actual circumstances in which we live. Many "modern" forms of pastoral care have been unsuccessful, however, because what was natural remained purely natural and was not sufficiently integrated into the proper nature of pastoral care.[23]

In pastoral care we are, therefore, servants and instruments of Christ. Our Lord Jesus Christ is *the* pastor; it is Christ who baptizes, confirms, etc. Hence it is the *Church* in which Christ lives and works which exercises the pastoral functions. The whole ecclesial community has a share in that task, but the Church has appointed some men with the charge of fulfilling that task in a special manner. For this she has ordained them, given them power and sent them; and for this they are trained. But the pastoral care that belongs to *all* is the extension of the work of Christ, that is, the continuation of the glorification of the Father by Christ and the sanctification of men that is directed to that end. God's Son became man, the Word became flesh. The Church is the Body of Christ, and every man must live the life of Christ through grace, a life of grace that must grow and attain its full flowering. That is why pastoral care is wonderfully characterized in the expression

---

[23]Cf., e.g., the three special issues of *Anima* dealing with love and pastoral care, vol. 8 (1953), pp. 113-196; with pastoral care and the phenomenon of dread (anxiety), *ibid.,* pp. 209-297; with nature and grace in pastoral care, vol. 9 (1954), pp. 1-84.

"the ministry of the Incarnation of the Word" (*Ministerium Incarnationis Verbi*).

To put it in a more concrete form, we should keep in mind that we can distinguish many facets in Christ's priesthood. For a long time we have been accustomed to distinguishing three principal aspects. Although these distinctions are not wholly indispensable, they are helpful when we wish to form an image of pastoral care.

To Christ the Teacher of the truth there corresponds the *office of teacher* or "prophet," i.e., of speaking on behalf of Christ. To Christ the High Priest corresponds the *priestly office* in the narrow sense. To Christ the King of all nations corresponds the *pastoral office* of shepherd. All three aspects of Christ's priesthood bring salvation, but they have a special relation to one another. The office of Teacher or "prophet" prepares the way for a life of grace, it proclaims God's grace. The administration of the sacred mysteries or sacraments, the priestly office in the strict sense, makes the life of grace come into being, makes it grow or, if need be, restores it. The pastoral office governs and guides the faithful; this covers a large field of activities, but its purpose is always to give birth to, develop, or restore the life of grace through Christ.

Those three "offices" are really aspects of the one office and must be seen in close connection with one another. The pastoral office is not the first one, for pastoral care is essentially a participation in Christ's threefold ministry. Now, since the essence of Christian life consists in existence and growth in the grace of Christ, in participation in divine life, the most essential element of pastoral care is the administration of the sacraments: baptism, the Eucharist and the other sacraments. For it is by them that the life of grace is established and given an opportunity to develop. Thus the offering of the Sacrifice and the administration of the other sacraments is the primary exercise of the office or function of pastoral care. For all others who do not have this office participation in those sacraments and that Sacrifice is the highest form of pastoral care, of "lay apostolate."

Those three aspects of the one office are most closely interconnected and cannot be exercised with perfect independence from one another. Just as Christ was Teacher, Priest and Shepherd on the Cross, so also the priest is teacher, priest and shepherd, when he celebrates the Eucharist; and all have a share in that. The same is true of all the sacraments. Even when no sacraments are administered, the pastoral office and the office of teacher—mostly exercised together—remain in close connection with and operate on the basis of the priesthood, in either a general or a special way. One aspect may be predominant at various times, but the other aspects will never be absent.

It is within the work of Christ, conceived in this way, that all pastoral activities must be seen. This also applies to visiting homes, working for youth groups, social groups, etc. When these activities are seen in that connection, and hence also in connection with the Eucharist and the administration of the other sacraments, it will not be so easy to let the variety of "external" activities degenerate into "activism", that is, into an activity with no spiritual core and with little or nothing to do with pastoral care and religion. Then also, there will be no danger of having too narrow a concept of pastoral work, for instance, of limiting it to purely parochial care.

Every priest is a pastor in the most essential sense of the word. Every lay person, likewise, has a share in pastoral care if he fulfills his task as a layman, even if he might not be numbered among those who are more or less officially "lay apostles." There are, of course, degrees of participation in pastoral care: a bishop and a parish priest share more fully in it than a priest-bursar in an institution. But the essentials are not wanting even in the latter. Our prayers also, and in particular the office offered by the priest in the name of the Church, belong to pastoral care. For instance, it is of very great value when priests who have a common charge of a parish pray that office together in the parish church.

In the light of what has been said, one can also discern what *practical* pastoral care means. The celebration of the Eucharist, the administration of baptism and of the other sacraments are the most practical pastoral works. However, "practical" is often confused with "pragmatic," that is, with that which is immediately useful, which offers here and now the greatest possibilities, which can most easily be attained for the present. Pastoral care is then no longer leadership, but simply an attempt to catch up with events. A sound "practical pastoral care" is a truly supernatural care that is well informed and takes account of actual circumstances.

Community and Person. Finally let us say a few words about pastoral care for the community and for the individual. Everything we have said was permeated with the idea that pastoral care takes place in and by the ecclesial community. When we stick to this principle, our pastoral care will not degenerate into treating the community as a nameless mass and its members as faceless individuals; it will not give modern man in the Church a feeling of isolation, as, unfortunately, has too often happened. Only when we start from the idea of the Church as the ecclesial community of persons shall we arrive at a true pastoral community care and at a corresponding care of the *persons* in this community. For the Church is a community of personal human beings with Christ as its Head. Hence we must keep well in mind both that we are a community and that every person has a particular value. The community as such, but also every person, must honor God, become holy and be happy. When pastoral care is de-

380

fined as the "sanctification of men," we run the risk of neglecting man's communal being.

We are presently living in a time when individualism and collectivism are fighting for supremacy and it is difficult to find the way to the true idea of community and hence of true personalism. In the process of developing that idea further and in combatting the tendency of over-estimating organization—which tendency is present also in pastoral care—it is necessary to put particular stress on the value of personality both for itself and for the community. We shall never attain to a true community if we do not cultivate personality. Orientation toward the community may never be lost sight of, lest we fall into individualism and reduce the person to a nameless face in a faceless mass.

THE LAY APOSTOLATE

Pastoral care that is exercised on the basis of the faithful's general priesthood and not on the basis of ordination to the priesthood, is usually called "lay apostolate." Just as much as it follows from the office of the ordained priest that he is called to a special function of pastoral care, so does it follow from the status of the layman that he is called to a general kind of apostolic pastoral work. Lay apostolate is not at all something that one does "as an extra" over and above one's duty, for "the laity derive the right and the duty to the apostolate from their union with Christ the head of the mystical body.[24]

Some particular tasks can be clearly indicated with respect to ordained pastors, but these are always within the totality of their priestly existence. In the case of the layman—and this term applies theologically also to religious who are not priests

---

[24]Vatican Council II's *Decree on the Apostolate of the Laity*, Ch. I, art. 3.

—the emphasis lies fully on his life and works as a layman in the Church and less on particular concrete tasks that could be spelled out. The general apostolic task of all faithful assumes particular forms in each man's life. The lay apostolate as such is neither a substitute for the priest's pastoral care nor a diluted copy of it. Rather, it has a value in its own right springing from the same root as that of the priest. The lay apostolate is not something that has been or can be "introduced" at a particular time. At most, the layman can be stimulated to fulfill his God-given role.

Pius XI and Catholic Action. In a certain sense the rise of Catholic Action was an occasion for confusion. Because of the way that Catholic Action was emphasized in connection with a certain historical situation, it became difficult to see this action as merely a specific determination of the general task belonging to every layman in virtue of his general participation in the priesthood of Christ.

Catholic Action began earnest with the rise of anticlericalism and anti-Churchism, especially in Italy. Pius XI has been called the first pope of Catholic Action, but the term itself was already used under Pope Pius X. It was Pope Pius XI (1922-1939) who strongly encouraged and even tried to define Catholic Action. In his first Encyclical, *Ubi arcana Dei* of December 29, 1922, he spoke very emphatically about the lay apostolate in a general sense. Addressing himself to the bishops he wrote: "On the other hand, remind the faithful also of the fact that by their cooperation in the works of the private and public apostolate under your guidance and that of your clergy . . . they will merit the holy title of 'a chosen race, a royal priesthood, a holy nation, a purchased people' (1 Peter 2:9)."[25]

---

[25]*A.A.S.*, vol. 14 (1922), pp. 673 ff.

Striking in that text is the strong, direct bond of such action with the hierarchy. Of course, the activity of the whole Church is under the guidance of the hierarchy; but in those words we find already elements of the definition of Catholic Action which the same Pontiff gave at a later date, namely, "Catholic Action is the participation of the laity in the hierarchical apostolate of the Church" (March 19, 1927). In a letter of July 30, 1928, the Pope defined it more precisely as: "The participation of the Catholic lay people in the hierarchical apostolate, for the defense of religious principles, for the development of a sane and sound social action, under the direction of the ecclesiastical hierarchy, outside and above all political parties, for the purpose of renewing Catholic life in the family and in society."

It is quite notable that throughout the pontificate of Pope Pius XI there was a constant emphasis on the layman's "cooperation in the hierarchical apostolate." This was already the case in the text of 1922, although the Pope then referred to the words of St. Peter which, however, have a more general purport. Secondly, since little stress was placed upon the general apostolic task of all the faithful but a correspondingly greater emphasis was given to official Catholic Action, it is easy to see how "lay apostolate" and "Catholic Action" became almost synonymous. When a distinction was made, the general apostolate was spoken of as "Catholic Action in the broad sense."

The rise of Catholic Action, however, strongly stimulated the idea that the laity has a general apostolic task, even when such activity is not immediately dependent on the hierarchy and has no official connection with Catholic Action.

Pius XII and the Lay Apostolate. Pope Pius XI's definition appeared inadequate. For this reason the allocution of his successor at the end of the first World Congress of the Lay

Apostolate, October 14, 1951, was of great significance.[26] Pius XII here distinguished a lay apostolate in the *improper* sense, i.e., the apostolate of good example, prayer and sacrifice, from the lay apostolate in the *proper* sense. The latter could be either organized or unorganized; and organized lay apostolate was subdivided into so-called Catholic Action and other forms, such as sodalities and religious societies. Pius XII described Catholic Action as the official lay apostolate, an instrument in the hands of the hierarchy.[27] As such, it enjoyed less freedom than other forms of lay apostolate. Moreover, the latter were in no way to be regarded as subservient to the former.

Unlike his predecessor, Pius XII did not speak of Catholic Action as a *participation* in the apostolate of the hierarchy but as a *cooperation* with the hierarchical apostolate. The reason undoubtedly was that the term "participation" too strongly suggested the idea that the members of Catholic Action were in some sense "taken up into the hierarchy." The same idea caused some theologians[28] to object to the notion that those members had received a kind of canonical mission or mandate rather than a simple task to fulfill in the Church.

Vatican Council II. Meanwhile the *Constitution on the Church* of Vatican Council II has declared that the lay apostolate is "a participation in the salvific mission of the Church itself" and that all members "through their baptism and confirmation are commissioned to that apostolate by the Lord Himself." However, "besides this apostolate . . ., the laity can also be called in various ways to a more direct form of

---

[26]A.A.S., vol. 43 (1951), pp. 748-792; English text in N.C.W.C. ed., *The Lay Apostolate—Its Need Today*. Cf. also *Actes du Ier congrès mondial pour l'apostolat des laiques*, 2 vols., Rome, 1952.

[27]*The Lay Apostolate—Its Need Today*, art. 29.

[28]Karl Rahner, *Schriften zur Theologie*, vol. II, pp. 339 ff.

cooperation in the apostolate of the hierarchy."[29] The layman's *participation*, then, is in the mission of the *Church*, the people of God, while his *cooperation* refers to the apostolate of the hierarchy.

Because Christ's redemption is essentially concerned with the salvation of *men*, it includes also "the renewal of the whole temporal order." The laity must take up this renewal as "their own special obligation," but this is not the whole extent of their task, for they exercise their apostolate in "both the spiritual and the temporal order."[30] They fulfill their task not only by the witness of their way of life but also by the spoken word and deeds. The laity's apostolic activity can be undertaken either on an individual basis or together as members of an organized group. All lay persons are called to the individual apostolate exercised by living a life of faith and, in certain circumstances and according to each one's abilities, also by the spoken or written word.[31] Group apostolate, on the other hand, lies wholly in line with man's social nature and with the Christian's membership in the people of God. The laity have the right to found and control apostolic associations, but the hierarchy can give explicit recognition to certain forms of apostolate or join them more closely with its own apostolic function.[32]

Pastoral Care, Apostolate, Missionary Work, and Specialized Spiritual Care

Above we have tried to sketch the characteristics of what is usually signified by the term "pastoral care." We must still point out certain practical distinctions that are sometimes made between "pastoral care," "apostolate" and "missionary

---

[29]Ch. IV, art. 33.
[30]*Decree on the Apostolate of the Laity,* Ch. II, art. 5 and 7.
[31]*Ibid.,* Ch. IV, art. 15-16.
[32]*Ibid.,* Ch. IV, art. 18-19 and Ch. V, art. 34.

work." In addition there is also the specialized care destined for particular categories of people.

Let us begin by noting that what was said regarding the definition of pastoral care is applicable to pastoral care in the narrow sense to be used here and also to the apostolate and missionary work. Every action of the Church has the three aspects of Christ's priesthood: the office of prophet or teacher, the priesthood and the office of shepherd. Whatever one may do in the Church's pastoral task, we must always keep in mind that that activity should be one of *maintaining, consolidating,* and *expanding* God's kingdom.

When this is presupposed, we can accept the threefold distinction that was made for practical reasons:

Pastoral care. By this we must then understand primarily the task of *maintaining* or taking care of those who belong to the flock (the *cura animarum*). *Parochial* care is the principal form of this care in its narrow and usual sense, but it is by no means its only form. Pastoral care—particularly at the present time—must never neglect the apostolic dimension, and its task certainly includes educating people in an apostolic mentality.[33]

Apostolate. This is the *consolidating* task of the Church in countries where she is already established and indicates her work with those who live outside the Church or are only weakly connected with her. The development and increased interest in this apostolate has been strongly influenced by the growing number of people who no longer practice their faith or have left the Church. Moreover, it has been vigorously stimulated by another important factor, namely, the new theology about the Church. For, a better understanding of the proper nature of the Church makes us realize more and more

---

[33]Cf. *Decree on the Pastoral Office of Bishops in the Church,* Ch. II, art. 30.

386

that, by taking care only of the faithful who are already in the Church, we are fulfilling only a part of our task.

Missionary Work. This is the planting and establishing of the Church in countries where she is not yet or only weakly present. It is in this sense that we speak of the *expanding* of God's kingdom.

Under the influence of the actual development in the Church, the terms "pastoral care" and "apostolate" as defined above, have received a more or less emotional overtone. Pastoral care is looked upon as the old-fashioned, self-satisfied and closed form of ministry. On the contrary, the apostolate is considered the modern form of ministry: fresh, youthful, mobile, not static but dynamic, with a lively openness for the needs of the Church, with an apostolic zeal especially toward those who are outside the Church or only feebly attached to it. If this be admitted, it would then be especially the apostolate that would emphasize the task of the laity, while there would be practically no place for it in the more traditional pastoral work. It is evident that if one looks at things in that emotional context, he shall be led to draw false conclusions and establish contrasts and oppositions where they do not really exist.

Specialized spiritual care refers to pastoral *or* apostolic work directed to special categories of persons, as distinguished by their profession, age, etc., such as: students, soldiers, religious, the sick and the aged. This "categorical" spiritual care is clearly either pastoral or apostolic: for example, the care of Religious is pastoral, while the care of a groups of dechristianized workers is apostolic. Often, however, "categorical" ministry is a combination of pastoral care and apostolate, for instance, among workers of a certain category, such as itinerant farm workers. According as either the pastoral or the apostolic aspect prevails, the ministry in

387

question will be called pastoral or apostolic; for instance, we speak of an industrial apostolate among factory workers in Europe and pastoral work among Catholic university students. The "categorical" ministry can also be organized parochially, as is sometimes done for students in Europe. But most of the time categorical ministry is not parochial and parishes are not categorical.

2. Changing Accents in Priestly Ministry

Today, those who are engaged *ex officio* in pastoral work are forced to seek new ways. Pastoral care has to accept the consequences flowing from the changes that are taking place in the whole of society and in the Church. The right conclusions, however, are not as easy to reach as those of a simple reasoning process. Nowadays it is very difficult to draw clear-cut conclusions. We can consider ourselves fortunate when we are at least able to see in what direction we are going. With respect to those changes taking place in priestly pastoral work, we can see that we are going in the direction of a greater emphasis on sacrament and word. Let us try to explain the matter a little more in detail.

DEMAND OF AUTHENTICITY

The great problems of life, the fundamental religious issues, are becoming more and more questions of vital and direct concern. There is great diversity in the way those questions are expressed, but we must admit that very many people today are asking themselves what the meaning of life is, whether God really exists, what we ought to think about Christ. No doubt, such thoughts are stimulated also by all sorts of publications, discussions, and particularly by certain literary works; but the true cause lies deeper. The expressions that are found in literature and also in plays (e.g., Sartre's) are, not the cause, but rather the crystallization of a widespread doubt about the meaning of life.

However, modern man is not always a sceptical doubter who more or less *a priori* excludes any positive answer. The man of today who is not totally carried away by difficulties or opportunities on the material level desires to get an answer to the great questions. Today's Catholic wants in particular to get an answer regarding the Church. What is the Church? He knows, of course, the catechism's answer to that question; but he is inclined to take that answer for what it is, and to seek a reply in line with real life. What is the Church as she presents herself to us in reality? Theology speaks about the Church as God's sign of salvation in this world. What shows that she is such a "sign of salvation"? What exactly is the message of the Church? The Gospel is the "Good News," the news that spells joy to all men. What does that mean while, all around us and also in the Church, we meet with so little interior joyfulness, so little acceptance of life? The Church maintains that she announces to us and proclaims the word of God, but is it truly God's word? What right has the Church to explain the word of God to us?

And so the questions constantly go back to the basic issue: what is the basis of the Church's far-reaching claims? What right has the Church to occupy herself with our personal life? If there is a God, why is my conscience not enough? Must the Church always intervene and tell me what I must and must not do in regard to God? Let the Church prove her credibility! Let her prove by the way she exists that she has the right to exist and that she is acceptable for men who are looking for an answer to the great questions of life.

The present situation does not permit any half-heartedness. Traditional answers and traditional positions are *a priori* at a disadvantage. Traditions are increasingly incapable of making a strong impression; traditional arguments, certainly

389

among the young, are no longer powerful. Modern man has suffered so many disillusionments that he examines very critically the real value of everything that presents itself as having great claims, especially if it should claim an evident right to impose obligations on men. This applies very clearly to the Church which maintains that she has the power and the task of insuring eternal salvation. Man has become spiritually deaf and blind to all sorts of promises because he has suffered so many disappointments.

Ant yet man still has a craving for what is good and true, and above all he looks for love. But, because he has been hurt numerous times, he has become distrustful. When deplorable things occur in society as a result of the doings of men, and particularly when this takes place in the Church community, voices are heard from all sides to the effect that "Didn't we know it all along?" Formerly reaction was likely to be: "It is probably not true"; but at present this is no longer the usual reaction. The Church, because she puts forward the greatest claims to being authentic and truthful, presently stands in a particularly exposed position. Man wants her to be what she claims to be. He does not desire so much that she adduce clear theoretical proofs of being Christ's Church but he wants her to show this by the authenticity of her life.

Even if the faithful of today realize better that there is a human and therefore sinful side to the Church, those who govern the Church and thus particularly represent her, are in a very precarious situation. Their life and deeds are becoming more and more the standard by which men gauge the credibility of the Church. Her leaders must realize that they will increasingly find a wall of distrust which they must first break through. The sceptical and soberly disillusioned man is even inclined to begin by denying true values before he accepts them with some reserve. Confidence is easily weakened; the idealism of modern man is very sensitive. We must not be astonished when we notice that "reasons which are in themselves unsound" make people fall away from the faith. Much more frequently today than in previous times, proofs and reasonings are disregarded while the concrete existential situations are taken as the norm. Easily, much too readily, men turn their backs to the "disappointing" Church.

Modern man, in spit of his seeming scepticism, is an idealist and is motivated by love; yet he is able to pierce through the veil of appearances. He goes to the heart of the matter even with respect to the Church, although he cannot say exactly what he is seeking. But he wants to get the authentic answers to his fundamental questions from those who minister to the Church. There is nothing he loathes more than thoughtless chatter and doing things as they have always been done. Although his own life may fall short of his standards and be full of compromises, he does not tolerate that sort of thing in the Church and in her ministers.

Theology, Bible exegesis, the new tendencies in moral theology and the liturgical movement are heading in the same direction: honesty, truthfulness, and the core of Christian existence. They are in some sense the answer to the questions asked by the faithful; they urge the Church's ministers to reflect on the fundamental questions of Christianity and of pastoral care. They do not merely present these ministers with the fundamental problems but also give them an indispensable support.

The priest, who faces the increasingly pressing questions of his fellow-believers and often recognizes in them his own questions, must not try to evade them but is obliged to delve deeply into them. He may not look upon those questions as wanton doubts against the faith but, on the contrary, as starting points, as questions of believing Christians who desire to live their life of faith more earnestly than of old. These questions point in the same direction as that of theological reflection, namely, to the authentic and true ministry of sacrament and word in an ecclesial community built on love.

THE CHANGED SOCIAL POSITION OF THE CHURCH

The changed social condition offers another pointer in the same direction. The medieval era of "Christendom" under Pope and Emperor is gone forever.[34] For many centuries that politico-religious order was looked upon as *the* realization of the right relationship between the Church and the world, or at least between the Church and the State. And this was maintained in spite of the almost constant difficulties which resulted for the Church. For many centuries, even to our own days, that pattern was presented in our textbooks of ecclesiastical public law as the normal situation that should be realized everywhere, to the extent that it was possible. It was recognized, of course, that this could not be achieved "for the time being" in all countries; but it was considered necessary to strive for the restoration of close cooperation of Church and State in which the Church could exercise a very strong influence in social life. As long as this was not possible, it was necessary to make a number of compromises in order to reach a liveable situation. This view shows a great lack of realism; "Christendom" is not at all required on principle.

In our present society the Church is thrown back upon herself. We do not mean that she is forced out of real life but that she is now called to be fully herself. She can no longer lean upon the State and she may not be a pillar of support for the State. Yet this does not exclude a certain cooperation between the two. Both Church and State, by their very nature, occupy an important place in the whole of society. But

---

[34]Cf. Albert Dondeyne, *Faith and the World,* pp. 305 ff.

there are also other factors that, together with Church and State, constitute the whole of human society. There should be cooperation between all those constituent factors, but this does not mean that they must be dependent, and certainly not that they must have a juridical bond. Moreover, no particular historical form of such a bond can ever be necessary on principle. One might imagine, on the basis of older theories, that the Church has been pushed out of the social polity; but it is more correct to say that the Church has gained a greater freedom to be fully herself. The Church is much less involved in temporal affairs than formerly; her ministers thus have greater freedom to pursue the work proper to them.

To this must be added the fact that the Church in many countries is more and more in the state of "diaspora," of dispersion. This is true not only of countries in which the Church's flock is widely scattered, as in Northern Germany and in Scandinavian countries, but applies also to so-called Catholic countries. If we are willing to be realistic, we have to admit that there also the Church's position has become that of a minority. Faithful Catholics are only a minority. This appears more clearly now that social pressure to participate in Church life, has greatly disappeared in those countries. The Church is no longer a dominating Church. This is even more evident when we contemplate the whole world. Since men see themselves more and more as being members of one world, we realize so much the better that we Christians constitute a minority.

GREATER RESPONSIBILITY OF THE LAYMAN

In spite of all that, the Church must desire and strive to make Christians live a total Christian life. "The Church" desires this and strives for it, that is, *the whole Church,* the whole ecclesial community. This Church strives for an ideal that does discern earthly values but nevertheless sees the

393

whole of life as Christianized, as permeated with Christ's spirit and life. The christianization of all the aspects of life is a permanent task of the Church, of all of us; and we are never permitted to withdraw from it or to let others take it away from us.[35]

A very first task of the Church is the Christian exercise of *charity*. Charity occupies a very special place within the more general exercise of Christian love of neighbor. In charitable works the love of neighbor acquires a concrete form toward men who are in need, whatever this need may be, and this can very considerably according to the circumstances of time and place. The Church has always considered the practice of charitable works a most important factor in Christian life and has even exercised it by special ministers, the deacons. But whether performed by deacons or others, the Church values charitable works as an "inalienable duty and right,"[36] as one of the first consequences flowing from the Gospel. But, within the ensemble of Christian influence, the Church has also a direct task with respect to married and family life, to education and social life, and to all other realms and situations of life in which man is involved as man or is asked to make a choice.

The question, however, is, Does that whole immense domain of Christian and ecclesial influence fall directly under the care of the Church's official ministers? By the very nature of things, the decisive word belongs to the leaders, to the hierarchy which was willed by Christ. It is the hierarchy that indicates the general lines and that decisively changes the direction at critical moments. This is to be expected, of

---

[35]Cf. *Decree on the Apostolate of the Laity,* Ch. II, art. 5. See also Bernard Haring, *The Liberty of the Children of God,* Alba House, 1966; Adrian L. van Kaam, *Personal Fulfillment in the Spiritual Life,* Dimension Books, 1966.
[36]Cf. *ibid.,* Ch. II, art. 8.

course, from the leaders of our community. The direct execution, however—and this can embrace a great deal—is a task that is, indeed, ecclesial but that does not in the first place belong to those officially charged with Church functions.

As a matter of fact, actual development is going increasingly in that direction. More and more the bishops appeal to the layman's own responsibility. An evident example at present is that in Europe the bishops, in contrast to what was the case a few decades ago, give only general norms concerning the structure of social organizations and leave to the lay people concerned the choice of the particular structure. Vatican Council II has endorsed this policy.[37] And an increasing number of functions are transferred to hands of lay people. This may still surprise a few simple souls, but in a short time we will consider it perfectly normal. The situation in the last century was such that it was simply necessary for priests to be the leaders in every field, even in politics. (The same phenomenon occured also among Protestant ministers.) But that time is gone.

The causes of that change are complex. If it is called a phenomenon of internal emancipation, we have no objection, provided that emancipation is not viewed as a sort of war of liberation. It is true, of course, that the clergy does not readily give up certain "vested interests," but this is a more or less natural human phenomenon of minor importance. The real point is that the layman now begins to take a more conscious part in ecclesial life. Furthermore, there is a growing number of lay people capable of taking over many functions, and in fact they are often better equipped than their priestly predecessors were able to be. We have only to think of laymen occupied in education, as teachers of practically every branch of learning, inclusive of theology, or the Catholic Press.

---

[37]Cf. *ibid.*, Ch. IV, art. 19.

We may add that in the present situation of the world, it is much better for the Church that the priests be not directly engaged in a number of fields in which laymen can do an excellent job. The required specialization demands such a thorough knowledge that priests who have received a predominantly theological formation simply cannot do justice to many areas, unless they are given the opportunity to study those special subjects for a sufficient number of years. In some countries, an additional reason is that the priest had best stay in the background because it is no longer "acceptable." Fortunately, this is not the case in the English-speaking world.

There is no reason to regret that change of the priest's situation. If the Church wishes to be truly the sign of God's salvation in this world, that sign will be much more significant when the whole people of God, the entire ecclesial community, actively speaks in this world.[38] The Church then appears before the whole of mankind as a community, not as a flock of sheep blindly following the shepherd. The magnificent biblical figure of the shepherd has sometimes been sadly misused. Christ certainly did not intend that the faithful should "sheepishly" follow their shepherds, but He meant to say that the shepherds must be good, trustworthy leaders.

This changed situation is also of great advantage for the full exercise of the priestly task, for this task can now receive full attention. But the change also means that we are forced to reflect again upon that priestly task. This increased attention to the proper task of the priest does not mean merely that more time can be devoted to it, but it also implies a change of attitude by which the "proper task," whatever this may be, can gain in intensity and quality. The layman's great-

---

[38]Cf. *ibid.*, Ch. III, art. 13 and ch. IV, art. 18.

er role may also have consequences with respect to the problem of the present scarcity of priests.

Back to the Sacristy? This whole change in the actual functions of the priest in no way means that he is relegated to the sacristy. His work is not to be confined to Church services as his one and only task, for he could not then do justice to his office. In the situation that is now developing, though not without growing pains, the priest will have more opportunity than formerly to keep in contact with his fellow believers for whom he has a special responsibility. There must be more contact between the priest and the *community* of *persons.*

We have already touched on this subject in connection with parochial life, but this question of contact, which is often neglected, also applies to the whole field of pastoral work. It must be a contact with a *community*—whatever its concrete structure might be—that consists of *persons.* Contact with this community as such must always be maintained, because it is indispensable for personal contact. Experience shows that there can be great differences in this matter. There are communities, especially parishes, in which the priests, precisely by the way they celebrate the sacraments and particularly by their way of preaching, have and maintain contact with their parishioners. In other parishes, however, the priests and the community are more or less strangers to one another. In the latter case the ecclesial community is not functioning and it will be very difficult to attain the good personal relationships required for proper pastoral care.[39]

PERSONAL CONTACT

Personal contact is so important that it deserves to be treated separately. In some countries there is unfortunately entire-

---

[39]Cf. J. Pascher, "Seelsorge vom Altare aus," *Anima,* vol. 5 (1950).

ly too little contact between priests and parishioners, even when people would greatly appreciate such contact. We used to speak of the "sacristy priest," but now there are other reasons for the estrangement between priest and people than a sort of "recluse" mentality on the part of pastors; and one gets the impression that in recent years, the separation has been getting wider. Some priests are so much "organization men" that they fail to contact their faithful personally; others are so busy with administrative affairs that they have "no time" for personal contact. Moreover, conditions of work (night shifts, "moonlighting," etc.) and modern habits of life—which sometimes reduce the home to an eating and sleeping station—may make it difficult for the priest to meet the families as a unit and have a truly personal contact with all its members.

Yet that personal contact is most necessary, and the priest should conscientiously ask himself what activities he must drop in order to include this essential task. We have already mentioned that some activities could and should be transferred to the hands of lay people. But we must also realize that it is not merely the priest's involvement in so much organizational work that prevents him from giving sufficient attention to his office of spiritual leader. The already mentional social conditions make that situation even more critical. It is most important, therefore, that priests and lay people, in joint deliberation, look for new ways for the priest to be given back to the faithful. In some countries like the United States, the priests often have kept close contact with their parishioners. But even here there are parishes so large that it is impossible for the pastor to know his people; and people go to and from church services in droves just as, during the week, they go to and from factories. Individual priests may be ingenious in finding a solution for such problems, but it seems most important that bishops, priests and people make a common effort to improve any situation that prevents priests from doing the things that must take first place in their ministry.

Visitations of Homes. In this respect, visitation of the home remains one of the most important forms of contact, particularly of personal contact. Sisters and legionaries of Mary can do much in this respect, but they cannot establish and maintain the particular and personal relation that should exist between a shepherd and his individual sheep.

It is unpleasant to hear parishioners remark that "no priest of the parish has ever crossed our doorstep"; and it is quite certain that many parishioners would appreciate more frequent visits. Most priests accept theoretically that home visitations for pastoral purposes are very useful. We say for pastoral purposes, and if that kind of visit is considered so important, we must see to it that it is undertaken to achieve that purpose. The "social" visits of some priests to families, usually the same ones, are sometimes productive of just the opposite of what a pastoral visit should aim at.

What then is the fundamental characteristic of a true pastoral visit? One could answer in a general way: it consists in this that, as their shepherd, the priest visits those families. And this we then explain further: it is ultimately meant to bring Christ to those people. "To bring Christ to people"; this the priest does when he offers the holy sacrifice, when he administers the sacraments, when he announces the word and gives pastoral guidance. But this is not done exclusively within the church building. Also in the visit to the home, the fundamental elements of pastoral care must be found namely, sanctification, proclamation of the word, and guidance. Of course, these elements do not appear in exactly the same way in family visits as in the ministry within the church building, nor are all the elements always present in the same measure.

399

The priest enters a home, sometimes to administer the sacraments or sacramentals, sometimes for the sake of proclaiming the faith in a suitable way adapted to the circumstances, or again to hold a pastoral conversation about some concrete problems.

However, it would be going too far to attempt to establish the necessity of home visitation on the basis of what we read in the Acts of the Apostles: "And they continued steadfastly in the teaching of the apostles and in the communion of the breaking of the bread . . . . breaking bread in their *houses* . . ." (Acts 2:1 ff.); and "I have kept back nothing that was for your good, but have declared it to you and taught you in public and *from house to house*" (Acts 20:20). Although there may have been some element of a "home visitation" in what St. Paul meant here, it was in the first place a preaching of the Gospel to groups of people gathered in particular houses. People came together there just as they came together when the Eucharist was celebrated "from house to house."[40]

In any case we must maintain that a certain type of visitation of homes is a pastoral work in which, in principle, all the elements of pastoral care find expression; in exceptional cases there might even be a celebration of the Eucharist (a thing that was formerly very common in Ireland). Keeping that presupposition in mind, we must next make a clear distinction between two aspects that find expression in home visitation: getting acquainted with the faithful who are entrusted to the priest's care, and pastoral contact with them.

It would certainly not be pastoral if home visitation meant nothing more than a means to know one's parishioners. This acquaintance is important but is not the principal thing, and

---

[40]Cf. Th. Blieweis, *The Diary of a Parish Priest*, Newman, 1965; K. Metzger, *Seelsorge auf der Strasse und in die Häusern*, 1945; R. Wick, *Franziskus in der Grosstadt*, Luzern, 1953.

it can, moreover, be achieved to a great degree by other means. There are pastors, even in cities, who know their parishioners very well, and yet not by means of home visitations. Some meet them at the doors of the church on Sundays, or at various parochial and other social gatherings. But this frequently does not satisfy the legitimate desire of parishioners who want more personal contact with their pastors. Some priests are satisfied with keeping the names of, and information about, their parishioners in their files. But the shepherd must know his sheep in a way that is more warm and personal than cold statistics. He must have pastoral knowledge, interest, love, care; he must have a priestly contact with his parishioners.

Contact, however, is possible in many ways. As we have said, the celebration of the Eucharist, the administration of the sacraments and the proclamation of the faith are essentially a contact between priest and people and of the people among themselves. In addition, there is contact through local groups and associations, through incidental meetings, etc. Home visitation is a particular form of contact between priest and faithful, but a form now imposed by Vatican Council II: "In fulfilling their office as shepherd, pastors . . . should visit homes and schools to the extent that their pastoral work demands."[41]

In most of the English-speaking world the circumstances are such that pastoral visitation of homes is appreciated. But such visits should not be based solely on the priest's obligation to know his flock, for this could lead to the notion that these visits are little more than a means to take the census of the parish. It is not always in the parishes in which such a census is most detailed and complete that the best contact exists between priest and parishioners.

---

[41]*Decree on the Pastoral Office of Bishops in the Church,* Ch. II, art. 30.

We should also make a distinction between a visitation of the *home* and a visitation of the *family*. Protestants sometimes speak of visits to the homes as "individual" or "personal" ministry. But this is not correct as a definition of the visitation of homes. Such a visitation might contain a certain amount of individual and personal ministry, but a visitation of the *family* as such is a most important form of home visitation. Many times a visit to the home is indeed a question of personal ministry, but it is then too often concerned only with marriage questions and not sufficiently with helping to form a Christian family life in our time.

It is useful to develop a few of those points more fully, namely those that concern:

1) The proper nature of the priestly visitation of homes and the importance of lay help in that matter;

2) The importance of the visitation of families;

3) The place of the visitation of homes in the context of pastoral care and in relation to the changed circumstances of our time.

The Character of Home Visitation. When a priest makes a home visitation, be it as pastor, assistant, missionary or in any other way that merits the name of priestly visit, he does it as a collaborator of the bishop of the diocese in whose power he participates and in whose name he exercises a pastoral function. To make a home visitation means to exercise one's priesthood and all three aspects of the priesthood find expression in such an activity. This is most clearly so in the visitation of the sick when the sacraments are administered in the home. It is also clear that the exercise of the teaching office and of pastoral guidance go together most of the time. But though in the latter case there is no question of administering sacraments, we must nevertheless look upon any instruction or guidance given there as an exercise of the priest-

402

hood, just as a sermon, as a form of proclaiming the Gospel, cannot be divorced from the totality of priestly activity. Even when certain distinctions are rightfully made, all exercise of the priesthood constitutes a unity. It consists in making the living Christ present among men.

Of course, no one has ever had any serious doubts about the priestly character of home visitations. But the question suggests itself whether we have not looked at it exclusively as belonging to the field of pastoral guidance, and whether such visitations have not practically tended to become purely human conversations. It is most important that the priest himself be deeply convinced of the fact that the visitation of the home is a function of his total priesthood; that is, it springs from the sacrament of priesthood which made him participate in Christ's priesthood and hence made him a distributor of the mysteries of God. But the people also must see clearly that it is as a priest that he makes a visit to their homes. And this, in fact, is what people also desire and expect. Of course, it is possible, and it does happen, that some will avoid engaging in any kind of serious talk; but this might be merely a "game of cat and mouse," to use a popular expression. They try to get away from serious subjects, but, at the same time, expect the priest to take up such topics. In truth, they find it strange if the "cat" does not try to catch the "mouse," be this the second or third such an attempt. Priests must have the courage to bring up the serious matters.

The priestly character of the visit must be evident, not only in their whole attitude, but also in the way the visitation of the homes takes place. The concrete form will be determined mostly, or in fact always, by the circumstances. Nevertheless, it is correct to put an emphasis on the hallowed character of the visit, as has been suggestion in many publications. All sorts of suggestions have been made: to connect a prayer with home visitations, not to forget blessing the patient in

403

the visiting of the sick, to restore the practice of the blessing of houses on the occasion of the yearly more or less official visits of the homes, and at least, when possible, to connect a priestly blessing with such visits.

Because the visitation of the home is a truly priestly work, there is a fundamental distinction between the home visit by a layman and by the priest, just as there is a difference between the general and the special priesthood. The home visitation by a lay person has, nevertheless, a high value; it is an exercise of the very real, spiritual, general priesthood and an exercise of the specifically Christian love of neighbor; but with respect to a home visitation by the ordained priest, the layman's visit is only a preparation or a complement.

At the beginning we said that all visitations of the home ultimately take place under the authority of the bishop who is the supreme pastor of the diocese. Hence it is not correct to maintain that only pastors and assistants can make "true" home visitations in their own parishes. *Per se* there should be no objection against other priests doing that kind of priestly work. The bishop can appoint other men and the pastor can invite other priests to help him in that function. Likewise, when a priest makes an incidental priestly visit to a home, a truly priestly character canot be denied to such a visit; for, by the fact that he is a priest and is lawfully exercising his priestly function, he is a collaborator of the bishop of the diocese in which he lives or is only a temporary resident.

The importance of the visitation of the home springs principally from the place which the family occupies in ecclesial life. The family is a truly Christian society within the context of the Church. Hence, St. Augustine speaks rightly about it as "the little Church," and he puts particular emphasis on the priestly function, in virtue of the general priesthood, of the father in the family. The family issues from marriage which is a sacrament. Whence the *Constitution on the Church* speaks of it as "the domestic Church."[42]

It follows that the Church not only attaches particular importance to a good family life, but that the hierarchy, the leaders of the Church, must also maintain a living contact with the family as such; hence not only with the persons who are members of a family but with the family-community as such.

This contact must, by its very nature, bear a priestly character. The priest comes into a family to sanctify it, to proclaim the faith and give direction to it. This, in practice, will take place in very diverse ways. In several countries recently, both theorists and people with practical experience have stressed that, at least once a year, the visitation of families should have a sacred character. In regard to the form that this visit should adopt there can be various opinions and it seems particularly important not to impose any rigid pattern.

Although every pastor is convinced of the importance of the family and will do his best to give it his support, awareness of the family as an ecclesial community is not particularly strong. And a more adequate program of home visitation cannot solve that problem. The whole structure of pastoral care really by-passes family life as such. The pastor will say that "the parish consists of so many families" but this is not much more than an administrative designation. That there are "so many souls in the parish" is more in harmony with the real situation. The same is true, of course, also of organizations and social life. They, too, by-pass the family. The problem admits of no easy solution, expecially because we should not try to return to the conditions of the old "closed" family. But it is important to recognize that there is a prob-

---

[42]*Constitution on the Church,* Ch. II, art. 11.

lem, for the priest's contact with the family as community belongs among the fundamental tasks of his pastoral care.

The Place of Family Visitation in Our Time. At present in many countries there are many complaints on the part of both clergy and faithful about the want of visitation of the homes. Perhaps too much is expected of such visitations. Some even call it the beginning and the end of all pastoral work which, no doubt, is an exaggeration. Perhaps that overemphasis has some connection with the impersonal character that increasingly permeates many human relations, which then cause a reaction calling for personal contacts. It is worthwhile asking whether it has ever been possible to be as intensively occupied with home visitations as is now desired in many places. Is it really possible to make an unhurried visit to al the families several times a year in a medium-sized parish?

Whatever importance one may attach to the pastoral visitation of homes, we must not forget that it may and should remain only one of the activities of a priest. In other words, we must always remember that the crucial matter is contact with the Church and the priest. This contact has greatly decreased in many parts of the Church and for large groups of people it threatens to become even less. It would be naive to attribute this principally to a want of home visitations; and it would be equally naive to expect a solution to be found in better and more frequent visitations of families. On the other hand, it is very true that because of the actual situation in our time, home visitation is certainly of the utmost importance.

It is very dangerous to make categorical statements about the causes leading to the loss of contact with the Church and the dechristianization that has taken place in several countries. Should we say that the rapid and often abrupt structural changes of modern society constitute one of the principal

406

causes of that dechristianization and diminished contact with the Church? Or is dechristianization at the source of the change that is taking place in society? Undoubtedly, both factors work together; but one cannot help getting the impression that the failure of the Church to adjust herself quickly enough to the structural changes is a major cause of the loss of contact resulting in the flagging of the faith and ultimately in falling away from the Church. However, visiting homes more frequently alone will not stem the tide. And if we were to neglect other means of contact in order to devote more time to home visitations, the situation could even get worse.

Hence it will be necessary to plan and look for a change in the organization of pastoral care, because in many places it is no longer adjusted to present circumstances. Within that new organization the visitation of homes will of necessity take a most important place. We shall certainly have to cast overboard many things that are now useless and outdated; and we shall have to entrust many things to lay people if only to give priests the time that is required for the visitation of homes. But this visitation remains only one of the means for restoring and maintaining contact.

3. An Updated Ideal of the Priesthood

Priests and laymen are seriously reflecting upon the way the priestly office should be viewed in our time. A number of doubts have arisen about this office. While these are related to the changed situation of the Church and the priest's place within the Church, at the same time, they also result from a new view of the structure of spiritual life.

SOCIAL POSITION

In a not too distant past a certain social position was also attached to the priesthood. In some countries this still is the case. We do not mean that the priesthood today no longer has any social consequences but rather that, not so long ago, many priests occupied a prominent position, in some countries more than in others, in state and society. They had all sorts of political and social offices and functions. A glaring example of this was the old Papal States before 1870. Practically all the offices were held by priests, bishops and cardinals. It is very difficult to recognize an exercise of the priesthood in such functions. Leaving aside the Papal States, with their exceptional position, there are a number of positions with respect to which one can at least doubt whether or not they are in harmony with the priestly character; for instance, being a member of parliament, a diocesan purchasing agent or insurance director.

While we do not wish to defend the extreme view that only an activity directly related to spiritual life can be called an exercise of the priestly office, it must be recognized that at the present time there is a clear shift toward a more direct exercise of the priestly office and an effort to avoid any other kind of function.

This is connected, in the first place, with the already-named change of the Church's position in the world. Without relegating the Church to a ghetto, we may rejoice that the Church is presently more and more free from too formal a link with the State. Her pastoral task thereby acquires greater freedom and the priesthood is purified from all sorts of elements which, although both very good and Christian, do not belong to the priestly office. Furthermore, a shift is also taking place within the Church, in the sense that functions are being transferred from the priest to the laity. As a result, the Church is becoming more ecclesial and, within her, the priest is becoming more the priest.

It is a well-known fact that change plays a role in the present problem of vocations for the priesthood. In previous times, when a Catholic boy went away "to study," it was understood that he was going to become a priest. For many boys, who showed a talent for a more intellectual function than their father's occupation, going to the seminary was the most natural thing to do. Something similar existed with respect to women's vocations for religious life. A girl who felt inclined to embrace a state of life in which she would be able to serve her neighbor almost naturally chose the religious life, because that function in a Catholic environment was practically always exercised by religious.

In view of the past historical situation, it is easy to understand all this, but now much has changed in that respect. All sorts of tasks that were formerly fulfilled by priests and religious are now performed by lay people, or at least also by lay people, and in a much more varied and specialized form. Young people now are presented with a much larger choice of intellectual and idealistic professions. There is no longer that "natural" choice of the priestly state. Moreover, the situation has changed to such an extent that now young men sometimes hesitate to enter the priesthood, in spite of their inclination to do so, because they are afraid that their superiors might give them a function in which they will not be able to work "as priests."

NOT A WAY OF LIFE
BUT A MINISTRY

Thus the first question that arises is, What does it mean to "work as priests"? Let us begin by noting that, if we wish to find a satisfactory answer to that question, it will be necessary to strongly emphasize the fact that the priesthood is an ecclesial office. It is pleasant to record that the priesthood is seen less and less as a personal gift for the priest and a particularly safe way to get into heaven. Ordination to the priesthood, of course, is a great gift of God; but this char-

409

acter of a gift is secondary to the conferring of an office. If a special emphasis is put on the personal gift, one is easily induced to be satisfied with all sorts of non-priestly functions. But if we stress the priesthood as primarily the fulfilling of an ecclesial office, one will be reluctant to accept functions that show no direct connection with the priesthood.

Stressing the priesthood as a particular form of Christian life has sometimes led to the view that "you can just 'as easily' get to heaven as a layman and also accomplish meritorious work for the Church." When we look at the priesthood from this standpoint, namely, that it is a meritorious way of life, that opinion cannot be refuted. But this is not the correct way to look at the priesthood. The desire to exercise the priestly office is not a direct choice of a way of life. Vocation in this respect is in the first place a vocation by the Church, an appointment to an office. Also, according to the present rules of Church Law, the fact that someone is perfectly suited for the priesthood does not yet give him any right to receive ordination. The bishops are not allowed to ordain more priests than they need (Canon 969). More emphasis should be placed on the fact that the Church can invite young men (or also older men) to accept the priestly office in the Church, if they have the will and ability to fulfill the necessary requirements of that office.

Along with the acceptance of this office, it is also necessary that in every case the candidate desire to exercise that office. A first great characteristic, in reality *the* great characteristic, of that office is that it means being at the service of the ecclesial community. He who becomes a priest must discard all thoughts of a brilliant career. What he chooses is a simple and inconspicuous life that brings with it great responsibilities but few human compensations. As Vatican Council II expresses it, candidates for the priesthood "should understand that they are not destined for domination or for honors but are given over totally to the service of God and to the pastoral ministry."[43] The priest opts for a most important function but, at the same time, a difficult one that often is a thankless task, the fruits of which are known mostly to God alone.

A priest must have a strong *awareness of the Church*. As a consequence, he must see his pastoral work as an extension and continuation of the work of Christ. This is the heart of the matter, and it must never be obscured by the variety of activities at the periphery of his office.

Further, he must have considerable *optimism* based on love and faith. Yet the priest must have a thorough knowledge of the true circumstances of life and must not simply picture the situation as being better than it really is. However, that actual situation is not completely determining; though there may be obstacles on all sides, he is justified in remaining optimistic. But this is the optimism of the Cross, which is at the same time the folly of the Cross. Christ's death on the Cross was apparently His greatest defeat. That supernatural optimism looks at things with a spiritual foresightedness; it does not desire immediate success. It knows that "just as Christ carried out the work of redemption in poverty and persecution, so the Church is called to follow the same route that it might communicate the fruits of salvation to men."[44]

The priest must possess a *practical* sense which is rooted immediately in a proper conception of his office, namely, that he must bring the men of this time to Christ.

The priest must always feel a great *responsibility* for the building of God's kingdom on earth and for the salvation of every man.

He must throughout life remain *faithful* to Christ. His fidelity must be able to withstand all difficulties. Because

---

[43]*Decree on Priestly Training,* IV, art. 9.
[44]*Constitution on the Church,* Ch. I, art. 8.

of that fidelity to Christ, he is also trustworthy with respect to the faithful: they can count on him.

The *simplicity* of the priest implies honesty, sincerity and self-effacement—a total engagement in the highest interests of mankind.

The spiriual life of the priest is based upon the fulfullment of his office. What is true of all Christians also applies to the priest, namely, that for too long his "spiritual life" has been built up as something more or less separate from his "ordinary life." The unity of life and works holds good in a particular way for the priest. He must sanctify himself by his work. If we admit that a Christian who does not exercise a high spiritual function can sanctify himself by his work, then this holds true in the highest degree in regard to the priest. There is no spiritual life that lies outside his work. Whence Vatican Council II's *Decree on the Ministry and Life of Priests* says: "Priests who perform their duties sincerely and indefatigably in the Spirit of Christ arrive at holiness by this very fact."[44a]

Theoretically speaking, it should not be difficult for the priest to attain that unity of life and work, but in practice he, too, suffers from the general want of appreciation of the idea that holiness is to be reached through his work. On the other hand, let us not forget that the fulfillment of the priestly office demands much meditation and prayer, not only his official prayer in leading the community and reciting his breviary, but also personal prayer. The fulfillment of his office requires that. Precisely because the priest of today finds it impossible to give much room to prayer and reflection amidst his work, he feels that something is not right in his priestly life. He feels that he is unable to be for his faithful what they expect him to be, namely, a leader in the spiritual life.

[44a]Ch. III, art. 13.

THE PRIEST IS NOT A
SOCIAL WORKER

The ecclesial community asks that the priest be a leader in the spiritual life, not a social worker. This expression has become more or less a slogan, like so many others that are heard nowadays. Nevertheless, we must not disregard the intention that lies behind it. On account of the present situation of the Church, the position of the priest in the Church, and the idea of the priesthood, the boundaries between the priestly office and other ecclesiastical functions, especially social functions have become somewhat blurred. We are presently searching for a purer determination of the priestly office. But it would not be correct—as we have already hinted—to consider the exercise of "direct pastoral care" as the only true exercise of the priestly office. If direct pastoral care were identical with parochial ministry, we would see this very clearly. But even if we include the various forms of specialized pastoral ministry under the concept of direct pastoral care, it is necessary to be very careful.

It is very easy to look upon parochial ministry as self-evidently the exercise of the true priestly office. But every parish priest knows from experience that one can legitimately question whether some of the activities he must perform are genuinely priestly. By this we do not mean to disparage his numberless forms of contact with his parishioners, but there are many time-absorbing occupations that belong more to the field of charity and the socio-economic situation of the parishioners. An exact boundary line, however, cannot be drawn here.

In the field of specialized ministry there are even much greater difficulties. Here we often meet with functions that are exercised by priests but which in reality belong more to the field of what is now called social work, although they are accompanied by pastoral work. At present the trend is

413

to entrust this charitable and social work more and more to lay people who have specialized in it. Nevertheless, there are still a good number of priests who are so much occupied with that kind of work that it is doubtful whether they really fulfill a pastoral task.

Some people, however, are inclined to judge this situation too quickly and too rigidly. The priestly office, in particular as teacher and pastor, permits many possible forms. Lately priests who teach "secular" subjects, such as physics and economics, are receiving much attention from some quarters. In view of historical circumstances it is understandable, though it may not be acceptable, that in some countries college education is almost entirely given by priest-teachers. This trend is now diminishing, however.

Strange as it may seem to some laymen, there have also been calls from among the laymen themselves who teach in colleges for retaining at least a few priest-teachers, not only for religion but also for "secular" subjects. The reason is not that certain "secular" subjects are closely connected with man's view of life, for that aspect can be confidently entrusted to competent Catholic laymen. But it is considered necessary that a few priests stand fully in the life of the students. In other words, it is thought that such priests can better fulfill their pastoral task when they are wholly taken up in the function of such schools and thus are fully integrated in the situation of the school and its students.

The same ideas can also be applied in other fields. In order that the priestly office be fulfilled, it may sometimes be necessary for priests to perform work which in itself does not belong to that office. For this reason Vatican Council II says that "all priests are sent as co-workers in the same apostolate, whether they engage in parochial or extra-parochial ministry. This is true whether they devote their efforts to scientific research or teaching, or whether by manual labor they share in the lot of the workers themselves . . ., or finally whether they fulfill some other apostolic tasks or labor designed for the apostolate."[44b] The important point is that the priestly *office* be taken as the norm. When this is done, one will not be inclined to consider the kind of work a priest does as less important than his priestly state of life. This standpoint leads of itself to a healthy limitation of functions that are considered suitable for priests.

THE WORKER-PRIESTS

A typical modern question in connection with what we have said above is the problem of the worker-priests in France. In Paris and other French cities, for instance in Marseille, a number of priests, with the permission of their bishop, wanted to build a bridge between the Church and the masses of laborers who are estranged from the Church and the priests. It is estimated that in the working-class quarters of Paris only from three to four percent practice their religion to the extent of making at least their Easter duty. This is the problem which the priests of the "mission of Paris" and others had to face. It was Abbé Godin, the author of *France Pagan?*, who began that special work. But through an accident, caused by over-fatigue, he died soon after the work had started.

The worker-priests always stressed the fact that they had not developed a special *method*, but that they lived rather in virtue of a *spirit*. They entered fully into the workers' milieu, to be there an example of real Christian life. At night, after they returned home from their work, they offered up the Holy Sacrifice in a working man's dwelling. Their principal task was bearing witness to an authentic and honest Christian life. They had no intention of forming cells, as the communists

---

[44b]*Ibid.*, Ch. II, art. 8.

are accustomed to doing. They were convinced that it was not *per se* necessary that this witnessing should be done by priests. On the other hand, they desired to make the priest present among the people and, further, considered it of the greatest apostolic importance that precisely priests should set the example of a truly Christian life, thereby also giving witness to a life that is truly that of a holy priest.

They disliked the name "worker-priests." They wanted to be priests just as other priests are professors, scholars, scientists, pastors or teachers. They did not want to be looked on as a curiosity and shunned publicity, although unfortunately they got much of it. The Archbishop of Paris had formally forbidden outsiders to go to the celebration of the Eucharist conducted by those priests. He issued that prohibition because he wished to prevent the worker families who went to such Masses from losing their freedom, for then the fruit of that work would be lost.

This kind of life demanded very much from those priests. Although each one lived alone in a workers' milieu, they belonged to a team whose members met once a week for a conference and recreation. They were obliged regularly to read Scripture, study theology and say their breviary to the extent that it was possible. There were never any delusions as to the precariousness of the situation of those priests. Long ago they themselves were of the opinion that this particular life really implied no greater moral dangers than life in a rectory; but they saw, nevertheless, a danger that they might become so identified with their surroundings that they would sympathize with the Communist movement because of their interior revolt against the inhuman living and working condition of the laborers.

Difficulties constantly increased, both internal difficulties among the worker-priests themselves and others from the outside created by opponents and by some press reports.

416

Finally on January 19, 1954, the French bishops in whose dioceses the worker-priests were active, laid down a drastic rule, after consultation with the Holy See.[45] It was decreed, among other things, that henceforth the priests would be allowed to consecrate only three hours a day to manual labor. The reason for that decision was as follows:

> The Church desires, before all else, to safeguard the priest's proper mission. She desires to give priests to the world of workers, priests who, amidst that world and for it, live a fully priestly life. Now, the priest is ordained to offer to God the worship of the whole people, in the first place by the celebration of the Mass and the public prayer of the office; he is also, among men, the distributor of the divine gifts by the preaching of the word of God and the administration of the sacraments. That is why the Church asks the priest whom she sends into the workers' milieu to perform manual work only for a limited time. Similarly, in order to safeguard the essential orientation of their priesthood, the Church asks them to renounce any temporal bond (that is, membership in workers' organizations). To avoid all confusion in the future, the priests engaged in the apostolate among the workers will no longer be known as "worker-priests" but as "priests of the workers' mission."[46]

This has, not quite unjustly, been called "the end of the worker-priests." As is well-known, a number of worker-priests, certainly at the beginning, were unwilling to obey that directive.

Hence, although the Church in no way desired to impede the special apostolate among the workers, the fact remains

---

[45]Cf. Claire Bishop,*France Alive,* Macmillan, 1947; Friedrich Heer, "The Priest-Workers in France," *Cross Currents,* vol. 4 (1954), pp. 262-274; Pierre Andreu, *Grandeurs et erreurs des prêtres ouvriers,* Paris, 1955.

[46]For the bishops' declaration, see "Déclaration épiscopale sur les prêtres-ouvriers," *L' actualité religieuse dans le monde,* no. 21, Feb. 1954, p. 8. For the statement of the position of the priests who refused to comply, see their collective work, *The Worker Priests,* Macmillan, 1957.

that a heroic experiment came to an end in a somewhat tragic way. It was said that the decree wanted to cling to the "traditional form" of priestly life in contrast with the form which the worker-priests had chosen. For it is true that the worker-priests did not primarily want to perform specific priestly tasks in the workers' milieu but that they wanted to set an example of a good Christian life. They believed that this should be done *also* by priests because, notably in France, the enmity toward Christianity and the Church, is strongly tainted with anticlericalism. Consequently, those priests thought that they had as their *special* priestly task to be present in the workers' milieu. And they thought it necessary to adopt a life that was wholly that of a worker, precisely as a means of giving that testimony.

Of course, there are also other examples of priests fulfilling functions that do not flow from their priestly office but at most can be looked upon as an opportunity for exercising a special form of priestly apostolate. Never before, however, had the question been raised as sharply as in the case of the worker-priests because never before has the contrast made itself felt as strongly as that between being-a-priest and being-a-worker. This fact is very revealing concerning the situation of the workers in some countries and the difficulties they meet with respect to leading a Christian life.

The big question, however, is whether the reason for the bishops' decree should be sought in the particular situation of the working class in those countries and in the difficulties experienced by the worker-priests, or should the reason be sought in the view that the priestly office should be exercised in a *direct* way.

In November, 1965, the Holy See agreed to let the worker-priest movement operate again on an experimental basis for three years. To avoid the dangers of the past, the worker-priests will be more carefully selected, and then trained in

418

sociological and economical issues lest they themselves fall for the Communist line. In the new experiment the worker-priests must live in communities and abstain from political activity, but they will be permitted to join labor unions.

THE SHORTAGE OF PRIESTS

A much-discussed problem in the Church today is that of the shortage of priests. That there is a problem cannot be denied, and yet it seems necessary to qualify the question a little and try to formulate it in a more exact way. We can begin by asking, for instance: Are there really too few priests? No doubt there are sections in the world where there is a want of priests. Well-known is the situation of South America. In mission countries the problem has special characteristics because there the needs can be called practically limitless. But in Europe and in North American the situation varies greatly according to countries, areas and dioceses; it is connected also with the above-mentioned problems of priestly existence. Much study has been given to the problem in Europe,[47] and also in America.

In the United States, according to the *Official Catholic Directory,* there were as of Jan. 1, 1965, 58,632 priests (35,-925 diocesan, and 22,707 religious) for a total Catholic population of 45,640,619. Many priests from abroad, notably from Ireland, labor in certain dioceses such as San Diego. The Glenmary Home Missioners were founded in 1939 for the care and conversion of souls in neglected "No-Priest-Land." Their 1962 statistics show that there are 710 counties in the U.S.A. that have no resident priests. According to the *National*

---

[47]Cf. the proceedings of the international workshop on this matter held in Vienna, October, 1954, *Die Europaische Priesterfrage,* Vienna, 1959.

Catholic Almanac of 1965 the number of United States overseas missionary priests is 3,518.

In Austria and some other parts of Europe there is a real scarcity of priests. It is particularly acute in the Archdiocese of Vienna for, of Austria's approximately six million Catholics, one third belong to the Archdiocese of Vienna. Austria has about 6,600 priests of whom about 4,300 are active in parochial work, i.e., an average of 1,440 parishioners per priest. Austria thus stands almost at the bottom of the list in Europe, for, on the basis of one priest for every thousand parishioners as the optimal ratio, there is a shortage of 1,700 in Austria (in Vienna alone the shortage is 1,000).

In Vienna the situation is truly very serious. The ratio there is one priest for more than 3,100 parishioners. Although the over-all figure of priests in Vienna is one for 1,393 Catholics, many priests are withdrawn from parochial work to give religious instruction in the schools. The Archdiocese of Vienna affects the statistics of the whole of Austria for, exclusive of Vienna, there is one priest for 803 Catholics and one engaged in parish work for every 1,393 Catholics. The situation is therefore much more varied that the total statistics would first lead us to believe. But in any case, Vienna suffers from a real dearth of priests. Little improvement is foreseen for the future because there is only one senior seminarian for 20,350 Catholics, in contrast with one for 8,180 in the other Austrian dioceses (hence in the whole of Austria one for 17,475 Catholics). We are speaking here about diocesan priests. In Vienna there are only about 200 parishes; there is an urgent need to establish many new ones, for 44 parishes have from ten to twenty thousand parishioners and 14 have more than 20,000.

The religious orders are also deeply involved in this crisis. In the whole of Austria there is one religious priest for 2,659 Catholics, as compared to one secular priest for 1,184 Cath-

420

olics. Almost half of the religious (45.5%) are engaged in parochial work. This, notably, is also the case with the thirty abbeys in Austria which together take care of 409 parishes (15% of the total). There is, of course, no reason why active religious orders should not be engaged in parochial works. However, this situation has not worked out well in Austria, especially for the Benedictines and the Cistercians. Their enormous abbeys stand almost empty and are scarcely able to provide for the needs of the parishes. Religious life suffers greatly on that account and this in turn is not conducive to fostering new vocations. Hence we must conclude that Austria and in particular Vienna are clearly in need of receiving help from outside which, in turn, raises all sorts of problems.

In Germany also there are great problems. There are difficulties especially in areas where Catholics are widely scattered. For in these areas the number of faithful has almost doubled because of the enormous immigration from the East. In sections where Catholics are rather widely scattered, there has always been a need for a great number of young, healthy and psychically strong priests. But this precisely is a great problem, for there are less vocations to the priesthood, the number of aged priests is increasing and, unexpectedly, there is an alarming increase of deaths among the younger clergy.

Up to this point we have spoken exclusively about the ratio of priests to Catholics. But this is not the proper way to approach the problem, because the mission of the Church and her priests may not be confined to Catholics. Sweden, for instance, has only sixty priests, eight of whom are natives; they have their hands full with the care of the widely-scattered 26,000 Catholics. Hence it is impossible for those priests to exercise a wide apostolate among the seven million non-Catholics. In Great Britain we find a similar problem. In Germany things are not different, especially when we think

421

of the great number of non-practicing Catholics who call for special attention. In this respect, of course, the situation in France is particularly complicated.

Ireland, which has only a few million inhabitants, in 1965 had 5,769 priests in the country itself, one for every 550 Catholics (*Irish Catholic Directory,* 1965). Besides these, more than 5,000 Irish priests labor in others countries, such as Great Britain, the United States and other English-speaking lands, and in mission territories (nearly 2,200 Irish priests in the territories that are under Propaganda). The number of vocations in Ireland continues to be high: 3,205, or one senior seminarian for every 1,000 Catholics. Thus the contribution of Ireland to other lands can be expected to continue in future years.

Holland also has a relatively high percentage of priests. At the end of 1963 it had 13,634 priests (one for every 340 Catholics). In the country itself there were 9,785 (one for every 507 Catholics), and of these 4,329 priests were working in parishes (one for every 1,146 Catholics). The others are active in education (about 1,880), in social, industrial and other special forms of apostolate. It would seem possible that many priests who are occupied in education, and especially in works of administration, could be freed for work abroad. The remaining 3,849 Dutch priests are laboring outside the country, in the missions or elsewhere. Notable in Holland is the proportion between diocesan and the religious clergy. Of a total of 13,634, only 4,369 are diocesan priests. The number of senior seminarians is 2,179 (one for every 2,277 Catholics).

Spain is, as in so many other respects, in a special situation also in regard to priests. Conditions vary greatly in the country itself. The northern dioceses have many priests: thirteen of them have an average of one priest for every 300 Catholics. In the six southern dioceses, on the contrary, there is an average of one priest for 2,300 Catholics. Spain is thus, at the same time, a country that can help other lands and one that has a need of priests. The dioceses that, vocation-wise, are rich must help first of all those that are poor. Nevertheless, Spain makes important contributions to other countries. Around twenty per cent of all the priests in South America have come from Spain, that is, 8,000 out of about 40,000. In some countries the proportion is very high: in Panama and Peru half of the clergy used to come from Spain; until recently in Venezuela and Puerto Rico about 84% came from Spain. The Spanish priests who go to foreign countries are generally religious. But, with respect to work in mission countries properly so-called, Spain does not contribute a great deal —less than six per cent of all the missionaries.

These figures plainly show how complicated the situation is. The question whether there are too few priests in Europe, or in America, cannot be answered with a simple Yes or No.

The Role of the Religious Clergy. An examination of the situation reveals that the countries in need of priests must expect help principally from religious orders. The general tendency in many countries seems to be that the number of religious priests grows more than that of the diocesan clergy. But the question has also been asked whether it is not precisely among religious that many reserves remain unused.

In France the number of secular priests decreased by sixty between 1948 and 1958, while the number of religious increased by 1,417 (26%). In Belgium there are 13 vocations for the diocesan clergy in comparison with 17 for the religious clergy for every 10,000 Catholics. The number of senior seminarians in the Belgian dioceses decreased fifteen per cent in ten years (from 1,750 in 1948 to 1,485 in 1957). In Holland that situation is particularly striking.[48] One hundred years ago

---

[48]Cf. *ibid.* the contribution of B. van Leeuwen.

the proportion between diocesan and religious clergy was still three to one. In the second half of the nineteenth century this began to change. In 1895 the number of ordinations of religious priests was for the first time higher than the ordinations of all the dioceses together. In 1937 the ratio was three new religious priests to one diocesan, and this proportion has since then remained practically the same. The reason for the great number of vocations to the religious priesthood is to be attributed, to a great extent, to the flowering of the missionary spirit, but also in Holland itself, the number of religious priests who are active in parochial work is relatively great.

In the United States the ratio of secular to religious clergy is about three to two (1965). Over the past ten years the secular clergy has increased by about 6,000 and the regular clergy by about 4,000; hence the proportion appears to be more or less stable. Many parishes are in the hands of religious priests, not only in new dioceses, but also in relatively old ones.

Thus both in Europe and in America the religious clergy are an important factor with respect to the whole question of the supply of priests. A matter of principle also is connected with it. The only true principle in this matter is, however, the fundamental equivalence of the secular and regular clergy. The rest is a question of practical regulation, of cooperation and mutual accomodation. Pope Pius XII, in his discourse to the Congress of Religious in 1950,[49] explicitly emphasized the equal value of the priestly office in the "secular form" (*forma saecularis*) and the "regular form" (*forma regularis*) and the equal value of their priestly activity.

Those words of the pope were apparently directed against the tendency to attribute to the secular clergy a priority in

---

[49]Cf. *A.A.S.*, vol. 43 (1951), pp. 26 ff.

the pastoral work in virtue of a sort of divine right, leaving to the religious clergy a purely "supplementary" role. For this reason the pope said that it is not an abnormal situation when a diocese is entirely entrusted to religious priests, and that it is wrong to imagine that a diocese can only temporarily be administered by them and should, as soon as possible, be transferred to the secular clergy. On the other hand, however, "in the care of souls the first place is held by diocesan priests . . . , for they have fully dedicated themselves in the service of caring for a single portion of the Lord's flock."[50]

Secular and religious priests also stand in the same relation to the bishop. The priesthood of both is a participation in the bishop's fullness of the priesthood. The religious exemption of orders and of some congregations is not concerned with the relation of their priestly office to the bishop, but it concerns their internal community life.[51] That is why also the regular clergy "can be said in a real sense to belong to the clergy of the diocese,"[52] the episcopal clergy. The clergy of a diocese consists of seculars and religious, constituting together "one priesthood with their bishop."[53]

On the basis of this fundamental equality it is then also possible to divide the work and functions in a diocese on practical grounds. One cay say that the seculars, by their incardination in a particular diocese and the "secular form" of their priesthood, are more suited for parochial work; but it must then be understood that other forms of pastoral work must not be excluded. We may say also that religious priests, in virtue of their community life and their life as religious, are generally more suited for mission work and for specialized

---

[50]Vatican Council II's *Decree on the Pastoral Office of Bishops in the Church*, Ch. II, art. 28.
[51]*Ibid.*, Ch. II, art. 35.
[52]*Ibid.*, Ch. II, art. 33.
[53]*Constitution on the Church*, Ch. III, art. 28.

forms of apostolate; but here again, it must be understood that they should not be excluded from parochial work.[54] It could be that particular orders and congregations prefer not to have any parishes, but it is not right to maintain that in general, parochial work cannot be reconciled with the "religious form" of priestly life.

One can take as a general rule that the religious priests should be active where the needs of the Church are greatest and where great mobility is required. They will have to orientate their efforts more by the needs of the Church than by the traditions of their institute.[55]

Hence in principle and in practice a high measure of collegiality and cooperation is necessary and possible between the religious and the secular clergy.

Ineffective Distribution of Clergy. All this illustrates that we must not indiscriminately speak about a shortage of priests in Europe and in North America. Priests, secular and regular, often are, with respect to place and activity, not properly distributed.

In France the situation is particularly lopsided: 21,000 priests work for 18 million people who live in the country; yet for the 24 million who live in cities there are only 7,200 priests in the parishes. There are 15,500 parishes in the country, of these a third number less than 300 parishioners. This situation is also present in some other countries to a greater or lesser extent. In some sections of Belgium also there are parishes that have very few parishioners. The same applies to Spain, although there the small parishes are generally without a pastor. In contrast with this, there is, for instance,

---

[54]Cf. the *Decree on the Pastoral Office of Bishops in the Church,* Ch. II, art. 35.

[55]*Ibid.,* Ch. II, art. 33-35; *Decree on the Religious Life,* art. 8.

the diocese of João Pessoa in Brazil which has only 37 priests for 850,000 Catholics.

Consequently, efforts are now being made to regroup parishes. A plan has been worked out in about twenty dioceses of France for the purpose of correcting that lopsided distribution of priests. Boulard[56] is of the opinion that 2,000 priests would immediately be made available if no parishes were maintained that have less than 500 souls. Laloux[57] proposed a plan for those country parishes that were too small: specialized groups of priests would combine parochial work in several places with the work of rechristianization, Catholic Action, etc. According to his plan a regional organization should be set up to determine which small parishes could be merged into pastoral districts.

Boulard and others, however, point out that it will not be enough to regroup parishes. In 1946 more than 7,000 French priests were engaged in education. This is one of the principal reasons for the shortage of priests in parochial work. Moreover, those priests are principally occupied in Catholic schools, while there are still too few teachers of religion for the State schools. But since 1946 that large number has been gradually reduced to 5,300.

However, this is not exclusively a French question. It exists also in Belgium, in parts of Holland, Switzerland, the United States and elsewhere. In the United States 12,346 priests are engaged in full time teaching duties, although more than 700 counties do not have a single priest to spread the faith. In Switzerland there are cities in which one parochial priest has the care of more than 2,000 Catholics; yet 741 priests teach 9,400 students in Catholic schools, that is, about one priest

---

[56]Cf. his book *Essor ou déclin du clergé français,* Paris, 1950.
[57]See his contribution in the book mentioned in footnote 47.

for every twelve students. There are seminaries in Switzerland where there is a ratio of one professor for slightly more than two students. In many small dioceses of Italy and the southern part of France, all the priests with above-average ability are employed in seminaries and withdrawn from direct pastoral work. This defect is now being remedied in Italy by means of regional seminaries in which generally a superior education is offered to future priests. In France, the senior seminarians of about thirty dioceses are brought together in ten seminaries, of which five are entrusted to the secular clergy and five to the Sulpicians. In this connection it is also fitting to mention the "Mission of France" (Pontigny): around 300 priests form a sort of interdiocesan auxiliary team for the benefit of the most dechristianized parts of the country.[58]

However, even a regrouping of the parishes and a reconsideration of the position of priest-teachers—though the value of this priestly work must not be denied—is not yet sufficient. There must be a willingness on the part of priests from relatively well provided dioceses to go to work in dioceses in which there is a scarcity of priests, and there must be a willingness on the part of bishops to provide that sort of assistance.[59] Religious must be ready to labor in whatever places are in the most critical condition. This willingness must exist not only within the country but also on an international scale. At the same time, enthusiasm alone is not enough, but careful planning also is needed. The forces that are available must be used in the most efficient way. Every diocese and every order or congregation has the obligation to help where it can. We are presently put in contact with other peoples in a mul-

---

[58]Cf. J. Faupin, *La mission de France,* Casterman, 1960.
[59]*Decree on the Pastoral Office of Bishops in the Church,* Ch. I, art. 6.

tiplicity of ways; we are brought face to face with people who suffer great need; we must do our best to help them in a well-planned and well-organized manner. This spirit, which must ultimately be based on Christ's words about the simplicity of the dove and the cunning of the serpent, must become characteristic of the activities of the Church.

EPILOGUE

This book ends with the door wide open. The changes in the Church, with which it is concerned, are still going on; the Church is in a period of transition. It is possible, indeed, to indicate in general in what direction she is going, but what the consequences will be God alone knows.

October 11, 1962, marked the beginning of Vatican Council II. In September of 1965 came its Fourth and last Session. Everything that has occurred during the sessions shows that the modern movement in the Church cannot be stopped. Even if, according to human standards, the Council were considered a failure, that movement will go on.

Changes have already been introduced, for instance, in the liturgy and in ecumenism, which a few years ago would have been thought impossible. Ideas about the nature of the Church, her relations with separated Christians, Jews, Muslims, in fact with all peoples with or without faith in God, questions about the role of the laity in the Church and many others are being discussed more and more, not only by the Council Fathers, but by clergy and laity in many parts of the world.

Those ideas and discussions naturally bring about a certain amount of tension. Although extremists are never absent from strong movements, we are permitted to say that the tensions exist among groups of men who are qually imbued with love for the Church and an orthodox belief in the Gospel. The present movement of reform is sincere, thoroughly ecclesial and therefore irresistible. As Pope Paul VI said in his Encyclical *Ecclesiam Suam*:

> We are taken up by the desire to see the Church of God become what Christ wants her to be, one, holy, and entirely dedicated to the pursuit of perfection to which she is effectively called. Perfect as she is in the ideal conception of her Divine Founder, the Church should tend towards becoming perfect in the real expression of her earthly existence . . . . This search for perfection fills her with groanings and prayers, with repentance and hope, with strength and confidence . . . .
>
> The Church will rediscover her renewed youthfulness not so much by changing her exterior laws as by interiorly assimilating her true spirit of obedience to Christ . . . .
>
> The Church today is more than ever alive. But it seems good to consider that everything still remains to be done; the work begins today and never comes to an end . . . . This is the ordinary task of our ministry, Venerable Brothers, which everything today stimulates us to *renew* and to make more devoted and intense.[1]

Vatican Council II has ended. But, in the words of Pope Paul VI, "its conclusion is not the end but the beginning of many projects"[2] in THE CHANGING CHURCH.

[1]*A.A.S.*, vol. 56 (1964), pp. 609 ff.; N.C.W.C. translation, *Paths of the Church*, art. 41, 51, 117.

[2]*Osservatore Romano*, Nov. 15, 1965, p. 1.

Index of Names

435

Index of Subject Matter

437